Unknown New England
By Jon Marcus

© 2003 by Jon Marcus. All rights reserved.

No part of this book may be reproduced, stored in a retrieval system, or transmitted by any means, electronic, mechanical, photocopying, recording, or otherwise, without written permission from the author.

ISBN: 1-4107-1825-5 (e-book)
ISBN: 1-4140-2002-3 (Paperback)

Library of Congress Control Number: 2003090680

This book is printed on acid free paper.

Printed in the United States of America
Bloomington, IN

1stBooks - rev. 09/29/03

For Elisabeth,
the newest New Englander

Table of *Contents*

Introduction vii

Unknown Boston and Eastern Massachusetts 1

Unknown Cape Cod and the Islands 55

Unknown Central and Western Massachusetts 73

Unknown Connecticut 94

Unknown Maine 114

Unknown New Hampshire 150

Unknown Rhode Island 164

Unknown Vermont 178

Unknown New England

The Old North Church. The *USS Constitution*. Harvard Yard. The White Mountains. Mystic Seaport. The mansions of Newport, R.I.

Been there. Seen those.

Sure, New England is home to many of America's most important historical, natural, academic, and cultural sites. Few places have as many internationally famous tourist destinations. But its woods, hills, craggy seacoasts, and historic cities are also full of extraordinary things you won't see on the standard travel maps, and attractions just as—if not more—interesting than the places that get all the ink.

A museum in landlocked Springfield, Massachusetts, for example, brimming with thousands of artifacts from the *Titanic*. The real Mulberry Street and other landmarks used as models by the children's author Dr. Seuss. The battlefield souvenirs of the oldest military organization in the Western Hemisphere, all but unnoticed in the heart of Boston's busy tourist district. The site of the first liquid-fueled rocket launch—birthplace of the space age.

Some of these spots relate to history you probably never knew, or have forgotten. The town in Vermont, for instance, that was the site of a little-known battle in the Civil War. New England's role in that war was disproportionate, beginning with the writing of the influential *Uncle Tom's Cabin* by Harriet Beecher Stowe in Brunswick, Maine, and ending with General Robert E. Lee's surrender at Appomattox Courthouse to Joshua Chamberlain—who also came from Brunswick. Both of their homes in that town remain intact. There's even a Civil War memorial in Massachusetts that was the gift of a Confederate.

There are also secrets about the oft-taught Revolutionary War exposed in unknown historic sites and small museums. The story of the battles that preceded Lexington and Concord, for instance, and of Paul Revere's *other* ride, months before the lanterns were hung in the steeple of the Old North Church. There's the little-known massacre carried out in Connecticut by British soldiers under hero-turned-traitor Benedict Arnold, the tea party hardly anyone remembers, the naval battle that took place five days before the Battle of Bunker Hill, the place where the American flag was raised for the first time, and the first-ever submarine, used against a British ship at anchor in 1776.

That's not the only history that may come as a surprise. It was in Maine, for instance—not Plymouth, Massachusetts—that the English planted their first colony in northeastern North America. Vermont was an independent country for 14 years. A corner of New Hampshire once broke away to form an autonomous republic. And there was an armed rebellion in Rhode Island that sought to overthrow the government. You can ponder the sites of presumed Viking settlements, mysterious

Introduction

Stonehenge-like ruins, and the tombstone of a 3,800-year-old Egyptian mummy—in a cemetery in Vermont. Connecticut, Maine and Massachusetts have their own ghost towns, and reputed vampires lie not entirely at rest in cemeteries in Rhode Island and Vermont.

New England's unparalleled record of inventiveness and ingenuity accounts for many of its secret treasures. The laboratory where Alexander Graham Bell invented the telephone is here, along with the auto supply store where Albert Champion invented the spark plug, the ruins of the towers that carried the world's first transatlantic wireless signal and first spoken radio broadcast, the remote facility in Maine that beamed the world's first satellite transmission, the first home in the world lit with electric lights, the places where the microwave oven and the birth control pill were invented, and the tenement where Charles Goodyear discovered the process for vulcanizing rubber (and an all-rubber desk he built as a gimmick to promote it). The first successful gasoline-powered car and motorcycle were invented in New England. So were the frozen French fry, the Graham cracker, the plastic pink flamingo, volleyball, the Quonset hut, the earmuff, the fishing reel, barbed wire, the dune buggy, the helicopter, and the "caterpillar" tracks that made possible the bulldozer and the military tank.

You can check out the world's largest revolving globe, the room in New Hampshire where the gold standard was secretly set, the Massachusetts town that was the model for Riverdale of the Archie comic books, and Al Capone's bar, transplanted from his hideout in Miami to a neighborhood restaurant in Boston.

There's a Cold War-era nuclear missile silo, the world's only known bull cemetery, the site of the first night baseball game, a prison built in an abandoned copper mine, the factory where the paper is made for all U.S. currency, the launch site of the first successful transatlantic balloon flight, the toothpick capital of the world, a 19th-century observatory where astronomers searched for evidence of life they believed existed on Mars, and the only public building that is half in Canada and half in the United States.

New England's lesser-known museums are bound to appeal to any taste or interest, and to residents and visitors alike. There's a museum in Maine dedicated to F.E. and F.O. Stanley, the brothers who invented the Stanley Steamer, and another about the odd life's work of a psychiatrist who studied the sexual orgasm; a museum at MIT devoted to famous pranks; and museums of fly fishing, ham radio, skiing, bad art, plastics, the Arctic, garbage, forestry, lifesaving, the Mack truck, solar vehicles, famous shoes, cuff-links, snowmobiles, amateur astronomy, antique radios, kerosene lamps, medical rarities, the wireless telegraph, celebrity dirt, and the Barnum & Bailey Circus.

Many of these museums may be largely unknown, but their holdings are superlative, including, among other things, the world's largest collections of mounted dinosaurs, holograms, shovels, thermometers, antique trolley cars, and Hollywood memorabilia. There is a collection of postage stamps second in size only to that in the Smithsonian, the largest collection of Irish materials outside of Ireland itself, the largest collection of British art outside Great Britain, and the only museum in America devoted to indoor plumbing. Unknown New England museums also boast the nation's largest collections of everything from diners to antique snowplows.

Hidden in these small depositories are such finds as the goggles worn by Wiley Post, the first man to fly around the world. There's a chair used by Pope Pius XII, Marie Antoinette's harpsichord, and the case that carried Louis XV's crown jewels. You'll find the world's largest ring, the boxing gloves and shoes worn by Rocky Marciano, Louis Pasteur's address book, life vests and deck chairs from the *Titanic,* a compass owned by Galileo, and a sloop sailed alone across the Atlantic in 1901 by a man who had no fingers.

Other hidden gems: drinking glasses used by Napoleon on St. Helena, the uniform of a Redcoat killed on the first day of the American Revolution, the skull of

Unknown New England

Blackbeard the pirate, a tree grown from a branch of Isaac Newton's apple tree, the world's first nuclear-powered submarine, a German staff car that was used in North Africa during World War II, a re-creation of Sherlock Holmes's fictional sitting room at 221-B Baker Street, the earliest known typewriter, the world's only authenticated pirate treasure, a rifle musket used at Custer's last stand, and the captain's silver setting from the *USS Maine,* the battleship whose sinking in Havana Harbor on February 15, 1898 provoked the Spanish-American War.

Also in these little-known attractions are the bones of a whale found mysteriously buried 150 miles from the ocean in Vermont, the last hand-cranked telephone switchboard in North America, Mussolini's telephone, an 1851 daguerreotype of the moon, Elvis Presley's gallstones, Ethan Allen's bar bill, and a full-sized replica of the bridge of the *USS Enterprise* from the original *Star Trek* television series.

Some of the least-expected sites of interest are not necessarily about New England—merely in it. The National Yiddish Book Center in rural central Massachusetts, for example, and the archives of the Nuremberg tribunals in Connecticut. Interested in Ernest Hemingway? His dog tags and other mementos of Hemingway's adventurous life are displayed in a virtually unknown Boston archive, a blue marlin he caught while he was writing *The Old Man and the Sea* is hanging in an obscure museum in Maine, and his fly-fishing tackle is on display in New Hampshire. How about Charles Lindbergh? You'll find the crate used to ship his *Spirit of St. Louis* home from Paris in a little town in Maine, while a piece of the airplane's fabric skin, and the necktie he wore on his famous flight, are in Connecticut.

Visitors can walk the trail John Chapman took when he left his boyhood home in Massachusetts, scattering apple seeds behind him. He would come to be known as Johnny Appleseed. They can see the earth's largest radio detector, built to listen for signs of other intelligent life in the universe, or visit the hospital operating room where anesthesia was first used, a home designed by Frank Lloyd Wright, the site of the first World Series, the only place in America that was shelled by enemy guns during World War I, and the real Pepperidge Farm.

Many of New England's famous homesites and birthplaces are also missing from the standard travel maps. They include the homes of Mark Twain, Horatio Alger, playwright Eugene O'Neill, horror writer Stephen King, Babe Ruth, movie directors John Ford and Cecil B. DeMille, Grandma Moses, Rudy Vallee, General and Mrs. Tom Thumb, Edgar Allen Poe, Jack Kerouac, the real Uncle Sam, James Abbott McNeil Whistler (and his mother) motion picture magnate Louis B. Mayer, baking baron John Sargent Pillsbury, and department store founders Marshall Field and R.H. Macy—whose first shop was in Massachusetts, not New York.

Tractor maker John Deere, Admiral George Dewey, and both Joseph Smith, the founder of the Mormon Church, *and* his successor, Brigham Young, were born in New England. Rudyard Kipling wrote *The Jungle Books* not in India, but in quiet Vermont town, near where Justin Morgan bred his famous horses.

Travelers can visit the landlocked place where Herman Melville authored *Moby Dick,* and a separate museum on Nantucket that tells the extraordinary true story on which the book was based; the house where Lizzie Borden was accused of murdering her parents with an axe; the home where Mary Baker Eddy founded the Christian Science Church; the unlikely New England setting where Clarence Mulford created cowboy hero Hopalong Cassidy; the red schoolhouse to which Mary's little lamb followed her one day; and "grandmother's house" to which the holiday classic takes us over the river and through the woods. In addition to Dr. Seuss's Springfield and Archie's Riverdale, you'll find the New England communities that inspired "Little Red Riding Hood," "Dogpatch" of the *Li'l Abner* comic strip, Thornton Wilder's *Our Town,* the steamy novel *Peyton Place,* even Peter Cottontail's briar patch.

There are extraordinary natural wonders, too, including the world's highest tide and the largest whirlpool in the Western Hemisphere. The Royal Lipizzan Stal-

Introduction

lions' summer home is here, and there's an equally anachronistic herd of buffalo roaming around a preserve in New Hampshire.

Why go to Monticello or Mount Vernon when Massachusetts has the birthplaces of presidents John and John Quincy Adams, John F. Kennedy and George Herbert Walker Bush; Connecticut of George W. Bush; New Hampshire of Franklin Pierce; and Vermont of Chester Alan Arthur and Calvin Coolidge? Kennedy, William Howard Taft, and Grover Cleveland had their summer White Houses here. And it is in little-known New England museums and historic homes, of all places, that you'll find President Abraham Lincoln's trademark stovepipe hat, the pen with which he signed the Emancipation Proclamation, a pass he hand-wrote the day before he was assassinated, and an exact full-sized replica of the Kentucky log cabin where he was born.

Some of these places relate to the long-overlooked history of women, blacks, native Americans, Jews, and other groups. There's Malcolm X's house, for instance, and the grave of a former slave credited with killing the British commander at the Battle of Bunker Hill. There's the story of America's only black whaling captain, an African prince who worked his way out of slavery, and the first academy to for black women in New England, which still bears the scars of the riot by a mob that shut it down. (It's not the only example of persecution in the supposedly progressive North; there also are white hoods worn by Ku Klux Klansmen preserved in a museum in Vermont, and a house in Massachusetts with slave quarters still attached.)

The homes remain of many well-known women from New England—including Abigail Adams, Emily Dickinson, Red Cross founder Clara Barton, Susan B. Anthony, Edith Wharton, Margaret Chase Smith, and Katharine Lee Bates, who wrote "America the Beautiful"—and some whose names are not well-known, including the first American women to discover a comet through a telescope, the first woman to navigate an American ocean-going vessel, a woman who disguised herself as a man and fought in the Revolutionary War, and the women who captured a British spy at pitchfork-point while their husbands were fighting at Lexington and Concord.

Contrary to popular belief, the first encounter between the Pilgrims and the natives was not a friendly one; you can visit the site of their brief skirmish. You can also see collections that show how local Indians manufactured objects for trade centuries before white settlement, including a flute made from a bone of a swan at a time when Europeans were still living in caves.

New England also is the home of the world's first Christian Science, Universalist, and Seventh Day Adventist churches, and the first Congregationalist, Episcopal and Baptist churches in America.

Even many of the people who live near these extraordinary landmarks and historic sites don't know about them. Yet almost every single one is staffed by enthusiasts and knowledgeable volunteers delighted to give tours. And most are free.

They may not be around forever, though. Some have already been lost, including a museum of antique outboard motors in New Hampshire and the Horse Cavalry Museum, which documented the surprising history of the nation's first cavalry unit—organized not in the wild West, but in Connecticut horse country in 1776; no one came riding over the hill when the lease ran out. The Nut Museum in Connecticut, an unparalleled collection of jewelry, art, and even toys made out of nuts (along with the world's largest nut, a 35-pound coco-de-mer grown on an island in the Indian Ocean), closed when its owner suffered health and financial declines. The Polaroid collection of instant photography by the likes of Ansel Adams and David Hockney went on the auction block along with the rest of the financially troubled company. There's a 300-pound piece of the Rock of Gibraltar in the lobby of Boston's Prudential Tower, trademark of the company that financed the building, but it was inexplicably concealed behind a wall when the interior was remodeled.

So don't wait. Discover the secrets of unknown New England.

Unknown New England

Advice for Visitors
Every place listed in this book can be visited, including the sites of the historic events described; in every case, street addresses are supplied, along with telephone numbers and operating hours where applicable. Most are open to the public, usually in exchange for a minimal donation, but often at no charge. Some are privately owned, and can be viewed only from the outside. Please respect property rights in these cases. Because so many of these destinations rely on volunteers, hours are subject to change; it's always best to call ahead. Some attractions also welcome guests by appointment during their off seasons or at times they are otherwise scheduled to be closed. All require advance notice for visits by groups. It's also a good idea to call ahead for holiday hours.

Acknowledgements
So many people provided information for, and enthusiasm about, this topic, it's impossible to thank them all. But my friends, family, and colleagues deserve special recognition for being patient with me as I endlessly detailed for them my most trivial discoveries. I'm also grateful to the Boston Athletic Association, *Boston Magazine,* the Bostonian Society, the Greater Boston Convention and Visitors Bureau, Northeastern University, the Society for the Preservation of New England Antiquities, and the Trustees of Reservation, and to Marc Abrahams, Liz Alcock, Mel Allen, Carol Aten, Patricia Crawford, John Dumville, Terri Evans, Elizabeth Fitzsimmons, Jack Fleming, Fran Golden, Marcia Harrison, Susan Cole Kelly, Nancy Marshall, Larry Meehan, Jerry Morris, Diane Viera, Katharine Webster, and Joe Wrinn. And a very special note of thanks to Bob Parsons for designing the cover.

Unknown Boston
and Eastern Massachusetts

Even Boston's famous landmarks and historic sites hold secrets: the eclectic museum of the oldest military organization in the hemisphere, hidden on the seldom-visited top floor of Faneuil Hall, for instance. Or the most complete collection of Ernest Hemingway memorabilia, buried deep inside the John F. Kennedy Library.

If anything, much of what people think they do know about the city's main attractions *isn't* true. Bunker Hill? We lost. "Don't fire until you see the whites of their eyes!"—ascribed to a zealous patriot—was actually a common military order. Faneuil Hall, the "cradle of liberty," was built with money from the slave trade. "Witches" and heretics were hanged on Boston Common. And not only was the story of Paul Revere's ride propaganda; neither his house, nor the Old State House, look much like they did when Revere was living, thanks to well-meaning but misguided preservationists. It was the Americans who started the Boston Massacre—marked by a circle of stones on State Street—over a bill owed to a wigmaker by a British officer. Even the pious Anglicans who worshipped in the Old North Church sat under statuary stolen by Boston privateers from defenseless ships at sea.

And yet, for every jingoistic myth, Boston's epic buildings, ships and cemeteries hide a dozen little-known truths. It is true, for example, that the steeple of the Old North Church was where two lanterns were hung to warn that British troops were traveling by sea the night Revere set out to sound the alarm. (He was arrested before reaching Lexington or Concord, despite what Henry Wadsworth Longfellow later wrote.) But the steeple was already famous. On September 13, 1757, a man named John Childs hurled himself from its 191-foot height in a rudimentary glider three times, once firing a pistol in midair, until the alarmed city fathers quickly passed a law against that sort of thing; there's a plaque describing the event on the wall of the church garden. The Old State House was home to the nation's oldest sitting court and first bicameral legislature, and the first place in the world where the public could watch its representatives do business. It also was one of the nation's first examples of historic preservation, but only after the city of Chicago offended local pride by offering to move it to Lake Michigan as a tourist attraction. On display inside is John Hancock's coat—evidence he was as small as his famous signature was large—and the lone vial of tea known to have survived America's most celebrated act of vandalism; the tea was confiscated as evidence

1

Unkown Boston and Eastern Massachusetts

against a sticky-fingered patriot caught smuggling it home from the Boston Tea Party in the cuffs of his leggings. The Boston Common is the nation's oldest public park, but it is also was where the modern game of American football was played for the first time in 1874. And everybody knows the *USS Constitution* is the oldest commissioned warship afloat, but it was also the first U.S. territory stepped on by a Catholic pope, Pius IX, when the ship visited Naples on a goodwill tour in 1849.

Acton

The statue on the town green is of Isaac Green, a 30-year-old father of four who was the first American killed at the battle at the North Bridge in Concord—the "shot heard 'round the world"—which launched the Revolutionary War.

Acushnet

Originally a grammar school, the Long Plain Museum reflects Acushnet's unexpected history as a whaling center with scrimshaw, harpoons and captains' portraits. There's also an authentic carpetbag of the type used by post-Civil War northern carpetbaggers. *1203 North Main Street; Sunday 1 to 4 June through mid-September; 508-763-8626.*

The actress who produced and performed in the play *Our American Cousins* at Ford's Theatre on the night President Abraham Lincoln was shot was so traumatized by the experience that she retired to a quiet 125-acre farm on the Acushnet River. The actress, Laura Keene, was knocked down when assassin John Wilkes Booth leaped from the president's box to the stage while trying to escape. The site of her house, which burned down in 1896 and was rebuilt in 1920, is marked with a plaque; nearby Laura Keene Avenue is named in her honor. *59 South Main Street.*

Amesbury

Cartoonist Al Capp, creator of the "Li'l Abner" comic strip, settled here after marrying the daughter of the local newspaper publisher; he is buried in Mount Prospect Hill Cemetery under his full name, Alfred Gerald Caplin. Capp started the strip in 1934, and drew it until 1977. Locals, perhaps uncharitably, are convinced he modeled Dogpatch –home of Li'l Abner, Mammy and Pappy Yokum, Daisy Mae, Fearless Fosdick, and Sadie Hawkins—on neighboring Seabrook, New Hampshire.

Once a busy manufacturing town with mills driven by the Powow River, Amesbury was the first place where the circular saw was used in 1781. One of the first nail factories was opened here in 1795; before then, people made their own. Later so many carriages and early auto bodies came from here that the town became known as the Detroit of the East. The Bartlett Museum reflects this industrial history with carriages and carriage parts, including the carriage of eccentric selectwoman Annie Webster, who left the rest of her fortune to her cat. *270 Main Street; Friday through Sunday 1 to 4 Memorial Day through Labor Day; 978-388-4528.*

The meeting house was a center of early New England life, and one of the last remaining 18th-century New England meeting houses is the Rocky Hill Meeting House, built in 1785. In 1789, George Washington spoke here. The original pulpit, finishings and fittings remain. *4 Portsmouth Road; by appointment; 978-462-2534.*

America's oldest continuously operated wooden boat shop, Lowell's Boat Shop is one of the nation's oldest businesses of any kind, and the birthplace of the dory. Opened in 1793 by Simeon Lowell, the ramshackle shop has produced an estimated 150,000 boats, many of them used to establish Gloucester as the fishing capital of the world. Today the shop serves as a working museum. *459 Main Street; Tuesday through Saturday 8 to 4; 978-388-0162.*

Unknown New England

Abolitionist and poet John Greenleaf Whittier spent most of his adult life here in a house he bought in 1836, which is impeccably preserved; even most of the paint and wallpaper is original. When Whittier's poetry didn't pay, he supported himself as a teacher and shoemaker until abolitionist editor William Lloyd Garrison became the first to publish his work. While he lived here, Whittier helped found the Republican Party. He is buried in Amesbury's Union Cemetery. *86 Friend Street; Tuesday through Saturday 10 to 4 May 1 through October 31; 978-388-1337.*

Andover

One of the great collections of American art is housed at a private high school: the Addison Gallery of American Art at Phillips Academy. The museum has several Winslow Homer masterpieces, including "The West Wind" and "Eight Bells," but it also boasts works by John Singleton Copley, John Singer Sargent, Georgia O'Keeffe, Edward Hopper, Jackson Pollock, Alexander Calder and Phillips alumnus Frank Stella. Founded in 1927, the Addison has 11,000 pieces in all; it was endowed by Thomas Cochran, who attended the school on a scholarship and went on to become J.P. Morgan's banking partner. *Phillips Academy, Main Street; Tuesday through Saturday 10 to 5, Saturday and Sunday 1 to 5; 978-749-4015.*

Samuel F. Smith composed the hymn "My Country 'Tis of Thee" in the house at 147 Main Street. The actual name of the song is "America," and the house, now known as the America House, is owned by Phillips Academy.

Harriet Beecher Stowe's grave is marked with a Celtic cross in the chapel cemetery at Phillips Academy, where her husband taught at the time of her death in 1896. They lived on the campus in what is now called Stowe House.

Native Americans were living in small communities in New England 12,000 years ago, following the last ice age. This largely unknown history of natives who lived here 7,000 years before the pyramids were built is a focus of the Peabody Museum, one of the nation's foremost repositories of archeological artifacts relating to native Americans, which has woven textiles dating back more than 1,500 years—rare because such cloths usually decay—indicating that cotton was already being cultivated here then. There are also figures carved from walrus tusks by Eskimos, and dioramas of 15th-century Indian life along the Merrimack River. *Phillips Academy, Main Street; Monday through Friday 9 to 5; 978-749-4490.*

Arlington

Born on September 13, 1766, Samuel Wilson was only 8 when British troops marched past his house on their way to the battles at Lexington and Concord on the first day of the Revolutionary War. And he did not have a white beard or wear a high hat. But he would become a patriotic icon: Uncle Sam. Wilson ended up a meat packer who provided casks of beef and pork marked with the federal monogram "U.S." for American troops during the War of 1812, and the legend began to grow that the initials stood for "Uncle Sam" Wilson. Congress made it official in 1961: Sam Wilson was the basis for Uncle Sam. The birthplace of Uncle Sam is marked with a huge memorial statue. *Massachusetts Avenue at Route 60.*

The first casualties of the Revolution didn't come only on the historic battlefields. Some of the bloodiest fighting of April 19, 1775, the first day of the war, occurred in a guerilla raid on a house where Patriot snipers had concealed themselves. A British flank guard surprised the snipers and fatally bayonetted the owner of the house—farmer Jason Russell—on his own front doorstep. One other colonist was killed; the rest saved themselves by blockading themselves in the cellar. Bullet holes from the skirmish on the first day of the Revolution still can be seen on the walls of the parlor, master bedroom and stairway. Next door, the local historical

Unkown Boston and Eastern Massachusetts

society operates the Smith Museum. Among other assorted artifacts, the museum displays a 42,000-year-old mastodon tusk discovered in 1959 in Spy Pond. *7 Jason Street; Friday through Sunday 1 to 5 mid-April through October 31. 781-648-4300.*

Ashland

The Boston Marathon started here, not in Hopkinton, when it was run for the first time on April 19, 1897. Seventeen runners crossed a starting line drawn in the dirt road outside Metcalf's Mill on the Sudbury River by Olympic sprinting champion Thomas Burke for the nearly 25-mile race to Boston in the first of what is now the oldest continuously operated marathon in the world. The starting line was moved to Hopkinton in 1924 to conform to new international standards. *Pleasant Street.*

Attleboro

Attleboro was once a major jewelrymaking center, a legacy reflected in the Attleboro Area Industrial Museum, whose collection includes the world's largest ring—the size 22 1/2 class ring designed for a husky Texas high school student in 1981; and the size 19-and-a-half Pro Football Hall of Fame ring given to Chicago Bears fullback Bronko Nagurski in 1963. The average size of a man's ring finger is 9 and a half. *42 Union Street; Tuesday through Saturday 10 to 4; 508-222-3918.*

Belmont

Built by Winslow Homer's uncle, the William Flagg Homer House was the backdrop for several famous Homer paintings, including "The Croquet Scene," which was set on the front lawn, and "Making Havelocks for the Volunteers," showing the women of the Belmont Women's Club rolling bandages for Civil War soldiers in front of the bay windows of the front parlor. *661 Pleasant Street; 617-484-4892.*

Beverly

President William Howard Taft had his summer White House here in friendly Republican territory, where his golfing partners included neighbors Senator Henry Cabot Lodge Sr. and Congressman Nicholas Longworth, who was married to Theodore Roosevelt's daughter, Alice. Taft spent the summers of 1909 and 1910 in a 14-room "cottage" on Woodbury Cove, which he leased from R.D. Evans, an immigrant who rose to become the president of U.S. Rubber, later Uniroyal. Tightened security and other problems prompted Taft to move farther inland for the summers of 1911 to 1912 to Parramatta, the hilltop estate of merchant Henry Peabody. Parramatta, at 70 Corning Street, has since been converted into condominiums; the R.D. Evans cottage was moved by barge to Peaches Point in Marblehead, and an Italianate garden planted in its place. The 15-acre garden, nestled in the foundations of Taft's summer White House, is open to the public. It features statues and plots of begonias, marigolds, roses, and snapdragons. *55 Ober Street.*

The birthplace of the American Navy is marked with a stone monument near where the 78-ton schooner *Hannah*—the nation's first commissioned warship—sailed off to intercept British military vessels in September, 1775. A month later, the outgunned *Hannah* was chased back into Beverly Harbor by the British ship *HMS Nautilus* and run ashore. But the *Nautilus* was also severely damaged by cannon firing from what is now Independence Park on shore. It was the first ocean-going naval engagement of the Revolution. *Route 1A at the Salem-Beverly Bridge.*

Almost as secret today as it was during the Cold War, the once-classified Army bunker here included three underground silos where missiles were concealed to defend against a Soviet bomber threat to the American mainland. The B-15 Boston Area Defense silo is now open on a limited basis, and an original 21-foot Nike Ajax

Unknown New England

guided surface-to-air missile is displayed there. The bunker was deactivated in 1963. *Beverly Airport, Henderson Road; by appointment; 978-922-5680.*

One of the 13 original copies of the Declaration of Independence is in the Beverly Historical Society & Museum, housed in Cabot House, itself built in 1781 by local privateer Captain John Cabot. Also here is the signet ring of Revolutionary War hero Nathan Hale ("I only regret that I have but one life to lose for my country") and Essex County Constable Andrew Elliott's staff of office used during the Salem witchcraft trials. The many portraits of ship's captain include several by Gilbert Stuart, and there is also an extensive collection of materials relating to President William Howard Taft. *117 Cabot Street; Wednesday through Friday noon to 4 October 1 through April 30, Tuesday, Thursday, and Saturday 10 to 4, Wednesday 1 to 9 May 1 through September 30; 978-922-1186.*

Models of ships, cars, trains and planes are among the 200,000 artifacts relating to New England transportation in the Walker Transportation Collection, which has particularly strong holdings of 19th-century railroad equipment and Ford auto models. *117 Cabot Street; Wednesday 7 to 10 p.m.; 978-922-1186.*

Eighteen-year-old David Balch was, according to him, tormented by witches as he lay on his sickbed in his family home, one of the oldest wood-frame houses in America, in 1690. Although Balch died of his illness, a servant testified two years later during the Salem witch trials that she had also seen these apparitions. Because so much time had passed, neither of the two women she accused was ultimately brought to trial. *448 Cabot Street; Tuesday through Saturday 1 to 4 Memorial Day through September 30; 978-922-1186.*

The Reverend John Hale, Beverly's town minister, thought the witch trials were a terrific idea, until his wife was accused of witchcraft in 1691. The hysteria died down before she was tried. The Hale Farm, which dates to the late 17th century, survives. *39 Hale Street; Saturday 1 to 4 July and August; 978-922-1186.*

It may have only been their summer home, but *Atlantic Monthly* editor Ellery Sedgwick and his wife, Jill, spared no expense when they built Long Hill in 1916. Impressed by the Isaac Hill House in Charleston, South Carolina, the Sedgwicks copied the exterior and bought all of the original interior decoration from that 1802 mansion, which had since become a dormitory for railroad workers. But it is the gardens that are truly noteworthy, with 400 species of plants, including Japanese cherry trees, plus imported Chinese gates and tile fences. Here the Sedgwicks entertained the likes of Robert Frost and Bertrand Russell. *572 Essex Street; gardens daily 8 to sunset, house tours by appointment; 978-921-1944.*

Boston

Oliver Wendell Holmes wrote in 1858 that Boston was "the hub of the solar system," and that the exact center was the Massachusetts State House. The center of the universe is now marked with a bronze medallion in the sidewalk; find the produce stand on the corner of Washington and Summer streets and look down.

A statue of Cy Young stares steely-eyed toward a granite home plate at the site of baseball's first World Series: the Huntington Avenue Grounds, built in 1901 to house the Boston Pilgrims of the new American League, and now part of the Northeastern University campus. The original home plate was exactly at this spot; left field was bordered by Huntington Avenue, right field by Gainsborough Street. Young pitched for the Pilgrims, later to become the Red Sox, against National League champions Pittsburgh in a best-of-nine series starting on October 1, 1903. More than 18,000 fans, double the stadium's capacity, came to the game, many standing in the outfield. Boston won the series in eight games. The Huntington Avenue Grounds closed after the 1911 season to be replaced by Fenway Park in 1912, but not before Young pitched the first perfect game of the 20th century there against Philadelphia on May 5, 1904. *Behind Cabot Cage, Northeastern University.*

Although local hopes today rise and fall (usually fall) on the fortunes of one well-known baseball team, Boston once was home to two. Braves Field, home of the Boston Braves from 1915 until 1952, is the sole physical reminder of the era before the Braves left Boston for Milwaukee in 1953, and then moved to Atlanta in 1964. The stadium, now Boston University's Nickerson Field, was the site of three World Series, in 1915, 1916 and 1948; the 1936 All-Star Game, won by the National League; and Major League Baseball's longest game, between the Braves and the Brooklyn Dodgers on May 1, 1920, which went 26 innings and ended in a 1-to-1 tie. Braves Field was also home at various times to the Boston Braves football team, the Boston—now New England—Patriots, and the Boston Breakers of the U.S. Football League. *Harry Agganis Drive.*

It was in the lobby of the Hotel Buckminster that a Boston bookmaker named Joe Sullivan made a secret deal with Chicago White Sox first baseman Chick Gandil to throw the 1919 World Series in what would become known as the Black Sox Scandal. Gandil was one of eight Chicago players banned forever from baseball when the scandal was uncovered. *645 Beacon Street.*

The Museum of the Ancient and Honorable Artillery Company

At the epicenter of the busiest travel destination in New England is a place where the solitude is punctuated only by the creaking of the floorboards.

The museum of the oldest chartered military organization in the Western Hemisphere occupies the top floor of Faneuil Hall, its eclectic collection spilling into anterooms and hallways. Yet few people even know it's there.

The Ancient and Honorable Artillery Company's accumulated artifacts represent a history that dates back to 1638. The walls are lined with paintings, portraits and pennants and an ornamental wooden molding interrupted by carved images of eagles bearing mortars on their wings. There is weaponry from swords to cannon, muskets to machine guns, medals, cannonballs, bullets and bricks from old forts, prisons and historic buildings. Even the benches in the meeting hall, where the Ancient and Honorable still meets for drills, are more than a century old.

Among the weapons on display: a 1917 German water-cooled machine gun, a swivel gun designed to be mounted on the rail of a ship, a Browning automatic rifle from World War I and an early Gatlin gun with its revolving barrel. So many antique muskets are exhibited that nobody has gotten around to labeling them all.

Members of the Ancient and Honorable have served on every battlefield from early colonial Indian wars to Desert Storm, accumulating a haphazard collection of mementos: arrowheads, antique saddles, shells fired in the Spanish-American War, a cannonball from the Battle of Bunker Hill, a Civil War surgeon's kit, elegant swords and scabbards worn for show, and the hoof of a horse named Charger, apparently a hero of the Charge of the Light Brigade in 1854.

The museum of the Ancient and Honorable Artillery Company on the top floor of Boston's Faneuil Hall, whose second-best-kept secret is the elevator installed in place of an old chimney during renovations in 1990. To reach the elevator, enter on the building's south side; Monday through Friday 9 to 5; 617-227-1638.

Once the U.S. Constitution had been written in 1787, copies were circulated to stimulate discussion. One of only nine remaining copies of the first edition of the

Unknown New England

Constitution, and one of the very few on public view, is in Boston's federal courthouse. *1 Courthouse Way; Monday through Friday 8:30 to 5; 617-261-2440.*

More than a third of the visitors to the *USS Constitution* miss the *USS Cassin Young*, a World War II destroyer moored barely 50 yards away. Named for a Congressional Medal of Honor winner who swam back to his burning ship and rescued survivors during the Japanese attack on Pearl Harbor, the 376-foot *Cassin Young* took part in action in the Pacific, including the Battle of Leyte Gulf. She was twice hit by kamikaze aircraft. Big Band-era music plays in the background on tours, which are far less crowded than those aboard the *Constitution*. *Charlestown Navy Yard; daily 10 to 5 mid-June through Labor Day, then daily 10 to 4; 617-242-5601.*

Paris has its sewers and Rome its catacombs, but one of Boston's most unusual attractions has to be the state-of-the-art sewage treatment plant that's cleaning up the famously polluted harbor. Three hundred and fifty years of dumping sewage straight into the ocean made Boston Harbor so filthy George Bush used it as a backdrop to assail then-Massachusetts Governor Michael Dukakis's environmental record when Dukakis was the Democratic presidential nominee in 1988. Now dolphins, loons and harbor seals have returned, beaches are back in business, and the $3.4 billion sewer plant on Deer Island has opened for tours. The 212-acre plant—so big employees ride bicycles inside to get around—treats 450 million gallons a day of waste from Boston and surrounding communities representing nearly half the population of the state. Reusable methane, hydrogen, ammonia and sulfur are recovered from the process and sludge is processed into fertilizer. The plant's 16 giant egg-shaped tanks, 14 stories tall, are connected by enclosed walkways 140 feet in the air, which offer unparalleled harbor views. The views on the 20-minute boat ride to the plant past the city's skyline aren't bad either. There is a museum exhibit in the now-abandoned steam-driven pumphouse on the island that was built to dump the city's waste into the ocean in the 19th century. *Ferries leave from the Charlestown Navy Yard; reservations required; 617-539-4248.*

Castle Island—no longer actually an island, having been connected to the mainland in 1891—is the site of the oldest continually used military fortification in the United States: Fort Independence, established in 1634. British troops seized the fort at the outbreak of the Revolutionary War, but American forces took Dorchester Heights above in a daring middle-of-the-night maneuver, quietly emplacing 59 cannon they dragged 300 miles from Fort Ticonderoga in New York, and the British evacuated, giving newly appointed commander General George Washington his first major victory. But Fort Independence also has a literary history. The friends of a Lieutenant Robert Massie, who was shot dead in a duel over a card game in 1817, sealed his killer alive in a wall with bricks and mortar, leaving him to die. A sullen private named Edgar Allen Poe, posted to Fort Independence 10 years later, heard about the incident and used it as the basis for his story, "The Cask of Amontillado." In 1905, workers repairing an abandoned casemate found a skeleton in military uniform buried in the wall. The man was never identified. *William J. Day Boulevard, South Boston; park daily dawn to dusk, Fort Independence tours given weekends and holidays noon to 3:30; 617-268-5744.*

The site of one of the most pivotal moments in Boston history is well off the beaten trail, and often missed: Dorchester Heights, where George Washington forced the occupying British to evacuate the city by secretly surrounding them with 59 cannon dragged 300 miles by oxen from Fort Ticonderoga on the night of March 4, 1776. When they awoke to find the cannon pointing down at them, the British fled. The event is commemorated by a 215-foot marble monument and a city holiday, Evacuation Day, each March 17. *456 West 4th Street, South Boston; grounds*

Unkown Boston and Eastern Massachusetts

open dawn to dusk, monument open Saturday and Sunday 10 to 4, Wednesday 4 to 8 Memorial Day through Labor Day; 617-242-5642.

The Boston Harbor Islands National Recreation Area

It was the ocean that made Boston. It furnished fish to feed it, berths for its trading vessels, and protection from its enemies. Then the city turned its back. The harbor became a dumping ground, a national embarrassment.

But now pollution has been flushed from Boston Harbor. Popular commuter ferries cross from seaside suburbs to rejuvenated docks. The murky, smelly veil has been lifted to reveal again the watery tableau that is American's front yard.

Quietly from it has been created the Boston Harbor Islands National Recreation Area, an attraction rich with historical, cultural and natural landmarks on a par with the Golden Gate and Statue of Liberty national parks, but still comparatively unknown and uncrowded.

At the center is George's Island, the spoke from which free water taxis shuttle passengers to the other islands. It is home to one of the largest forts on the East Coast open to the public, the astonishingly well-preserved Civil War-era Fort Warren.

More than 3,000 Confederates were imprisoned here, including Confederate Vice President Alexander Hamilton Stephens. There were several executions, including that of a prisoner's wife known only as the Woman in Black, who dressed as a man and smuggled herself onto the island in a bid to free her husband. Her last wish was to be hanged in women's clothing—black drapes from the mess hall fashioned into a crude dress. Since then, there have been more than 20 sightings of a ghost-like figure dressed in black; there are even court-martial records of sentries who shot at this apparition.

Nearby Lovell's Island has a history of shipwrecks, the most famous that of a packet ship from Maine that sank in a blizzard in 1786. With no shelter, all 13 passengers and crew perished. In 1782, the French man-of-war *Magnifique* went aground here, laden with gold coins that were never found and are presumably still buried. Lovell's Island also has an underwater tunnel, a dubious submarine defense built so that explosives could be set beneath the channel.

The largest island, Peddock's, also has a giant fort, but it's an eerie ruin, abandoned after World War II and overgrown with trees. Built in the 1890s, Fort Andrews housed artillery and, later, antiaircraft guns and observation stations. More than 1,000 Italian prisoners were held there during World War II. The small white wooden church beside the pier was used by summer residents of the now-abandoned cottage community that shared the island with the fort. One islander working in her garden found what turned out to be the remains of an Indian man who lived 4,100 years ago, the oldest skeleton ever discovered in New England.

Boston Light, the quintessential lighthouse and the nation's oldest, stands on Little Brewster Island. Built in 1716, it stands 98 feet high and is visible for 16 miles. Occasional tours are given, but the best view is from the ocean-facing ramparts of Fort Warren.

The Boston Harbor Islands National Recreation Area is open from 9 a.m. to sunset from early May to mid-October. Ferries to George's Island operate from Long Wharf in Boston, Hewitt's Cove in Hingham, and Pemberton Point in Hull. From George's Island, there are free water shuttles to Lovell's, Peddock's, Gallop's, Grape and Bumpkin islands. Call 617-223-8666.

Hundreds of samples of distinguished dirt line the shelves of the Museum of Dirt, including soil specimens from the pyramids of Egypt and the Great Wall of China, the grassy knoll in Dallas, the LBJ Ranch, Nicole Brown-Simpson's front

Unknown New England

walkway, the bridge at Chappaquiddick, and the *Baywatch* beach. Samples have been donated by celebrities including Robert Redford and Vannah White; Barry Manilow contributed dirt from his driveway, columnist Dave Barry some of his dryer lint. There are also letters from Prince Charles and others politely declining to contribute to the collection. *35 Drydock Street; by appointment; 617-574-4800.*

Sixty-five billion dollars. That's how much money is processed at the Federal Reserve Bank of Boston *every day* around the clock. And you can watch as three million checks and more than six million cash notes are counted, shredded (one-third of all one-dollar bills that arrive here never leave) and impounded (the Boston Fed finds about 50 counterfeit bills per day). Built in 1977, the 33-story building itself is made of anodized aluminum and affectionately referred to by the locals as the Washboard Building. *600 Atlantic Avenue; tours of check-processing department for groups only, by appointment; 617-973-3464.*

By the late 19th century, Boston's narrow, crooked streets were so clogged it was said pedestrians could walk to work on the roofs of the obstructed trolley cars. This notorious traffic is what prompted the city to build the first subway system in the Western Hemisphere, opened in 1897. Two of the vintage workhorse streetcars that carried generations of commuters are on display on an abandoned siding in the Boylston Street station of what is now called the Massachusetts Bay Transit Authority: No. 5734, a boxy 1924 model; and the cigar-shaped no. 3295, designed in 1936. Both have been restored to the color and condition of their long years in daily service through the tunnels and along the network of surface tracks that radiated from the city center. Similar streetcars rode the rails until the current generation of light rail vehicles replaced them in the 1970s; a few still do, on the free shuttle that connects the Cedar Grove and Ashmont stations on the Red Line. That Mattapan connector, by the way, crosses Cedar Grove Cemetery, lovingly designed by a man named Frederick Safford only to see these rails laid down right through the middle of it. Safford vowed to haunt the line forever, and employees of the MBTA swear they've seen his apparition on cold and foggy winter nights.

Open to members only, the private Boston Athanaeum allows visitors for tours during limited hours if they have made advance reservations. What isn't widely known is that the first two floors of this largest membership library in North America are open at any time, including part of an art collection so valuable it formed the nucleus of the Museum of Fine Arts. One of the oldest cultural institutions in America, The Athanaeum has amassed 750,000 books since it was founded in 1807, from George Washington's personal library to the world's largest collection of Confederate imprints, books, and pamphlets, gathered by historian Francis Parkman after the Civil War. The art includes works by John Singer Sargent, Gilbert Stuart and others, and even a bust of Washington from Thomas Jefferson's dining room at Monticello. *10½ Beacon Street; Monday through Friday 9 to 5, Saturday 9 to 3:30; tours Tuesday and Thursday at 3; 617-227-0270.*

While serving in Congress from the 11th Massachusetts District beginning in 1946, John F. Kennedy lived at the Bellevue Hotel at 122 Bowdoin Street, beside the State House. It remained his legal voting address until his death. The building is now condominiums. The bachelor congressman spent Sunday afternoons in Booth 18 of the nearby Union Oyster House eating lobster stew and reading the newspapers, a custom memorialized by a small brass plaque in the booth.

Edgar Allen Poe was born in Boston, the son of actors, and wrote his first book here. But he never liked the city. No matter; Poe's birthplace is marked with a plaque at the corner of Boylston Street and Edgar Allen Poe Way.

Unkown Boston and Eastern Massachusetts

Even the period street scene out the window is authentic at the Dr. H. Martin Deranian Dental Museum, a re-creation of a 19th-century dentist's office so complete it looks as if the dentist just hung up his waistcoat and left the room. The display, at the Tufts School of Dental Medicine, includes a drill operated by a foot pump, and the "key," an extraction tool Oliver Wendell Holmes once called "a diabolical instrument of apprehension and agony." *One Kneeland Street, seventh floor; Monday through Friday 9 to 5.*

The nation's third-oldest stock exchange, the Boston Stock Exchange opened in 1834 to trade the stocks of New England-based companies. Today it trades 2,000 nationally listed equities and 200 high-growth companies. Visitors can watch from a gallery above the trading floor where there are artifacts displayed from the history of business in New England, including 17th-century shipmaking tools, Indian trading beads, and modern-day products ranging from Fig Newtons to Gillette razors. The trading floor is just above a 2,100-square-foot steel-clad vault where, in 1950s, a cabal of business leaders called the Boston Coordinating Committee met secretly at what was then the headquarters of the Boston Safe Deposit & Trust Company to talk business and politics. The group was nicknamed "the Vault." *100 Franklin Street; Monday through Friday 9:30 to 4 by appointment; 617-235-2000.*

Overshadowed by the great Chicago fire 13 months before, the great Boston fire of 1872 remains to this day the fourth-costliest conflagration in history. It killed 33 people, claimed 776 buildings, flattened 65 acres, and prompted fearful city leaders to impose a 125-foot height restriction on new construction. But the federal Customs House was exempt from this law, and became Boston's first skyscraper when the 16-story tower was added in 1913 to the original 1837 base. Now a luxury hotel, the Customs House has a small and little-known collection just above the ground-level lobby of art and artifacts from Salem's Peabody Essex Museum, including maritime paintings, Chinese export vases and tea sets, navigation instruments and telescopes, and a 19th-century painted wooden toy horse and rider from Zanzibar. *3 McKinley Square; always open; 617-310-6300.*

Distant from the city's other landmarks, the 1796 Harrison Gray Otis House is often overlooked, but is perhaps the best-preserved historic home in Boston. Its surprisingly festive and colorful decorations are startling compared to the washed-out interiors of most historic houses. In fact, microscopic paint and fiber analysis used to restore the house confirmed that homes built following the Revolutionary War were brightly decorated in keeping with the optimism of the new nation. Otis was a lawyer, congressman and later mayor of Boston who made his fortune developing nearby Beacon Hill. He also was a friend of the architect Charles Bulfinch, who designed this house and also was the architect of the U.S. Capitol building. *141 Cambridge Street; Wednesday through Sunday 11 to 5; 617-227-3956.*

Until the first successful use of ether in a surgical procedure at Massachusetts General Hospital on October 16, 1846, patients were forced to endure the knife without anesthesia. That day, considered the dawn of modern surgery, dentist William T.G. Morton placed a glass inhaler with an ether-soaked sponge over the mouth of patient Gilbert Abbott while Dr. John Collins Warren removed a tumor; the sponge and a replica of the inhaler are on display in the operating room, now known as the Ether Dome. Often overlooked in a corner of the room is the 6th-century BC mummy of an Egyptian stonecutter named Padihershef, given to the hospital in 1823. *Bulfinch Building, Massachusetts General Hospital; Monday through Friday 1 to 3; 617-726-2206.*

Despite the fact that they themselves had fled religious persecution, the ruling Puritans banished Boston's first Jewish resident, Solomon Franco, in 1640; another

Unknown New England

of Boston's earliest Jews had to convert to Christianity before he could join the Harvard faculty—to teach Hebrew. Jews from Europe started to arrive in larger numbers in the 18th century and were granted full rights of citizenship in 1821, though they were not allowed to be buried in the state until 1844. By 1900 there were 40,000 Jews in Boston; today there are 200,000. The only synagogue in Boston remaining from the great era of immigration, the Vilna Shul, has been restored as a monument to this heritage. Built in 1919 by Jews from the Lithuanian city of Vilna (now called Vilnius) the shul is a hybrid between a European synagogue and a colonial New England meeting house, though it has traditional separate seating for women, who had their own door in the alley on the right. The two-story Ark of the Covenant was carved by Jewish artisans who formerly crafted wooden ponies for carousels in Eastern Europe. Services at the shul ended in 1985. *14-18 Phillips Street; Sunday 1 to 3 April through November; 617-523-2324.*

Though Jews finally won the right to be buried in Massachusetts in 1844, the state's first legally authorized Jewish cemetery was relegated to then-distant East Boston. Still, it was better than shipping the deceased to Rhode Island, the West Indies, or even Europe, as had been done before the opening of the Temple Ohabei Shalom Cemetery. The cemetery's evolution reflects the expansion of the Jewish population in Boston. Among those buried there: Isaac Rosnosky, the first Jewish member of the state House of Representatives. *Wadsworth and Horace streets.*

Built with small donations collected over more than 50 years by a Catholic missionary order called the Don Orione Fathers, the Madonna Queen National Shrine is a 35-foot, six-ton bronze-and-copper statue of the Madonna 216 feet above sea level overlooking East Boston from Orient Heights. The statue, dedicated in 1954, is a replica of one atop Mount Mario in Rome sculpted by an Italian Jew, Arrigo Minerbi, as a gesture of gratitude to the order for helping him escape the Nazis during World War II. An observation deck in the tower offers unparalleled views of the airport below and the city skyline just across the harbor. *111 Orient Avenue, East Boston; daily 10 to 7; 617-569-2100.*

Rose Fitzgerald Kennedy was born July 22, 1890, at 4 Garden Court in the North End, now privately owned.

Although it's one of the nation's oldest parking structures, built in 1927, the garage at 600 Commercial Street in the North End is more significant as the site of the Brinks robbery on January 17, 1950, when seven men wearing rubber masks entered the second-level counting room via Prince Street and took $2.7 million, by far the largest single cash robbery up to that time. After an investigation that cost $29 million, the men were arrested just 11 days before the statute of limitations expired. The original counting room walls are gone, but the tile floor remains.

Benjamin Franklin's birthplace is marked by a plaque at 17 Milk Street. The house burned down in 1810.

Tucked away off the lobby of an office building at the heart of the financial district is the room where one of the most important technological advancements in the modern era came about: the laboratory where Alexander Graham Bell invented the telephone. Bell's lab was where the Boston University professor and determined inventor sent the first coherent spoken message—"Come here, Watson, I want you!"—on March 10, 1876. Originally at 109 Court Street, the attic laboratory was painstakingly disassembled when that building was torn down in 1959 and reassembled in the headquarters of what was then the New England Telephone and Telegraph Company (a plaque marks the spot of the original site in front of what is now the John F. Kennedy Federal Building). It looks exactly it did at the time Bell

11

was preparing sketches and models for the first telephone patent, which was granted March 7, 1876 (and is on display here); old city maps were consulted to re-create the view from the window as it would have appeared at that time. The window itself is original, as are the timbers, rafters, sheathing and floorboards, all authenticated by Bell's assistant, Thomas A. Watson, himself. Also on exhibit are the world's first commercial telephone, and the first telephone switchboard, which was installed at 342 Washington Street on May 17, 1877. *Verizon Building, 185 Franklin Street; Monday through Friday 9 to 5.*

Behind the bland façade of another telephone company building near the exact spot where the telephone was invented is hidden a museum devoted to the telephone, including early models made in the 1870s by Thomas Watson, Alexander Graham Bell's laboratory assistant. There are about 300 telephones in all here, dating from between 1876 and 1954, along with antique switchboards and related equipment, including an elaborate 1890 telephone booth with ornate carpeting and curtains. *Cambridge Street at Sudbury Street; by appointment; 617-743-1167.*

Nothing of historical significance happened at the Nichols House, though Daniel Webster lived next door for three years. What makes it special is that it's one of only two houses on Beacon Hill that's open to the public, providing a unique glimpse behind the walls. It also proves one incontrovertible truth about the pricey homes along these fabled streets: They're not as cozy as they look from the outside. Designed by Charles Bulfinch, the typical Federal-style townhouse was built in 1804 as one of four connected row houses, and each of the narrow levels is windowless at both ends with space for barely two rooms. Furnished with Flemish tapestries and oriental rugs, the house was left as a museum by Rose Standish Nichols, the last of her family to live there, who died childless in 1961, and whose dour countenance looks down from above the fireplace. *55 Mount Vernon Street; Thursday through Saturday 12:15 to 4:15 February 1 through April 30, Tuesday through Saturday 12:15 to 4:15 May 1 through October 31; 617-227-6993.*

While almost completely unknown, the 1808 William Hickling Prescott House on Beacon Hill is opened to the public by its owner, the Massachusetts chapter of the Society of Colonial Dames, a society of women whose ancestors lived in North America in 1776 or earlier. Prescott himself, who lived in the house from 1845 until 1859, was left nearly blind by a freak accident at Harvard, where he was struck in one eye by a crust of bread, yet he became a renowned historian of Spanish royalty and South American and Mexican history and was an integral member of Boston society. A portrait he owned of Cortez hangs in the house, and a secret stairway he built can be seen hidden behind a library bookcase. The Colonial Dames also have one of the largest collections of original 18th-century costumes and clothing, and a rare Simon Willard clock. *55 Beacon Street; Wednesday, Thursday, and Saturday noon to 4 April 1 through October 31, Wednesday noon to 4 November 1 through March 31; 617-742-3190.*

After her literary success, Louisa May Alcott lived here on Beacon Hill with her parents and sisters. She also died in this house off Louisburg Square on March 6, 1888, two days after the death of her father, Bronson. *10 Louisbourg Square.*

Julia Ward Howe, who wrote "The Battle Hymn of the Republic," lived on Beacon Hill with her husband, Samuel Gridley Howe, founder of the Perkins Institution for the Blind. Together they organized the Committee of Vigilance to protect fugitive slaves, and entertained the likes of Ulysses S. Grant. *32 Mount Vernon Street.*

Edwin Booth, brother of Lincoln assassin John Wilkes Booth, also lived on Beacon Hill. *29A Chestnut Street.*

Unknown New England

So determined was he to preserve his grandmother's opulent 1859 Victorian mansion, Charles Hammond Gibson Jr. roped off many of the rooms while he was still living there and made his guests sit on the stairwell instead of on the furniture. One of the first houses in the Back Bay, the Gibson House was also one of the most modern in the country at the time, with gas lighting, indoor plumbing and central heating; its interiors and servants' quarters look the way they did when the house was built. The Italian renaissance Revival-style brownstone still has its embossed leather wallpaper, walnut woodwork and imported carpets. It was left by Gibson in 1954 as a museum and home of the New England chapter of the Victorian Society. *137 Beacon Street; Wednesday through Sunday 1 to 4 May 1 through October 31, Saturday and Sunday 1 to 4 November 1 through April 30; 617-267-6338*

The Black Heritage Trail and African Meeting House

Like the history it chronicles, Boston's other freedom trail is steep and uneven. The Black Heritage Trail commemorates the affluent free black community that settled on Beacon Hill, where seeds of abolition grew. Park rangers serve as tour guides on the 1.6-mile route through the neighborhood that now is Boston's most elite address.

The first Africans in Boston, as elsewhere in the colonies, arrived as slaves in 1638. By 1705, there were the beginnings of a free black community, and there were more free blacks than slaves at the close of the American Revolution.

The oldest home built by blacks, and possibly the oldest built by anyone on Beacon Hill, was shared by black Revolutionary War hero George Middleton and Louis Glapion. The 1797 house is at the top of Pinckney Street, one of Beacon Hill's most picturesque. At No. 86 lived John J. Smith, a free black who returned to Boston from the California gold rush and became a barber. Smith's shop was a center of abolitionist activity and his house served as a rendezvous for fugitive slaves.

Central to the trail, and its first stop, is the 1897 Robert Gould Shaw 54th Regiment Memorial, an imposing high-relief bronze commemorating the all-black Civil War company from Boston that was the subject of the movie *Glory*. The frieze is dominated by the likeness of its white colonel, Robert Gould Shaw, who led the July 18, 1863 assault on Fort Wagner in Confederate Charleston, South Carolina. When it was built, the monument bore only the names of the regiment's white officers; the names of blacks who died were not added until 1982.

Nearby is the African Meeting House, the oldest standing black church in the nation. The hall's religious purpose was to be eclipsed by the political and abolitionist activities it hosted. The New England Anti-Slavery Society was founded in 1832 in the basement, and abolitionist Frederick Douglass made more than 30 speeches in the building, his principal platform in the early years of his career. William Lloyd Garrison founded the New England Anti-Slavery Society there in 1832. The meeting house has been called "the single most historic architectural monument to the human and civil rights victories of the African American in the United States."

On exhibit inside are Colonel Shaw's ceremonial sword, a handwritten speech recounting the assault on Fort Wagner and delivered at the White House by a sergeant from Shaw's regiment, a diagram of an 18th-century slave ship and copies of Garrison's abolitionist newspaper, *The Liberator*.

The African Meeting House is at 8 Smith Court on Beacon Hill in Boston, where guided and self-guided tours of the Black Heritage Trail are available. The trail also is marked with street signs; daily 10 to 4 Memorial Day through Labor Day, then Monday through Saturday 10 to 4; 617-725-0022.

The French Library arose from the local chapter of the organization France Forever, formed in July 1940 during the German occupation of France. Today it serves as a cultural center for expatriates and francophiles, though <u>political posters from World War II</u> are part of its art collection, which is open to the public. The library is housed in the Back Bay mansion built in 1867 for the wealthy Codman family; the salon was based on the Empress Josephine's private parlor at Malmaison. *53 Marlborough Street; Tuesday through Thursday 10 to 8, Friday and Saturday 10 to 5; 617-266-4351.*

The <u>oldest genealogical society in America</u>, founded in 1845, the New England Historic Genealogical Society occupies the former New England Merchants Bank, which served the wealthy Brahmins of the Back Bay, and its richly appointed lobby is open to the public—complete with the original safe. There the society displays selections of its historic art holdings, including works by John Singleton Copley and Rembrandt Peale, and curiosities including <u>the key to the prison cell where John Brown was held</u> before the fiery abolitionist was hanged for his raid on Harpers Ferry. *101 Newbury Street; Tuesday, Friday, and Saturday 9 to 5, Wednesday and Thursday 9 to 9 April 1 through November 30; Tuesday, Thursday, Friday, and Saturday 9 to 5, Wednesday 9 to 9 December 1 through March 31; 617-536-5740.*

Among Boston's countless firsts—the first digital computer, first human organ transplant, first newspaper in America, first trade union, first post office, first commercial bank, first credit union, first passenger elevator, first YMCA, first American hockey team, first public housing project—the city also had <u>the first cooking school</u>. Fannie Farmer's School of Cookery opened in the Back Bay in 1902. The building is now condominiums. *40 Hereford Street.*

The oldest historical society in America, founded in 1791, the Massachusetts Historical Society has an extraordinary collection of artifacts, including <u>the pen with which President Abraham Lincoln signed the Emancipation Proclamation, a copy by Thomas Jefferson of his original draft of the Declaration of Independence, and a table made from three pieces of the dome of the United States Capitol</u>, used at the inaugurations of Lincoln and President Ronald Reagan. Among the art holdings are works by John Singleton Copley and Gilbert Stuart, a portrait by John Trumbull of George Washington commissioned by Jefferson for Monticello, and a painting of Peter Faneuil by John Smibert, who also designed Faneuil Hall. *1154 Boylston Street; Monday through Friday 10 to 4 by appointment; 617-536-1608.*

<u>The tree beneath which Boston's Sons of Liberty met to protest British taxation</u> was unceremoniously cut down by occupying Redcoats in 1775 because of its symbolic value. But the site where the elm tree stood is marked by a bas relief made by ship carvers in 1850. *Liberty Tree Block, Boylston and Washington streets.*

<u>One of the deadliest building fires in American history</u>, the fire at the Cocoanut Grove night club on November 28, 1942, took 492 lives—second only to a 1903 Chicago theater fire that killed 602—and led to sweeping changes in fire codes and burn treatment. The fire is believed to have been started by an electrical short behind a fake coconut tree in a basement bar called the Melody Lounge; patrons trying to flee the overcrowded club were trapped behind revolving doors and locked fire exits. A plaque marks the site of the tragedy. *Piedmont Street.*

<u>Two chairs from the Cocoanut Grove nightclub</u>, confiscated by the city's arson squad after the deadly 1942 fire there, are among the more unusual artifacts in the Boston Fire Museum, housed in a former fire station built in 1891. The building still has its original brass fire poles and is crowded with historic fire apparatus, including an 1868 Button hand pumper, a 1905 hand-drawn ladder truck, a 1945 Ward LaFrance engine, and a 1966 American LaFrance. There are also two Amoskeag steam fire engines, one each from 1882 and 1896; once horse-drawn, they are

Unknown New England

now hooked up to even rarer Christie front-drive motor trackers. The museum also has the fire memorabilia accumulated over his lifetime by Boston Pops conductor Arthur Fiedler, a collection of helmets and badges from all over the world so vast only about a tenth of it can be shown at any one time. *344 Congress Street; Saturday noon to 4 April through October; 617-482-1344.*

    The Boston Public Library has a largely unknown collection of art on free public display, including works by John Singleton Copley, Winslow Homer, James Abbott McNeil Whistler, John James Audubon, Rembrandt, Goya, Picasso, Toulouse-Lautrec, Rockwell Kent, and Alfred Stieglitz. There are also murals, including John Singer Sargent's "Judaism and Christianity," which he considered his greatest achievement, showing the development of world religions, on the third floor of the McKim Building; and "The Quest of the Holy Grail," by Edwin Austin Abbey, with 150 life-sized figures illustrating the legends of King Arthur. In its research room, the library exhibits some of its rare book holdings, which include Shakespeare first folios and the personal papers of President John Adams. *700 Boylston Street; Monday through Thursday 9 to 9, Friday and Saturday 9 to 5, Sunday 1 to 5, closed Sunday June through September; 617-536-5400.*

    How secret is the memorial to anarchists Sacco and Vanzetti by Gutzon Borglum, the sculptor of Mount Rushmore? So secret it was kept out of public view for 60 years. Italian immigrants Nicola Sacco and Bartolomeo Vanzetti, executed August 23, 1927, for the murder of a factory payroll manager, were memorialized by Borglum in 1937. But so controversial was their case, the monument was three times rejected by the city; even today, it is displayed in an anteroom on the little-trafficked third floor of the Boston Public Library's McKim Building. The library also has Sacco and Vanzetti's ashes and the death masks taken after they were executed. *700 Boylston Street; Monday through Friday 9 to 5; 617-536-5400.*

    Baptist minister Francis Bellamy wrote the Pledge of Allegiance in 1892 in this building, now known as the Pledge of Allegiance Building; there is a memorial plaque at the Columbus Avenue entrance. *142 Berkeley Street.*

    Built by E.M. Statler, the famous hotelier who coined the phrase "location, location, location," the Park Plaza Hotel has its own small museum devoted to this city-within-a-city, built in 1927. The hotel was one of the first to have in-room radios, with its own radio station that broadcast from the penthouse. There also were such amenities as circulating ice water, a 30-chair barber shop to accommodate traveling salesmen, "servidoors" allowing laundry to be delivered without disturbing the guests—even a hospital on the 14th floor. A 1944 bill for $7.86 is on display. "How came you charge so much for your rooms?" the guest scrawled on the invoice. Every U.S. president since 1927 has slept here. *Lobby alcove, 64 Arlington Street; 617-426-2000.*

    The world's oldest annual marathon, the Boston Marathon has its own museum—though almost no one knows about it—tracing the colorful history of the ace all the way back to the origins of long-distance running itself: the day the Greek Pheidippides ran from ancient Marathon to Athens to deliver the report, "Rejoice! We conquer," and dropped dead. For its part, the Boston Marathon was run for the first time in 1897, a year after a contingent from the Boston Athletic Association returned from competing in the first modern Olympics, held in Greece. Of course, few modern sports require less equipment than marathon running, and the museum consists mostly of photographs, newspaper clippings, maps, T-shirts, trophies and running shoes. But what owners: Johnny Miles, Johnny Kelley, Bill Rodgers, Alberto Salazar, Joan Benoit Samuelson, and others. There is even a bronzed pair of Kelley's Size 8 running shoes; he ran the marathon 61 times, win-

15

ning it twice. *40 Trinity Place, fourth floor; Monday through Friday 9 to 5; 617-236-1652.*

Part of the collection of the Sports Museum of New England hangs on the fifth and sixth floors of the FleetCenter, including the Beanpot Trophy given to the winner of the annual hockey tournament between the city's four major universities, plus Marvin Hagler's boxing gloves, and a bleacher bench that was in Fenway Park from 1912 until 1933. *Causeway Street; Tuesday through Saturday 10 to 5, Sunday noon to 5, except during games; 617-624-1234.*

Few people have heard of Pierre Lallement, but he is considered the Henry Ford of bicycling. Lallement sold his patent for the two-wheel pedaled bicycle to Albert Pope, who founded Columbia Bicycles, the first major bicycle manufacturer in the United States, in this building in 1897. *219-223 Columbus Avenue.*

Albert Champion invented the spark plug in his South End auto supply store in 1907. *541 Tremont Street.*

The world turned inside-out, the Mapparium is a stained glass globe 30 feet in diameter that shows the planet's land mass on its spherical interior. Designed and built between 1932 and 1935 by the Christian Science Church, which is headquartered here, it is the only map of its kind in existence, made of 608 glass panels kiln-fired and fixed in a bronze framework. A glass bridge crosses the sphere, whose acoustics make it possible to hear a whisper from across the room. Around the globe has been built the Mary Baker Eddy Museum for the Betterment of Humanity, which features exhibits about the church founder and the *Christian Science Monitor* newspaper, which is published next door. *250 Massachusetts Avenue; Tuesday through Friday 10 to 9, Saturday 10 to 5, Sunday 11 to 5; 617-450-7110.*

By the time Boston University got serious about collecting the personal papers of historic literary and political luminaries, most already had been taken. So the university turned its attention to the living: stars of stage and screen, 20th-century journalists and authors, screenwriters, producers, directors and comic strip artists. Today, BU's Twentieth Century Archive boasts the world's largest collection of Hollywood memorabilia, including Fred Astaire's dancing shoes, the laurel wreath Claude Rains wore in *Caesar and Cleopatra*, Rex Harrison's Tony Award for *My Fair Lady*, Gene Kelley's Oscar for *An American in Paris*, and all the original drawings of "Little Orphan Annie," "Dennis the Menace," and "Li'l Abner." Many of the items are on display in a little-known exhibit room on the first floor of the university library. Bette Davis, who grew up in nearby Somerville and Newton, contributed 119,000 documents, including her school report cards, 111 scrapbooks she pasted together herself, and her leather-bound copy of the *All About Eve* script, opened to the famous party scene where she says: "Fasten your seat belts. It's going to be a bumpy night." "It's so lovely for someone to want one's memoirs," Joan Fontaine is reported to have said when BU came for hers. *Mugar Memorial Library, 771 Commonwealth Avenue; Monday through Friday 9 to 4:30; 617-353-3696.*

More than 80,000 documents relating to the Reverend Martin Luther King are on display in the library at Boston University, where the civil rights leader earned his doctorate in 1955. Among them: correspondence with Rosa Parks and Malcolm X, and King's BU transcript. The university was allowed to keep the papers after winning a 1993 case brought by King's widow. *Third floor, Mugar Memorial Library, 771 Commonwealth Avenue; Monday through Friday 9 to 4:30, Saturday and Sunday 9 a.m. to 10 p.m.; 617-353-3696.*

Unknown New England

The Photonics Center at Boston University studies the elements of light, a discipline that has been cross-fertilized with art to create <u>a collection of light-based art</u>. Among the unique works on display in and around the building: the "Photonics Mast," outside the southwest façade, cylindrical waveguides with high-intensity light sources at their ends. "First Light," inside, is a 12-foot-by-14-foot series of digital images inspired the Dylan Thomas line, "Light breaks where no sun shines." Another work is activated by people moving on the stairway. A self-guided tour is available beginning at the center's office on the ninth floor. *8 St. Mary's Street; Monday through Friday 9 to 5; 617-353-8899.*

Born in a New York hotel to a father who was an actor perpetually on tour, <u>playwright Eugene O'Neill died of pneumonia in his room at the Shelton Hotel</u> on November 27, 1953. "Born in a goddam hotel room and dying in a hotel room!" O'Neill sniped as he lapsed into a coma. The hotel is now a Boston University dormitory. *91 Bay State Road.*

Once the preeminent tryout town for American live theater, Boston was the place where shows were tested, tweaked and occasionally put out of their misery before they went to Broadway. *The King and I*, *South Pacific*, *Camelot*, *Mame*, Thornton Wilder's *Our Town*, and Richard Burton's *Hamlet* all opened here. An unknown Marlon Brando starred in the 1947 pre-Broadway run of *A Streetcar Named Desire*. The Rogers and Hammerstein musical *Away We Go* opened in 1943 to terrible reviews; rewritten and renamed, it went on to Broadway success as *Oklahoma!* A display of mementoes in the lobby of the Emerson Majestic Theater remembers the era when Boston had more than 50 theaters, with 1920s ticket envelopes, brass coat-check stubs, and theater programs including one from the tryout of *Of Thee I Sing*, the first Pulitzer Prize-winning musical. *219 Tremont Street; open during performances; 617-824-8000.*

The son of a sea captain, William Haynes became a silversmith who specialized in flutes. Today the William S. Haynes Company, opened in 1888, is <u>the oldest continuously operating manufacturer of handmade flutes in the United States</u>, whose flutes are used by musicians including Jean-Pierre Rampal and Kathy Chastain. Only during World War II did the Haynes Company put aside flutemaking to manufacture parts for radar, which was being developed at MIT. The factory has free tours. *12 Piedmont Street; 617-482-7456.*

Confiscated by the Japanese government as scrap metal near the end of World War II, <u>a 325-year-old ceremonial bell from a Japanese religious shrine</u> survived the war intact and was taken home to Boston as a souvenir by sailors on the *USS Boston*. Asked if they wanted it returned, Japanese diplomats replied it should be left in Boston as a gesture of world peace; the Japanese Peace Bell remains on display today in the Kelleher Rose Garden in the Fenway. *Park Drive.*

Phineas Gage's contribution to neurology was unintended. He was a construction worker helping lay a railroad line through Cavendish, Vermont, on September 13, 1848, when a four-foot iron bar propelled by an accidental dynamite explosion shot through the frontal lobe of his brain. Incredibly, Gage lived, although his personality completely changed, teaching doctors so much about brain function that the incident still appears in modern textbooks. Gage's perforated skull and the iron bar that pierced it are in the Warren Anatomical Museum, <u>one of the world's greatest collections of medical rarities</u>. Off limits for years because of lack of space, the collection has been disinterred from the vaults of Harvard Medical School and quietly returned to public view, along with the National Archives of Plastic Surgery and other holdings. Among them: 1898 x-rays of the imperial couple Nicholas II and Alexandra, showing not only their hands and wrists but the jewelry they were wearing; photographs of President James A. Garfield's spine, complete with holes left by his assassin's bullets; graphic views of Civil War wounds; early foam rubber breast implants; a colony of the mold from which the first batch of penicillin was developed in 1928; and the Storer Collection of Medical Numismatics, the world's largest collection of medical coins and medals. *10 Shattuck Avenue, fifth floor (Warren) and sub-basement (other collections); Monday through Thursday 8 a.m. to 11 p.m., Friday 8 to 7, Saturday 9 to 5, Sunday noon to 11; 617-432-4888.*

In a city of colorful politicians, James Michael Curley was the most colorful of all, winning a term as mayor even while under indictment for mail fraud. A son of Irish immigrants, Curley became a state representative, governor and congressman. But he is mostly remembered as mayor, a position he held off and on from 1914 until 1950. Even while indicted for setting up a phony mining syndicate, "the Rascal King" won back his seat in City Hall in 1945 by the largest margin ever up to that time. Convicted and imprisoned in 1947, he served only five months before his sentence was commuted by President Harry Truman, and returned to finish his term. Curley, who died in 1958, is buried in Old Calvary Cemetery. You'll recognize his house by the shamrocks. *350 the Jamaicaway, Jamaica Plain; 617-635-4105.*

Beer has always been an ingredient of Boston's history. The Pilgrims settled in Plymouth rather than continuing their journey at sea because "our victuals were spent, especially our beere," one later wrote, and many a Revolutionary War-era protest was plotted in a Boston tavern. By the early 1900s, there were 22 breweries in Boston's Jamaica Plain section, more breweries per capita than in any other U.S. city. One has been revived: the Boston Beer Company, which offers tours of the brewery where it makes some of its Samuel Adams draft beer for the Boston market. Adams himself inherited his father's malt house on State Street after graduating from Harvard in 1748, but turned out to be better at brewing rebellion than beer, and the business quickly folded. *30 Germania Street, Jamaica Plain; tours Thursday at 2, Friday at 2 and 5:30, Saturday at noon, 1, and 2, and also Wednesday at 2 in July and August; 617-522-9080.*

The military hospital where the colonial wounded were taken from the Battle of Bunker Hill, the Georgian-style Loring-Greenough House had been built in 1760 by Joshua Loring, an American who served as an officer in the Royal Navy and had fled for his safety. It also later served as headquarters for General Nathanael Greene, the youngest brigadier general in the Continental Army and confidante of George Washington who rose to the post of quartermaster general. *12 South Street, Jamaica Plain; Saturday and Sunday noon to 3, Tuesday 10 to noon Memorial Day through Labor Day, Satursday and Tuesday 10 to noon Labor Day through Memorial Day; 617-524-3158.*

Overshadowed by the far more famous Mount Auburn Cemetery, the 280-acre Forest Hills Cemetery boasts one of the nation's finest collections of 19th-century sculptures, including five by Lincoln Memorial designer Daniel Chester French. It was designed in 1848 by Henry A.S. Dearborn, the same horticulturist who helped create Mount Auburn, with rolling hills, trees, gardens, terraces, and man-made ponds; Dearborn liked it so much more, he had his own parents' remains moved to Forest Hills from Mount Auburn. Among the 100,000 other people buried there are poet Anne Sexton, *Barron's* founder Clarence Walker Barron, playwright Eugene O'Neill, author Edward Everett Hale, abolitionist William Lloyd Garrison, Boston Celtics star Reggie Lewis, and poet e.e. cummings—whose name on his gravestone is spelled in capital letters. There is a monument erected by Cunard to its employees lost at sea; a bronze eagle in memory of Kitchell Snow, the first man to land at what is now Logan International Airport, who died in a plane crash when he was 23; and the grave of John Souther, who invented the steam shovel and the auto-

Unknown New England

matic sprinkler. One of the oddest monument is the memorial to Louis E. Mieusset, who died at the age of 5 in 1886; he is depicted in a small boat, now kept under glass. *95 Forest Hills Avenue, Jamaica Plain; daily dawn to dusk; 617-524-0703.*

Human rights activist Ella Little-Collins served as surrogate mother of her brother, Malcolm Little, later to be known as Malcolm X; her house was Malcolm X's boyhood home beginning in 1940. Little worked in Boston as a soda jerk, a busboy at the Parker House Hotel, and, eventually as a burglar; it was that line of work that landed him in 1946 in Charlestown Prison and Norfolk Prison Colony, where he joined the Nation of Islam. He returned to his sister's house after he was paroled in 1953, and founded Mosque Number 11 of the Nation of Islam at 10 Washington Street in Dorchester in 1954. He would later be replaced as minister in Boston by Louis Farrakhan. His sister's home is privately owned today by other relatives, but there is a commemorative marker at the site. *72 Dale Street, Roxbury.*

New England's only museum devoted exclusively to African, Caribbean and African-American art, the Museum of the National Center for Afro-American Artists has, among other things, the burial chamber of the Nubian king Aspelta, ruler of the largest empire on the Nile until modern times, who lived in the 6th century BC. On the walls of the re-created burial chamber are hieroglyphics that were found there from the Egyptian Book of the Dead. The museum is housed in Oak Bend, a neo-Gothic Victorian mansion built in 1870. *300 Walnut Avenue, Roxbury; Tuesday through Sunday 1 to 5; 617-442-8614.*

Named for the meeting house built at its top in 1873, Meeting House Hill in Roxbury is one of Boston's oldest neighborhoods; now primarily populated by new immigrants, it was once among the city's swankiest addresses. John "Mad Jack" Percival, who commanded the *USS Constitution* on her famous around-the-world cruise starting in 1844, lived at 309 Bowdoin Street; his house is now the rectory of St. Peter's Church, the city's first major Roman Catholic church, whose construction began a rapprochement between local Protestants and Catholics. Mary Jane Safford-Blake, one of the first female gynecologists, lived at 5 Percival Street.

A window on another time surrounded by a busy urban neighborhood, the 1747 Shirley-Eustis House was the Georgian-style mansion of Royal Governor William Shirley, commander-in-chief of all British forces in North America; it is the only remaining country house in America built by a British royal colonial governor. The house was later occupied by Massachusetts Governor William Eustis. *33 Shirley Street, Roxbury; Thursday through Sunday noon to 4; 617-442-2275.*

The only Braille publishing house in New England and one of just five in the United States, the National Braille Press offers tours of the 1927 plant where written material is transcribed, proofread with the help of a 72-volume Braille dictionary, and put onto metal plates for embossing. A third of the 35 employees are blind or visually impaired. *88 St. Stephen Street, Roxbury; tours Monday through Friday 8:30 to 5 by appointment; 617-266-6160.*

A lot of history is packed onto Fort Hill; even if it wasn't, the view of downtown Boston from Highland Park at the top is unequaled. You can find it by the water standpipe, modeled on the turret of a Disney-worthy Bavarian castle, a surreal landmark towering over Roxbury. The tower stands on the site of Roxbury High Fort, built by Henry Knox in June 1775 to help end the British occupation of Boston. The park itself was landscaped by Frederick Law Olmsted in 1895.

The town center of once-independent Roxbury, little-visited John Eliot Square is named for the Christian missionary to the Indians who translated the Bible into the Algonquin language. The restored 1750 Dillaway-Thomas House, which serves as a visitor center, was <u>headquarters for the Continental Army during the siege of Boston in 1775</u>, and the Roxbury Burying-Ground boasts better examples of 17th- and 18th-century tombstones than its famous counterparts downtown. Within walking distance lived Unitarian minister and author of *The Man Without a Country* Edward Everett Hale at 12 Morley Street and abolitionist leader William Lloyd Garrison at 125 Highland Street. *183 Roxbury Street, Roxbury; Wednesday through Friday 10 to 4, Saturday and Sunday noon to 5; 617-445-3399.*

William Monroe Trotter, a Harvard graduate, <u>the first black Phi Beta Kappa</u>, and founder of an early civil rights newspaper called *The Guardian*, opposed the accommodationist racial policies of his time; he was arrested in 1903 for throwing a stink bomb into the audience during a speech by the more conservative black leader Booker T. Washington at the African Zion Church on Columbus Avenue. Trotter helped establish the Niagra Movement in 1905, which led to the formation of the National Association for the Advancement of Colored People. His beliefs and tactics were models for the civil rights movement of the middle 1900s. His home, where he lived from 1899 to 1909, is a national historic landmark, though it is not open to the public. *97 Sawyer Avenue, Dorchester.*

Overshadowed by the John F. Kennedy Library and Museum across the parking lot, the Commonwealth Museum displays the holdings of the Massachusetts Archives and Massachusetts Historical Commission, specializing in the simple items of everyday life in a state with an extraordinary history—a ball used for lawn bowling in the 1600s, for example, even though the game was then illegal in the colony. There are also epic documents including <u>the 1629 parchment charter issued by King Charles I that established the colony of Massachusetts Bay in 1629, a law against witchcraft passed in 1692, Paul Revere's bill for sounding the alarm that the British were coming (he was paid 10 pounds, four shillings), and the original state constitution, the oldest in the world still in use</u>. *220 Morrissey Boulevard, Dorchester; Monday through Friday 9 to 5, Saturday 9 to 3; 617-727-9268.*

<u>The most famous utopian experiment in America</u>, Brook Farm was founded in 1841 by transcendentalists following the anti-materialistic principles of the French social philosopher Charles Fourier. Its members shared manual labor and were paid equally whether they were milking cows or writing poems. Poems were likely preferred, considering that Nathaniel Hawthorne and other literary lights were involved. But fires and poor farmland doomed the commune, which disbanded in 1847; Hawthorne sued for the return of his investment. Ruins of the original houses can still be seen; the old print shop is intact. *Baker Street, West Roxbury.*

When rival underbosses and the feds turned up the heat on Al Capone in 1927, he went south to Palm Island in Biscayne Bay near Miami, paying cash for a 14-room Spanish-style estate that had been built by brewer Clarence Busch; it was there that he hid out during the St. Valentine's Day Massacre. Ironically, it was Capone's lavish spending on the house that would ultimately give prosecutors the evidence they needed to successfully prosecute him for tax evasion. One of those expensive furnishings was a massive room-length mahogany bar. <u>Al Capone's bar</u> today is in a Boston restaurant, the Stockyard, whose owners bought it in Atlanta in an auction. *135 Market Street, Allston; 617-782-4700.*

Braintree

The U.S. Military Academy on the west bank of the Hudson River in New York was already 15 years old when Braintree native General Sylvanus Thayer took over, but so thoroughly did he revamp the school that he is known as <u>the father of West Point</u>. Thayer remained superintendent until 1833, when he returned to his

Unknown New England

birthplace and took over the job of building Boston Harbor's military fortifications, including Fort Warren on George's Island. In 1867, he retired from the military and founded and endowed the Thayer School of Engineering at Dartmouth. Thayer's house, built in 1720 by his great-great grandfather, has his traveling writing desk, saber, commission signed by Abraham Lincoln, and one of only three surviving Dublin-style New England dovetail press cupboards, a piece of furniture literally pressed together instead of being pegged or nailed. *786 Washington Street; Saturday and Sunday 10 to 4:30 mid-April through mid-October; 781-848-1640.*

The Ernest Hemingway Archive

You won't find any signs leading to the Ernest Hemingway archive, but the stuffed impala over the fireplace and the mangy lion skin across the floor give it away.

The author's manuscripts and letters line one wall, written on the backs of tailor bills, train tickets and whatever else was handy. But it is the assortment of objects Hemingway accumulated in his real-life adventures that make this collection as unique as it is unknown.

Here is the cartridge bag he carried as an ambulance driver during World War I, and pieces of the shrapnel taken from his legs when he was wounded by a mortar shell in Italy in 1918. Hemingway's infatuation with the Red Cross nurse Agnes von Kurowski while he recuperated from this injury was the basis for *A Farewell to Arms*. Here also is the author's wallet and its contents: a World War II correspondent's visa, his 1946 Montana fishing license, a picture of his son John and—who would have expected it?—tough-guy Ernest Hemingway's AAA membership card.

The animal trophies, Mary Hemingway said, give the room "some feeling of Ernest." It was she who chose to give the Hemingway collection to the John F. Kennedy Library, passing up the Library of Congress because, she said, "I hated the idea of Ernest being stuck there in the ground in those dark corridors with so, so many other people."

Simply getting the collection here was an adventure in international intrigue, danger, honor and romance worthy of, well, Hemingway. Some of his work—including the manuscript of *Death in the Afternoon*—was recovered from the back room of Sloppy Joe's Bar in Key West, where the author was a regular, and from the basement of the Ritz Hotel in Paris. Fidel Castro, an admirer, allowed the author's widow to retrieve some papers he had left in Cuba, and President Kennedy agreed to let her go despite a travel ban imposed amidst the tensions heightened by the Bay of Pigs invasion. The battered steamer trunks that followed Hemingway through Europe on his many travels were packed for the last time with his manuscripts and letters and loaded aboard a fishing boat for Tampa.

Still stenciled, simply, HEMINGWAY, they now are part of the collection that crosses the facts of his life with his fiction.

To enter the Ernest Hemingway Room at the John F. Kennedy Library in Boston, go to the security desk beyond the gift shop on the first floor; Monday through Friday 8:30 to 4:30; 617-929-4523.

Brockton

Once the world's largest producer of footwear, Brockton boasts an obscure but extraordinary museum of shoes in the 1767 homestead of a shoemaker named Jeremiah Beals, tracing the evolution of American shoemaking from Indian moccasins to walking shoes. Also on display is celebrity footwear including Ted Williams's baseball spikes, shoes worn by Charles Lindbergh, President Gerald Ford's golf shoes, running shoes used by presidents Jimmy Carter and Bill Clinton, comedian

21

Unkown Boston and Eastern Massachusetts

Jay Leno's loafers and the size-24 shoes worn by Primo Carnera, world champion Italian boxer of the 1930s. *216 North Pearl Street; Sunday 2 to 4; 508-583-1039.*

The boxer Rocky Marciano, born here on September 1, 1923, is memorialized by the local high school stadium, where teams nicknamed the Brockton Boxers play, and by the community's slogan: City of Champions (former world middleweight champ "Marvelous" Marvin Hagler also was from Brockton). Marciano dropped out of that high school and worked in a shoe factory like his father; it was not until 1947, when he was 24, that he began to box. He knocked out former heavyweight champ Joe Lewis in 1951 and, in 1952, took down Jersey Joe Walcott in Philadelphia to win the world championship. Marciano retired in 1959 with a 49-0 record, 43 of them knockouts, and died in an airplane crash on August 31, 1969. Rocky Marciano's boyhood home is at 168 Dover Street. The boxing gloves and shoes Marciano wore while fighting Walcott are in the city historical museum. *216 North Pearl Street; Sunday 2 to 4; 508-583-1039.*

The world's first practical standardized central power system, built by Thomas Edison, was switched on at 6:15 p.m. on October 1, 1884, lighting a Brockton barber shop, billiard hall and several other businesses and leading directly to today's distribution of electricity from a central source. Edison had chosen Brockton for his demonstration because its progressive businessmen were willing to work with him. One, Colonel J.J. Whipple, later Brockton's mayor, allowed his home to be the first in the world to be lighted by Edison's standard central system; the house still stands at 42 Green Street. So does the electrical plant itself, now offices, at 60 School Street. The city's historical museum has a rare display of some of the earliest standardized incandescent bulbs dating back to 1873 and other equipment developed by Edison. *216 North Pearl Street; Sunday 2 to 4; 508-583-1039.*

Brookline

Joseph P. Kennedy bought a nine-room colonial revival-style house in Brookline in 1914 and moved there with his bride, Rose Fitzgerald Kennedy; two years out of Harvard, Kennedy was a bank president with interests in the stock market and film industry, and wanted to ride the trolley with the bluebloods. The master bedroom on the second floor would be President John F. Kennedy's birthplace, where he came into the world May 29, 1917. "We were very happy here," Rose Kennedy, who died in 1995, reminisces on a recording eerily used to narrate guided tours, "and although we did not know about the days ahead, we were enthusiastic and optimistic about the future." In fact, all four Kennedy children born in this house met tragic fates: JFK, who was assassinated; Joseph P. Jr., and Kathleen, both killed in airplane crashes during World War II; and Rosemary, who was lobotomized. In 1921, the growing family moved to a bigger house nearby at 51 Abbottsford Road. The future president was baptized and served as an altar boy at St. Aidan's Catholic Church on Freeman Street and attended the Noble and Greenough lower school next door, now the site of a high-rise apartment complex, and the Edward Devotion School on Harvard Street. *83 Beals Street; Wednesday through Sunday 10 to 4:30 May 1 through October 31; 617-566-7937.*

Joseph and Rose Fitzgerald Kennedys' graves are in Holyhood Cemetery. *Walnut Avenue at Amarillo Road.*

Frederick Law Olmsted literally changed the landscape of America. He designed New York's Central Park, the U.S. Capitol and White House grounds, the layout of the 1893 Chicago World's Fair, and the Emerald Necklace of linked green space from Boston Common to Franklin Park. He also helped to push for the protection of the Yosemite Valley as a park. Olmsted's home and office, the world's first professional practice of landscape architecture, are hidden behind a spruce

Unknown New England

pole archway entrance to the estate he called Fairsted, where he moved in 1883 and worked until his retirement in 1895. The grounds were landscaped to illustrate what he saw as the ideal suburban lifestyle, including a tiny grotto in a sunken garden. *99 Warren Street; Friday through Sunday 10 to 4:30; 617-566-1689.*

Cambridge

The spreading chestnut tree of Henry Wadsworth Longfellow's poem *The Village Blacksmith* stood outside the blacksmith's house at 56 Brattle Street. The blacksmith's house is still there; ironically, the tree was cut down and made into a chair as a gift for Longfellow by well-intentioned local children. That chair now sits to the right of the fireplace in the study of his home, which is open to the public. Longfellow first stayed in the house as a boarder in 1837; his father-in-law bought it for him as a wedding present, and he lived at this address until his death in 1882. The study appears as it did when Longfellow wrote his famous poems there, but it had previously served as George Washington's headquarters when the Continental Army was encamped at Cambridge Common. *105 Brattle Street; 8:30 to 5 Wednesday through Saturday mid-May through October 31; 617-876-4491.*

The route of William Dawes, who rode to Lexington and Concord to warn that the British were coming on April 18, 1775, is marked with horseshoes in the pavement alongside Cambridge Common. Often missed by visitors to Harvard University across Massachusetts Avenue, the Common is also where more than 16,000 colonial soldiers pitched their tents at the onset of the Revolutionary War, and where George Washington took command of the Continental Army. A slice of the tree under which he first spoke to the troops is at the Hooper-Lee-Nichols house.

Originally part of a neighborhood of summer homes with then-unimpeded views of the Charles River, the Hooper-Lee-Nichols House is the oldest house in Cambridge, built in 1685 by Dr. Richard Hooper. Hooper died almost as soon as the house was finished, and his widow purportedly ran it as a tavern of ill repute to make ends meet. The most notorious tenant, however, was Dr. John Webster, who confessed to killing Dr. George Parkman over a gambling debt after parts of Parkman's body turned up in his Harvard Medical School office. It was the most sensational murder case in 19th-century Boston. Slices of the house's floors and ceilings have been ingeniously cut away and hinged for a closer look at their original construction. *159 Brattle Street; Tuesday and Thursday 2 to 5; 617-547-4252.*

Harvard University's museums are a world-class secret. Probably the least known is the vast Museum of Cultural and Natural History, dedicated to nothing less than "the study of life on earth," with one of the world's foremost geology collections plus endless botany, zoology, archaeology and ethnology exhibits. The highlight is a remarkable one-of-a-kind display of 3,000 glass flowers, precise reproductions of delicate flowers and flower parts handcrafted over 50 years by father-and-son glass blowers for use as instructional tools for future botanists. There are also skeletons of dinosaurs and other animals now extinct, among them a 42-foot crocodile; and a zoo's worth of stuffed birds and animals. The field journals and correspondence by Ivy League anthropologists on Third World expeditions read like movie scripts. *26 Oxford Street; daily 9 to 5; 617-495-3045.*

The 1650 university charter, the oldest corporate charter still in use in the Western Hemisphere, is in the Harvard University archives, which also has John Hancock's John Hancock from the days he served as Harvard treasurer, and library records showing what Ralph Waldo Emerson and Henry David Thoreau read when they were students. This is also where they keep the keys to Harvard, used at the inaugurations of every university president since 1846, although they don't actually open anything. *Pusey Library; Monday through Friday 10 to 4:45; 617-495-2461.*

23

Unkown Boston and Eastern Massachusetts

Built in 1903, Harvard Stadium is the nation's first permanent football stadium. *North Harvard Street.*

Hidden in the basement of a science building is the Harvard Collection of Historical Scientific Instruments, one of the three largest university collections of its kind in the world, with 15,000 items dating from 1450 to the present, including a telescope purchased by Benjamin Franklin and a compass owned by Galileo. *Science Center; Tuesday through Friday 10 to 4; 617-495-2779.*

An unused storage room in a Harvard chemistry lab is the little-known home of the Museum of Improbable Research, repository of the Cambridge-based journal *Annals of Improbable Research*, whose annual Ig Nobel Awards honor scientific research that cannot and should not be reproduced. Here visitors will find a piece of Barney the Dinosaur preserved in formaldehyde, an inflatable Nixon doll used in an Ig Nobel ceremony as part of a demonstration of the prize-winning medical report "Transmission of Gonorrhea through an Inflatable Doll," and the beard of an actual Nobel Laureate. *By appointment; 617-491-4437.*

The oldest library in the United States, second in size only to the Library of Congress, Harvard's Widener Library is named for Harvard graduate Harry Elkins Widener, who went down on the *Titanic*. But while Widener is no longer open to the public (thanks to snotty scholars who complained about chatty tour guides), the rare book collection housed next door in Houghton Library has an elegant exhibition hall that shows selections from its unparalleled holdings. The collection includes everything from Shakespeare first folios to the papers of Leon Trotsky. *Harvard Yard; Monday through Friday 9 to 5, Saturday 9 to 1; 617-495-2441.*

The first black to earn a doctorate at Harvard, NAACP co-founder W.E.B. Dubois lived at 20 Flagg Street.

Often bypassed in favor of that other university across town, the Massachusetts Institute of Technology has an unparalleled permanent collection of contemporary art displayed around its Charles River-side campus, including sculptures by Alexander Calder, Henry Moore and Louise Nevelson. A self-guided tour to the works is sold at MIT's List Visual Arts Center, a museum designed by MIT alumnus I.M. Pei, where rotating exhibits are shown. *20 Ames Street; Tuesday, Wednesday, Thursday, Saturday, and Sunday noon to 6, Friday noon to 8; 617-253-4680.*

Louis Pasteur's address book is among the artifacts in the collection of the Dibner Institute, a museum of the history of science and technology. Also on exhibit: 18th-century static electricity collectors, early lightbulbs including Westinghouse test models, some of the first telegraphic transmission keys, and pieces of the first transatlantic telegraph cable. The museum also has a plaster copy of Isaac Newton's death mask, the parchment on which he tried to calculate the dimensions of the Temple of Solomon, and his proof of the *Principia Mathematica*, laying out his theories of physics. The Newton memorabilia at the institute is the second-largest collection of its kind in the world. *Burndy Library, Massachusetts Institute of Technology, 38 Memorial Drive; Monday through Friday 9 to 5; 617-253-8721.*

It may not look like much from the outside, but the MIT Museum has, among other things, the world's largest collection of holograms, and art created using the electronic strobe, developed at MIT by the late Harold "Doc" Edgerton, known as "the man who stopped time." The strobe light allows photographers to capture phenomena that are otherwise too fleeting to be seen, such as a bullet piercing an apple, a drop of milk falling on a flat surface, and a balloon as it pops. There are also moving sculptures, in the literal sense of the word, some of them operated by

Unknown New England

hand cranks. *265 Massachusetts Avenue; Tuesday through Friday 10 to 5, Saturday and Sunday noon to 5; 617-253-4444.*

Who says MIT students don't have a sense of humor? The school's legacy of practical jokes and pranks is so rich, it has its own museum. The Hall of Hacks boasts the full-sized police car school officials found one morning sitting atop the university's signature dome in 1994, complete with a box of doughnuts on the front seat, the original "Nerd Crossing" sign that appeared one day on Massachusetts Avenue, a device once used to make it snow inside a dormitory, and the weather balloon that arose from the playing field during the 1982 Harvard-Yale football game; at the same game, unknowing Harvard fans raised placards they thought spelled out "Beat Yale," but actually read: "MIT." *265 Massachusetts Avenue; Tuesday through Friday 10 to 5, Saturday and Sunday noon to 5; 617-253-4444.*

One of the world's best, and nation's oldest, maritime collections, the Hart Nautical Gallery at MIT was opened in 1921. Endowed by Francis Russell Hart, a member of the Class of 1885 who rose to become president of the United Fruit Company, it has more than 35 full-hull ship models originally used as teaching aids at MIT's Pratt School of Naval Architecture, now called the Department of Ocean Engineering, among them the *USS President*, a frigate similar to the *USS Constitution*, and the most famous of all America's Cup racers, the metal-hulled *Reliance*, which won the cup in 1903. *55 Massachusetts Avenue; daily 9 to 8; 617-253-5942.*

The navigation instruments that made it possible for man to land on the moon are on exhibit at the Charles Stark Draper Laboratory, where they were developed. Draper pioneered the guidance and inertial navigation systems for the Apollo program, submarines and missiles. The company's progenitor, Charles Draper, invented the extraordinarily accurate Mark XIV gunsight used by U.S. anti-aircraft gunners to shoot down enemy planes in World War II. A Mark XIV also is shown, along with a model of a Mars probe designed in 1957 but never launched. *Lobby, 555 Technology Square; Monday through Friday by appointment; 617-258-2605.*

To this day, no one knows who secretly put a granite bench dedicated to the writer Virginia Woolf in a quiet waterside stand of pines at Fresh Pond Reservation in 1994, inscribed with a passage from the novel *Orlando*: "There are wild birds' feathers—the owls, the nightjars. I shall dream wild dreams. I should lie at peace here with only the sky above." After the mystery received worldwide attention, however, the city let it stay. *Fresh Pond Parkway.*

Canton

The oldest continually operated weather station on the continent, the Blue Hill Observatory has been around for so long, readings were originally taken there by kite. The observatory was founded in 1884 as a private scientific station for the study of the weather, the atmosphere and climate, and pioneered the measurement of atmospheric radiation and other phenomena. The first weather readings were taken February 1, 1885, and have continued uninterrupted since then, producing the most consistent climate record in North America. Some of those early kites are on view, along with early instruments including antique barometers still in use. The bas relief on the exterior is a copy of a fresco from the Tower of the Winds in Greece. *Washington Street; by appointment; 617-696-0389.*

Cohasset

The brig *St. John*, packed with immigrants from Galway fleeing the Irish potato famine, was practically in sight of Boston and passengers were celebrating their arrival when the ship was dashed on an underwater ledge off Cohasset in a storm on the night of October 7, 1849 Ninety-nine passengers drowned while the crew escaped in the only two lifeboats. The captain's writing desk and a passenger's trunk from the ill-fated *St. John* are part of the collection of the Cohasset Maritime Museum. The museum also has models of several Donald McKay clipper ships, including the *Great Republic*, the largest ever built, which was launched from McKay's East Boston shipyard. *Elm And Main Streets; Tuesday through Saturday 1:30 to 4:30 June 1 through September 30; 781-383-1434.*

Concord

The surviving lantern of the two hung in the steeple of the Old North Church to warn that the British were coming on the eve of the Revolutionary War isn't in the church; it's in the Concord Museum, which traces the history of this town from the time of the Native Americans who lived here first, followed by rebellious colonists in the 18th century and America's leading literary figures in the 19th. Ralph Waldo Emerson's study has been moved to the museum and rebuilt so exactly that the sunlight enters the same way it did in his house, which is across the street. The museum also has the single largest collection of Henry David Thoreau artifacts, including the bed, desk and rocking chair from his cabin at Walden Pond. There are weapons used by both sides in the battles of Lexington and Concord, and a veritable forest of colonial standing high chests and grandfather clocks. *200 Lexington Road; Monday through Saturday 9 to 5, Sunday noon to 5; 978-369-9609.*

Part of the Underground Railroad, the 1720 house now used as a gallery for the Concord Art Association has a secret room to hide escaped slaves behind a panel on the first floor reached through a trap door in an upstairs bedroom. So well-designed was the chamber, it was not rediscovered until 1922. The house is also unique in that it was the work of an early woman architect, Lois Howe, and home to American Impressionist artist Elizabeth Wentworth Roberts, 18 of whose works are on display. *37 Lexington Road; Tuesday through Saturday 10 to 4:30, Sunday noon to 4:30; 978-369-2578.*

Ralph Waldo Emerson encouraged his friends to move to Concord in a bid to build an intellectual utopia; the Alcotts lived a block away, and Nathaniel Hawthorne next to them. As for Emerson's house, where he lived from 1835 until his death in 1882, it was comparatively undistinguished. Operated as a museum by his descendants, the house looks much as it did when Ralph lived there, complete with his books, furniture, the robe he wore while preaching, his beaver hat—even his dressing gown. *28 Cambridge Turnpike; Thursday through Saturday 10 to 4:30, Sunday 2 to 4:30 mid-April through October 31; 978-369-2236.*

Louisa May Alcott wasn't the only one of transcendentalist Bronson Alcott's daughters who was creative. Her sister May drew pictures on the wall of their house in Concord, and her sister Anna was an actress who performed to audiences seated in the parlor. May's drawings and Anna's makeshift stage survive in the house, called Orchard House because it was at one time in an orchard. The house was as eccentric as its occupants. It was built in 1857 by joining together two 18th-century houses, leaving peculiar nooks and crannies and a steeply slanted floor. As for Louisa, she wrote her semiautobiographical classic *Little Women* sitting at her bedroom window. *399 Lexington Road; Monday through Saturday 10 to 4:30, Sunday 1 to 4:30 April 1 through October 31, Monday through Friday 11 to 3, Saturday 10 to 4:30, Sunday 1 to 4:30 November 1 through March 31; 978-369-4118.*

Sleepy Hollow Cemetery is the final resting place of such luminaries as Nathaniel Hawthorne, Ralph Waldo Emerson, Henry David Thoreau and Louisa May Alcott, who succumbed to mercury poisoning she contracted as a Civil War nurse. The headstones tell their own story. Thoreau, for example, died at only 44, and Alcott outlived her father, Bronson, by just two days. One of the most interesting monuments, however, was sculpted by Lincoln Memorial designer Daniel Chester French to three men of the same family killed in the Civil War and commissioned by their lone surviving brother. *Bedford Street; daily dawn to dusk; 978-371-6299.*

Danvers

The biggest secret about Danvers is that it's actually Salem. Danvers was originally known as Salem Village Parsonage, and it is here that many of the witchcraft incidents associated with Salem actually took place. The foundation of the house where Elizabeth Parris and her cousin, Abigail Williams, concocted the tales that caused the witchcraft hysteria in the first place starting in 1692 is at 67 Centre Street. The Osburn house at 273 Maple Street was the home of the first victim, Sarah Good, who was hanged, and Rebecca Nurse, who denounced the young girls and was also hanged; her sons are said to have secretly retrieved her body from its unmarked grave and buried it in the yard. A memorial to the 25 men, women and children killed as witches was erected in 1992 at 176 Hobart Street, near the site of the meeting house where the witchcraft trials themselves were held.

At more than 300 years, the Endicott pear tree is the oldest living fruit tree in America. *Endicott Street.*

Dedham

The sound of toilets flushing in the adjacent theater restroom is an appropriate accompaniment for a visit to the Museum of Bad Art, which specializes in "art too bad to be ignored." These works are so artless that only one of every 10 nominees is bad enough to be accepted. Highlights include a painting of a Hindu goddess at the beach with a radio and umbrella, a pointillist study of a fat man in a towel, and the composition *Sunday on the Pot with George*. *Dedham Community Theater basement, 580 High Street; Monday through Friday 6:30 to 10:30, Saturday and Sunday 1:30 to 10; 781-325-8224.*

The oldest wood-frame house in North America, the Fairbanks House was built in 1636 for farmer Jonathan Fairbanks and occupied by his descendants until 1904; fully 90 percent of the original framing is intact. *511 East Street; Tuesday through Saturday 10 to 5, Sunday 1 to 5 May 1 through October 31; 781-326-1170.*

Dover

A sex scandal that rocked Boston society took place in a seven-room English country cottage where an eccentric Boston mayor named Andrew Peters hid his teen-age mistress, Starr Faithfull, during a seven-year affair beginning in 1919; he was 45 at the time, and married. The main room of the house has 33-foot ceilings painted blue with "stars" that light up at the flick of a switch representing the sky as it appears in March, the month of Faithfull's birth. Her mysterious death years later made headlines, though while Peters's career would end in embarrassment and disgrace, he was never implicated in the case. *Old Colony Drive.*

The Dover Pharmacy still sells lime rickeys from its old-fashioned soda fountain, as it has since World War II, mixed in a Hamilton Beach blender that goes back even farther than that. *60 Centre Street; 508-785-0166.*

A gentle trail rises through a New England wood of oak, maple, beech and birch trees, to a flat rock ledge left by an ancient glacier. Silent but for the sound of birds and a burbling brook, the forest seems as distant from civilization as it's possible to get. All the more startling, then, to part the curtain of skinny white pines that mark the entrance to the ledge, step out, and come upon ... the Boston skyline. In fact, this place, Noanet Peak, is only 19 miles from downtown, part of the 695-acre Noanet Woodlands. Noanet Brook powered the Dover Union Iron

Unkown Boston and Eastern Massachusetts

Company, which made nails, part of the unexpected industrial legacy of what is now decidedly a bedroom suburb; a spur trail leads to the ruins of the iron mill. In all, 10 miles of color-coded trails cross the soft forest floor of the preserve, populated only by warblers, woodpeckers, orioles and other birds; the blue trail leads to the 387-foot peak, with its extraordinary views of Boston. *Dedham Street; daily dawn to dusk, with a ranger on duty weekends and holidays; 508-359-6333.*

A powderhorn carried by Thomas Larrabee, a local farmer who helped row Washington across the Delaware, is one of the treasures of the Sawin Museum of local history. *Dedham and Centre streets; Saturday 1 to 4 April through June and September through November; 508-785-0567.*

Duxbury

This is the town where the Pilgrims eventually really settled, among them John and Priscilla Alden, who traveled the two miles across Plymouth Bay to Duxbury with some of their 10 children in 1632 and built a tiny cottage that survives to this day. The house, since expanded, is furnished with period antiques donated by the Aldens' descendants, who meet there for reunions. John and Priscilla Alden are buried in the Old Burial Ground on Chestnut Street, where other Pilgrims' gravestones betray the harsh conditions of the early settlement when entire families could be wiped out in a week by fever. *Alden Street; Monday through Saturday noon to 4 mid-May to mid-October; 781-934-9092.*

On the highest point of the peninsula that faces southeast into Plymouth Bay is the Miles Standish Monument, a 116-foot granite tower topped by a 14-foot statue of the Pilgrims' militia leader, built in 1898. The view from the top reaches as far as Provincetown, 25 miles east. *Crescent Street; daily dawn to dusk; 508-866-2580.*

Founded by the Weyerhauser family of lumber industry fame, the Art Complex Museum is built of Douglas fir with a rolling roof to mimic ocean waves. But the building is only part of the attraction. Inside are some of the family's art acquisitions, including one of the largest contemporary ceramics collections in the United States, Rembrandt's "The Descent from the Cross by Torchlight," a Tiffany stained-glass window, and a complete Japanese teahouse reassembled on the grounds, where authentic tea ceremonies are held the last three Sundays of June, July and August. *189 Alden Street; Wednesday through Sunday 1 to 4; 781-934-6634.*

The largest shipowner in America at the time his house was built in 1808, Ezra Weston II was so rich and powerful he came to be called King Caesar. Now a museum, the King Caesar House reflects this status, with rare and expensive French wallpaper and a Spanish mission bell taken by pirates during a raid in the Caribbean and recaptured by one of Weston's ships at sea. The fleet was based at the massive stone wharf opposite the house. In 1869, the first indirect transatlantic cable from France was laid with Duxbury as its American terminus via the French island of St. Pierre off the coast of Newfoundland. The cable office was in the basement of 670 Washington Street, which is now a private home, but the museum has several pieces of the cable itself and some of the original telegraph equipment, almost all of which still functions. *120 King Caesar Road; Wednesday through Sunday 1 to 4 mid-June through September 30; 781-934-6106.*

Easton

So successful was the Ames Shovel Company that, by 1879, two-thirds of all the shovels in the world were made here, and North Easton came to be known as "Shovel Town." The mansion built by Frederick Lothrop Ames with his resulting fortune now is part of the Stonehill College campus, which uses it to house the world's largest collection of shovels. The Ames Shovel Archive has 784 shovels,

Unknown New England

including "entrenching" shovels from the War of 1812, an iron potato scoop shovel, and 24 silver-plated shovels from the 1876 Centennial Exhibition in Chicago. *Donahue Hall, 320 Washington Street; by appointment; 508-565-1403.*

Part of the wealthy Ames shovel family, Oakes and Blanche Ames were accomplished in their own right, he as <u>a world-renowned botanist who specialized in orchids</u> and she as <u>president of the Massachusetts Women's Suffrage League</u> who used her talents as an artist to support the cause of women's rights. Their 15-room mansion, Borderland, built in 1911, sits on 1,800 acres of lawns, woods and fields, and looks like an English castle. The chandelier in the dining room is a replica of Columbus's ship the *Santa Maria*; the two-tiered library has 6,000 books; and there is a trophy room of Civil War artifacts related to Blanche Ames's father, General Adelbert Ames, and her grandfather, General Benjamin Butler, who was governor of Massachusetts. *Massachusetts Avenue; grounds open daily dawn to dusk, house Sunday 1 to 3 and Friday by appointment; 508-238-6566.*

The Ames men fancied themselves gentleman farmers, importing bulls for breeding. So expensive was this hobby that the animals were given formal burials when they died. The site of <u>the world's only known bull cemetery</u> is beside the Holy Cross Fathers Archive building on the Stonehill College campus.

H.H. Richardson, designer of Boston's Trinity Church—ranked by the American Institute of Architects as one of the 10 greatest public buildings in the nation—is considered the pre-eminent 19th-century American architect. <u>The greatest single concentration of H.H. Richardson buildings</u> is in Easton: five in all, including the railroad station, which now serves as the home of the Easton Historical Society. The society has self-guided tours of the Richardson buildings, all in walking distance. *80 Mechanic Street; second Sunday of each month 1 to 5; 508-238-7774.*

Essex

Nearly 4,000 vessels were built in Essex beginning in 1668, but only five survive. <u>One of last five surviving Essex schooners</u> is on display, albeit on land, beside the Essex Shipbuilding Museum: the *Evelina M. Goulart*, which fished the North Atlantic from Canada to the Carolinas for 50 years and twice held the record for the most swordfish caught in a single voyage. Inside the museum, housed in the 1835 Essex Central School, is a collection of 20 ship models on loan from the Smithsonian Institution, among other maritime artifacts. *28 Main Street; Wednesday through Sunday noon to 4; 978-768-7541.*

The house built in 1730 by a man named Jonathan Cogswell on land that had been granted to his great-grandfather 100 years earlier looks like an old farmhouse from the outside, but the inside is filled with <u>one of the nation's most important collections of folk art</u>, acquired over 50 years by longtime Society for the Preservation of New England Antiquities director Bertram Fletcher and his wife, Nina, who bought Cogswell's Grant as a summer home in 1937. The collection includes primitive paintings, furniture, Shaker boxes, weathervanes and decoys. *Spring Street; Wednesday through Sunday 11 to 5 June 1 through October 15; 978-768-3632.*

Fairhaven

<u>A British cannon captured by John Paul Jones</u> is still emplaced at Fort Phoenix, the ruins of a Revolutionary War-era fort built to protect New Bedford Harbor; cast in 1690, the cannon bears the imprint of the royal lion head with crown, but proved no match for attacking British troops who captured the fort and blew it up on September 5, 1778. Later rebuilt from the ashes—and given its new name—Fort Phoenix was used to ward off a War of 1812 attack by the *HMS Nimrod* on June 13, 1814. The fort was decommissioned in 1876. *Old Fort Road; daily dawn to dusk.*

Unkown Boston and Eastern Massachusetts

Joshua Slocum spent 18 months on Poverty Point fitting out a broken-down oyster boat in which he would become the first man to sail alone around the world in 1898. Slocum's voyage aboard the 36-foot *Spray* started in Boston on April 24, 1895, and ended more than 46,000 miles later at Newport, Rhode Island, on June 27, 1898. On July 3 of that year, Slocum sailed the *Spray* back to Fairhaven, where a memorial commemorates his feat. *Pilgrim Avenue.*

Some of the most beautiful municipal architecture in the country is the legacy of Fairhaven's native son and Standard Oil founder Henry Huttleston Rogers, a friend of Mark Twain and benefactor of Helen Keller. Rogers built and paid for almost every public building in his home town: the high school, Rogers Grammar School, Masonic hall, Cushman Park, Unitarian Memorial Church and Millicent Library, whose stained-glass window by the London firm of Clayton & Bell includes the likeness of Rogers' daughter Millicent as the winged Muse of Poetry. "It is the ideal library," said Twain, a frequent visitor. Rogers, who was born in Fairhaven in 1840, even gave the town its public water system. A tall granite shaft in front of Fairhaven High School was erected by the town in 1912 as a memorial to Rogers, inscribed in Latin with the words: "If you would see his works, look about you." Rogers' boyhood home is at 39 Middle Street; his grave, at Riverside Cemetery.

John Cooke, one of the original, and longest-surviving, *Mayflower* Pilgrims, is buried at Burial Hill.

Fall River

The house where Lizzie Borden took an ax and gave her mother 40 whacks (and where, when she saw what she had done, she gave her father 41) is now a museum and bed-and-breakfast inn. Borden was actually acquitted of the charges that she killed her wealthy father Andrew and stepmother Abby in their Greek Revival-style home on August 4, 1892. Still, Lizzie, then 32, was forever ostracized; she died, unmarried, in 1927 at the age of 67. Officially, the deaths remain unsolved. The house has been reopened as a museum of Borden memorabilia and a six-room inn with period artifacts, ouija boards, books related to the case, and video editions of a movie it inspired. Guests get the same breakfast that the Bordens ate on the morning of their murders, as established in the autopsies: bananas, jonny-cakes, and sugar cookies. *92 Second Street; 508-675-7333.*

The hatchet with which Lizzie Borden was accused of murdering her parents is the highlight of the Fall River Historical Society museum, which also has a blood-stained camisole and bedspread from the house, photos of the victims' shattered skulls and locks of their hair, and the chair from the cell where Lizzie was held while awaiting trial. Lizzie Borden and her parents are buried together in Oak Grove Cemetery. There also is an odd display about 19th-century mourning customs, including photographic portraits of dead people. *451 Rock Street; Tuesday through Friday 9 to 4:30 April through mid-November, Tuesday through Friday 9 to 4:30 and Saturday and Sunday 1 to 5 June through September; 508-679-1071.*

Madeleine Astor's life vest from the *Titanic*, a section of the ship's wooden railing and a chair from its Turkish bath are among the artifacts in the little-known Fall River Marine Museum, which also has a 28-foot model of the ill-fated liner created by Twentieth Century Fox for a 1952 film about the tragedy with Barbara Stanwyck and Clifton Webb. Mrs. Astor survived, but her husband, John Jacob Astor, was lost; the chair and railing were recovered by ships sent to retrieve the bodies. The museum also has the seaman's union log of Frederick Fleet, the lookout who spotted the iceberg. *Battleship Cove; Monday through Friday 9 to 5, Saturday noon to 5, Sunday noon to 4; 508-674-3533.*

Unknown New England

Longer than two football fields and as tall as a nine-story building, the *USS Massachusetts* was the first and last American battleship to fire its guns in World War II; it anchors Battleship Cove, the world's most complete collection of historic fighting ships, including the destroyer *USS Kennedy*, named for President John F. Kennedy's older brother, Joseph P. Kennedy, the first vessel to stop a Soviet-chartered ship during the Cuban blockade in 1962; the World War II sub *USS Lionfish*; two PT boats, one of them used in JFK's inaugural parade; and the *Hiddensee*, operated by the former East Germany and given to the U.S. Navy after German unification. There are also landing craft like those used on D-Day, and a rare Japanese manned torpedo of the type sent on suicide missions at the end of World War II. *Battleship Cove; daily 9 to 5 April 1 through June 30, daily 9 to 5:30 July 1 through Labor Day, daily 9 to 4:30 Labor Day through March 30; 508-678-1100.*

Tiny steam engines and visitor-operated N-gauge model railroads chug their way around a 1930 Pennsylvania Railroad passenger coach, the fitting venue of the Old Colony & Fall River Railroad Museum, which also has a full-sized New Haven Railroad diesel car, a caboose, and the only surviving New Haven 40-foot boxcar; railroads have since switched to 50-footers. *Central and Water streets; Thursday through Sunday noon to 5 July 1 through Labor Day, then Saturday noon to 4 and Sunday 10 to 2 through mid-November; 508-674-9340.*

Framingham

A former slave credited with killing the British commander at the Battle of Bunker Hill, Peter Salem had been freed in exchange for enlisting in the colonial army. During the battle on June 17, 1775, he is said to have shot British Major John Pitcairn when Pitcairn ordered the American troops to lay down their arms and surrender. Suddenly leaderless, the British were temporarily stunned, giving the Americans time to retreat before they ran out of ammunition. Salem, who died on August 16, 1816, is buried in Framingham's Old Burial Ground. *Main Street.*

A fife played during the Revolutionary War, with the original accompanying songbook, is a highlight of the collection in the Old Academy Museum, a former school built in 1837 that now serves as the local historical museum. *Vernon and Grove streets; Wednesday and Thursday 10 to 4, Saturday 10 to 1; 508-872-3780.*

Freetown

A Revolutionary War engagement that came 10 days before shots were fired in Lexington or Concord, the Battle of Freetown on April 9, 1775, ended with the capture by Patriot militiamen of ordnance stockpiled on the property of a British colonel, who promptly fled to Canada. The story is retold in the museum of the Freetown Historical Society, which also has a large Civil War collection, and antique cars including a 1928 Franklin and 1931 Ford Model A. *1 Slab Bridge Road; Sunday 1 to 4 and Monday 10 to 4 July and August, then Monday 10 to 4; 508-644-5310.*

Gloucester

Clarence Birdseye, the inventor of frozen food, noticed that fish frozen stiff when caught were still fresh when thawed out months later. In 1924, he developed a company called General Seafoods Corporation in Gloucester to develop the process commercially. Birds Eye frozen peas, spinach, meat and fish went on sale in 10 grocery stores in Springfield on March 6, 1930. A plaque marks the site of Birdseye's original building. *33 Commercial Street.*

The largest collection of works by Gloucester native Fitz Hugh Lane, one of America's foremost maritime artists, is the centerpiece of the Cape Ann Historical Museum. The museum has 139 paintings and drawings by Lane. It also has the

Unkown Boston and Eastern Massachusetts

Centennial, a Gloucester dory used by Alfred Johnson on his first solo sail across the Atlantic in 1876, and the Gloucester sloop *Great Republic*, in which Howard Blackburn also sailed alone across the Atlantic in 1901—despite the fact he had no fingers. *97 Pleasant Street; Tuesday through Saturday 10 to 5; 978-283-0455.*

Judith Sargent Murray was the great-great aunt of artist John Singer Sargent, but she also was accomplished in her own right as a writer, early equal rights advocate and co-founder with her husband of Universalism in America. Murray also was the first American-born woman to write plays that were produced. Her Georgian-style home has been restored to the way it would have looked in 1790, when she lived there, and includes pencil etchings Sargent drew when he was 4, his oil portraits of his parents, and his traveling painter's palette. *49 Middle Street; Friday through Monday noon to 4 Memorial Day through Columbus Day; 978-281-2432.*

The Independent Christian Church was the first Universalist church in America. *Church and Middle streets.*

A jumble of towers, turrets, gables, and fake windows, Beauport was the fantasy home of early 20th-century collector and interior designer Henry Davis Sleeper. Sleeper, who designed interiors for such celebrity clients as Joan Crawford and Fredric March, spent 27 years building his own house, beginning in 1907, on land overlooking Gloucester Harbor. It has secret passageways, hidden skylights, and 40 rooms filled with his vast collections of antiques, including a regimental banner carried by Massachusetts forces in the Revolutionary War. The wooden curtains in the library were originally used in a hearse. After Sleeper died, the house was bought and preserved by Charles and Helena McCann, heirs to the Woolworth fortune. *75 Eastern Point Boulevard; Monday through Friday 10 to 4 mid-May through mid-September, Monday through Friday 10 to 4, Saturday and Sunday 1 to 4 mid-September through mid-October; 978-283-0800.*

During the 1930s, eccentric entrepreneur Roger Babson, the founder of Babson College, had inspirational mottos carved into huge stones in the area called Dogtown straddling the Gloucester-Rockport line. The sayings— "Keep Out of Debt," "Never Try, Never Win," and many others—can still be seen; maps are available in local bookstores. Babson, who was born in Rockport, ran for president as the candidate of the National Prohibition Party and came in third behind Franklin D. Roosevelt and Wendell Wilkie. In 1948, he created the Gravity Research Foundation to try to prove that gravity could be harnessed for energy. *Dogtown Road.*

Halifax

The lid of a casket used to ship home a casualty of the Civil War is in the Museum of Halifax. John Soule died in North Carolina of a fever; his family used the casket, stamped with his name, to patch a floor, until it was rediscovered. *Route 106; Wednesday 1 to 5 and the third Sunday of each month 2 to 4; 781-293-3163.*

Haverhill

The home town of artist Bob Montana, Haverhill was the model for Riverdale in the Archie comics, right down the statue of *The Thinker* that stands in front of both Haverhill and Riverdale high schools. Archie, Veronica, Jughead and the gang were inspired by Montana's classmates at Haverhill High; he sketched them in 1941 on a napkin in the Chocolate Shop on Merrimack Street. The shop has since closed, but it has been immortalized as the Choklit Shoppe on fictional Riverdale's Main Street. Montana drew the Archie characters until his death in 1975.

The first Macy's parade was held not in New York City, but on July 4, 1854, in Haverhill, where R.H. Macy got his start in the retail business by opening a dry

Unknown New England

goods store in 1851. Macy sold the store in 1858 and, with financial backing from Haverhill's Caleb Hunking, established his famous New York department store. The building that housed R.H. Macy's first department store remains, although it has undergone several major renovations. *70 Merrimack Street.*

Macy's wasn't the only 20th-century rags-to-riches story that began in Haverhill. Movie magnate Louis B. Mayer got his start here in 1907 when he bought a rundown theater he renamed the Orpheum; within nine years had built New England's largest movie theater chain. Mayer left in 1916 to found what would become MGM. He lived at various times on Temple Street and Hamilton Avenue.

A button taken from a British soldier's uniform and presented to the town by George Washington is in the Buttonwoods Museum, Haverhill's historical museum. So is the desk and poker table used by Theodore Roosevelt's Navy Secretary, William Moody, who was a Haverhill native and the prosecutor in the Lizzie Borden case; and a mirror from one of Louis B. Mayer's original local movie theaters. The museum is named not for Washington's button, but for the graceful buttonwood trees that once stood on the site. *240 Water Street; daily 10 to 5; 978-374-4626.*

A prisoner of marauding Indians who escaped by killing 10 of her captors, Hannah Duston is memorialized in a statue in G.A.R. Park. The story is more complicated than it sounds, however. Abenaki Indians killed 27 people in their March 15, 1697 raid, and kidnapped Duston, her infant child, and 13 others. But six of the Abenakis that she killed on her escape were women and children, and Duston returned with their bloody scalps to collect a cash bounty. *G.A.R. Park, Main Street.*

The birthplace of abolitionist, poet, and newspaper editor John Greenleaf Whittier, the Whittier Family Homestead appears much as it did in the 1820s, when he made it the subject of his poems "Snowbound," "In School Days" and "Barefoot Boy." *305 Whittier Road; Tuesday through Saturday 10 to 5, Sunday 1 to 5 May 1 through October 31, Friday and Sunday 1 to 5, Saturday 10 to 5 November 1 through April 30; 978-373-3979.*

Hingham

Major General Benjamin Lincoln, who accepted the British surrender at Yorktown to end the Revolutionary War, lived at 181 North Street; the home is still owned by his descendants. Lincoln is buried in Old Ship Cemetery.

When Thomas Andrews Jr. received a license to operate a tavern in 1702, it was on the condition that he "send his customers home at reasonable hours with the ability to keep their legs." The Old Ordinary, so called because it served ordinary home-cooked food along with drink, now is a museum with an authentic 17th-century tap room. The other rooms are filled with 18th- and 19th-century furniture; the garden is attributed to Frederick Law Olmsted. *21 Lincoln Street; Tuesday through Saturday 1:30 to 4:30 mid-June through mid-September; 781-749-0013.*

The First Parish Meeting House, commonly known as the Old Ship Church, is the oldest church in continuous use in the United States. Built by ship carpenters in 1681, the sanctuary looks like the inside of an overturned boat. *107 Main Street.*

Hull

Once they had electrified the branch railroad that served the summer hotels on Nantasket Beach, civic boosters started casting about for something else to do with electricity. So they strung up lights and held the world's first night baseball game, between two Boston department store teams, in September 1880. *L Street Field.*

33

Unkown Boston and Eastern Massachusetts

The only gun that ever hit an enemy ship in Boston Harbor was a field piece emplaced at Fort Independence on Telegraph Hill in Hull, which fired at British ships raiding Boston Light on July 31, 1775, and turned the tide of that battle to the patriots' advantage. Part of the ramparts of the fort can still be seen, along with the 1897 defenses that were located on the same site and known as Fort Revere, and subsequent structures built to protect the harbor during World Wars I and II. There are six 18th-century cannon, a World War I gun, a memorial to French soldiers who served in the American Revolution, and a museum in the officer's quarters with a rare working World War I crystal field radio and other military artifacts. The harbor views remain extraordinary. *Farina Road; Monday through Friday 1 to 4, Saturday and Sunday 11 to 4 July 1 through Labor Day; 617-727-4468.*

Joshua James is considered the greatest American lifesaver, estimated to have rescued more than 1,000 people from the time he was 15 until he died of a heart attack on a beach on March 19, 1902, while stepping out of a surfboat at age 75. That boat, the *Nantasket*—one of only four surviving surfboats built for the Massachusetts Humane Society, precursor to the Coast Guard—is in the Hull Lifesaving Museum, a station of the U.S. Life Saving Service built in 1889. The museum has other historic rescue equipment, shipwreck artifacts, the fourth-order Fresnel lens from the Gurnet Point Lighthouse, a radio room, and medals given for rescues off Hull. *1117 Nantasket Avenue; Wednesday through Sunday 10 to 4 Memorial Day through Labor Day, then Friday through Sunday 10 to 4; 781-925-5433.*

Once threatened with destruction, but now restored, the Paragon Carousel alongside Nantasket Beach, is one of the nation's largest surviving carousels, with 66 horses, rare Roman-style chariots, a Wurlitzer organ, and a panel with an original oil-painted portrait of Charles Lindbergh, who once flew over Hull and dipped his wings. The carousel was built in 1928 and was part of Paragon Park, a hugely popular but now-defunct seaside amusement park. *205 Nantasket Avenue; daily 10 to 9 mid-June through Labor Day; 781-925-0472.*

Ipswich

Once the summer home of Chicago bathroom fixture king Richard Crane, Castle Hill is a Stuart-style, 59-room mansion finished in 1927 on 800 acres, including a broad grand lawn half a mile long that ends at the ocean's edge. The entrance hall alone is 63 feet long with a ceiling 16 feet high; the landscaping was designed by Frederick Law Olmsted and completed by landscape architect Arthur Shurcliff; and the faucets are made of sterling silver. *Argilla Road; grounds daily dawn to dusk, house tours in the summer by appointment; 978-356-4351.*

Systematically killed off so open land could be used for grazing livestock, wolves have now disappeared from most areas of the United States. The North American Wolf Foundation raises British Columbian gray timber wolves to teach about wolves and encourage their protection. Begun with five pups donated by other facilities, the pack at the foundation's Wolf Hollow has since grown to more than 15. *114 Essex Road; Saturday and Sunday 1 to 5; 978-356-0216.*

Augustine Heard operated one of the most profitable mercantile houses in China in the 19th century, and the furniture and art he accumulated fills his house in Ipswich. The Federal-style mansion, built in 1795, also has the largest single collection of works by artist Arthur Wesley Dow, who painted countless scenes of his native Ipswich; one of the nation's finest collections of antique carriages and sleighs; and early dolls and toys. *54 South Main Street; Wednesday through Saturday 10 to 4, Sunday 1 to 4 May 1 through mid-October; 978-356-2811.*

Unknown New England

Ipswich has the most 17th-century houses still standing of any town in America; one, Whipple House, is open to the public as a museum. An herb garden by Arthur Shurcliff, designer of gardens at Colonial Williamsburg, fronts the 1655 timber-frame home. *1 South Village Green; Wednesday through Saturday 10 to 4, Sunday 1 to 4 May 1 through mid-October; 978-356-2811.*

Lincoln

A house built by Walter Gropius, founder of the Bauhaus School in Germany and one of the fathers of modern architecture, is left just as he designed it for himself after coming to the United States in 1938 to teach at Harvard. The house incorporates such features as glass block, acoustical plaster, chromed banisters and welded steel, and furniture and fixtures designed at the Bauhaus School, which Gropius directed from 1919 until 1928. There are also works of art given to him by friends including Laszlo Moholy-Nagy and Josef Albers, and an outside spiral staircase Gropius built for his daughter so she didn't have to introduce visiting friends to her parents. *68 Baker Bridge Road; Wednesday through Sunday 11 to 5 June 1 through October 15, then Saturday and Sunday 11 to 5; 781-259-8098.*

Summer home of wealthy Boston merchant John Codman, Codman House remained in his family's possession until 1968, when his descendants left it as a museum complete with the original furniture and many personal possessions. Built in 1740 and later renovated by the architect Charles Bulfinch, the Georgian-style mansion is one of the most accurate representations of an historic house. Among the contents: 11 of the 100 paintings by French, Italian and Dutch masters snatched up at bargain prices by Codman's brother, Richard, from once-wealthy Europeans in need of cash after the French Revolution. The grounds include a hidden Italianate garden and a reflecting pool filled with waterlilies. *Codman Road; Wednesday through Sunday 11 to 5 June 1 through October 15; 781-259-8843.*

Lowell

Lowell's 19th-century status as a leading city of the industrial revolution also left it a legacy relating to immigration, feminism and labor unrest. All of those things come together at the Boott Cotton Mills Museum, which shows not only the technology that built great fortunes, but also the conditions under which the workers—women and then immigrants—were forced to work for long hours at low pay. Young women worked 16-hour days, six days a week here, with mandatory church services on Sunday. They formed one of the earliest labor unions to petition for a 10-hour work day and held one of the first strikes, in December 1828. *400 Foot of John Street; Monday through Saturday 9:30 to 5, Sunday 11 to 5; 978-970-5000.*

Among the French Canadian families drawn to Lowell to work in the mills were the parents of Jean-Louis Lebris Kerouac, who was born on March 12, 1922, at 9 Lupine Road in the Little Canada tenement neighborhood. A monument to Jack Kerouac, the name he would later use while helping to define the Beat generation in books including *On the Road*, now stands near the site of a building where Kerouac's father was a printer while his mother worked in a shoe factory. The memorial consists of eight granite pillars inscribed with the opening passages of five Kerouac novels that were modeled on his life in Lowell, along with passages from *On the Road* and other works. Kerouac quit college in 1941 and worked as a sportswriter at the *Lowell* Sun while writing his first book, *The Town and the City*, in which Lowell appeared as the fictional town of Galloway. *Kearney Square.*

Jack Kerouac's grave is in Edson Cemetery. He was 47 when he died on October 21, 1969. *Gorham Street.*

Unkown Boston and Eastern Massachusetts

Although he preferred to deny it, artist James Abbott McNeil Whistler's mother gave birth to him here on July 11, 1834. Whistler's father, George Washington Whistler, had come to Lowell to serve as chief engineer of the canals and locks. But Whistler spent most of his working life in Europe, which is why so few people know about his birthplace here. Today the home, built in 1823 by the canal company, has been turned into the Whistler Museum of Art, which has a dozen Whistler prints of the Thames and Chelsea section of London, where he spent most of his life, and a full-sized copy of his famous "Portrait of the Painter's Mother," by Whistler's cousin, Edith Fairfax Davenport; the original is at the Musee d'Orsay in Paris. There also is a portrait of Whistler's father by William Elwell. As for Whistler, he hated to be reminded of his hometown, telling friends he was from Baltimore. "I shall be born when and where I want, and I do not choose to be born in Lowell," he once said. *243 Worthen Street; Wednesday through Saturday 11 to 4; 978-452-7641.*

The Sports Museum of New England showcases the countless great moments in regional sports history with, among other things, life-sized statues of bigger-than-life heroes Bobby Orr, Larry Bird, and Carl Yastrzemski. *25 Shattuck Street; Tuesday through Saturday 10 to 5, Sunday noon to 5; 978-452-6775.*

Ruth Elizabeth Davis—better known as the actress Bette Davis—was born here on April 5, 1908. *22 Chester Street.*

New England's only museum devoted solely to quilts, the New England Quilt Museum has an 1825 quilt by ancestors of Lizzie Borden, and "Achipelago," considered one of the greatest quilts of the 20th century. *18 Shattuck Street; Tuesday through Saturday 10 to 4 January through April, Tuesday through Saturday 10 to 4 and Sunday noon to 4 May through December; 978-452-4207.*

Lynn

Mary Baker Eddy, founder of the Christian Science Church, turned to prayer |after suffering a fall here when she was 45. It was here that Eddy completed her book *Science and Health with Key to the Scriptures,* the basis of her new religion. *12 Broad Street; Friday and Saturday 10 to 4, Sunday 1 to 4; 781-593-5634.*

Manchester

Bought in 1871 by Thomas Jefferson Coolidge, U.S. ambassador to France and grandson of President Thomas Jefferson, Coolidge Point is a 58-acre combination of forest, wetlands, beach and rocky shore. And while Coolidge's estate is gone, the extraordinary grand lawn that led from the house to the sea remains, a reminder of how the other half lived during the North Shore's "Gold Coast" period. President and Mrs. Woodrow Wilson and Crown Prince Olaf of Norway were guests. *Summer Street; trails dawn to dusk, ocean lawn open Saturday only; 978-356-4351.*

Marblehead

The famous painting *Spirit of '76* by Archibald Willard, showing a ragtag Revolutionary War fife and drum trio, hangs not in a museum, but in Abbott Hall, Marblehead's town hall. It was given to the town by Marblehead native General John Devereaux, whose son was the model for the young drummer in the 1876 work. *Washington Street; Monday, Tuesday and Thursday 8 to 5, Wednesday 7:30 to 7:30, Friday 8 to 5, Saturday 9 to 6, Sunday 11 to 6 Memorial Day through Columbus Day, then Monday, Tuesday and Thursday 8 to 5, Wednesday 7:30 to 7:30, Friday 8 to 1, Saturday 9 to 6, Sunday 11 to 6; 781-631-0000.*

Marblehead native Elbridge Gerry was a signer of the Declaration of Independence, represented Massachusetts at the Constitutional Convention, and was vice president under James Madison. But he has been immortalized for reorganizing an

Unknown New England

electoral district in favor of his party while governor in 1812, shaping it like a salamander to pick up the most possible friendly votes. Hence the term "gerrymandering." Gerry's home, now privately owned, still stands. *44 Washington Street.*

The huge colonial home he inherited from his father wasn't grand enough for merchant Robert Hooper, so in 1745 he attached an addition—not to the back, but to the front, where a shallow façade leads to the five-story 1728 original. Hooper's enormous home has 14 fireplaces and a ballroom built with the fortune he earned in the codfishing industry. There's even a tunnel from the wine cellar in his basement to the wharves; the bedrooms on the second floor were built at an angle to make the captain feel as if he were on board one of his ships. Called King Hooper thanks to his philanthropy, he was nonetheless forced to flee to Nova Scotia during the Revolutionary War because of his support for the British. Hooper's ghost reputedly sits in a corner of the ballroom and stares out the window at the home of his arch rival, Colonel Jeremiah Lee across the street. *8 Hooper Street; Monday through Saturday 10 to 4, Sunday 1 to 5; 781-631-2608.*

Hooper's competitor and adversary—even though their wives were sisters—Jeremiah Lee wanted a house even grander. True, the four-story Georgian-style Jeremiah Lee Mansion is made of wood shaped into blocks to simulate stone, but Lee otherwise cut no corners when he built the most elegant home in the colony in 1768. The entrance hall is 16 feet wide, the marble fireplace in the state drawing room is flanked by original hand-painted wallpaper depicting Roman ruins, the wooden banister spindles are hand-carved, and the kitchen fireplace features a rare mechanical spit. Colonel Lee owned a fleet of 27 ships and was one of the first heroes of the Revolutionary War, dying of exposure after carrying ammunition to his fellow colonists at Lexington and Concord on April 19, 1775. President George Washington, accompanied by the Marquis de Lafayette, visited his widow here after the war to show his gratitude. *161 Washington Street; Monday through Saturday 10 to 4, Sunday 1 to 4 June 1 through October 15; 781-631-1768.*

Marshfield

Reginald Fessenden, a chemist and electrical engineer, sent the first spoken radio broadcast in history from the 420-foot tower of the National Electric Signaling Company at Brant Rock on Christmas Eve, 1906. Fessenden could be heard by telegraph operators on ships hundreds of miles away as he spoke and played *O Holy Night* on his violin. A second broadcast was picked up as far away as the West Indies. Fessenden also unintentionally broadcast the first transatlantic wireless communication to Europe when a conversation he was having with a radio operator in Plymouth about a technical problem was overheard in Scotland. The remains of the original tower base survive. *Ocean Street.*

The tea party no one remembers occurred December 19, 1773, three days after the Boston Tea Party, when Marshfield residents drinking in a tavern decided to find all the British tea they could and burn it on what is now known as Tea Rock Hill. The tavern, which was called Bourne's Ordinary, still stands. *7 Library Plaza.*

Rebellious colonists weren't the only ones holding secret meetings in the days before the Revolutionary War. Dr. Isaac Winslow, great-grandson of town founder and *Mayflower* passenger Edward Wilson, had a secret chamber in his house where he met with others loyal to England; the entrance is off the "bridal chamber" on the second floor of the Winslow House, now a museum. On the grounds of the house is the law office of Daniel Webster, who lived in Marshfield and represented it in Congress. A champion of American nationalism, Webster ran for president in 1836, but lost, though he served under secretary of state under President William Henry Harrison. In his office are his chair and a suit of his clothes. His phaeton is in

37

Unkown Boston and Eastern Massachusetts

the carriage house, along with a Concord coach used to carry passengers to Hingham, where it connected with a packet ship to Boston. Webster, who died in 1852, is buried in Governor Winslow Cemetery. *Careswell and Webster streets; Wednesday through Sunday 11 to 3 mid-June through mid-October; 781-837-5753.*

Mattapoisett

Two drinking glasses used by Napoleon on St. Helena are among the treasures taken home to Mattapoisett by its shipbuilders and sea captains and now on display in the Mattapoisett Museum. Most of the whaling vessels in the Nantucket and New Bedford fleets were built here, including the *Acushnet*, on which Herman Melville sailed, and the *Wanderer*, the last ship to go whaling under sail from New Bedford. Housed in an 1821 former church, the museum has tools from the old shipyards, and the town's first piece of fire apparatus, an 1821 hand-pumper. *5 Church Street; Tuesday through Saturday 1 to 4 July and August; 508-758-2844.*

Medford

Grandmother's house, to which the holiday classic takes us "over the river and through the woods," was the holiday destination of its author, abolitionist and poet Lydia Maria Francis Child. Child originally titled the verse "A Boy's Thanksgiving Day" when she wrote it in 1844. She would have taken a horse-drawn sleigh from her own house, which still stands on the corner of Salem and Ashland Streets, over the Mystic River and through the woods to her grandparents' home, known as the Paul Curtis House after the shipbuilder who was its first owner. *114 South Street.*

Medford also inspired the Christmas carol "Jingle Bells," written here by James Pierpont, who lived at 87 Mystic Street, a popular sleigh route. Pierpont borrowed the only piano in town from a woman who, on hearing the tune, said she thought it was a "merry little jingle," and that became its title when the song was copyrighted in 1857. The town has put up a plaque honoring both Pierpont and his famous song. *High and Forest streets.*

The Medford Historical Society holds the nation's third-largest collection of Civil War photographs, including some by the photographer Matthew Brady. About 3,000 of the 5,000 prints in the collection are calling card-sized portraits that were popular with generals and other officers. The society's museum also has the cradle used by author, abolitionist and poet Lydia Maria Francis Child; and documents, including sailing orders, owned by a northern slave trader, Thomas Fitch, who died in Medford. *10 Governors Avenue; Sunday 2 to 4; 781-391-8739.*

Killed by a train, purportedly while pushing a baby elephant off the tracks, Jumbo the circus elephant was stuffed and given to Tufts University by its owner, P.T. Barnum, one of the university's founders. But the luckless pachyderm was burned in a fire in 1979. Jumbo's ashes are in a peanut butter jar in the athletic director's office—athletes rub the jar for luck before their games—and Jumbo himself is memorialized with somewhat more dignity in a statue on the quad. His tail is in the Tufts archives, along with P.T. Barnum's papers. *Boston Avenue.*

The Isaac Royall House, built in 1732, is the only house in the North that still has slave quarters attached. Slaves here worked in the home itself and on the surrounding farm until Royall, a British loyalist, fled in 1775. Slavery was outlawed in Massachusetts in 1783. *15 George Street; by appointment; 781-396-9032.*

The Peter Tufts House is considered the oldest brick house in America, built in 1674. *350 Riverside Avenue.*

Unknown New England

Merrimac

Edwin Howard Armstrong, the inventor of FM radio, should have enjoyed great fame and fortune. To this day, his inventions are in every radio and television set manufactured. Instead, the radio networks, which preferred not to make the costly switch from AM at the time, harassed, sued, and ultimately bankrupted him, and he has been widely forgotten. On February 1, 1954, exactly 21 years after patenting FM radio, Armstrong put on his hat, scarf and gloves and jumped 13 floors to his death. He is buried in Merrimac, his wife's home town. *Locust Grove Cemetery.*

Middleborough

Mercy Lavinia Warren Bump, born in Middleborough on October 31, 1841, had grown to only 32 inches by the time she was 21. She used her small size to her advantage, performing on a Mississippi River steamboat, and then signing on with P.T. Barnum's Circus. There she met and married Charles Sherwood Stratton and the couple became world famous as General and Mrs. Tom Thumb, eventually returning to her home town and building themselves a miniature house with lower-than-average countertops and steps, across the street from Mrs. Thumb's birthplace on Plymouth Street; even from the outside, the extra-low windowsills are evident. Both homes survive, though they are privately owned. After Tom Thumb died in 1883, his widow married an Italian dwarf, Count Primo Magri, who is buried in St. Mary's Catholic Cemetery. A wealth of General and Mrs. Tom Thumb's personal property is on display in the Middleborough Historical Society museum, including their miniature clothing and gifts from such dignitaries as Queen Victoria and the Emperor of Japan, who gave the couple a miniature teakwood table and chairs. *18-20 Jackson Street; open July and August, hours vary; 508-947-1969.*

The museum of the Massachusetts Archaeological Society, the Robbins Museum of Archaeology displays some of its 70,000 artifacts covering 12,000 years of history. Most are from Massachusetts, including a pictograph of a turtle etched in stone thousands of years ago, and ancient pendants carved in the shapes of animals and people. *17 Jackson Street; hours vary; 508-947-9005.*

Milton

The birthplace of President George Herbert Walker Bush is at 173 Adams Street. Bush was born here to Dorothy Walker Bush and Prescott Bush, later a U.S. senator, on June 12, 1924. The house, which still stands, is privately owned.

To punish Massachusetts for the Boston Tea Party, the British instituted the Coercive Acts in March 1774, annulling the state charter and prohibiting the loading or unloading of ships in Boston Harbor until the crown was compensated for its losses. In response, a list of grievances against the king was drawn up, most significant among them that the colonists should arm themselves and form their own militia. The so-called Suffolk Resolves, the first step to revolution was drafted on September 9, 1774, at the home of a man named Daniel Vose, now known as the Suffolk Resolves House—mainly because it was the only mansion big enough to hold all the delegates. *1370 Canton Avenue; by appointment; 617-333-9700.*

The pair of lions in the doorway of the Captain Robert Bennet Forbes House to ward off evil spirits are a sampling of a remarkable collection of goods from the China trade brought back by the maritime merchant. The 19th-century Greek Revival-style mansion remained in the Forbes family almost without interruption and is impeccably preserved, right down to the four-story lighthouse-style staircase, deep tin bathtub nestled in a wooden base, bells pulled to summon servants, and other architectural eccentricities. The house overlooks Quincy Bay and the Neponset River, where Forbes' clipper ships once docked on their return from Asia; inside, there are so many items from the Orient that the house was previously called the China Trade Museum, including decorative tiles on an upstairs porch that wish a visitor infinite good luck, and fine Chinese furniture held together without nails or glue. In the back yard is an exact replica of the Hodgenville, Kentucky, log cabin where Abraham Lincoln was born, built by a Forbes descendant who admired Lincoln. *215 Adams Street; Sunday and Wednesday 1 to 4; 617-696-1815.*

The grave of ice cream magnate Howard Johnson is in Milton Cemetery.

Nahant

The locals bill it as the first lawn tennis game in America: the bout between two bored vacationers, cousins James Dwight and David Sears Jr., in the summer of 1874 in the back yard of an aunt's vacation home. In fact, a game had been played two months before at a Staten Island cricket club. No matter; a marker at the site still claims the distinction for Nahant. What is true is that, by August of the next year, there were enough players to launch the first tennis tournament in America on that same flat stretch of seaside lawn, and Dwight and Sears went on to become the national men's doubles champion and organize the U.S. Lawn Tennis Association in 1881. *Swallows Cave Road.*

Natick

One of the most extraordinary small museums in New England, the Natick Historical Society museum in the basement of Bacon Free Library has the uniform of a Redcoat killed on the first day of the American Revolution, a pocket watch taken from a fallen British soldier after the Battle of Bunker Hill, and a copy of one of the first books printed in America: a Bible translated into the Algonquin language by John Eliot, a self-appointed Puritan apostle who converted the Indians here to Christianity. The Takawambait pulpit desk, built by the Indians for Eliot, is in the museum, which also has epaulets owned by Natick native Henry Wilson, vice president under Ulysses S. Grant, a whole aviary of mounted birds, an ear trumpet, colonial-era toasting irons, a World War II ration book, and Indian dolls and beadwork. *58 Eliot Street; Tuesday 6 to 8:30 p.m., Wednesday 2 to 4:30, Saturday 10 to 12:30 p.m., closed Saturday in July and August; 508-647-4841.*

Ulysses S. Grant's vice president, Henry Wilson, lived at 33 West Central Street and owned a shoe shop, since restored as a memorial, at Mill and West Central streets. Chairman of the important Senate Committee on Military Affairs during the Civil War, he became vice president in 1872 and died in office in 1875.

Horatio Alger Jr.'s father lived at 16 Pleasant Street in South Natick, where Alger was a frequent resident. The author whose name became synonymous with the American rags-to-riches stories he wrote, Alger died in his sister's house at 31 Florence Street. Horatio Alger's grave is in Glenwood Cemetery. *Glenwood Street.*

Part of the U.S. Army's research-and-development arm, the Soldier Systems Center focuses exclusively on improving military food, clothing, shelter and other support systems—including mobile showers, heaters, even laundries—tested in facilities that can simulate the hottest and the coldest conditions on the planet. This is where C-rations were replaced with the modern meal, ready to eat (MRE), which has a shelf life of at least three years, and can be air-dropped without parachutes. Tours are offered periodically. *617-233-4300.*

Five hundred species of plants have been identified in the Audubon Society's Broadmoor Sanctuary, and 150 kinds of birds that make their presence known with their soothing, omnipresent chirping. The sanctuary's nine miles of walking trails fan out over 624 acres of woodlands and wetlands, including along Indian Brook, which flows into the Charles River. A boardwalk allows people to look in on sala-

Unknown New England

manders, amphibians and freshwater shrimp in vernal pools where they breed. *Eliot Street; visitor center open Tuesday through Friday 9 to 5, Saturday and Sunday 10 to 5, trails open daily dawn to dusk; 508-655-2296.*

Needham

Entire museums are devoted to the artist Newell Convers Wyeth and his famous family, but his hometown has 14 of N.C. Wyeth's paintings and illustrations hanging in the public library. The father of Andrew Wyeth and grandfather of Jamie Wyeth, N.C. Wyeth was born in Needham on October 22, 1882, and used the town as the backdrop for many of his works and illustrations for *Scribner's* magazine and other publishers. On display are his "The Walk in the Snow," drawn for Robert Louis Stephenson's *David Balfour*; "The Chimneys," which depicts a scene from Jules Verne's *The Mysterious Island*; and "Charles River Scene." *1139 Highland Avenue; Monday through Thursday 10 to 9, Friday 10 to 5:30, Saturday 9 to 5, Sunday 1 to 5, closed Sunday in June, July and August; 781-455-7559.*

N.C. Wyeth's famous painting "Christmas Morning" is in the Needham Historical Society museum; it shows his home in Needham and his grandfather, Swiss-American botanist Denys Zirngiebel, who introduced the French carnation and Swiss pansy to America. The museum also has trophies, tickets, equipment and programs from the nation's oldest Thanksgiving Day high school football rivalry, the annual bout between Needham and Wellesley, which began in 1882. *53 Glendoon Road; Monday and Wednesday 8:30 to noon and 7:30 to 9; 781-455-8860.*

New Bedford

Designed by then-Lieutenant Robert E. Lee in 1846, massive Fort Taber never saw action; by the time it was completed, the Civil War was almost over. (Another officer involved in its construction was Captain Henry Robert, who later wrote *Robert's Rules of Order*.) But Fort Taber is distinguished as the only military fortification in America with a lighthouse on top of it to replace Clark's Point Light, which it displaced. The site commands an unequaled 360-degree view of Buzzard's Bay. *Brock Avenue; daily 9 to 5; 508-979-1745.*

The home of Sergeant William H. Carney, the first black recipient of the Congressional Medal of Honor, is at 128 Mill Street. A member of the all-black 54th Massachusetts Regiment made famous in the movie *Glory*, Carney took the American flag from the fallen standard-bearer and carried it under fire to the Confederate parapet of Fort Wagner in South Carolina during a brutal battle on July 18, 1863. Wounded, he nonetheless returned with the colors to tell his colleagues: "The old flag never touched the ground, boys." The home is now privately owned.

Known as the Black Liberty Bell, the bell in New Bedford's Liberty Hall was rung to warn escaped slaves when bounty hunters were nearby. After a fire destroyed the building, the bell was melted into a plaque that tells its story, and placed in the wall of the building now on the site. *Purchase and William streets.*

The only historic whaling merchant's home on the East Coast open to the public, the Rotch-Jones-Duff House shows vividly how profitable the whale trade could be. The grand 1834 Greek Revival-style mansion was designed by Richard Upjohn, founder of the American Institute of Architects and today reflects several periods of its long history, including a 1930s-era Art Deco bathroom upstairs with chest-level showerheads to keep women's hair from getting wet. *396 County Street; Monday through Saturday 10 to 4, Sunday noon to 4; 508-997-1401.*

The "Whalemen's Chapel" of Melville's *Moby Dick*, the Seamen's Bethel was built by locals concerned about the "arduous and licentious lifestyles" of sailors.

Unkown Boston and Eastern Massachusetts

Inside are cenotaphs bearing the names of men lost at sea, with accounts of their deaths. The pew where Melville sat during his 1840 visit is marked with a plaque. In an example of life imitating art, the bow-shaped pulpit was added in 1956 to conform to the film version of *Moby Dick* starring Gregory Peck. *15 Johnny Cake Hill; daily 10 to 4 May through Columbus Day, Monday through Friday 11 to 1, Saturday 10 to 5, Sunday 1 to 5 Columbus Day through April; 508-992-3295.*

The world's largest ship model, the 89-foot replica of the whaling bark *Lagoda*, is in the New Bedford Whaling Museum, the largest museum in the world devoted to American whaling history. Built in 1826, the *Lagoda* was one of the most profitable whalers ever. Also on display: the only blue whale skeleton on view in the world. The skull alone weighs two tons. *18 Johnny Cake Hill; daily 9 to 5 and until 9 p.m. on the second Thursday of each month; 508-997-0046.*

On April 28, 1944, more than a month before the invasion of the Normandy Beaches in World War II, a top-secret practice exercise went horribly wrong. As the U.S. 4th Infantry Division practiced landing in a secluded bay in England, a German submarine began to attack. Thinking it was part of the drill, the servicemen did not return the fire, and 749 of them were killed. A World War II-era Sherman tank here serves as a memorial to the soldiers killed in the Exercise Tiger tragedy; it is surrounded by 749 cobblestones, one for each of the casualties. *477 Park Street.*

The oldest active fire station in Massachusetts when it was closed in 1979, Station No. 4—built in 1867—now houses a fire museum with apparatus even older. There are 1840s hand pumpers, 1880s horse-drawn steam fire pumpers, a 1900 ladder truck and hose wagon, and 1927 and 1928 Ahrens Fox pumper trucks. *51 Bedford Street; daily 9 to 4 June through August; 508-992-2162.*

Newbury

Built in 1654 with just two rooms, the Coffin House boasts an adult cradle made to soothe grown family members who were old or sick. *14 High Road; Saturday and Sunday 11 to 4 July 1 though Labor Day; 978-462-2634.*

Dedicated to the era of the hand-operated fire pumper, the American Hand Fire Engine Society has four hand fire pumpers ranging from 1840 through the late 1860s. *Zero Morgan Avenue; by appointment; 978-465-3948.*

Newburyport

The original purpose of the Newburyport Maritime Society, founded more than 200 years ago by 171 local sea captains, was to help the widows of any members lost at sea. But by the 1850s, it was also serving as a "cabinet of curiosities" to which returning seafarers would contribute souvenirs they had acquired on their journeys around the world. Now those curiosities are the secret treasure of the Custom House Maritime Museum: a spear lined with shark's teeth from the South Pacific, an ostrich egg engraved in scrimshaw, even a feng shui dial once mistaken for an Oriental compass. The 1835 Classical Revival-style Custom House itself was designed by Robert Mills, architect of the Washington Monument and the Treasury Building, shown on the back of the $10 bill. *25 Water Street; Monday through Saturday 10 to 4, Sunday 1 to 4 April through December; 978-462-8681.*

Captain William Hunt died at sea before his elegant Federal-period mansion was completed, and his widow rented half of it out to John Newmarch Cushing Jr., who bought the house outright in 1818. Today the Cushing House Museum is filled with exotic teak and ivory from the China trade, a collection of miniatures by 18th-century artist Laura Coombs Hills, and portraits of merchants and sea captains by

Unknown New England

the deaf-mute artist John Brewster Jr. *98 High Street; Tuesday through Friday 10 to 4, Saturday 11 to 2 May 1 through October 31; 978-462-2681.*

Built at the end of the 17th century, the Spencer-Peirce-Little farm was the country seat of wealthy merchants. In the attic is graffiti including signatures from generations of occupants, sketches of ships, and other subjects. *5 Little's Lane; Wednesday through Sunday 11 to 5 June 1 through October 15; 978-462-2634.*

One of the nation's best birdwatching areas, Plum Island's ocean, salt marsh, mud flat, freshwater pond and mixed forest habitats attract herons, egrets, loons, grebes, snowy owls, rough-legged hawks, and 15 to 20 species of warblers. The Parker River National Wildlife Refuge offers self-guided tours. *978-465-5753.*

Newton

The congressional office of five-term U.S. House Speaker Thomas P. "Tip" O'Neill has been reassembled at his alma mater, Boston College, complete with his desk, first used by Grover Cleveland. It was O'Neill who said: "All politics is local." *O'Neill Library, Boston College; Monday through Saturday 11 to 4; 617-552-8297.*

Boston College holds the largest collection of Irish materials outside of Ireland itself, selections from which are on display in an exhibit room, including paintings by Irish artists, a 19th-century Irish harp, Waterford crystal, silver, and other items. *Paul Burns Library, Boston College; Monday through Friday 9 to 5. 617-552-3282.*

After founding the Christian Science religion, Mary Baker Eddy became disgusted with the yellow journalism of the early 20th century, some of which was directed at her own controversial contention that prayer could heal physical illness. Though she was already 86, it was in this estate, purchased with the copious profits from her writing, that she founded the *Christian Science Monitor* in 1908, personally reviewing the editorials daily. She lived here until her death in 1910, tended by a staff of 20. The first edition of the *Monitor* is on display. So are 10 of Eddy's carriages, one of the nation's largest private carriage collections. *400 Beacon Street; Friday and Saturday 10 to 4, Sunday 1 to 4; 617-566-3092.*

Johnny Kelley ran the Boston Marathon 61 times winning twice and finishing second seven times—once after falling behind on the steep rise through Newton, which Kelley immortalized by naming it "Heartbreak Hill." A statue near Heartbreak Hill shows Kelley as the 27-year-old winner of the 1935 race and as an 84-year-old finishing his last run before retiring in 1992. It was paid for by an admiring fellow runner. *Commonwealth Avenue at Walnut Street.*

North Andover

The Moseley Iron Bridge is the oldest iron bridge in Massachusetts and one of the oldest riveted wrought-iron bridges in America. The bridge, which once carried Canal Street in Lawrence, was restored by civil engineering students after it collapsed in 1990. It now spans the reflecting pool at Merrimack College, and has been designated a national historic civil engineering landmark in the company of the Hoover Dam and Golden Gate Bridge. *315 Turnpike Street.*

Phillips Brooks wrote the song "O Little Town of Bethelem" in his summer home here. *168 Osgood Street.*

Norton

The father of American golf, Francis Ouimet was a 20-year-old caddy at the Brookline Country Club who won the 1913 U.S. Open, ending British dominance of golf. The Massachusetts Golf Museum has his jacket, medals, clubs, and other items relating to the history of golf in the state. *300 Arnold Palmer Boulevard; Monday through Friday 10 to 5; 774-430-9100.*

Peabody

Convicted of killing 11 women between 1962 and 1964, Albert DeSalvo is commonly (though not universally) believed to have been the Boston Strangler. DeSalvo was himself stabbed to death by fellow inmates. The grave of the man believed to be the Boston Strangler is in Puritan Lawn Cemetery. *Lake Street.*

Plymouth

Plymouth's history of European settlement began centuries before the Pilgrims. As early as 1004, Thorwald, son of the Viking Eric the Red, purportedly landed at Gurnet Point, claimed it, was promptly killed by Indians, and is buried here. In 1606, the area was visited again, this time by the French explorer Samuel de Champlain. Today on Gurnet Point stands Plymouth Light, the oldest wooden lighthouse in America, built in 1769 and hit by a British cannonball during the Revolutionary War. After a fire, it was replaced by the current tower in 1843.

The most complete collection of Pilgrim possessions is not at Plimoth Plantation, but in the less well-known Pilgrim Hall Museum, which has, among other things, William Bradford's Bible, Myles Standish's sword, and the cradle of Peregrine White, the first child of English settlers in New England, born aboard the *Mayflower* while it was anchored in Provincetown Harbor before coming to Plymouth. *75 Court Street; daily 9:30 to 4:30 except January; 508-746-1620.*

The oldest wooden courthouse in America, the Old Court House was built in 1749; John Adams argued cases here. One of the nation's longest-used municipal buildings, it served as town hall until 1953. The gallows, last used in 1875, also are on display. *Town Square; daily 11 to 5 mid-June through Columbus Day; 508-830-4075.*

Four black slaves who fought in the American Revolution were granted their freedom in return, along with 94 acres apiece. The four—Quamany Quash, Kato Howe, Plato Turner, and Prince Goodwin—are buried in Parting Ways Cemetery. *Route 80.*

Quincy

Native Americans called this triangular-shaped hill "Mos," for "arrowhead," and "wetuset," for "hill." That's how the unimpressive looking Moswetuset Hummock came to be the place where Massachusetts got its name. The hill is in the Wollaston Beach Reservoir. *Quincy Shore Drive; daily dawn to dusk; 617-727-5293.*

Arguably the most historic house in the United States, the Adams National Historic Site was home to not one, but two presidents, John Adams and John Quincy Adams. Later residents included Charles Francis Adams, U.S. ambassador to Great Britain during the Civil War, and literary historians Henry and Brooks Adams. The site includes the two adjoining modest saltbox houses where the presidents, father and son, were born, and the impressive mansion where they later lived, which is crowded with 78,000 artifacts from their eventful lives including the first furniture used in the White House, the desk on which the Massachusetts constitution was drafted, and the imprint used by John Adams to seal the Treaty of Paris ending the Revolutionary War and by John Quincy Adams to seal the Treaty of Ghent that ended the War of 1812. In one of the strangest coincidences of American history, John Adams and Thomas Jefferson both died on July 4, 1826, exactly 50 years after the signing of the Declaration of Independence, Adams in his upstairs study here and Jefferson at Monticello. Both Adamses and their first ladies are interred

Unknown New England

next door in the United Parish Church. *Visitor center at 1250 Hancock Street; daily 9 to 5 April 19 through mid-November; 617-770-1175.*

The Quincy Homestead was the seat of one of America's most influential political dynasties, home at one time or another to Dorothy Quincy, wife of John Hancock, and Colonel John Quincy, grandfather of Abigail Adams and namesake of President John Quincy Adams. *34 Butler Road; Wednesday through Sunday noon to 4 Memorial Day through Columbus Day; 617-472-5117.*

The need for nails, tools and cooking utensils led to the creation of America's first iron blast furnace by John Winthrop Jr., less than 25 years after the Pilgrims first landed at Plymouth, and 130 years before the Revolutionary War. The riverside site has since been known as Furnace Brook. *Crescent and Hall Streets.*

The first commercial railroad in the United States was opened here on October 7, 1826, to carry granite from the Quincy quarries across Boston to the site of the Bunker Hill Monument in Charlestown. Some of the original iron wheels still sit beside two historic markers at the start of the actual track bed. *Ricciuti Drive, Blue Hills Reservation; 617-698-1802.*

The ice cream Howard Johnson made in 1925 for his drug store soda fountain was so popular that he started selling it from roadside stands distinguished by their eye-catching orange paint. By 1940, there would be 130 Howard Johnson's restaurants, known for their orange roofs, cupolas, Simple Simon-and-the-Pieman logo, and toasted hot dog rolls in paper sleeves. The mirror, menus and other contents of Howard Johnson's soda fountain are in the Quincy Historical Society museum, the former Adams Academy school for boys, founded by John Adams on the site of John Hancock's birthplace. It also has Adams artifacts including John Adams' wedding vest. *8 Adams Street; Monday through Friday 9 to 4; 617-773-1144.*

The first Dunkin' Donuts also is in Quincy, where founder Bill Rosenberg opened a shop he initially called Open Kettle in 1948. That has since led to 5,000 more in the U.S. and 40 other countries. *534 Southern Artery; 617-472-9502.*

Kilroy was here first. James J. Kilroy, a Fore River Shipyard inspector, took to certifying the bulkheads of the ships he had examined with the legend "Kilroy was here," and a chalk doodle. The idea caught on. The shipyard now is home to the U.S. Naval and Shipbuilding Museum, whose main attraction is the 700-foot *USS Salem*, the world's only preserved heavy cruiser, which was built here and was the Sixth Fleet flagship in the Mediterranean. There is also a collection of ship models, guns, bombs, and personal effects from both world wars. *Route 3A; daily 10 to 5 Memorial Day through Labor Day, then Saturday and Sunday 10 to 4; 617-479-7900.*

A combination grist and lumber mill, the 1802 Souther Tide Mill was powered by water trapped during high tide, and then released. Named for shipwright John Souther, who operated a boatyard at the site, the ramshackle wooden structure is one of only six surviving tidal mills in the United States. Grain from Quincy farms was processed into flour here, then shipped from the adjacent wharves to other cities on the East Coast, and to Europe. *Route 6A.*

Revolutionary War Colonel Josiah Quincy was progenitor of three mayors and a president of Harvard. His house is a now maintained as a museum. *20 Muirhead Street; Saturday and Sunday 11 to 5 July 1 through Labor Day; 617-227-3956.*

Unkown Boston and Eastern Massachusetts

Rockport

Tired of drunkenness among their husbands, the women of Rockport, led by Hannah Jumper, raided every tavern in town one July day in 1857, and smashed barrels open with axes; the gutters reportedly ran with rum. A room devoted to Hannah Jumper is part of the Sandy Bay Historical Society museum, which also has ship models and early fishing artifacts in an 1832 house made of local granite. *40 King Street; daily 2 to 5 mid-June through mid-September; 978-546-9533.*

Salem

Blackbeard, history's most notorious pirate, terrorized his victims by his physical appearance alone, with a beard that almost covered his face. He captured more than 40 ships during his brief but infamous career, which lasted from 1713 until he was killed off North Carolina in 1718. They don't talk about it much, but the skull of Blackbeard the Pirate is in the Peabody Essex Museum, the oldest continually operated museum in the country, founded in 1799. Blackbeard's skull is displayed here only periodically or loaned for exhibits at other museums. *128 Essex Street; Monday through Saturday 10 to 5, Sunday noon to 5 April 1 through October 31, then Tuesday through Saturday 10 to 5, Sunday noon to 5; 978-745-9500.*

The wooden cane of George Jacobs Sr., who was executed during the Salem witch trials, is in the Phillips Library, an often-overlooked extension of the Peabody Essex Museum. Also on display: witch trials victim Rebecca Nurse's arrest warrant, and depositions of her accusers. *132 Essex Street; Tuesday, Wednesday, and Friday 10 to 5, Thursday 1 to 8; 978-745-9500.*

Salem has a less well-known legacy that has nothing to do with witches: It was once among the nation's busiest and wealthiest ports. At its peak, Salem's fleet comprised 200 vessels; the fortunes they earned built the Federal-style homes around Salem Common and along Chestnut Street. But its shallow harbor doomed Salem's seagoing trade after 1850, when merchant ships grew too big to come here. Salem has the only remaining 18th-century wharves in the country, now part of the Salem Maritime National Historic Site. Also preserved is the home of Elias Hasket Derby, America's first millionaire, so rich he imported the bricks for his house from England and built a half-mile wharf for his fleet. Next door is the 1819 Custom House, where Nathaniel Hawthorne was surveyor of the port in the 1840s; it was where Hawthorne conceived *The Scarlet Letter*. The gilded eagle over the door, and the 7,420-pound iron safe, are testimony to the more than $20 million collected here from the 5 percent import duty between 1789 and 1840—accounting for fully half the revenues of the national government. *174 Derby Street; daily 9 to 5 September 1 through July 31, daily 9 to 6 in August; 978-740-1650.*

Ever since a shipwreck stranded a man named Moulton there for three wintry days in the early 1600s, the twin islands off Salem have been known as Great and Little Misery. Their more recent history has been equally unhappy. A resort went bust, and the ship *City of Rockland* wrecked here. Now Great and Little Misery are open to the public, littered with the ruins of a casino and summer cottages, a seaplane hangar, a saltwater swimming pool, and the shipwreck, only partially submerged. There are two beaches. *Ferries from Salem Willows daily Memorial Day through Labor Day, then Saturday and Sunday in the fall; 978-356-4351.*

The world's first home to be lit with electric lights was owned by Moses G. Farmer, who hooked up a platinum burner lamp of his own invention powered by abattery in the basement in July of 1859. *11 Pearl Street.*

Unknown New England

The Gardner-Pingree Mansion and the Captain Joseph White Murder

The condemned man finished off his second cup of coffee. He drank it black. "Come," he told his guards. "Let's get this hanging over."

They walked together from his cramped cell to the prison door. It opened on a restless crowd of 5,000 men and women, more than a third of all the citizens of Salem. Six months after he was killed in his sleep, Captain Joseph White would be avenged.

The sheriff nudged the subject of the mob's attention forward through the prison courtyard to the scaffold. There he was allowed a last request: to stand free and untied on the gallows for a minute. He turned to let a nervous deputy adjust the noose around his neck. He felt the rope burn as another tied his wrists. "Have you anything to say?" the sheriff asked theatrically.

The crowd fell silent.

"No," said the condemned man.

The drop swung open. His fingers tightened on the handkerchief in one last mortal spasm. Three minutes later, he was dead.

It was 8:44 a.m. Tuesday, September 28, 1830. They had just hung a man for a murder the whole town knew he didn't commit.

So ended one of the most extraordinary cases of 19th-century Massachusetts: the killing of a powerful and wealthy Salem sea captain by brigands in the employ of his niece's ne'er-do-well husband, who was after a share of the old man's fortune. Smith was found by a servant, stabbed 13 times in the heart by a killer who had entered his second-story bedroom on a ladder late at night.

"Nothing is going on but murder and robbery," Oliver Wendell Holmes, then a student at Harvard, wrote to a friend. "Poor old Mr. White was stabbed in the dark, and since then the very air has been redolent of assassination."

The murderer, Richard Crowninshield, was quickly caught; he would become part of the case's celebrity cast. Daniel Webster was the prosecutor. Nathaniel Hawthorne reported on the case for the Boston newspapers. The scion of a prominent and wealthy family, Crowninshield himself was the nephew of the secretary of the Navy under presidents Madison and Monroe.

"Whenever in after times our children shall read of this murder, they will shudder at the thought that the assassin and his confederates were all sons of New England, and of respectable and affluent families," Hawthorne wrote. "The object was money, the crime murder, the price blood."

Crowninshield hanged himself in jail, however, depriving the vengeful local populace of its vengeance. The stand-in who was executed on the gallows that September morning was Frank Knapp, younger brother of the man who planned the murder; he was condemned to death merely for serving as a lookout.

White's murder is no longer widely remembered. But his house, with his room arranged exactly as it was the night that he was killed, today is called the Gardner-Pingree Mansion, and is open to the public, part of the Peabody Essex Museum.

The Gardner-Pingree Mansion is at 128 Essex Street, Salem; Monday through Saturday 10 to 5, Sunday noon to 5 April 1 through October 31, then Tuesday through Saturday 10 to 5, Sunday noon to 5; 978-745-9500.

Scituate

The carageen, or moss, that grows on seaside rocks has traditionally been scraped off and made into such things as puddings and toothpaste. In Scituate, mossing was a veritable industry. The Scituate Maritime and Irish Mossing Museum, in the 1739 Captain Benjamin James House, boasts the only mossing exhibit in the country. It also has a room full of shipwreck artifacts, including two doors, a

Unkown Boston and Eastern Massachusetts

life jacket, a piano key, and luggage tags from the coastal steamer *Portland*, which went down in a gale in 1898 that sank 359 ships and killed 500 people; and equipment used to rescue the crew of the *Etrusco*, an Italian freighter that went aground off Scituate in 1956 in one of the area's last big shipwrecks. Local shipbuilding history is also told. More than 1,000 ships were built here, including the *Columbia*, for which the Columbia River in the Northwestern United States was named by its captain, Robert Gray, the first man to cross the Columbia River Bar. *The Driftway; Saturday and Sunday 1 to 4 July 1 through Labor Day; 781-545-1083.*

Sharon

Deborah Sampson Gannett was a woman who disguised herself as a man and fought in the American Revolution, enlisting in the 4th Massachusetts Regiment under the name Robert Shurtleff. She fought in several battles and was wounded twice but was not found out until a doctor examined her when she contracted typhoid fever in 1783. Gannett was honorably discharged and voted a soldier's pension by Congress in 1805; when she died in 1827, her husband, Benjamin Gannett, became the first man to receive a widow's pension. Deborah Gannett is buried in Rockridge Cemetery in a grave marked with both her name and the name "Robert Shurtleff," and there is a statue of her in front of the public library with an Army coat over one shoulder and a rifle hanging from one arm. *11 North Main Street.*

Sherborn

In one of the oddest juxtapositions in New England, the Sherborn war memorial stands beside a private peace memorial on the town's main street. Erected by a pacifist abbey on the grounds of its school, the peace memorial is an eight-foot bronze statue of Mohandas Gandhi surrounded by various religions' prayers for peace, with shrines to conscientious objectors and civilians killed in war. The war memorial, built by the town, is a statue of a female figure called "Memory" by the sculptor Cyrus Dallin, famous for his monument to Paul Revere behind the Old North Church and his likeness of an Indian astride a horse in front of the main entrance to Boston's Museum of Fine Arts. *Washington and Main streets.*

Somerville

Prospect Hill, then called Mount Pisgah, was the place where the American flag was raised for the first time on January 1, 1776, the day the Continental Army came into formal existence. The flag, commonly called the Grand Union, consisted of 13 red and white stripes, but with the British Union Jack instead of white stars on a blue background in the upper left-hand corner. There are panoramic views of greater Boston from the top of the hill. *Prospect Hill Parkway.*

South Dartmouth

The Lloyd Center for Environmental Studies has sea life and marine mammal skeletons, but from its observation deck you can also watch harbor seals in the winter and migrating birds in the summer in the marshes where they actually live. *430 Potomska Road; Monday through Friday 8 to 4, Sunday 11 to 4, trails open daily dawn to dusk; 508-990-0505.*

Sudbury

Babe Ruth's House was christened Home Run Farm by Ruth when he bought it for $10,000 in 1923—even though he had already been sold to the New York Yankees by Red Sox owner Harry Frazee. Ruth liked to speed here in his Stutz-Bearcat, paying neighborhood kids to watch out for the sheriff. *558 Dutton Road.*

While it is known that young Mary Sawyer nursed a young lamb back to health, and that the lamb came with her to the Redstone School one day in 1817,

Unknown New England

it is not certain whether hers is the story used by Sarah Josepha Hale, who wrote the famous nursery rhyme "Mary Had a Little Lamb" in 1830. Hale steadfastly claimed she made it up. Nonetheless, the one-room school to which Mary's little lamb followed her was moved from its original site in Sterling by auto magnate Henry Ford and rebuilt here in 1927. *Route 20 at the Wayside Inn; Wednesday through Sunday 11:30 to 5 mid-May through mid-October; 978-443-1776.*

Swampscott

The holder of 696 patents, Elihu Thomson was the inventor of the wattmeter, a practical method of measuring the electricity used by a home or business, opening the way for the practical distribution of electric power; with this device, he became a co-founder of the General Electric Company in 1892. Thomson also invented arc lights, generators, and electric welding machines. His mansion now serves as Swampscott's town hall. *22 Monument Avenue.*

Tewksbury

Housed in a 19th-century state hospital for patients with infectious and chronic diseases, the Public Health Museum displays the history of medicine in all its gore, with glass catheters, a primitive stomach pump, restraining cuffs, and patent medicines including Lydia E. Pinkham's Blood Purifier. There are also handwritten patient discharge notes, one describing the condition of an elderly patient as "used up." *East Street; Wednesday 1 to 4 and by appointment; 978-851-7321.*

Waltham

The American industrial revolution began here when Robert Lowell built the nation's first power loom beside the Charles River in 1814 based on designs he had secretly memorized while on a visit to Manchester, England. Lowell eventually branched out to what was then East Chelmsford, which was renamed Lowell in honor of his family. But it is Waltham that can claim the first mill in America where spinning and weaving were done in one operation under the same roof, the first time women were employed in large numbers and paid for their labor—even the first labor strike.The Charles River Museum of Industry, housed in the power plant connected to the original mill, chronicles the milestones of this largely forgotten history. *154 Moody Street; Monday through Saturday 10 to 5; 781-893-5410.*

Waltham's industrial legacy includes automobiles, principally the company begun in 1903 by one-time bicycle manufacturer Charles Herman Metz, the son of German immigrants. The largest manufacturer of automobiles east of Detroit, the Metz Company was sunk by the same German torpedoes as the *Lusitania*, which stirred up anti-German sentiment. But the Waltham Museum has a Metz buckboard made here in 1903, and Metz cars from 1913 and 1915. The famous Waltham Watch Company, which helped pioneer mass production of interchangeable parts in 1854 and made the timepiece a common personal possession, is also represented. The museum is in the one-time home of James Baker, who was the watch company's first employee. *196 Charles Street; Sunday 1 to 4:30; 781-893-8017.*

The Robert Treat Paine Estate, a Romanesque-Byzantine-style mansion designed for Paine by the famous architect H.H. Richardson, was the home of the attorney who prosecuted the British soldiers involved in the Boston Massacre, served as a delegate to the Continental Congress, and was a signer of the Declaration of Independence. Paine also was the first attorney general of Massachusetts, and a justice of the state Supreme Judicial Court. But he is best-known as the author of the pamphlet, "Common Sense," which called for American independence. *100 Robert Treat Paine Drive; Tuesday and Wednesday 1 to 4; 781-893-0162.*

Unkown Boston and Eastern Massachusetts

Chargé d'affaires in London after the Revolutionary War and later governor and U.S. senator from Massachusetts, Christopher Gore entertained the Marquis de Lafayette, Daniel Webster, and James Monroe in his opulent home. Now a museum, Gore Place has such mementos as the suit Gore wore when presented to the king, and his 19th-century billiard table. *52 Gore Street; Tuesday through Saturday 11 to 5, Sunday 1 to 5 April 15 through November 15; 781-894-2798.*

The robe and desk of the first Jewish member of the U.S. Supreme Court are on display at Brandeis University, itself named in honor of Justice Louis D. Brandeis. Brandeis was appointed to the high court in 1916 by Woodrow Wilson. The university also has Brandeis's books and furniture from his home, and unrelated artifacts including the death masks of the anarchists Sacco and Vanzetti, and a permanent exhibit of 19th- and 20th-century Jewish ceremonial items such as spice boxes, scrolls and a sabbath table. Opened in 1948, Brandeis is the only nonsectarian Jewish-sponsored college or university in the United States. *Goldfarb Library; Monday through Friday 9 to 5; 781-736-4685.*

The Rose Art Museum at Brandeis University boasts what is widely recognized as the finest collection of 20th-century art in New England, with works by Willem De Kooning, Marsden Hartley, Robert Motherwell, Robert Rauschenberg, and others. *415 South Street; Wednesday through Sunday noon to 5; 781-736-3434.*

The Boston Celtics Hall of Fame overlooks the team's training facility, where visitors can watch players work out on the court surrounded by replica championship banners. On display are such items as Larry Bird's sneakers, Jo Jo White's team jersey, warm-up uniforms from the early 1900s, and classic photos. *Healthpoint Fitness and Wellness Center, 840 Winter Street; Monday through Friday 7 a.m. to 9 p.m., Saturday and Sunday 7 to 7; 781-522-2222.*

Percy LeBaron Spencer was testing a vacuum tube called a magnetron in his laboratory at the Raytheon Company on October 8, 1945, when he noticed that a chocolate bar in his pocket had begun to melt. Rather than advancing radar, as he had intended, Spencer had discovered what would become a common kitchen appliance, making this small complex of industrial buildings the place where the microwave oven was invented. Raytheon filed a patent on the discovery, calling it the Radar Range, and it went on the market in 1947. But early models were five feet tall and cost $3,000, discouraging consumers almost as much as their mistrust of the technology. When a prototype was installed in the home of Raytheon director Charles Adams, his cook immediately quit. *Seyon and River streets.*

Wareham

Every inch of the world's largest thermometer museum is covered with thermometers, more than 3,000 of them—some even hanging from the ceiling. The oldest, which dates to 1830, is embedded in a French woodcut of a hunter and a deer under a tree. There are also thermometers set in cuckoo clocks, the Eiffel Tower, and a framed photograph of Dale Evans; and in pictures of Christ on the cross, President Franklin Delano Roosevelt, and John F. and Robert Kennedy. *49 Zarahelma Road; by appointment; 508-295-5504.*

Better-known in Japan than in America, Captain John Kendrick was the first American to land in Japan, which he visited in 1791 after stopping in the Pacific Northwest for furs to trade. The Japanese called the former privateer the "redhaired barbarian." The Captain John Kendrick Maritime Museum is in his house, which was built in 1745, but of his personal possessions there survives only a teacup he sent home to his wife. The other artifacts relate to a later owner, Captain

Alden Besse, including his spyglass, telescope, sextant, and charts. *102 Main Street; Saturday and Sunday 1 to 4 July and August; 508-291-2274.*

Watertown

The scoreboard that hung in the old Boston Garden now lords over a replica parquet floor in the food court of the Arsenal Mall—itself a former Civil War arsenal—put there by then-mall owner Stephen Karp, a lifelong sports fanatic who paid $40,000 for the treasure. Sixteen feet tall and 14 across, the electric Garden scoreboard still works. *485 Arsenal Street.*

Twin brothers Francis E. and Freelan O. Stanley, the inventors of the Stanley Steamer, proved the potential of their new contraption at the world's first auto show in Cambridge in 1898 by setting a speed record of 127 miles per hour—a record that still stands in that size and weight class. Flush with their success, the Stanleys rented a converted bicycle shop in Watertown, where they filled 100 orders before selling out to *Cosmopolitan* publisher John Brisane Walker, who opened the Stanley Motor Carriage Company. The factory where Stanley Steamers were built still stands; about 11,000 of the Stanleys' "Locomobiles" were assembled there before the factory was closed in 1924. *44 Hunt Street.*

Watertown has one of the nation's oldest Armenian communities, drawn here by jobs at a rubber plant that operated in the town during the late 1800s and early 1900s. It also has the nation's principal depository of artifacts that survived the Armenian genocide. The Armenian Library and Museum of America tells the story of the Armenian diaspora in cultural artifacts and personal property that took the long, dangerous route to the United States, including a five-foot, 100-pound copper tray depicting Jesus and the apostles that was carried across the mountains to Lebanon by an Armenian fleeing the 1915-1922 massacre by the Turks. Also on display is a memorial to the nearly two million Armenians killed, framed by Adolf Hitler's 1939 comment justifying the Holocaust: "After all, who today remembers the extermination of the Armenians?" *65 Main Street; Tuesday 1 to 5 and 7 to 9, Friday and Sunday 1 to 5; 617-926-2562.*

One of the most famous female sculptors of her time in the world, Harriet Hosmer was born in Watertown in 1830, and the public library has a bust of Hesperus by Hosmer, her sculpting tools, her liquor flask, and photographs of her other statues. As an eccentric expatriate living in Rome, Hosmer also served as the model for Hilda in her friend Nathaniel Hawthorne's *The Marble Faun*. *Hunnewell Room, Watertown Public Library, 123 Main Street; Monday through Thursday 9 to 9, Friday and Saturday 9 to 5, Sunday 1 to 5 September 1 through June 15, then Monday through Thursday 9 to 9, Friday 9 to 5, Saturday 10 to 2; 617-972-6431.*

The first school for the blind chartered in America, the Perkins School for the Blind has a museum with raised-print precursors to Braille, antique six-key Braille writers, and a display showing how the blind have been depicted in art. There are also artifacts relating to famous students, including Helen Keller's handwriting samples, and doilies crocheted by Laura Bridgman, the first blind and deaf person educated in America. *175 North Beacon Street; by appointment; 617-924-3434.*

Wellesley

A tree grown from a branch of Sir Isaac Newton's apple tree is on the Babson College campus, whose founder, pioneering stock analyst Roger Babson, attributed the boom-and-bust cycle of the modern-day economy to Newton's law of action and reaction. The original tree is the very one from which an apple fell on Newton's head in 1665, leading to his theories of gravity. Babson also imported Isaac Newton's study when the physicist's home in London was torn down in 1913. The room

Unkown Boston and Eastern Massachusetts

has been reassembled here, with its original wall paneling, fireplace and mantelpiece. *Horn Library; Monday through Friday noon to 4, 781-239-4570.*

A revolving globe three stories tall spins outside Coleman Hall at Babson College. Built in 1955, the 28-ton sphere is 28 feet in diameter and was once the biggest world in the world. It was restored and rededicated in 1993.

Secret love letters exchanged by the poets Robert Browning and Elizabeth Barrett now are available for everyone to see, along with the very door from Barrett's father's house in London under which the notes were slipped. Robert and Elizabeth Barrett Browning eventually married in 1846 and settled in Italy, but their correspondence is at Wellesley College along with a Harriet Hosmer cast of their clasped hands. *Margaret Clapp Library, Wellesley College, 106 Central Street; Monday through Friday 10 to noon and 1 to 5; 781-283-2129.*

A series of 15 interlinked greenhouses simulating every climate on earth, from desert to rainforest, the Margaret C. Ferguson Greenhouses are filled with more than 1,000 kinds of living plants, including rice, papyrus and bamboo, and the finest collection of tropical plants in New England. Built in 1922, the complex of greenhouses is adjacent to a 22-acre botanic garden. *Wellesley College; daily 8 to 4.*

Pritzker Prize-winning Spanish architect Rafael Moneo's first American commission, the Davis Museum at Wellesley College houses selections from a permanent collection of works by Alexander Calder, Willem deKooning, Monet, Cezanne, Sir Joshua Reynolds, John Singleton Copley and woman artists including Louise Nevelson, Angelica Kauffman, and Anne Whitney. *106 Central Street; Tuesday through Saturday 11 to 5, Sunday 1 to 5; 781-283-2051.*

The showcase garden of the Massachusetts Horticultural Society, Elm Bank once was the estate of Benjamin Pierce Cheney, founder of the company that was a forerunner to American Express; the name was given by an earlier owner who planted elm trees along the adjacent Charles River. After years of neglect, Asian and Italianate gardens laid out in the 19th century by Frederick Law Olmsted have been restored and a 36-acre horticulture center and experimental garden added. The trial garden is one of only 13 experimental gardens in North America that test new plant varieties to evaluate their performance in each climate. *900 Washington Street (Route 16); Monday through Friday 8 a.m. to dusk; 617-933-4900.*

Wenham

One of the world's largest collections of dolls, the Wenham Museum's 5,000 dolls aren't all glass-faced and frilly. There are kewpie dolls, an Eskimo doll carved out of walrus tusk, a Boston Red Sox mascot doll given after the team won the World Series in 1915, one of the world's finest collections of British toy soldiers, and dolls once owned by Queen Victoria, Czar Nicholas, Admiral Byrd and Cecil Rhodes. The museum also has dollhouses including a three-foot-tall Addams Family house based on the Charles Addams illustrations, and six operating HO train layouts so realistic you can look through the windows of the engines and see the gauges. *132 Main Street; Tuesday through Sunday 10 to 4. 978-468-2377*

Westford

There are 50 different species of live butterflies inside a 3,100-square-foot glass atrium at the Butterfly Place, where as many as 500 butterflies at a time flutter around colorful plants and shrubs. Visitors can walk among the butterflies in the 27-foot-high atrium, which is kept at a butterfly-friendly temperature of 80 de-

Unknown New England

grees, or watch them through an observation window. *120 Tyngsboro Road; daily 10 to 4 in March, daily 10 to 5 April 1 through Columbus Day; 978-392-0955.*

Weston

A life of study persuaded Eben Norton Horsford, a Harvard chemistry professor, that Vikings under the command of Leif Ericson's brother, Thorwald, had not only brought their longboats into Boston Harbor six centuries before the Pilgrims, but rowed them up the Charles River as far as a place called Norumbega, a name Horsford speculated was derived from "Norway." The presumed Viking settlement of Norumbega is marked by stone tower with a plaque at the base recounting these claims. The Vikings purportedly arrived around the year 1000. Look closely and you'll see other signs of this New England Viking legacy, including a bronze statue of Leif Ericson at the end of the Commonwealth Avenue Mall near Kenmore Square in Boston. And the supports of the Longfellow Bridge between Boston and Cambridge are carved in the shape of longships bound upriver. *Norumbega Road.*

Second in the size of its collection only to the Smithsonian Institution's National Postal Museum, the Cardinal Spellman Postal Museum has some of the world's rarest stamps, including stamps collected by President Dwight Eisenhower, General Matthew Ridgway, and Francis Cardinal Spellman, archbishop of New York—more than two million stamps in all. Among them: the first adhesive stamp, made in 1840; sheets of President John F. Kennedy memorial stamps signed by his widow, mother, and two brothers; and stamps created secretly by Polish inmates in a German World War II prisoner-of-war camp to communicate among themselves. *235 Wellesley Street; Thursday through Sunday noon to 5; 781-768-8367.*

Built in 1768, the Golden Ball Tavern was owned by a wealthy British loyalist around the time of the Revolutionary War and was a base for British spies. The owner, Isaac Jones, ultimately switched sides, but not before his house was raided by colonial rebels who burst in on his wife and their newborn son. The door broken down by the mob remains; so does the original furniture, which shows the evolution of the house over 200 years. From the tavern days, shards of beer mugs and the outline of the bar can still be seen. *662 Boston Post Road; Wednesday 9:30 to noon, Sunday 1:30 to 4 April through November; 781-894-1751.*

Weymouth

Born in 1744, Abigail Smith lived here until she was 20, when she was courted by John Adams and became Abigail Adams, wife of one president and later mother of another. Her tiny wooden crib is still in the house, which was restored in 1947 with bricks contributed by other first ladies. Some of the bricks came from the White House when it was undergoing various renovations. *180 Norton Street; Tuesday through Sunday 1 to 4 July 1 through Labor Day; 781-335-4205.*

Woburn

A ventilator cowl from the *USS Maine*, whose sinking in Havana Harbor sparked the Spanish-American War, is on the town common. A local veterans group successfully petitioned for the relic in 1913. *Main and Pleasant streets.*

The tenement where Charles Goodyear discovered the process for vulcanizing rubber in 1839 shows how poor he was at the time. Goodyear never fully profited from his discovery; though named for him, the Goodyear Tire and Rubber Company was founded in 1890, three decades after he died. *286-292 Montvale Avenue.*

Franklin D. Roosevelt called Benjamin Thompson one of the five most intriguing figures in history. That may have been an understatement. Born a poor farm boy in Woburn in 1753, Thompson enamored himself to the daughter of a wealthy

Unkown Boston and Eastern Massachusetts

family in Rumford, Maine, married her, and became accepted into high society. A loyalist, he was a spy for the British against the Americans during the siege of Boston, later commanding a British cavalry regiment that saw action in New York and South Carolina before leaving America—and his wife—for Bavaria. There he was enobled as Count Rumford, and it is this name by which he is more widely known as the father of thermodynamics. Extending this work into practical use, he was the inventor of the Rumford Fireplace, shallower and therefore more efficient than conventional fireplaces, and the Rumford Roaster. He also studied lunar observations, gunpowder, shell velocity, and nutrition, and is believed to have been the inventor of the folding bed. A statue of Rumford stands before the Woburn Public Library, and his birthplace is preserved as the Rumford Birthplace National Landmark, a gambrel-roofed farmhouse built in 1714 that contains his cradle, models of his experiments, paintings of his many mistresses, and a copy of his portrait by Thomas Gainsborough. It was Gainsborough's only portrait of an American. *90 Elm Street; Wednesday through Saturday 1 to 4:30; 781-933-0781.*

Unknown Cape Cod
and the Islands

The secret of Cape Cod, Martha's Vineyard and Nantucket isn't only where to go; it's when. It's in the winter—not the crowded summer—that the Cape and Islands slow to a quiet, peaceful pace, reminders of an age when it was possible to walk alone on a secluded beach, take a drive along a country road without another car in sight, or stretch out unmolested before the fireplace in the parlor of a bed-and-breakfast inn. Temperatures are milder than on the mainland, moderated by the ocean air on all sides; the prices drop as quickly as the crowds, and there are holiday festivities amidst the weathered shingles and wooden steeples of picture-postcard Cape and island towns. It's even possible to see a life vest from the *Titanic* in an unknown Martha's Vineyard museum that isn't open in the summer.

History here stretches back farther than almost anywhere in the United States—so far that much of it has been forgotten. It was in Provincetown, for instance, not Plymouth, where the Pilgrims first set foot on land, and their first encounter with Indians was in Eastham—and it wasn't friendly. No matter; the French definitely, and the Vikings probably, got here first. Cape Cod was fired on by the British in the War of 1812 and the Germans during World War I, the only place in America to be shelled during that conflict; the scars of both attacks remain, if you know where to look—including in what is now a restaurant men's room. Leaders of the American Revolution lived here, Grover Cleveland had his summer White House on Cape Cod, and President John F. Kennedy is still synonymous with it.

This was the world center of whaling, pirates roamed the waters just offshore, and shipwrecks litter the craggy reefs and shallows. But the dramatic coastline also inspired writers and artists from Edward Hopper to Eugene O'Neill, and provided the perfect geography for the first wireless telegraph transmission from the United States to Europe and the first transatlantic cable from France. This nautical legacy also left behind the world's only town clock that strikes the time in ship's bells.

Barnstable

Although it ranks in importance with the Boston Tea Party, the protest march at Barnstable's Old Colonial Courthouse has been overlooked by history. In <u>one of the first mass uprisings against colonial rule</u>, more than 1,500 people disrupted a court session here on September 27, 1774, to protest an unpopular British ruling dictating how jurors were to be selected. Later converted to a church, the 1772 building now is home to an organization dedicated to the preservation of Cape Cod history. *Rendezvous Lane at Route 6A.*

Unknown New England

Barnstable's Otis family was a bunch of overachievers. James Otis was <u>one of the first leaders of the American Revolution</u>. Less well-known was his sister, Mercy Otis, <u>America's first woman writer</u>. She wrote patriotic poetry and political plays and in 1805 published her three-volume history of the Revolutionary War. The site of the Otis homestead is marked by a memorial boulder in a meadow diagonally across the road from the West Barnstable post office. *Route 6A.*

Once William Sturgis had given his house, his book collection and part of his fortune for the town to build what is now called Sturgis Library, he figured that he might just as well leave his wallet. So he did, along with his <u>pocket watch that traveled around the world three times</u>, no small feat in 1863. Built in 1644 as the home of the Reverend John Lothrop, the Sturgis is <u>the oldest building in the United States used as a library</u>. Since Lothrop held Sunday meetings in the parlor, it also is <u>the oldest surviving structure in American where religious services were regularly held</u>. The library has the so-called Bishop's Bible, brought by Lothrop to America in 1605; when it was burned through by a candle in 1634, he restored from memory the missing passages. *3090 Main Street (Route 6A); Monday, Wednesday, Friday 10 to 5, Tuesday 1 to 8, Thursday 1 to 5, Saturday 10 to 4; 508-362-6636.*

West Barnstable-born John "Mad Jack" Percival commanded the *USS Constitution* on an epic 52,279-mile, 495-day around-the-world cruise starting in 1844, making her the first American warship to circumnavigate the globe. He got his nickname when, during a stop in China, he started a diplomatic row by trying to rescue a French bishop imprisoned there. There is <u>a memorial to Mad Jack</u> in the wall of Northside Cemetery, where he is believed to be buried. *Route 6A.*

The Wampanoag chief Iyanough, for whom the Barnstable village of Hyannis and the Wianno section of Osterville are named, died in 1621 after being chased into a swamp by Pilgrims. There is a statue of Iyanough on the Hyannis village green, and his grave is marked with a sign off a highway. *Route 6A, Cummaquid.*

The <u>wheel from the steamship *Portland*</u>, which went down with all hands in the great gale of November 27, 1898, has resurfaced at the Centerville Historical Museum, which boasts a large and varied collection of 19th-century maritime items including the remarkable prosthetic leg made for Captain James Worrell, complete with a leather foot and hinged heel in a boot. The surrounding neighborhood is notable for its unparalleled number of sea captains' homes; at the peak of its maritime period, Centerville was home to 104 captains. *513 Main Street; Monday through Saturday noon to 5 June 1 through October 31; 508-775-0331.*

Ever since family patriarch Joseph Kennedy bought a summer home in Hyannisport, the village has been closely tied to the Kennedy clan. Their years here are commemorated in the John F. Kennedy Memorial Museum in the former town hall in Hyannis. There are photographs, a videotape narrated by Walter Cronkite about President Kennedy's Hyannisport years, and oral histories recorded by friends. Though JFK lost the vote for president in predominantly Republican Barnstable, he made his 1960 election-night victory speech in the armory building here; the family church, St. Francis Xavier, whose altar was given by the Kennedys as a memorial to Joseph P. Kennedy Jr., is near the museum. *397 Main Street; Monday through Saturday 9 to 5, Sunday noon to 5 mid-April through October 31, Wednesday through Saturday 9 to 5 November 1 through mid-December; 508-790-3077.*

Overlooking the ocean off Hyannis where the president once sailed from his summer compound in Hyannisport is <u>a memorial to John F. Kennedy</u> consisting of a fieldstone monument with the presidential seal and the inscription: "I believe it is important that this country sail and not sit still in the harbor." *Ocean Street.*

Unkown Cape Cod and the Islands

The <u>oldest continuously operated boatyard in America</u>, the Crosby Boatyard, opened in the mid-1700s, was famous for the Wianno sailboat, and the wooden "Crosby Cat," a faster, more stable sailboat favored by commercial fisherman; John F. Kennedy had a Wianno Senior made by the Crosbys, which is on display outside the John F. Kennedy Library and Museum in Boston. *West Bay Road.*

The Osterville Historical Society has a Crosby Wianno sailboat like the one owned by JFK, and a Crosby Cat in its boat collection. Inside the society's 1824 Jonathan Parker House is <u>Jean Baptiste Adolphe Gilbert's painting of George Washington at Valley Forge</u>. Wealthy families including the du Ponts and Mellons settled in Osterville's exclusive Oyster Harbor section in the 1920s; letters and photographs from that period are also on display. *Parker and West Bay roads; Thursday through Sunday 1:30 to 4:30 mid-June through Columbus Day; 508-428-5861.*

Once the busy custom house that served Cape Cod, the red brick Trayser Museum was built in 1856 and, when the custom house was moved, became the post office. Today it holds the collection of the Barnstable Historical Commission, including <u>the veritable Cadillac of horse-drawn hearses</u>: a sleek, glass-sided number that was the best and last horse-drawn hearse used in Barnstable County. There also is the original four-cell 1690 jail, complete with authentic 17th-century graffiti on the walls; and a maritime collection that includes gifts made out of shells by sailors for their sweethearts. *Route 6A; Tuesday through Sunday 1:30 to 4:30 Father's Day through Columbus Day; 508-362-2092.*

The Pilgrims weren't the only Britons exiled for their religious beliefs. Barnstable was founded by a group of Congregationalists who were thrown out of the mother country a few years later and settled here in 1639, establishing <u>the first Congregational church in America</u>, now known as the West Parish Meeting House. At first the congregation met at Sacrament Rock, which was blasted through to build Route 6A but has been pieced back together and can be seen across that road from the Barnstable-West Barnstable Elementary School. The current church dates from 1717. On the Sunday before every Thanksgiving—Henry Jacobs Day—members dress in period costume and re-enact a 17th-century-style service. *2049 Meeting House Way; 508-362-4445.*

Famous <u>husband-and-wife folk artists</u> are commemorated in the Cahoon Museum of American Art, a one-time colonial tavern that now is an unsung museum of folk, marine, and American Impressionist art. The 1775 building was the home and studio of Ralph Cahoon and his wife, Martha, whose work forms the bulk of the collection. The Cahoons became famous for their folk paintings on furniture, wood, and even Masonite; Ralph Cahoon specialized in depicting mermaids knitting, playing golf, fishing, and in other poses before rough-hewn New England backdrops of lighthouses and hot air balloons. *4676 Falmouth Road; Tuesday through Saturday, 10 to 4 February through December; 508-428-7581.*

Bourne

Set up in 1627 by the Pilgrims as an outpost for trade with the Dutch in New York and the local Wampanoag Indians, the Aptucxet Trading Post was <u>the first commercial enterprise in English-speaking North America</u>, using polished bits of quahog shells, or wampum, as currency. The building now on the site encompasses the original foundation, hearth and fireplace; the remainder is a replica based on references in Governor William Bradford's History of Plimoth Plantation. Also here is the 200-pound Bourne Stone, which some claim to be <u>proof of a Viking settlement on Cape Cod</u> centuries before Columbus. The Wampanoags were first to find the stone, with its mysterious inscription, and they brought it to the site of the Bournedale Indian Church, where it was given a position of honor as the threshold. Only

Unknown New England

hundreds of years later, when the church was moved and somebody turned the stone over, was the inscription rediscovered and determined by some scholars to be runic, or Viking. While the link remains in dispute, the local ocean rowing club has named itself the Vikings. *24 Aptucxet Road; Monday through Saturday 10 to 4, Sunday 2 to 5 May 1 through Columbus Day; 508-759-8167.*

Grover Cleveland's summer White House was a palatial Tudor-style mansion on a point jutting into Buzzards Bay; called Gray Gables, it had its own railroad station built for his exclusive use. Cleveland bought the house after his first term as president ended in 1889 and before his second began in 1893. When he died, it was turned into an inn and then a private residence before burning down in 1975. But Cleveland's private railroad station survives, and has been moved to the Aptucxet Trading Post. The site of his home is at the end of Presidents Road.

Bourne native Major General Leonard Wood had as colorful a career as anyone in American history. Wood preceded Theodore Roosevelt as commander of the "Rough Riders" in Cuba, helped capture Geronimo, and ran for the Republican presidential nomination in 1920. An Army surgeon, he was military governor of Cuba from 1898 until 1902, and lost to Warren Harding for the GOP nomination—though not until the 10th ballot. Harding made Wood governor general of the Philippines. Fort Leonard Wood in Missouri is named for him. The sleigh in which his father, also a doctor, made his winter rounds is at the Aptucxet Trading Post; the house where he was born is now privately owned. *866 Shore Road.*

Like many sea captains, William Burgess took along his wife on lengthy voyages. But when Burgess died at sea during an around-the-world trip, his wife, Hannah Rebecca Burgess, became the first woman to navigate an American ocean-going vessel. Her log, and some of the exotic artifacts she brought home with her from China and other ports, are in the Jonathan Bourne Historical Center in the Burgesses' home town, which was named for Bourne when it broke away from Sandwich in 1884. *30 Keene Street; Tuesday 9 to 3; 508-759-6928.*

Built in 1957 for the headquarters offices of Bethlehem Steel's shipbuilding division, a unique room-sized Lucite "ocean" with models depicting more than 100 years of shipbuilding has been retired to the Massachusetts Maritime Academy, and restored. The display in the Captain James Hurley Library is divided into two half-circles, one for military ships and one for merchant ships, including the World War II battleship *Massachusetts*, the aircraft carrier *Lexington*, the cargo ship *Alcoa Pathfinder*, the inaugural liberty ship *Patrick Henry*, the submarine *Narwhal*, the first deep-sea oil rig *Texas Towers*, and the Spanish-American War Monitor *Olympia*, Admiral Dewey's flagship in the Battle of Manila Bay. Built—like many of the originals—at the former Bethlehem shipyard in Quincy, the models "float" on the largest blocks of Lucite ever cast and also include the *Thomas B. Landers*, the world's first seven-masted schooner. Because there weren't enough nautical names for seven masts, the sailors on the *Landers* named them after the days of the week. *101 Academy Drive; Monday through Friday 9 to 4; 508-830-5035.*

One of the original masts from the *USS Constitution* stands as a monument for Massachusetts Maritime Academy graduates lost at sea, along with a statue of a mariner with a sea bag. *Maritime Memorial Park.*

The third-largest vertical-lift drawbridge on the continent, the Buzzards Bay Bridge is 270 feet high and 544 feet long; only bridges in Chicago and New York are longer. The bridge is still lowered nightly for trains to pass. Their cargo these days? Cape Cod's garbage. The bridge is visible from the canal access roads.

Unkown Cape Cod and the Islands

Brewster

Set on 383 acres of museum- and publicly owned conservation land, the Cape Cod Museum of Natural History has expansive windows overlooking a salt marsh and Cape Cod Bay beyond. With bird feeders hung outside, the Marshview Room allows for unparalleled <u>indoor birdwatching</u>. Binoculars are provided. The museum also offers nature walks around the area with knowledgeable guides. *Route 6A; Monday through Saturday 9:30 to 4:30, Sunday 11 to 4:30; 508-896-3867.*

Operated as an industrial site for more than 300 years, the Brewster Mill is powered by Stony Brook, which drops 26 vertical feet in its two-mile journey to Cape Cod Bay. Begun in 1663 as a grist mill to grind grain into meal and flower, the site became <u>America's first woolen factory</u> in 1814. But perhaps the most coveted product made here in the 19th century was ice cream. Corn is still ground for sale in the summer by volunteers in the lower level of the last mill building built here, whose upper level is a museum with an eclectic collection including antique ice cream freezers that pre-date refrigeration. Stony Brook is also a herring run where saltwater herring return each April and May to spawn. You'll find them during high tide, though not in numbers as high as when colonists described the stream as black with fish; since that time, pollution, obstructions, and overfishing have thinned the run. *Stony Brook and Satucket roads; Thursday through Saturday 2 to 5 May and June, Friday 2 to 5 July and August;. 508-896-9521.*

Chatham

The Atwood House of the Chatham Historical Society, built in 1752 by sea captain Joseph Atwood, is now a museum chronicling the town's long maritime history. The collection includes <u>a sofa from the ward room of the *USS Constitution*</u>, a rare bottle of whale oil, paintings of Chatham ships in Asian ports, and portraits of Chatham sea captains painted by Frederick Wight, for whom the art museum at UCLA is named. Town life is depicted on extraordinary murals painted in the 1930s and 1940s showing Christ coming ashore in a dory and living among the locals. *347 Stage Harbor Road. Tuesday through Friday 1 to 4, Saturday 9:30 to noon early June through late September; 508-945-2493.*

Founded by a retired executive of the New York Central System, the Chatham Railroad Museum has as its centerpiece a standard-issue <u>New York Central caboose built in 1900</u>, sitting at the platform as if awaiting an engine. The museum is in the original 1887 station of the Chatham Railroad Company, a small shore line that mostly carried fish and other freight. Service on the line ended in 1937. *153 Depot Road; Tuesday through Saturday 10 to 4 mid-June through mid-September.*

The Chatham Aviation Display exhibits <u>more than 150 model airplanes</u> in authentic colors and markings, mostly from World War II; in the background, Big Band music plays, and aviation documentaries run on a monitor. There also are exhibits of aviation posters, goggles, maps, and aerial reconnaissance photos. *Depot and Hitching Post roads, daily 1 to 4 June through September; 508-945-6082.*

<u>You can stay overnight in the historic Monomoy Point Lighthouse</u>, built in 1823 and decommissioned in 1923, in the middle of the 2,750-acre Monomoy National Wildlife Refuge. There's no electricity or running water in the keeper's cottage, but a guide will prepare dinner by lanternlight. *Saturday mid-May through mid-June and mid-September until October 1, and Tuesday, Thursday, and Saturday mid-June though mid-September; 508-896-3867.*

Dennis

Opened in 1927 in a converted Unitarian meetinghouse, the Cape Playhouse is <u>America's oldest professional summer theater</u>. Bette Davis worked here as an

Unknown New England

usher before making her debut on the Playhouse stage, and others who have performed here include Gregory Peck, Ginger Rogers, Humphrey Bogart and Tallulah Bankhead. The adjacent Cape Cinema, built in 1930, has <u>one of only three surviving murals by the artist Rockwell Kent</u> (both of the others are in Washington, D.C.) covering the huge vaulted ceiling; at the time, it was the largest single mural in the world, a modernistic depiction of the heavens in blue, gold and orange with pairs of embracing lovers floating among the galaxies and constellations. Kent refused to come in person to Massachusetts to install the mural as a protest against the executions of the anarchists Sacco and Vanzetti. *Route 6A; Monday through Saturday mid-June through early September; 508-385-3911.*

Rockwell Kent is also represented in the Cape Museum of Fine Arts, whose topic is <u>Cape Cod's contribution to American art</u>. The permanent collection includes works by the likes of Henry Hensche, Oliver Chaffee, and sculptors Gil Franklin and Verujan Boghosian. *Route 6A on the grounds of the Cape Playhouse; Monday through Saturday 10 to 5, Sunday 1 to 5 mid-May through mid-October; 508-385-4477.*

A veritable zoo of <u>animal figures carved from driftwood</u> is part of the whimsical collection at the Jericho Historical Center, called that because when it was given to the town the walls were falling down. Since restored, the 1801 sea captain's house is a collection of odd objects contributed by locals, including a hand-pumped vacuum cleaner. *Old Main Street and Trotting Park Road; by appointment; 508-394-0206.*

The Congregational Church of South Dennis boasts <u>the oldest operating pipe organ in America</u>, dating from 1765 and installed here when the church was built in 1835, and a chandelier once lit with whale oil. The cemetery is filled with the graves of sailors lost at sea. *218 Main Street; 508-394-5992.*

Eastham

Contrary to popular belief, <u>the Pilgrims' first encounter with American Indians</u> was not at all a friendly one. Angered by the earlier kidnapping of fellow tribesmen by an English slave dealer, Nauset Indians fired arrows at the Pilgrims; they shot back with their muskets. Both sides withdrew uninjured. Today, First Encounter Beach is one of Cape Cod's more peaceful places. *Samoset Road.*

<u>Three of the original passengers on the *Mayflower*</u> are buried in Old Cove Cemetery. *Corliss Way.*

Near the end of World War I, on July 21, 1918, three barges pulled by the ocean-going tug *Perth Amboy* were sunk off Nauset Beach by the German submarine *U-156*. <u>A door from the *Perth-Amboy* riddled with German bullets</u> is one of the unexpected items on display in the Schoolhouse Museum, which also has <u>one of the original beams from Boston's Old North Church</u>, replaced during a renovation. *Nauset Road; Monday through Saturday 1 to 4 Memorial Day through Labor Day, then Saturday 1 to 4 through September 30; 508-255-0788.*

<u>A beach shack like the one in which the author Henry Beston spent the winter</u> writing his famous book *The Outermost House* is preserved by the Eastham Historical Society behind its Swift-Daley House. Vacationers in the 1930s and 1940s would spend their weekends in the rustic beach shacks, picnicking and fishing along the sandy shore; the historical society has furnished this rare survivor with typical mismatched dinnerware and castoffs of the period. Built in 1741, the Swift-Daley House itself has never been significantly altered, and still has its original wide board floors. It is furnished in a mix of eras from the 250 years in which it

Unkown Cape Cod and the Islands

was occupied. *Route 6; Monday through Friday 1 to 4 June 1 through Labor Day, then Saturday 1 to 4 in September; 508-240-1247.*

<u>Three lighthouses hidden in the woods</u>, the so-called Three Sisters Lights were built in 1838 and gradually moved back from the eroding shore, two in 1918 and one in 1923, before finally being replaced and reunited in a quiet clearing hidden in the woods along a marked path off Cable Road in the Cape Cod National Seashore.

Fort Hill

Near the bony elbow of Cape Cod is an enclave where the birds can still drown out the passing traffic, where the *Mayflower* got its first glimpse of the New World, and where there is natural beauty so overpowering that the locals spend their lunch breaks watching as the churning ocean pounds the beach.

All of this secluded splendor awaits behind a narrow wooded side street just a mile and a half shy of the wide main entrance to the Cape Cod National Seashore and yards from the busy four-lane road that is the curse of weekend visitors.

Fort Hill is a surfside Shangri La, a pastoral escape where the cacophony of Cape Cod is one of light and color, not of noise or crowds.

It was here that the Nauset band of Wampanoag Indians lived as fishermen and farmers, where the French explorer Samuel de Champlain dropped anchor 15 years before the Pilgrims settled, where the *Mayflower* first sighted land, where merchantmen and pirates were shipwrecked, where a whaling captain built one of the finest homes of its kind on Cape Cod, and where the author Henry Beston spent a winter alone with a journal in his "outermost house." "The great rhythms of nature, today so dully regarded, have here their spacious and primeval liberty," wrote Beston in his 1929 classic work of Cape Cod literature.

Fort Hill is the southernmost outpost of the inland portion of the National Seashore, preserved as a park with hiking trails, meadows and a small sign at the Eastham-Orleans line that is the only clue to its location.

Many of the walking trails lead to Skiff Hill, where there is a 20-ton boulder used for decades by the Wampanoags to grind and polish their stone tools. Below this cliff is the tidal marsh where Champlain landed on an exhibition from Quebec in 1605. He found the area surrounded by the thatched houses of the Nauset Indians and fields planted with corn and squash.

Champlain named the spot Port de Mallebarre, or "Port of Dangerous Shoals." The same shoals chased the Pilgrims away on November 9, 1620, when they neared the shore but turned and sailed north to Provincetown's protected harbor.

Centuries later, sea captain Edward Penniman built what was then the biggest house in town here, which still stands. The French Second Empire-style home is one of the most outstanding sea captains' houses on Cape Cod. The lower jaw of a finback whale arches over the entrance. Penniman's also was the first house on the Cape to boast both indoor plumbing and a kerosene chandelier.

For all that Fort Hill offers, it is equally attractive for what it doesn't: Noise. Traffic. Bicyclists. Swimmers. Surfers. Barely a fraction of the five million annual visitors to the National Seashore find their way here.

It is, wrote Beston, "the last fragment of an ancient and vanished land."

Fort Hill Road, Eastham; daily dawn to dusk; Penniman House open April through late October with tours Saturday at 10 by reservation; 508-255-3421.

Falmouth

Katharine Lee Bates, <u>the writer of "America the Beautiful,"</u> was born at 16 Main Street on August 12, 1859. It was on a visit to the Rocky Mountains in 1893 that she was inspired by their "purple mountain majesties" to write the famous hymn, whose words are inscribed on her gravestone in Oak Grove Cemetery on

Unknown New England

Palmer Avenue. There also is a statue of Bates on the grounds of the Falmouth Public Library a few blocks from her home on Main Street. *508-548-4857.*

It was just as memorable as "Don't fire until you see the whites of their eyes," or, "Don't give up the ship." But Falmouth townspeoples' answer to the captain of the British brig *HMS Nimrod* when he demanded they surrender their guns during the War of 1812 has largely been forgotten. "Come and get 'em!" they purportedly responded. When the *Nimrod* subsequently fired its cannon, it left several permanent mementos: cannonball holes, one each in what is now the men's room of the Nimrod Restaurant at 100 Dillingham Avenue, and one in the Elm Arch Inn at 26 Elm Arch Way. The shot that hit the inn landed harmlessly in a feather bed.

Several of the cannonballs fired at Falmouth by the *Nimrod* are preserved in the Conant House Museum, along with the ship's log; whaling tools and mementos of the years-long voyages to the Pacific made by Falmouth's whalers; and Katharine Lee Bates' books, photographs and papers. *55 Palmer Avenue; Monday through Thursday 10 to 4 mid-June through mid-September; Saturday and Sunday 1 to 4 mid-September through October 31; 508-548-4857.*

Instrumental in introducing inoculation for smallpox in 1797, Dr. Francis Wicks lived on Falmouth's village green in a Federal-style home that has one of the few authentic widow's walks remaining on Cape Cod. A surgeon's mate in the Revolutionary War when he was just a boy, Wicks became a doctor and his home, now the local historical society museum, is full of antique medical equipment. *65 Palmer Avenue; Monday through Thursday 10 to 4 mid-June through mid-September; Saturday and Sunday 1 to 4 mid-September through October 31; 508-548-4857.*

Founded in 1881, the Woods Hole Science Aquarium is the oldest aquarium in the United States, established by the National Marine Fisheries Service as a holding area for fish used in research projects. It has dinosaur-like wolf fish, puffer fish, and string-like bluespotted cornetfish, which can grow to six feet. There's also a kind of fish called tautogs that lie around waiting for their food to swim by; so lethargic are the tautog, there's a sign on the tank that says "No, They're Not Dead." Stranded and sick seals also make their homes here; seal feedings are at 11 and 4. *Albatross and Water streets; Monday through Friday 11 to 4; 508-495-2001.*

A full-sized model of the spherical cabin on the deep submergence vessel *Alvin,* which helped explore the *Titanic,* is in the exhibit center of the Woods Hole Oceanographic Institution, the nation's largest independent marine research and engineering laboratory. Guests can sit in the 7-foot-diameter mock-up of the cabin from *Alvin,* used on the second mission to the *Titanic* after it was found by WHOI scientists. The exhibit center, in a former Methodist church, also has displays and videos about WHOI research, including the *Titanic* discovery and the study of undersea hypothermal vents. The institution's famous research ships, including the *Knorr,* which found the *Titanic,* can often be seen from Waterfront Park, and there are free summer weekday tours by reservation. *15 School Street; Friday and Saturday 10 to 4:30 and Sunday noon to 4:30 in April, Tuesday through Saturday 10 to 4:30 and Sunday noon to 4:30 in May, Monday through Saturday 10 to 4:30 and Sunday noon to 4:30 Memorial Day through Labor Day, Tuesday through Saturday 10 to 4:30 Tuesday through Saturday and noon to 4:30 Sunday Labor Day through October 31, Tuesday through Friday 10 to 4:30 November and December; 508-289-2663; for institution tours, call 508-289-2252.*

So highly regarded it's been called a national treasure, the Marine Biological Laboratory in Woods Hole has a visitor center with exhibits about the marine research conducted here, and about evolution and molecular biology, with live specimens of baby toadfish and sea urchins. Tours leave from here for what was

Unkown Cape Cod and the Islands

once known as the "supply department": a storehouse full of sea life fated to become the subjects of experiments, mostly relating to biomedical research. *100 Water Street; Tuesday through Friday 10 to 2 January through April, Monday through Friday 10 to 4 May and June, Monday through Friday 10 to 4, Saturday and Sunday 11 to 3 July and August, Monday through Friday 10 to 4, Saturday 10 to 3 September, Monday through Friday 10 to 3 October through December; 508-289-7423.*

Yankee thrift is memorialized at the Woods Hole Historical Museum. When a hurricane blew down a forest of cedars, the frugal locals used the wood to build a fleet of dories. One is in the boat barn of the museum, along with a spritsail boat whose mast was hinged to travel under bridges. There's also a huge historic diorama of the town. *579 Woods Hole Road; Tuesday through Saturday 10 to 4 mid-June through mid-September with local walking tours Tuesday at 4; 508-548-7270.*

Harwich

Private Brooks Academy was <u>one of the first schools of navigation in the country</u>; it is now a museum of, among other things, tools used for cranberry harvesting; Harwich had <u>the nation's first commercial cranberry bog</u>. *80 Parallel Street; Wednesday through Saturday 1 to 4 June through mid-October; 508-432-8089.*

Nineteenth-century collectibles comparable to Currier and Ives prints, Rogers group statuary was popular beginning around the time of the Civil War for its depiction of clustered figurines ranging from soldiers at a conference to people playing chess. One of the largest surviving collections of Rogers statuary is in the Brooks Free Library. So valuable are the fragile plaster figures that about 56 pieces from the library's collection were stolen one night while most of the residents were attending a town meeting. They have never been recovered. The library still has more than 30 figures on display. *739 Main Street; Monday and Wednesday 10 to 6, Tuesday noon to 8, Thursday through Saturday 10 to 4. 508-430-7564.*

Mashpee

Arriving colonists tried to convert the original residents of Mashpee, the Wampanoag Indians, to Christianity, building churches for them. One, called the Old Indian Meeting House, has been converted into the Mashpee Tribal Museum, with re-creations of Wampanoag wigwams and tools. Built in 1793, the meeting house sits beside a herring run active in the spring. *483 Great Neck Road (Route 130); Monday through Saturday 10 to 2; 508-477-0208.*

Unlike most of the rest of New England, the peaceful 135-acre Lowell Holly Reservation off a side road on Conaumet Neck has not been cleared, burned or plowed in 200 years. It offers an unparalleled and undisturbed variety of American beech, red maple, sweet gum, black birch, pitch pine, and holly trees as. *South Sandwich Road; daily dawn to dusk; 617-539-1400.*

Orleans

After attacking the ocean-going tug *Perth-Amboy* and three barges off the coast of Orleans on July 21, 1918, the German submarine *U-156* turned its guns on the town, which became <u>the only place in America shelled by an enemy during World War I</u>. Curious residents rushed to the beach to watch as the shells landed harmlessly behind them. Word was sent to a Navy base in Chatham, which launched a seaplane to scare the sub away. *U-156* was reported sunk in the North Sea a month later. A plaque marks the site of the shelling. *Off Nauset Heights Road.*

When British Captain Richard Raggot of the *HMS Spencer* demanded a ransom to spare the town's saltworks from destruction during the War of 1812, the townspeople scoffed, and, when a party came ashore, the local militia held them off. <u>The</u>

Unknown New England

ransom demand is in the Meeting House Museum of the Orleans Historical Society in a former Universalist church, along with a collection of ships' logs and the musket owned by homegrown Revolutionary War hero Isaac Snow. There are also pieces of ships wrecked during the great gale of 1898 that sank the steamer *Portland* and hundreds of other vessels. *River Road and Main Street; Tuesday through Saturday 10 to 1, Thursday 6:30 to 8:30 July and August; 508-240-1329.*

The U.S. terminal for the first transatlantic cable between the United States and France starting in 1891, the French Cable Station looks almost exactly as it did when it carried the news of Charles A. Lindbergh's landing in Paris in 1927 and the invasion of France by Germany in 1940. The original instruments and other equipment, which are no longer in use, remain, along with samples of the underwater cable. *41 South Orleans Road; Monday through Saturday 1 to 4 mid-June through Labor Day, then Friday through Sunday 1 to 4 in September; 508-240-1735.*

Apparently all the good records had been broken by the time Englishmen John Ridgeway and Chay Blythe left from here in 1966 on the first successful transatlantic crossing in a dory. A plaque marks the spot. *Nauset Harbor.*

The tanker *Pendleton* broke in two so quickly in the blizzard of February 18, 1952, it barely had time to send a rescue call. But the 36-foot Coast Guard Rescue Boat 36500 with a crew of four braved the 60-foot seas and saved 32 of the 33 men clinging to the hull. The Coast Guardsmen were awarded the U.S. Gold Life Saving Medal for their efforts. Today *Boat 36500*, which has been restored, can be seen moored at Rock Harbor from June through September. *508-240-1329.*

Provincetown

Privateers and pirates didn't only operate in the Caribbean. There were pirates aplenty off New England, including "Black" Sam Bellamy, who terrorized the coast until his ship, the former slaver *Whydah*, was wrecked in a storm off what is now Wellfleet in 1717. Rediscovered in 1984, the wreck of the *Whydah* has yielded 200,000 artifacts from coins to cannon, many of them on display at the Expedition Whydah Sea-Lab and Learning Center; it is the world's only authenticated pirate shipwreck treasure. Legend has it Bellamy was sailing to Cape Cod to pick up his mistress after a year at sea in which he captured more than 50 ships. *16 MacMillan Wharf; daily 10 to 7 June through Labor Day, daily 10 to 5 May, September, and October, 10 to 5 Saturday and Sunday November and December; 508-487-8899.*

Drawn by the ethereal light, artists have made Provincetown their home for more than a century, since Charles Hawthorne founded the Cape Cod School of Art here in 1899. The Provincetown Art Association and Museum has an unparalleled collection of the works of Hawthorne, Edward Hopper, Robert Motherwell, Claes Oldenburg, William Merrit Chase, Mary Fassett, Andy Warhol, Joel Meyerowitz and many other Provincetown artists and photographers. *460 Commercial Street; noon to 4 Saturday and Sunday October through April, noon to 5 Saturday and Sunday April and May, noon to 5 Sunday through Thursday and noon to 5 and 8 to 10 Friday and Saturday Memorial Day through July 4 and September, noon to 5 and 8 to 10 daily July 4 through Labor Day; 508-487-1750.*

Provincetown calls itself America's oldest continuous art colony, and grateful artists have for decades left the town examples of their work. The resulting unparalleled town art collection hangs in the high school, police department, town-run nursing home, and 1885 town hall, which has more than 60 works on permanent exhibit. The biggest, on the back wall of the town hall's front lobby, are two murals depicting life in the fishing village in the 1930s painted by longtime Provincetown observer and modernist Ross Moffett. Charles Hawthorne's celebrated "Crew of the Philomena Manta," a view of Provincetown fishermen returning home, is in the main corridor. A map describing the art in town hall is available for free. *260 Commercial Street; Monday through Friday 8 to 5; 508-487-7000.*

The tallest all-granite structure in the United States, the 252-foot Pilgrim Monument is hard to miss, but the adjacent museum is often overlooked. It was in Provincetown, not Plymouth, that the Pilgrims first came ashore on November 11, 1620; they stayed for five weeks before finding the soil too sandy to settle. While anchored here, the Pilgrims wrote the Mayflower Compact, the first democratic document written in America, declaring each other "straightly tied to all care of each other's good." The museum has the cannon from the *HMS Somerset*, which laid siege to the town during the Revolutionary War, and a reconstructed captain's cabin from a whaling ship. Two famous sons are represented: Arctic explorer Donald MacMillan, and Eugene O'Neill, the first American playwright to win the Nobel Prize. There are wolves, a polar bear and an Eskimo kayak brought back from the Arctic by MacMillan, for whom the town's main wharf is named and who is buried in Town Cemetery; and mementos relating to O'Neill, who lived in Provincetown for 12 years, during which time his play *Bound East for Cardiff* debuted at the Provincetown Playhouse. *High Pole Hill Road; daily 9 to 7 July and August, 9 to 5 April, May, June, September, October, and November; 508-487-1310.*

The Race Point Lighthouse is separated from the nearest paved road by two and a half miles of sand dunes, so distant that it is a Race Point lighthousekeeper who is credited with being the inventor of the dune buggy. The light, built in 1816, allows paid overnight stays. *Tuesday June 1 through September 30; 508-896-3867.*

An original 1862 station of the U.S. Life Saving Service, the Old Harbor Life Saving Station was moved from Chatham to Provincetown in 1977 and now is a museum with original rescue apparatus including a surfboat and a gun that shot a rope to grounded vessels. Beach rescue drills are re-enacted Thursday evenings in the summer. *Race Point Beach; daily July and August, hours vary; 508-349-3785.*

Sandwich

Opened 17 days before the Panama Canal, the Cape Cod Canal is the world's widest sea-level canal. First proposed in Pilgrim times, the idea of building the canal was resurrected by George Washington during the Revolutionary War as a means of evading the British blockade. But it was not until 1907 that the Cape Cod Construction Company dug its first shovelful of dirt. The canal was opened seven years later by then-Assistant Navy Secretary Franklin D. Roosevelt. It is now run by the U.S. Army Corps of Engineers. A scale model of the canal and artifacts from its construction are displayed in a visitor center, which also has a 41-foot patrol boat and live radar and sonar images. *66 Ed Moffit Drive; Friday through Sunday 10 to 5 mid-May through mid-June and September 1 through mid-October, Wednesday through Sunday 10 to 5 mid-June through August 31; 508-833-9678.*

Almost certainly the oldest house on Cape Cod, the Hoxie House, built around 1637 (the exact date was lost in a fire at town hall), has been restored to its 17th-century appearance with furniture on loan from Boston's Museum of Fine Arts. Certainly the oldest post-and-beam saltbox, it was a private home until the 1950s—though it still had no running water, electricity, or heat. *Route 130; daily 10 to 5 June through Columbus Day; 508-888-1173.*

The oldest house in America continuously occupied by the same family, the Wing Fort House was built in 1641 by Stephen Wing, a Quaker. Wing was routinely dragged before the Plymouth court in the 17th century by Pilgrims who were not particularly fond of Quakers, but he persevered, and the house is still owned by his descendants. Inside, among other things, is a hooked rug made by a Wing who

Unknown New England

was a whaling captain; such pursuits were common among men at sea. *69 Spring Hill Road; Thursday through Saturday 10 to 4 mid-June through mid-September; 508-833-1540.*

The Sandwich Friends Meeting House Wing helped found in 1657 is now <u>the oldest Quaker congregation in America</u>. Its current building, the third on this site, went up in 1810, and is still heated with wood-burning stoves. *Quaker Meetinghouse Road; services Thursday at 6 and Sunday at 10:30; 508-888-4181.*

The <u>creator of Peter Cottontail, Grandfather Frog, and Reddy Fox</u>, Thornton W. Burgess was born in Sandwich in 1874. The Thornton W. Burgess Museum in the home of his aunt, Arabella, has original manuscripts and illustrations from some of his 170 books. The "smiling pool" of Burgess's stories, a pond shaped like a smile whose real name is Boiling Springs, is next door. *4 Water Street (Route 130); Monday through Saturday 10 to 4, Sunday 1 to 4 April through October; 508-888-6870.*

<u>Peter Cottontail's Briar Patch</u>, where Burgess set his famous stories, is now the 57-acre Green Briar Nature Center. Live turtles, rabbits, iguanas, and other animals are on display, along with a 1903 jam kitchen that still preserves and sells jelly made in the original kitchen and heated by sunlight, making this the <u>oldest commercial solar-cooking operation in the country</u>. *6 Discovery Hill Road; Tuesday through Saturday 10 to 4 January through March, Monday through Saturday 10 to 4, Sunday 1 to 4 April through December; 508-888-6870.*

The Sandwich Fish Hatchery raises more than 80,000 trout per year to stock ponds around the state. The fish, in their various stages of development, can be seen close-up, and even fed. *Route 6A; daily 9 to 3; 508-888-0008.*

Truro

When the two-masted brig *Jason* wrecked in 1893 a mile north of Ballston Beach, 24 of her crew of 25 were lost. The sole survivor grabbed onto a bale of jute, a material used to make rope, which was the vessel's cargo. <u>Jute from the *Jason*</u> is part of the collection of the Truro Historical Museum, tucked away in a former grand summer hotel. There is also other flotsam, including chairs, books and glassware from one of the most famous shipwrecks, that of the steamer *Portland*, which went down in 1898. But the highlight is <u>a Pilgrim musket and the only known surviving powder bag carried aboard the *Mayflower*</u> on its voyage to America. *Lighthouse Road; daily 10 to 4:30 June 1 through September 30; 508-487-3397.*

The <u>oldest lighthouse on Cape Cod</u>, Highland Light in Truro was the subject of an extraordinary engineering feat when it was moved 453 feet to safety from the eroding shore. Now reopened, it's one of the only lighthouses in which visitors are allowed all the way up to the lantern room, 69 winding steps and 183 feet above the sea. On display inside the keeper's house are artifacts relating to the light, including early lenses. *Lighthouse Road; daily 10 to 5:45 May 1 through October, open until sunset July and August; 508-487-1121.*

So popular was Swedish opera singer Jenny Lind in the mid-1800s, a riot broke out when her concert in Boston was oversold and she was forced to sing for free from atop a 55-foot stone tower at the Fitchburg railroad depot. When that tower was about to be demolished in 1927, a wealthy attorney had it shipped it to property he owned in North Truro, and rebuilt. The tower can be seen from Highland Light. *Lighthouse Road.*

Unkown Cape Cod and the Islands

When the 120-foot German bark the *Frances* came aground the day after Christmas in 1872, all hands were saved, but the ship itself was wrecked. Today its black hull can be seen at low tide, making it the only 19th-century shipwreck off Cape Cod still visible. *Head of the Meadow Beach.*

Although—or perhaps because—they had no electricity, telephones or running water, the 17 isolated rustic dune shacks built as shelters along the coast of Cape Cod by the Coast Guard in the 1920s and 1930s came to serve as inspirational retreats for some of the greatest American writers and artists including Jack Kerouac, Norman Mailer, e.e. cummings, Jackson Pollack and Eugene O'Neill, who spent all or part of summers in them. Threatened with demolition, the shacks have been preserved as national historic sites after the longest federal court case in American history—which took 25 years to be resolved. *High Head Beach at Peaked Hill Bar.*

Wellfleet

So vast is the ocean from this point, it seems you could see Europe. In fact, this was the first place in America you could hear it. The first transatlantic wireless transmission was sent from here, an exchange of messages in Morse code between President Theodore Roosevelt and British King Edward VII on January 19, 1903. Nor was that the last historic communication here; on the night of April 14, 1912, the station would receive the distress call from the *Titanic*. Though erosion has taken a toll, there are significant remnants of the transmitter station. Half of the original site has eroded, but the concrete foundations and the anchors that held the guy wires remain, and there's a model showing how it worked. It's also a great place from which to see the sandy shoreline, pounding ocean, and surreal landscape of gnarled pines and white cedars of the outer Cape. *Wireless Road; 508-349-3785.*

The long reach of this small town is reflected in the Wellfleet Historical Society Museum, a former general store. Included in the collection is memorabilia related to Marconi, including souvenir plates made to commemorate the first transatlantic wireless transmission, and pieces of the original transmission tower. There are also exhibits relating to Wellfleet native Lorenzo Dow Baker, who had nothing to fill the holds of his ship on a return trip from delivering mining equipment to South America in 1870, so imported bananas into the United States for the first time, and soon became the founder of the United Fruit Company. Then there was Luther Crowell, inventor of the square-bottom paper bag, who also designed a helicopter-like aircraft in 1862, though it never flew. Some of Crowell's patents are in the museum. So is the rocking chair of Sarah Atwood, one of the first female lighthouse keepers, who took over Mayo's Beach Light at Wellfleet Harbor from her ailing husband around 1822. *266 Main Street; Tuesday and Friday 10 to 4, Wednesday, Thursday, and Saturday 1 to 4 late June through early September; 508-349-9157.*

The clock on the First Congregational Church is the only town clock in the world that strikes the time in ship's bells. The day is divided into six four-hour "watches" beginning with first watch at noon, and bells are chimed each half hour: one bell at 12:30, two at 1, three at 1:30, up to eight at 4, when the cycle repeats. *200 Main Street.*

Yarmouth

Built in 1889 as an apothecary by Thacher Taylor Hallet and run by his descendants even today, Hallet's Drug Store still has its original marble-topped soda fountain with swivel stools and, up a narrow staircase on the second floor, a little-known museum with a random collection of artifacts from the store and local history: World War II ration checks, old medicines in their original bottles and posters for everything from Lucky Strikes to record hops at a local dance hall. *Route 6A; Monday through Saturday 8 to 5 March through December; 508-362-3362.*

The Reverend Anthony Thacher and his wife, Elizabeth, were making the seemingly safe sea journey from Ipswich to Marblehead in 1635 when a storm wrecked their ship. The Thachers watched their five children drown while they themselves floated to safety in their baby's wooden cradle. So touched was King Charles I by their story, he granted Thacher land on Cape Cod, where a 1690 reproduction of the cradle is in the Winslow Crocker House, built in 1780 by a Thacher descendant who also was an avid collector of the early American furniture that fills the home. *250 Route 6A; Saturday and Sunday 11 to 4 June 1 through October 15; 508-362-4385.*

The home of Edward Gorey, known for his macabre black-and-white illustrations famous from the opening of PBS's *Mystery* series, is now a museum devoted to the late artist and writer, filled with skulls he collected, 45,000 books, and roving cats. *8 Strawberry Lane; Wednesday through Saturday 10 to 5, Sunday noon to 5 May through September, then noon to 5 Thursday through Sunday; 508-362-3909.*

Martha's Vineyard

Martha's Vineyard's Seamen's Bethel is not only comparatively unknown; it's seldom visited, since it's closed in the summer, and open only by appointment in the winter. Hebrew for "House of God," a bethel provided harbor for sailors while their ships were in port; many left souvenirs of their travels in gratitude for this hospitality—which is how the Martha's Vineyard bethel came to be in possession of a life vest from the *Titanic* given by a sailor from the *Carpathia*, which picked up survivors of the ill-fated liner after it went down on April 15, 1912. The bethel also has whale tooth and walrus tusk carvings, and ships in bottles. *110 Main Street, Vineyard Haven; 508-693-9317.*

The decline of the whaling industry began in 1871 when 33 whaling ships—including two from Martha's Vineyard—were caught and crushed in heavy ice while hunting whales in the Arctic. What came to be known as the Great Arctic Whaling Disaster followed by 12 years the discovery of oil in Pennsylvania, which had already begun to dry up the market for whale oil. A lithograph of the disaster hangs in the Martha's Vineyard Historical Society museum. *Cooke and School streets, Edgartown; Tuesday through Saturday 10 to 5 mid-June through early October, Friday 1 to 4, Saturday 10 to 4 October through mid-December, Saturday 10 to 4 mid-December through mid-March, Wednesday through Friday 10 to 4, Saturday 1 to 4 mid-March through mid-June; 508-627-4441.*

Hidden among the pines and oaks of Chappaquiddick is a Japanese garden, the 14-acre Mytoi Japanese garden, whose red fretwork bridge is framed in daffodils, flowering dogwoods, azaleas, rhododendrons, Hanoki cypress, and holly, designed by landscape architect Hugh Jones. *Dike Road; daily dawn to dusk; 508-627-7689.*

It's an odd name to have seared itself into the national consciousness, but Chappaquiddick will forever be remembered as the place where U.S. Senator Edward Kennedy, then 37, crashed his Oldsmobile off the Chappaquiddick Bridge on July 18, 1969. His passenger, Mary Jo Kopechne, was killed. The Dike Bridge, which spans the 150-foot channel at the end of a long dirt road, was rebuilt in 1995. *Dike Bridge Road, Chappaquiddick.*

One of the finest lighthouse lenses ever made, with 1,009 individual prisms to maximize the beam's intensity, has been retired to a miniature lighthouse tower built especially to display it by the Martha's Vineyard Historical Society. The first-order Fresnel lens was originally installed in the Gay Head Lighthouse in 1856 after first being exhibited at the World's Fair in Paris. The society's collection includes sign-language instructions dating from a period in the 1800s when the island's small gene pool led to widespread hereditary deafness. There are also logbooks, ship models, scrimshaw, harpoons, and treasures brought back from the South Pacific. Outside, in the carriage shed, is a Hawaiian canoe carried on a whaling ship as a souvenir. *59 School Street, Edgartown; daily 10 to 4:30 July 5 through Columbus Day, then Wednesday through Friday 1 to 4 and Saturday 10 to 4; 508-627-4441.*

The Vincent House is the oldest home on Martha's Vineyard, built in 1672. One of the three rooms is furnished in the style of the 17th century, one in the 18th, and one in the 19th, and construction techniques are laid bare including the mud and clay insulation between the rough-hewn roof boards. The former owners raised as many as 11 children at a time in these three rooms and the attic. *Main and Church streets, Edgartown; 10:30 to 3 daily May 1 through Columbus Day; 508-627-4440.*

The Tiffany stained-glass windows aren't the only distinctive feature of St. Andrew's Church, built in 1899; the pulpit is the bow of a dory from the schooner *Northern Lights. 34 North Summer Street, Edgartown; 508-627-5330.*

A tree brought from China in a flower pot by Captain Thomas Milton when it was still a seedling is now the oldest pagoda tree in North America. Milton also built the house the tree now shades. *South Water Street, Edgartown.*

While its first white settlers called it "Martha's Vineyard" purely for symbolic purposes, wine is now made on the island. Founded in 1971, the Chicama Vineyards is the first bonded winery in Massachusetts. *Stoney Hill Road, Tisbury; Saturday 1 to 4 January through May and mid-October through mid-November, Monday through Saturday 1 to 4 in May, Monday through Saturday 11 to 5 and Sunday 1 to 5 June 1 through Columbus Day, Monday through Saturday 11 to 4 and Sunday 1 to 4 mid-November through December; 508-693-0309.*

Perversely, the native Indians on Martha's Vineyard avoided being wiped out by the arriving whites because they converted to Christianity. The blend of these two very different cultures is reflected in the secluded Indian Burying Ground and Chapel in Christiantown, whose gravestones reflect both pagan and Christian imagery. *Christiantown Road, West Tisbury.*

One of the two known carousels built by Charles W.F. Dare, the Flying Horses is the nation's oldest platform carousel. Brought to the island in 1884, it is now a national historic landmark, and still gives rides. *Circuit Avenue Extension, Oak Bluffs; Saturday of Easter weekend through Columbus Day, hours vary; 508-693-9481.*

A living museum on the outside, the famous cottages of the Martha's Vineyard Camp Meeting Association are off-limits on the inside—except for one. The Cottage Museum is the only place to see the inside of an Oak Bluffs cottage, with an exhibit of typical furnishings and memorabilia including the rocking chair where President Ulysses S. Grant sat when he visited. There's also an original magic lantern film projector lighted with a wicker candle. *1 Trinity Park, Oak Bluffs; Monday through Saturday 10 to 4 mid-June through September 30; 508-693-7784.*

The island's Civil War memorial was, ironically, the gift of a Confederate, Charles Strahan, a newspaper editor who settled on the Vineyard after the war and hoped to foster reconciliation. *Sea View Avenue, Oak Bluffs.*

Unknown New England

There are two Martha's Vineyard lighthouses open to the public in the summer, from half an hour before sunset until half an hour after: East Chop Light and Gay Head Light. At Gay Head Light, visitors are allowed into the light chamber, where they can watch the two lights rotate. *Gay Head Light, Lighthouse Road in Gay Head, Friday through Sunday, mid-June through Labor Day; East Chop Light, East Chop Drive in Oak Bluffs, Sunday mid-June through Labor Day; 508-627-4441.*

Although she didn't live in Chilmark, friends of the playwright and part-time Martha's Vineyard resident Lillian Hellman pulled strings so she could be buried there. The author of *The Children's Hour*, *The Little Foxes*, *Toys in the Attic* and other famous works, she was equally well-known for defying the House Un-American Activities Committee in 1952, and for her affairs with the likes of Dashiell Hammett. Hellman's grave in Abel's Cemetery is marked by a stone inscribed with a feather pen. Also in Abel's Cemetery is the grave of John Belushi, a summer resident of Chilmark who once said the Vineyard was the only place he could get a good night's sleep. Belushi died of a drug overdose. *South Road.*

On one side of the little-known Menemsha Hills Reservation, 150-foot sand cliffs overlook Nobska Point, the town of Falmouth and the Elizabeth Islands; on the other, Prospect Hill—at 308 feet, the highest point on the Vineyard—offers spectacular views of Menemsha and Gay Head. The conservation area is lush with blueberries, bearberries, and heath; harbor seals bask on the beach, deer and red-tailed hawks in the forest. *North Road, Chilmark; 508-693-3678.*

Nantucket

Moby Dick? True story. The Nantucket whaler *Essex*, the basis for Herman Melville's *Moby Dick*, was rammed by a whale off the coast of South America in 1820. But Melville didn't tell the whole tale. Survivors of the *Essex*, who escaped in three whaleboats, resorted to cannibalism to stay alive, drawing lots to decide which of them would be murdered and eaten; the short straw was drawn by the luckless teenage cabin boy, a nephew of the captain. The personal journal of *Essex* crewman Thomas Nickerson, is in the Nantucket Whaling Museum. Built 1847 as a candle factory, the museum building still has the original beam press used to press spermicetti from sperm whales into candles. The press is the only one of its kind in the world. *13 Broad Street. Saturday and Sunday 11 to 4 December through April 30, Thursday through Monday 11 to 4 May 1 through Memorial Day, Monday through Saturday 10 to 5 Memorial Day through Labor Day. 508-228-1894.*

The Folger-Franklin Memorial Fountain marks the birthplace of Abiah Folger, the mother of Benjamin Franklin. Overlooking fields, it's a good place to imagine what Nantucket looked like then. *Madaket Road.*

Like many Nantucketers, Absalom Boston became a whaling captain who ultimately bought his own ship, the *Industry*. Unlike other mariners, however, Boston was America's only black whaling captain, who also had an all-black crew, part of the significant black community on Nantucket that left behind the nation's second-oldest surviving meeting house built by free blacks for their own use; the oldest is in Boston. Now called the African School and Church, the building, at York and Pleasant streets served as a school for black children until Nantucket's public schools were integrated, then became the African Baptist Church, and later was used as a warehouse. Though their contributions are not widely known, blacks served in integrated crews on whaling ships, and even as officers, and the maritime route was as important as the Underground Railroad in helping slaves escape to freedom. Abolitionist Frederick Douglass fled in this way in 1838, working as a sailor on a ship that took him north; he made his first speech before a mixed audience three years later at the Nantucket Athenaeum. Captain Boston's portrait

Unkown Cape Cod and the Islands

hangs in the Nantucket Whaling Museum, and he is buried in the Colored Cemetery behind the current-day Martha's Vineyard Hospital. *29 York Street; Tuesday through Saturday 11 to 3, Sunday 1 to 3 July and August; 508-228-9833.*

The first American woman to discover a comet through a telescope, Maria Mitchell was America's first woman astronomer, the first woman professor of astronomy at a U.S. university—Vassar, where she was hired in 1865—and the first woman elected to the American Academy of Arts and Sciences. Mitchell discovered what is now called Comet Mitchell on October 1, 1847, from the roof of the Pacific National Bank building, still standing at the head of Main Street, where her father worked as a cashier. The telescope she used that night is in her birthplace, now the Maria Mitchell House and Museum of Astronomy, along with her eyeglasses, her desk from Vassar, and other items; she is buried in Prospect Hill Cemetery. *1 Vestal Street; Tuesday through Saturday 10 to 4 mid-June through Labor Day, then Friday and Saturday 10 to 4 through Columbus Day; 508-228-2896.*

The Maria Mitchell Association operates two observatories: the Vestal Street Observatory at 3 Vestal Street, which gives tours Saturday at 11 September 1 through June 1; and the Loines Observatory at 59 Milk Street Extension, which has evening viewings Friday at 8 September 1 through June 1. *508-228-8690.*

Generously described as the size of a two-car garage, the Maria Mitchell Aquarium nonetheless crams a lot of local aquatic life into its small space, formerly the station for the tiny island railroad. *28 Washington Street; Tuesday through Saturday 10 to 4 mid-June through Labor Day; 508-228-5387.*

Built in 1806 with massive oak timbers reinforced by iron straps, Nantucket's Old Gaol is one of the nation's oldest surviving prison buildings. It wasn't as tough as it looks; prisoners were often allowed to go home at night. Still, there were several escapes, including one of a 15-year-old boy who climbed through the chimney. He was caught, and the chimney rebuilt with a smaller flue. *15R Vestal Street; Monday through Saturday 10 to 5 Memorial Day through Columbus Day; 508-228-1894.*

In the early 1800s, Nantucket was the whaling capital of the world, with 88 ships. Its decline began with the Great Fire of 1846, which destroyed the wharves and much of the business district at the same time that demand for whale oil fell. The horse-drawn equipment used to fight the giant fire has been preserved in the Fire Hose Cart House, a former fire station built in 1886. *8 Gardner Street; Monday through Saturday 10 to 5 Memorial Day through Columbus Day; 508-228-1894.*

The second-oldest lighthouse in America, the squat but picturesque Brant Point Light was built in 1746; only Boston Light is older. The current wooden tower on the site, just 26 feet tall, was built in 1901. The grounds, though not the lighthouse, are open to the public. *Easton Street.*

The 260-acre Northland Cranberries bog is one of the largest cranberry bogs in the world. *Milestone Road.*

The fastest, largest and most luxurious passenger liner in the Italian fleet, the *Andrea Doria* was also advertised as the safest—until she became the victim of a thick Nantucket fog. On July 25, 1956, the *Andrea Doria* was hit by the Swedish-American liner *Stockholm* 60 miles off Nantucket, and immediately began to sink. All but 52 passengers and crew were saved; all the victims died in the collision. Artifacts recovered from the ill-fated *Andrea Doria* are on display at the Nantucket Life Saving Museum, including silverware from the opulent dining rooms. The museum also has a surfboat from the Massachusetts Humane Society, a precursor to

71

Unknown New England

the Coast Guard; quarterboards from wrecked ships; and lighthouse lenses. *158 Polpis Road; daily 9:30 to 4 mid-June through Columbus Day; 508-228-1885.*

Nantucket's Coffin School was <u>a tribute to his island relatives by a British admiral who fought against the colonies</u> during the Revolutionary War. Boston-born Admiral Sir Isaac Coffin, an intimate of Lord Nelson, established the school in 1827, when Nantucket had no public school. The building now on the site is the successor to the original, and houses the Egan Institute of Maritime Studies, with exhibits relating to Nantucket history—including 19th-century paintings by Elizabeth Rebecca Coffin, a student of Thomas Akins, and a portrait of Coffin by Akins. *4 Winter Street; daily 9 to 5 end of May through mid-October; 508-228-2505.*

Unknown Central and Western Massachusetts

It's hard to believe that Theodor Geisel saw anything on Mulberry Street in Springfield that would influence his life, or ours'. But there, wedged between the dentists' offices and bleak apartment buildings, survive the familiar cheerful, plump Victorians whose fading colors once were bright enough to stir the man we came to know as Dr. Seuss. This was Geisel's grandparents' neighborhood, which he immortalized with *And To Think That I Saw It On Mulberry Street*, the first of his 48 children's books. Like many places in his native city, it inspired illustrations that seem otherworldly, but are based on real buildings, cars, and motorcycles, and on animals and even people who actually lived here.

The legacy of Dr. Seuss is just one of the surprises hiding in the hills of central and western Massachusetts. Inland Springfield also is the unlikely setting for a one-of-a-kind museum devoted to the tragedy of the *Titanic*, for example, with relics taken from the ship by the survivors as it sank. It was here that the famous Springfield rifle was produced—and the M-1 machine gun, which General George S. Patton called the greatest weapon ever made—in the nation's longest-operating armory, now a museum. The first successful gasoline-powered car and the first gasoline-powered motorcycle were also built here.

Such inventiveness was hardly confined to Springfield. Great Barrington was the first city in the world to be lit with AC electricity like that in use today. Orange has the first factory in the United States designed expressly to assemble cars. Eli Whitney, the inventor of the cotton gin, was born here. So was Milton Bradley, Johnny Appleseed, and Sylvester Graham, inventor of the Graham cracker. The first liquid-fueled rocket was launched in western Massachusetts, opening the way for travel into space. The birth control pill was invented in central Massachusetts. So was the plastic pink flamingo, the first known typewriter, and the smiley face. There's a hydroelectric power station 10 stories tall 700 feet underground, and the world's largest radio receiver built to listen for alien signals from space.

This intellectual legacy also extends to literature. Towering figures from reclusive poet Emily Dickinson to dictionary writer Noah Webster lived here. So did W.E.B. DuBois, and Susan B. Anthony. You can find Alice's Resturant of the famous Arlo Guthrie ballad, the world's largest private holding of Russian books, and one of the world's largest collections of Yiddish books, films and music.

The history on exhibit here is deep and wide. It begins with the fossils of dinosaurs, including the first confirmed evidence of a dinosaur to be found in North America. The home of the little-known general who commanded the American Revolutionary forces before George Washington is here. So is the only place

Unknown New England

outside the National Archives that has original copies of the Declaration of Independence, Articles of Confederation, Constitution, and Bill of Rights.

This was the birthplace of American Red Cross founder Clara Barton, film director Cecil B. DeMille, and department store magnate Marshall Field, and the final resting place of the man known as Grizzly Adams and a German U-boat commander who nearly perfected missiles that could have opened U.S. cities to attack.

Then there are the destinations that defy classification: the ghosts of the lost towns wiped out by the Quabbin Reservoir, the real-life village of Podunk, the factory where the paper is made for all U.S. currency, the only museum devoted exclusively to indoor plumbing, and a 105-foot white domed Buddhist peace pagoda.

Adams

Not only is Susan B. Anthony's birthplace still standing; so is the simple Quaker meetinghouse on Friend Street where the suffragette who campaigned to win women the right to vote was inspired to live a life of social activism. In 1872, Anthony led a group of women to the polls in New York and was arrested, marking the beginning of the suffragette movement. *East Road at East Street.*

Amherst

Notoriously reclusive poet Emily Dickinson lived all but a few years of her life here inside the house her grandfather built in 1813. Born in the house in 1830 to a stern father, she rarely left, writing and cultivating the plants in the conservatory, and dying here in 1886. The home is now a faculty residence owned by Amherst College, but much of it is open to the public, including the second-floor bedroom where she did most of her writing; her bed and the rest of her furniture is still here, too, though Dickinson's desk and chair are in Harvard's Houghton Library. On a nightstand is a photograph of her overbearing father. Dickinson is buried in West Cemetery at Triangle and North Pleasant streets. *280 Main Street; Wednesday and Saturday 1 to 5 March and November through mid-December, Wednesday through Saturday 1 to 5 April, May, September, and October, Wednesday through Saturday 10 to 5 and Sunday 1 to 5 June through August; 413-542-8161.*

Original manuscripts and personal mementos of Emily Dickinson and Robert Frost are also on display in the Jones Library, which has four of Dickinson's handwritten poems, her calling card, and trim from her bonnet. Frost taught at Amherst College and lived off and on in Amherst for three decades. The Frost manuscripts include woodcut prints and blocks used to illustrate his books. *43 Amity Street; Tuesday 10 to 5, Wednesday through Saturday 10 to 1 and 2 to 5; 413-256-4090.*

Not all tories fled rebellious Massachusetts at the outbreak of the conflict with the crown. Amherst's John Nash's Tavern was one of the places British loyalists met openly during the Revolutionary War. And while a few were jailed briefly, they appealed and regained their freedom, though they were stripped of their rights to vote and bear arms for the duration of the conflict. The sign that hung outside John Nash's Tavern is part of the collection of the Amherst History Museum, which is in the home of Simeon Strong, one of the most vocal British loyalists in Amherst. It didn't hurt him much; Strong, a lawyer, went on to become a justice of the state Supreme Judicial Court after the war had ended. *67 Amity Street; Wednesday through Saturday 12:30 to 3:30 February through November; 413-256-0678.*

"Noah's Raven," the first confirmed evidence of a dinosaur to be found in North America, is part of the collection of the Pratt Museum of Natural History at Amherst College. The footprints were found in 1802 in South Hadley, 40 years before dinosaurs were identified as a fossil group and at a time when most people still unquestioningly believed the biblical accounts of creation. The museum also has other fossils, meteorites, and skeletons of prehistoric beasts, and stuffed passenger pi-

Unkown Central and Western Massachusetts

geons and other birds, 100 of them once owned by John James Audubon. *Route 9 at Route 116; Saturday 10 to 4, Sunday noon to 5 mid-June through August 31, Monday through Friday 9 to 3:30, Saturday 10 to 4, Sunday noon to 5 September 1 through mid-June; 413-542-2165.*

One of the founders of Amherst College, Noah Webster wrote sections A through K of the first American dictionary here beginning in 1812, before moving to New Haven, Connecticut, where he finished the alphabet. Webster was already 43 when he began the dictionary during a time when people in different parts of the country spelled, pronounced and used words differently; it took him 27 years to finish. It was Webster who gave us American spellings for such words as "color" and "theater" to differentiate them from the English versions. Webster's home stood near 62 Main Street; there is a statue of him on the Amherst College campus.

The Center for Russian Culture at Amherst College is the world's largest private holding of Russian books, manuscripts, newspapers, and periodicals. It includes an art gallery with Stalinist-era murals and pictures by the Russian-Jewish artist Chaim Livshitz. *Webster Hall, Amherst College, Route 9 at Route 116; Monday 9:30 to noon and 2:30 to 4 and Wednesday 9:30 to 1:30; 413-542-8453.*

Hidden in this unlikely rural New England setting is one of the world's largest collections of books, film and music in Yiddish: the National Yiddish Book Center, which is working to rescue the 1,000-year-old language that combines German grammar and vocabulary with Hebrew, Aramaic, Slavic, and other dialects. The center, on the campus of Hampshire College, has preserved 1.5 million volumes of Yiddish books, original recordings of Yiddish theater, film and music, and even Jewish recipes. An attached museum has a working Yiddish linotype machine from *The Jewish Daily Forward* in New York, the last of its kind in the world. The sign at the exit, which reads *A hartsikn dank*, means, "Thanks for visiting" in Yiddish. *1021 West Street; Sunday through Friday 10 to 3:30; 413-256-4900.*

The Edward Carle Museum of Picture Book Art, named for the author and illustrator of *The Very Hungry Caterpillar* and 70 other works, is the only museum in the United States devoted to children's books, with rotating exhibitions of international children's artists and hands-on art rooms for kids. *125 West Bay Road; Tuesday through Saturday 10 to 4, Sunday noon to 4; 413-658-1100.*

Ashfield

The birthplace of the legendary film director Cecil B. DeMille is in Ashfield, though mostly by accident. DeMille's father, a lay preacher, and his mother were passing through town when she went into labor on August 12, 1881, in the home of the couple that owned the Ashfield House Hotel, where they were staying. He went on to direct such masterpieces as *The Ten Commandments, Cleopatra*, and *The Greatest Show on Earth.* The house is now privately owned. *347 Main Street.*

The anti-Catholic, anti-immigrant Know-Nothing Party, which was briefly popular in the 1850s, was strongest in Massachusetts, where a Know-Nothing was elected governor. Even here, its members—all native-born Protestant men—met secretly. Exactly how secretly is made clear in the Ashfield Historical Society Museum, a former general store with a concealed room with a round hole in the door for a lookout. Also in the museum is a microscope made in 1843 by Alvan Clark, the Ashfield native and optics pioneer who invented the refractor lens still used in telescopes. *457 Main Street; Saturday 1 to 3 July 1 through Columbus Day.*

Unknown New England

Ayer
Established in 1917 as a staging point for soldiers destined for the World War I battlefields of Europe, Fort Devens served the same role during World War II, when it was the training site for nurses, chaplains, cooks and bakers and the Women's Army Corps. Decommissioned in 1995, it has left behind extraordinary monuments to history. One of them, oddly enough, is the grave of a German U-boat commander, Kapitan Leutnant Friederich Steinhoff, who surrendered to authorities at New Hampshire's Portsmouth Navy Yard at the end of the war, and then committed suicide. Steinhoff, commander of the *U-873*, was one of the developers of the

---

Robert Goddard and The Birthplace of the Space Age
The only objects soaring into space these days from Pakachoag Hill in Auburn are golf balls. But look closely: A four-foot granite obelisk marks the spot beside the first tee of the Pakachoag Golf Course where the space age began. It was here, on March 16, 1926, that Robert Goddard launched the world's first liquid-fuel rocket, making what was then his Aunt Effie's farm the Kitty Hawk of aeronautics.

Goddard's tiny rocket rose 41 feet, stayed aloft for two and a half seconds, built up a speed of 60 miles per hour and fell into a cabbage patch 184 feet away.

Goddard would go on to launch a larger craft in Auburn, with instruments, in 1929, this time drawing ambulances and police and an order from the state fire marshal banning further rocket tests in Massachusetts.

His work didn't end; it only moved. He built 35 successful rockets, including one launched in New Mexico that was the first to break the speed of sound, and developed gyro stabilizers, guidance systems, turbopumps and automatic recovery by parachute. His variable-thrust motor led to the development of rocket planes such as the X-15. Every rocket since designed relies on his inventions, which Wernher von Braun would call "the blueprint(s) for our exploration of outer space."

You wouldn't know it to look at them. The gawky metal tower Goddard used to launch that first-ever liquid-fuel rocket is on exhibit in the library named for him a few miles away at Clark University in Worcester, where he taught physics. A large permanent display at Clark includes the nozzles, cones and steering control fins used on later Goddard rockets, some with tin parts cut from coffee cans. But there also is a powerful reminder of the extraordinary consequences of this labor: a copy of his autobiography that was taken to the moon by the first astronauts to go there.

The people of Auburn, who had so disdained the "useless moon rockets" that disturbed their cows, have since built a memorial to Goddard in the middle of town. Its centerpiece: a huge surplus Polaris missile near a full-sized model of his tiny pioneering rocket, which stood just 10 feet tall and weighed a mere six pounds.

Among other things, the Clark museum displays several of his patents for a "rocket apparatus." There is a telescope he used to follow rocket trajectories, a combustion chamber and nozzle built in 1937 and the steering cones and control vanes used on various incarnations of his rockets.

There also is a letter Goddard received from *Popular Astronomy* in 1901, after he submitted a proposal for space travel. "The impossibility of ever doing it is so certain that it is not practically useful," the magazine's editor replied.

The Pakachoag Golf Course, site of the launching of the world's first liquid propellant rocket, is on Pakachoag Hill in Auburn. There is a memorial to Goddard at the roadside and a marker on the launch site. There also is a park in Goddard's memory behind the Auburn Fire Department; its centerpiece is an old Polaris missile, but don't miss the full-size replica of Goddard's first successful rocket. The Clark University exhibit is on the ground floor of the Robert Goddard Library in the center of the campus. It is open Monday through Friday 9 to 5. Call 508-793-7461.

Unkown Central and Western Massachusetts

submarine-launched missile, which, had it been perfected by the Germans, could have been fired on American coastal cities. He is, ironically, buried near a replica of the 80-foot tower Robert Goddard used in 1929 to launch some of the world's first liquid-fueled rockets from here after his neighbors in Auburn objected that his experiments were scaring their cows. Erected on the exact site in 1963, the tower recognizes Goddard as the father of the space age. *Jackson Road at Route 2.*

Becket

At the time America's leading couple of the dance, Ted Shawn and Ruth St. Denis, bought an old farm known as Jacob's Pillow and founded the company that would popularize modern dance; members included Martha Graham. The Jacob's Pillow Dance Festival continues to present modern dance, and its history is chronicled in a museum of programs, costumes, props, contracts, and other items. *George Carter Road; two hours before performances, or by appointment; 413-637-1322.*

Belchertown

People here are still a little sensitive about the name of their town. It wasn't their idea. They proposed the name Cold Springs, but the legislature wanted to honor Royal Governor Jonathan Belcher when they incorporated Belcher's Town in 1761. That's one of the stories recounted at the Stone House Museum, built of sturdy local fieldstone as a wedding present from a father to his daughter. Inside is the Union Army uniform of a 14-year-old Civil War drummer named Myron Walker, and 32 pieces of Rogers Group statuary—three-dimensional Normal Rockwell-style depictions of country life and historical scenes that were enormously popular in the late 19th century. Next door is the restored printing office of the *Belchertown Sentinel,* which started publishing in 1915, including the original hand-set letterpress and the first edition. *20 Maple Street; Wednesday and Saturday 2 to 5; 413-323-6573.*

The world's largest man-made drinking water reservoir when it was built beginning in 1930, the Quabbin Reservoir flooded 39 square miles and four towns. It is now a wilderness with bald eagles, loons, coyote, and deer, and a few ruins of the towns now gone. A visitor center displays photographs of the creation of the reservoir. Next door is the Windham Dam, with unobstructed views of the reservoir; and Windsor Park, with a hiking trail that ends at a lookout tower on Quabbin Hill. There are also cellar holes, including one just outside Gate 40, on the east side of the reservoir, that marks the home of "Popcorn" Snow, a 19th-century eccentric who lived on popcorn and milk and designed his own metal casket with a window so his loved ones could be certain he was dead. When the reservoir was built, Popcorn and the others buried in the former towns of Dana, Enfield, Greenwich and Prescott were dug up and reburied in Quabbin Cemetery, which also has the monuments moved from the commons of the obliterated towns. Trail guides also are available at the visitor center. *485 Ware Road; daily 9 to 4:30; 413-323-7221.*

Boylston

Tower Hill Botanic Garden is home to the Worcester County Horticultural Society, with seasonal displays of more than 95,000 flowering bulbs, 350 types of trees and shrubs, 119 antique varieties of apples, and the "Secret Garden," an area of fragrant plants around a fountain and reflecting pool. *Church Street; Tuesday and Thursday through Sunday 10 to 5, Wednesday 10 to 8 May through August, then Tuesday through Sunday 10 to 5; 508-869-6111.*

Unknown New England

Charlemont
A huge bronze statue of an Indian standing on a nine-ton boulder greets the sunrise in a memorial to the five tribes that lived along the Mohawk Trail. The Hail To The Sunrise Monument includes a pool with stones inscribed by 100 tribes and councils across the United States. America's first scenic auto route, built in 1914, the Mohawk Trail runs from the town of Florida to North Adams along a route first blazed by the Mohawks. *Route 2 at Indian Bridge.*

Charlton
John Capen Adams, the larger-than-life 19th-century bear-tamer and animal trainer known as Grizzly Adams, is buried here under a flamboyant headstone commissioned by circus showman P.T. Barnum. *Bay Path Cemetery, Route 31.*

Chelmsford
President Franklin Pierce's high chair is in the Barrett-Byam House, the museum of the historical society here in the town where Pierce's grandparents lived. The museum also has a musket ball a Civil War soldier considerately sent home to his mother after it was removed from his leg, and decorative glass bowler hats, canes and other unlikely items made in their spare time by workers at a local windowpane factory. *40 Byam Road; by appointment; 978-256-2311.*

Cheshire
What better way for Cheshire to salute newly elected President Thomas Jefferson on January 1, 1802, than with a 1,450-pound hunk of cheese, 18 inches thick and four feet in diameter. The cheese was so big, it had to be drawn by oxen and then put on a ship to Washington, where it was placed on public display and served to guests at the White House for three years. The Cheshire Cheese Monument is a replica of the press that made the famous cheese. *Church and School streets.*

Chicopee
Move over H.G. Wells; Edward Bellamy imagined the future far more accurately in his little-known book *Looking Backward*, in which a modern-day Rip Van Winkle named Julian West falls asleep in 1887 and awakens in the year 2000. Bellamy predicted an industrialized army, equal rights for women, universal higher education, even shopping malls; the book was one of the most popular utopian works ever written. Edward Bellamy's house has been preserved, and inside it every copy of the utopian newspaper he published, first editions of *Looking Backward* and personal items. Bellamy never lived to see the 20th century, never mind the 21st; he died in 1898. *91 Church Street; by appointment; 413-594-6496.*

The nation's largest Air Force Reserve base, Westover Air Force Base is the home of the 439th Airlift Wing, which flies troops, supplies and equipment all over the world in 16 enormous C-5 Galaxy cargo planes. The base was a staging point during the Berlin Airlift, and headquarters of the Military Airlift Command through 1955. The world's second-largest aircraft, a single C-5 can carry 50 tons of cargo. Public tours are available. *413-557-2020.*

Colrain
A patron of the arts, G. William Pitt collected 19th-century theater memorabilia from a time when actors and actresses worked on stage and not on film or television. His collection has been preserved in Pitt's summer home here, including Sara Bernhardt's umbrella; an Elizabethan-era bed owned by Edwin Booth, a well-known Shakespearean actor and brother of assassin John Wilkes Booth; not particularly good paintings of the Catskills by Joseph Jefferson, who created the role of Rip Van Winkle on stage; and costume handbags carried on stage by America's first great opera diva, Lillian Nordica. *8 Main Road; by appointment; 413-624-3917.*

Unkown Central and Western Massachusetts

Conway
Chicago department store magnate Marshall Field was born here on his family's farm in 1834. The house is gone, but Field built his home town a library as a gift. Marshall Field Memorial Library is noted for its limestone exterior and copper dome; there are portraits of Field and his parents in the elegant wood-paneled reading room. *1 Elm Street; Monday, Wednesday and Friday 3 to 8; 413-369-4646.*

Cummington
The house where 19th-century poet and newspaper editor William Cullen Bryant lived as a child served again as his retirement home at the end of his career as editor of the influential *New York Post*. Bryant bought back the house and spent the last 12 summers of his life here; it was here that he translated the *Iliad* and the *Odyssey* just before his death in 1878 at the age of 84. On display at the William Cullen Bryant Homestead are souvenirs from his travels, including a silk robe from Turkey and a grease lamp from a Middle Eastern mosque. The house is furnished just as he left it, down to the wooden dumbbells at the foot of his bed and the rod he used for pull-ups inside the closet doorframe. Bryant's exercise regimen included pole-vaulting over his bed; he also walked 15 miles a day around his 195-acre property. *Bryant Road; Friday through Sunday 1 to 5 late June through Labor Day, then Saturday and Sunday 1 to 5 through Columbus Day; 413-634-2244.*

Dalton
The factory where the paper has been made for all U.S. currency since 1842, Crane & Company patented a method to embed silk threads into banknote paper to foil counterfeiters, an idea used to this day, though the silk has been supplanted by a security filament on which Crane also holds the patent. The company's history is recounted in a museum in a mill built in 1844 on the Housatonic River to make paper out of cotton instead of wood. Inside the mill, with its original rough-hewn beams, are hand molds used there from 1801 to 1831; samples of paper used for currency; disposable paper collars popular after the Civil War; and the invoice for paper sold to Paul Revere to print America's first money in 1775. *Routes 8 and 9; Monday through Friday 2 to 5 June 1 through mid-October; 413-684-2600.*

Deerfield
Known as "the country Smithsonian," the Memorial Hall Museum of the Pocumtuck Valley Memorial Association has an eclectic collection including the Sheldon House door, a heavy wooden barrier studded with nails to withstand attack when Deerfield was the westernmost English outpost; it was nonetheless beaten down with axes during an Indian raid in 1704, when about 50 residents were killed and 100 taken captive. There is also a halter made by Mohawk Indians around 1746 to restrain the hostages they took from such raids, the traditional way they added to their tribes at a time when war and disease were decimating their numbers. There's also the nation's oldest surviving rag doll, which belonged to a blind girl named Clarissa around the time of the American Revolution, and which has no face since Clarissa couldn't see—but elongated fingers and toes she could feel and play with; and a 200-year-old schoolbook in which a child wrote: "remember me." *10 Memorial Street; daily 9:30 to 4:30 May 1 through October 31; 413-774-3768.*

East Brookfield
After a Worcester newspaper reporter set his stories in a section of East Brookfield in dispatches chronicling slow small-town life, summer visitor George M. Cohan, the actor and songwriter, picked up on it in his vaudeville routines as a metaphor for nowheresville. The name of the section? Podunk. This is the actual

Unknown New England

Podunk, a hamlet of about 100 people northeast of Quaboag Pond (formerly Podunk Pond), settled in 1686 by the first in a long line of stoic Yankees. Cohan suggested that if a joke played in Podunk, it could get laughs anywhere. *Podunk Road.*

Erving

As early as the 17th century, French explorers traveling down the Connecticut River claimed this area for their king, Louis XIV, at one point climbing to the top of an outcropping in the middle of the river and breaking a bottle of wine at the top, so impressed were they at the view. French King Rock then stood 16 feet above the surface of the river, but appears far less grand since a hydroelectric dam raised the water level. The dam's owner operates the Northfield Mountain Recreation and Environmental Center and gives boat rides on an oversized replica of the *African Queen*. There are also tours of the underground generating facilities cut into the rock to channel power from the dam, which is used only during peak electricity demand. The power station is in a cave 10 stories tall 700 feet below the surface; longer than a football field, it was the biggest facility of its kind in the world when it was built in 1972. *Route 2; daily dawn to dusk; boat rides given Father's Day through mid-October, power station tours by appointment; 800-859-2960.*

Erving Castle, on Hermit Mountain, was the homesite of a Scottish hermit named John Smith, who lived for 30 years beginning in the 1860s in a cave and hand-built wooden shack. So famous was he that European royalty are said to have visited him here in 1872; eventually he stopped selling blueberries in favor of receiving visitors, who gave him clothes and food. *Erving State Forest, Route 2.*

Fitchburg

Bequeathed over the years by local industrialists and others, the collection of the Fitchburg Museum includes a bas relief by Fitchburg-born sculptor Henri Fantin-Latour and 40 works by Eleanor Augusta Norcross, a Fitchburg native who painted in Paris and whose personal collection formed the core of the collection. There are also European paintings and prints, antiquities from Greece and Rome, and American art by the likes of Mary Cassatt, Georgia O'Keeffe, Edward Hopper and James A.M. Whistler. *185 Elm Street; Tuesday through Sunday noon to 4; 978-345-4207.*

Objects relating to Fitchburg's history of industrial inventiveness fill the Fitchburg Historical Society Museum, among them a model of the first pneumatic drill, which was invented here, along with a bag-filling machine that revolutionized seed-packet filling. *50 Grove Street; Monday, Tuesday, and Thursday 10 to 4, Wednesday 10 to 6, first two Saturdays of each month 10 to 1; 978-345-1157.*

Franklin

America's first public library, the Franklin Public Library was opened when the man for whom the town is named, Benjamin Franklin, was asked in 1786 to contribute a bell. He responded with an offer of books instead, characteristically pronouncing that "sense" was preferable to "sound." The books Franklin gave are still housed in the library, which boasts murals of scenes from Greek mythology, a marble foyer and a reading room paneled in Spanish mahogany. *118 Main Street; Monday through Thursday 9 to 9, Friday and Saturday 9 to 5; 508-520-4940.*

Horace Mann, the father of American public education, was born here May 4, 1796. It was while serving as state secretary of education that he started a movement for better schools and teaching. The site of his house is marked by a monument to Mann. *East Central Street.*

The oldest one-room schoolhouse still in operation, the Red Brick School opened in 1832. *Lincoln Street.*

Unkown Central and Western Massachusetts

Red Brick School scrapbooks, a working crank Victrola and other items are on display at the Franklin Horace Mann Museum, a former meeting house. *Washington Street at Colt Road; Sunday 1:30 to 5:30 May 1 through September 30; 508-541-3107.*

James H. Nason, the inventor of the coffee percolator, is buried here in a cemetery that has no name. Nason, a Franklin native, developed the first successful percolator in 1865. *West Central and Union streets.*

Gardner

Gardner produced four million chairs a year in its heyday in the 1920s, earning it the name "Chair City of the World." Its legacy is memorialized in a giant wooden chair, 20 feet tall and weighing 3,000 pounds, and in the Gardner Museum—not the Isabella Stuart Gardner Museum of Art, but a museum devoted to furniture-making whose walls are hung with chairs and other furniture, including an 1857 wooden baby bouncer. Also on display are paintings by Harrison Cady, the Gardner native who illustrated Thornton Burgess's *Peter Cottontail* books. Cady lived across the street from the one-time library that serves as the museum. *28 Pearl Street; Tuesday through Sunday 1 to 4 mid-March through mid-December; 413-632-3277.*

Grafton

The birthplace and original workshop of the famous Willard clock, the Willard House and Clock Museum is in the house built in 1718 by Joseph Willard, the first white settler in what later became Grafton. It was here that his grandson, Benjamin Willard made clocks in a small workshop in 1776, beginning a three-generation clockworking legacy. There are 70 Willard clocks on display. *11 Willard Street; Tuesday through Saturday 10 to 4, Sunday 1 to 4; 508-839-3500.*

Great Barrington

It was the Dutch, not the English, who first laid claim to this part of the state in 1692. But when English settlement began, the two sides more or less tolerated each other. The town history collection, on the second floor of the Ramsdell Public Library, includes a Dutch courting mirror traditionally given by a potential husband to the family of his intended, and a Dutch wine bottle. It also has the musket of an officer of the British 52nd Regiment of Grenadiers, picked up on the battlefield at Bunker Hill by a Great Barrington man. *Main Street; by appointment; 413-528-1357.*

One of the first instances of armed colonial resistance to British rule happened here, nearly a year before the battles at Lexington and Concord. It was here, on August 2, 1774, that 1,500 local men armed with muskets, blocked the entrance to the courthouse after the king abolished the jury system and appointed royal judges. The judges were politely escorted out of town. The site of the incident is now the town green. *Main and Castle streets.*

The first city to have its homes and streets lit with AC electricity like that used today, Great Barrington provided a willing laboratory for William Stanley, a summer resident who leased an old rubber mill and installed a 25-horsepower steam engine to generate 500 volts that was transmitted through two wires along Main Street. There he proved on March 6, 1886, that the current could be reliably controlled with regulating transformers of his own design. Stanley's generator operated only between 4 p.m. and midnight, as electricity was not considered necessary in the daytime. The foundations of the rubber mill remain; there is a monument to Stanley across the street. *Cottage Street.*

William Stanley's confederate, Great Barrington-born Franklin Pope, helped develop the first high-voltage transmission line over which electricity was carried

Unknown New England

seven miles to Great Barrington in 1894. Ironically, Pope died of electrocution in his cellar while replacing a fuse. His house is now an inn. *518 South Main Street.*

The site of W.E.B. Du Bois' boyhood home is marked with a monument. Du Bois helped found the NAACP in 1909. He died in West Africa in 1963. *Route 23.*

Friends introduced Herman Melville and Nathaniel Hawthorne on a hike up Monument Mountain in 1850, but a thunderstorm forced them to seek shelter in a cave. There they began a long friendship and, when he completed *Moby Dick*, Melville dedicated it to Hawthorne. The mountain itself is named in honor of an Indian maiden whose forbidden love for a cousin led her to leap to her death from the summit. *Route 7; daily dawn to dusk; 413-298-3239.*

Alice Brock, the "Alice" of Arlo Guthrie's "Alice's Restaurant Massacree," lived—as the 1967 song says—"in the church nearby the restaurant, in the bell-tower, with her husband Ray." It was there that Guthrie visited Alice and Ray Brock for Thanksgiving in 1965, the period recounted in his famous ballad. Today the Trinity Church serves as the Guthrie Center, home to Guthrie's recording company and an organization he founded that provides spiritual and cultural exchanges. *4 Van Deusenville Road; Tuesday through Friday 11 to 4; 413-528-1955.*

Hadley

The huge 1782 barn that serves as the Hadley Farm Museum is barely big enough to contain a collection that provides a glimpse into farm life from the days of oxen-powered plows, cheese presses, and butter churns. The highlight is the collection of horse-drawn vehicles, from a stagecoach to a clipper sleigh, peddler's cart and mowing machine. *208 Middle Street; Tuesday through Saturday 10 to 4:30, Sunday 1:30 to 4:30 Memorial Day through Columbus Day; 413-584-3120.*

Harvard

Built to listen for signs of other intelligent life in the universe, the earth's largest radio detector sits atop a hill in Harvard. The Billion-Channel Extraterrestrial Assay, or BETA, is a collaboration between Harvard University and the Smithsonian Institution to pick up signals from space. While the observatory is off-limits to the public, the 84-foot radiotelescope can be seen from Littleton County Road.

Transcendentalist Bronson Alcott, father of Louisa May Alcott, came here with his family in 1843 to start one of America's first communes, a utopian community called Fruitlands, short for "fruits of the land"; while the experiment was short-lived, the site now serves, in part, as a museum of the Transcendentalist movement. There are also collections relating to the Shakers, native Americans and Hudson River School artists. *Old Shirley Road; Monday through Friday 11 to 3, Saturday and Sunday 10 to 5 mid-May through mid-October; 978-456-3924.*

Heath

"America's Stonehenge," the Burnt Hill stones are an unexplained collection of some 40 rectangular boulders weighing as much as 500 pounds standing on end. Some point to the spot where the sun rises on the summer solstice and sets on the winter solstice; others toward Mount Greylock and other high peaks of the Berkshires and the Green Mountains of Vermont. The rest remain a mystery. The hill is privately owned, but open to the public by appointment. *Route 2; 413-337-4454.*

Holyoke

The two-hundred-million-year-old tracks of the meat-eating dinosaurs Eubrontes Giganteus are a highlight of the Dinosaur Footprints Reservation. These dinosaurs, more than 20 feet long, lumbered through the Triassic-era mud, leaving three-toed footprints 15 inches long. *Route 5; daily, dawn to dusk; 413-684-0148.*

Unkown Central and Western Massachusetts

The Holyoke factories owned by William Skinner were at one time the world's largest produces of satin linings, and the mansion Skinner built in 1874 is gilded with the profits. The mansion, called Wistariahurst, is richly ornamented with leather wall coverings, parquet floors, vaulted ceilings, and elaborate woodwork. Stones with real dinosaur fossils were even brought in to pave the driveway. A frugal Yankee at heart, Skinner took a few money-saving shortcuts that can be seen on closer inspection. The "marble" is really painted plaster, for example. *238 Cabot Street; Wednesday, Saturday, and Sunday 1 to 5; 413-534-2216.*

Looking for a new game to be played indoors, local YMCA physical education director William Morgan put up a net and told two teams of players to volley back and forth with a ball. He called it "mintonette." Within a year, the name of the game would be changed to volleyball. The Volleyball Hall of Fame honors the history of the sport and also has a model court where visitors can practice jumping and hitting. *444 Dwight Street; Friday through Sunday noon to 4:30 July and August, then Saturday and Sunday noon to 4:30; 413-536-0926.*

Atlantic salmon that swim up the Connecticut River to spawn get a boost over the Holyoke Dam on an elevator for fish that lifts them 52 feet over the dam into a 300-foot chute. About a half-million salmon annually take the fish elevator. A viewing area is opened during the May spawning season. *Route 116; 413-659-3714.*

Lancaster
Luther Burbank, history's foremost plant breeder, was born here on March 7, 1849. Burbank developed more than 800 strains and varieties of plants. A memorial inside Fort Devens marks the site of his birthplace. *Whittemore Hill.*

Lenox
The first woman to be awarded the Pulitzer Prize for fiction, in 1921, Edith Wharton lived here in a mansion called The Mount. It was here that she was inspired to write the short story "Ethan Frome," in which Lenox is thinly disguised as "Starkfield"; Ethan Frome's pivotal and crippling sledding "smash up" was based on an actual event that occurred in the hill behind 48 Stockbridge Road. Fashioned after a 17th-century English estate, The Mount has 29 rooms and gardens Wharton designed herself. *Plunkett Street; house daily 9 to 5, grounds daily 9 to 6 Memorial Day through Columbus Day, weekends 9 to 3 in May; 413-637-1899.*

An unparalleled private collection of Cubist art hung in a Bahaus-style house, the almost completely unknown Frelinghuysen Morris House and Studio was once the home of abstract artists and collectors George L.K. Morris and Suzy Frelinghuysen. Among the works here are murals, paintings, and sculptures by Picasso, Braque, Miro, and Gris, arranged by the collectors themselves in the house they built in 1941 of stucco and glass brick. *92 Hawthorne Street; Thursday through Sunday 10 to 4 late June through Labor Day, then Thursday through Saturday 10 to 4 through Columbus Day; 413-637-0166.*

Although Alice Brock gave up the business in 1979, Alice's Restaurant, made famous in the song by Arlo Guthrie, continues to operate. It's now called the Apple Tree Inn. *10 Richmond Mountain Road; 413-637-1477.*

Leominster
The son of a farmer who fought in the Revolutionary War, John Chapman became a nurseryman, migrating to western Pennsylvania, then Ohio, then Indiana, until he became so well-known he was immortalized—as Johnny Appleseed. The birthplace of Johnny Appleseed is marked with a plaque and a statue of him stands on West Street. *Johnny Appleseed Lane; 978-534-2302.*

Unknown New England

A short distance from the tanneries of Worcester, Leominster made an industry out of processing cattle horns discarded by the slaughterhouses into combs. Its legacy as the Comb City continued through the plastics era. Today the world's largest collection of women's combs is in the Leominster Historical Society museum, among them combs made for special occasions and combs made of materials such as tortoise shell and steel. There also is a related exhibit of jewelry and other objects made of human hair, including a woven basket. *17 School Street; Tuesday, Wednesday, and Saturday 9 to noon; 978-537-5424.*

After celluloid was invented in 1869, Leominster's comb-making factories switched from tortoise shell and bone to plastic; one of the companies, Union Products, became the home of the plastic pink flamingo. The National Plastics Center and Museum tells the history of the plastics industry with a display of products ranging from plastic billiard balls made by the discoverer of artificial cellulose, John Wesley Hyatt, to the first black Barbie doll. There also is a plastics hall of fame with the likes of Earl S. Tupper of nearby Shirley, the inventor of Tupperware. The gift shop sells those pink flamingos, a quarter of a million a year of which are still produced. *210 Lancaster Street; Wednesday through Saturday 11 to 4; 978-537-9529.*

Leverett

The 105-foot white domed New England Peace Pagoda is the work of the Nipponzan Myohoji Buddhist order, dedicated to the eradication of all weapons. On the steep trail to the isolated hilltop site, which is open to the public, are the ruins of an earlier temple that burned down. *Cave Hill Road; 413-367-2202.*

Monson

The seven generations of the Keep family, which lived here for 150 years, were well-named; they hardly ever threw anything away. The Keep Homestead Museum, as a result, boasts what is believed to be the nation's largest collection of buttons, including political, military, decorative glass, and other kinds, some so small they can only be truly seen only through a magnifying glass. *35 Ely Road; first Sunday of each month 1 to 3 April 1 through December 1; 413-267-4137.*

Montague

Blocked for decades by dams, spawning Atlantic salmon have resumed their migration up the Connecticut River to spawn thanks to a series of "fish ladders." The fish swim up a narrow succession of artificial pools. Visitors can watch from a viewing area during the May spawning season. *First Street; 413-659-3714.*

New Salem

The streets leading from the center of this town end at the gates to the Quabbin Reservoir, under which the rest of it is underwater. The Swift River Valley Historical Society tells the story of the section of the town lost when the reservoir was built, and of the four neighboring communities that were eliminated altogether: Dana, Enfield, Greenwich and Prescott, including a 1920 fire truck from Dana. Each is represented by photographs, paintings, signs, town records, and everyday items. *40 Elm Street; Wednesday and Sunday 2 to 4 July and August; 978-544-6882.*

Northampton

The "electric horse" exercise machine President Calvin Coolidge used in the White House is in the Calvin Coolidge Memorial Room of the Forbes Library. Coolidge lived in Northampton from the time he graduated college in neighboring Amherst in 1895. Calvin Coolidge's house was at 21 Massasoit Street, now privately owned; his law office was on the second floor of 25 Main Street. Coolidge served as mayor of Northampton and rose swiftly to the state legislature, the governor's of-

Unkown Central and Western Massachusetts

fice, and the vice presidency before becoming president in 1923. The house where Coolidge died was a 12-room estate called the Beeches, where he and his wife moved after leaving Washington; it still stands at the end of dead-end Hampton Terrace. The library has Coolidge's papers from the terms he served as governor and vice president, and his personal presidential papers, along with the original furniture from his law office, and the voting box in which he cast his ballots. *20 West Street; Monday through Wednesday 11 to 3; 413-587-1014.*

Sylvester Graham, the inventor of the Graham cracker, lived and baked here. *111 Pleasant Street.*

A series of interconnected greenhouses built beginning in 1895, the Lyman Plant House at Smith College house 2,500 types of plants encircled by Frederick Law Olmsted-designed gardens. *College Lane; daily 8:30 to 4; 413-585-2740.*

North Adams
The 30-foot span across the a 60-foot-deep cavern here is the only natural marble bridge in America; now a part of Natural Bridge State Park, it has stood for 550 million years over Hudson Brook below. *Route 8; daily dawn to dusk Memorial Day through mid-October; 413-663-6312.*

Orange
The first factory in the United States designed expressly to assemble cars was built here in 1900 by Carl, Frank, Charles and William Grout, whose Grout Brothers steam car had been patented in 1896. The Grouts switched from steam to gasoline engines in 1906. Today the building houses a tire dealership. *275 East Main Street.*

A 1904 Grout steam car built in Orange is the centerpiece of the Orange Historical Society Museum. The car has no windscreen; the water tank sits in the front, and the boiler underneath the driver's seat. "All you need to start it is a match," was the catchy slogan. The museum also has original New Home and White Company sewing machines, which were also built in Orange. *41 North Main Street; Sunday and Wednesday 2 to 4 mid-May through October 1; 978-544-3141.*

The Peace Statue in Orange Memorial Park depicts a World War I military veteran explaining to a child the futility of war. A plaque beneath the statue reads: "It Shall Not Be Again." It is dated 1934. *South Main Street.*

Oxford
The birthplace of Clara Barton, Civil War nurse and founder of the American Red Cross, was built shortly before she was born there in 1821. In it are Civil War and Red Cross memorabilia, including the field desk that could be carried from battlefield to battlefield, and on which she wrote thousands of letters to the families of wounded soldiers. Barton is buried in North Cemetery in a grave marked with a red granite cross. *68 Clara Barton Road; Wednesday through Sunday 11 to 5 Memorial Day through Labor Day, then Saturday 11 to 4 through December; 508-987-5375.*

Pepperell
With their husbands and sons off fighting the British at the start of the Revolutionary War in 1775, the women of this town began to suspect that British spies were crossing the Nashua River on their way from Canada to Boston. Led by Prudence Wright, the women donned men's clothes and lay in wait at Jewett's Bridge, where they captured a British captain who was carrying dispatches to the enemy. They turned him in at pitchfork-point. The place where the women of Pepperell caught a British spy is marked by a monument near the bridge. *Groton Street.*

Unknown New England

Petersham

Established in 1907 by Harvard University as a base for research in forestry, the Fisher Museum of Forestry is nestled in 3,000 acres of remote forest. But its most interesting feature is the 23 dioramas embedded in the walls, with <u>miniature scenes of forests and farms that follow the natural history of New England</u>. The first shows the landscape as seen by the first colonial settlers, who cleared almost all of it for farming. There is also forest equipment on display, and there are hiking trails through the woods. *Route 32; Monday through Friday 9 to 5; 978-724-3302.*

Pittsfield

One of the few museums with art, history and science are under one roof, the Berkshire Museum, founded in 1903 by paper magnate Zenas Crane, has the 19th-century buggy thought to be subject of Oliver Wendell Holmes's poem "The Wonderful One-Hoss Shay"; transformers and other early inventions of the Stanley Electric Company, which later became part of General Electric; works of art by John Singleton Copley and Rembrandt Peale; and <u>a 26-foot stegosaurus</u>. *39 South Street; Monday through Saturday 10 to 5 and Sunday noon to 5; 413-443-7171.*

<u>The desk on which Herman Melville wrote *Billy Budd*—and the bread box where his wife found the manuscript after he died</u>—are in the Berkshire Athenaeum's Melville Memorial Room. The desk is from the New York apartment where Melville wrote the book. The exhibit room also has carved items Melville collected in the South Pacific when he served on a whaling ship, and a large scrimshaw collection given to this landlocked town by a collector who admired him. *1 Wendell Avenue; Monday, Wednesday and Friday 9 to 5, Tuesday and Thursday 9 to 9, Saturday 10 to 5 July and August, then Monday through Thursday 9 to 9, Friday 9 to 5 and Saturday 10 to 5; 413-499-9480.*

Princeton

The largely forgotten but extremely bloody 17th-century conflict called King Philip's War belies the myth that Indians and white settlers coexisted peacefully. In fact, King Philip, the name the settlers gave the Indian leader Metacom, was the son of Massasoit, who had helped the Pilgrims during the early years at Plymouth. The Indians attacked beginning in 1675. When the conflict ended 14 months later, more than half of all white settlements had been destroyed, and one out of 10 colonists killed. The Indians died in even greater numbers, and often brutally. One of King Philip's captives, Mary White Rowlandson, was freed here when a settler who had taught some of the Indians negotiated for her release atop a huge flat rock, now known as Redemption Rock. *Route 140.*

Sheffield

The Sheffield Declaration, <u>one of the first petitions of grievances against British rule</u>, was drafted in 1773 in the home of Colonel John Ashley, a surveyor and lawyer. The home would also be the site of a less well-known but historic proclamation of independence eight years later when <u>a black servant, Mum Bet, sued and won her own freedom</u> in a precedent-setting test of the fledgling Massachusetts constitution. The Colonel John Ashley House, which is open to the public, adjoins Bartholomew's Cobble, a wildflower and fern preserve with more than 800 types of plants, 240 species of birds, and the Bailey Natural History Museum, with mounted birds and skulls of native animals from shrews to bears. *Weatogue Road; house Saturday, Sunday, and Monday 1 to 5 Memorial Day through Columbus Day, reservation daily dawn to dusk, natural history museum daily 8:30 to 4:30; 413-229-8600.*

Unkown Central and Western Massachusetts

Shelburne

When the trolleys stopped running across the Deerfield River in 1927, their 400-foot bridge sat abandoned until local women decided to plant shrubs, vines, and 500 varieties of flowers on each side of a stone path and wisteria on the frames that had supported the electrical wires for the trolley, creating the world's only bridge of flowers. Still tended by the Shelburne Falls Women's Club, the bridge is lit up at night and decorated for the holidays each December. *Bridge Street.*

The last surviving Shelburne-to-Colrain trolley is stubby little Number 10, which carried freight from the rail yard in Shelburne Falls to the mills in Colrain and passengers on the return trip. Old Number 10 spent much of its retirement serving as a chicken coop. It has since been restored. *Route 2 at Shelburne Center Road.*

Shrewsbury

The home of the man who commanded the American Revolutionary forces before George Washington, General Artemus Ward, contains Ward's military cap and vest, the general's highboy, and other items. As senior officer of the Massachusetts militia, Ward commanded the American troops at Bunker Hill and other battles until Washington arrived to take command; he then became one of Washington's senior officers. *786 Main Street; Thursday and Friday 10 to noon and 1 to 4, Saturday 10 to noon and 1 to 5, Sunday 1 to 5 April 15 through November 30; 508-842-8900.*

The Worcester Foundation for Experimental Biotechnology—which, despite its name, is in Shrewsbury—was the laboratory where the birth control pill was developed in 1954 by Dr. Gregory Pincus and several colleagues; it would take until 1960 before the pill was approved for sale in the United States. Pincus is buried in Mountain View Cemetery. The building biotechnology foundation is now a part of the University of Massachusetts Medical School. *222 Maple Avenue.*

South Hadley

The odd collection of ephemera amassed by wealthy Holyoke silk manufacturer Joseph Skinner now fills a former Congregational church built in 1846, which was itself moved from nearby Prescott before the town was flooded to create the Quabbin Reservoir. The Joseph Skinner Museum, on the grounds of Mount Holyoke College, has a little of everything, including cigar store Indians, ancient Egyptian furniture, a World War II swastika armband, figureheads from ships, and George Washington's autograph. *35 Woodbridge Street; Wednesday and Sunday 2 to 5 May 1 through October 31; 413-538-2085.*

Springfield

Theodore Geisel, or "Dr. Seuss," was born at 22 Howard Street and raised at 74 Fairfield Street, near Forest Park and the city zoo, which both supplied a wealth of models for the landscapes and animals of his imagination. The world of *Horton Hears A Who*, for instance, looks much like Forest Park, while the castle in *The Five Hundred Hats of Bartholomew Cubbins* was modeled on the Howard Street Armory. Springfield's people also fueled Geisel's imagination. He apparently recalled the real-life John McGurk, a clerk, and August Schneelock, a mailman, when he made up McGurk and Sneeloch's Store in *If I Ran The Circus*.

Springfield brothers Charles and J. Frank Duryea built the first successful gasoline-powered automobile in 1892; it won America's first auto race that year, from Chicago to Evanston, Illinois, and back. The Duryea Motorwagon Company, the nation's first gasoline automobile manufacturer, opened in 1895, turning out 13 cars that year. The company closed in 1898 because of a rift between the brothers, but the building where the Duryeas were assembled survives. *5159 Taylor Street.*

Unknown New England

The Springfield Armory

For a peace-loving country, the United States has spent much of its history at war. Just how much is evident in the city that supplied the guns.

The Springfield Armory was the nation's first and, for almost 200 years, principal manufacturer of military firearms—among them the famous Springfield Rifle and the M-1 machine gun, which General George S. Patton called the greatest weapon ever made. Established in 1794 by George Washington, the armory was closed in 1968, but now displays the largest collection of military guns in the country. Worldwide, only the British Royal Armory has more.

For historical impact, though, the Springfield Armory's more momentous contribution was actually the interchangeable part, perfected and used here on a large scale for the first time. Many of the crude original machines and instruments that transformed storefront industry into mass production also are displayed.

For all this, the armory and its museum remain a virtual military secret.

Among the 6,100 firearms in the collection are Dwight D. Eisenhower's M-14 machine gun and the slender French-made game rifle Confederate President Jefferson Davis was embarrassed to be caught with at the end of the Civil War. There's also a rifle musket that was used at Custer's last stand, the Battle of Little Bighorn—though it is not known by which side

The first guns made here were copies of the French Charleville, a 69-caliber musket with a muzzle loader. The original 40 workers managed to assemble one gun a day, compared to 5,000 a day produced by 14,000 employees at the peak of production during World War II, when guns were finally completely machine-made.

The armory's most famous product was the rifle named for it. The Springfield Rifle would become the mainstay of the infantry in World War I. Its last gasp of glory was the M-1, a semiautomatic rifle invented here in 1924. More than 6.5 million M-1s were eventually produced. Several experimental versions are on display, along with the target from the first successful test firing.

The Springfield Armory went on to design grenade launchers and aircraft-mounted rotary cannon used heavily in the Vietnam War. But its demise came when most of the work was shifted to private industry.

Several of the most intriguing guns in the museum are not American: a captured 9-mm German Luger, for example, and a menacing Soviet AK-47. There is a 15th-century halberd and a 14th-century hand cannon, one of the earliest firearms. The armory even has a mint-condition Thompson submachine gun, its fat magazine recalling the violence of Prohibition.

There are guns damaged in firing, or hit by bullets or by lightning. But for bizarre, nothing can surpass the "'Organ of Muskets," made from gun barrels, which inspired Henry Wadsworth Longfellow, after a visit, to write a peace poem. "This is the Arsenal," Longfellow wrote. "From floor to ceiling, like a huge organ, rise the burnished arms ... Ah! What a sound will rise, how wild and dreary, when the Death- Angel touches those swift keys!"

The Springfield Armory is open daily from 10 to 5; call 413-734-8551.

The first gasoline-powered motorcycle—and the first to be commercially produced—the Indian Motocycle was invented here and built in a factory the locals called the Wigwam from 1901 until 1953. The wing that housed the engineering department now serves as the Indian Motocycle Museum (there was no "r"), with 40 antique motorcycles, all in working order. Most are Indians, but there are also classic Harley, Yale, Henderson, Cleveland, Simplex, Excelsior, Pope and Hercules bikes, plus posters, helmets, racing trophies, patches, a unique collection of 5,000 toy motorcycles, and the tools used by Oscar Hedstrom to invent the motorcycle. On the third Sunday in July, owners and enthusiasts come here from all over the

Unkown Central and Western Massachusetts

country for Indian Day. *33 Hendee Street; Monday through Sunday 10 to 4 March through November, Monday through Sunday 1 to 4 December through February; 413-737-2624.*

Abolitionist John Brown lived in Springfield from 1846 until 1849, running a wool business that doubled as a front for his work helping escaped slaves. John Brown's safe from his office here is in the Connecticut Valley Historical Museum. The city's legacy as a car-making capital is also represented. The museum has a three-wheeled Knox automobile, the third manufactured in Springfield; it was built in the late 1890s. Also in the museum are some of the first clamp-on ice skates, which were made in Springfield; shampoo bottles from the Breck Company, which was based here; and advertisements featuring the original "Breck girls." There's also a statue memorializing Dr. Seuss. *State and Chestnut Streets; Wednesday through Friday noon to 4, Saturday and Sunday 11 to 4; 413-263-6800.*

A severe economic depression after the American Revolution gave way to the little-known Shay's Rebellion, led by a former captain in the Continental Army, Daniel Shays. Shays and his followers objected to high taxes, high salaries for public officials, and other policies. They marched on Springfield to capture the arsenal, but were stopped in a brief battle on January 25, 1787. Though the rebellion failed, it had one pivotal outcome: it led to the strengthening of the federal government. The site of Shay's Rebellion is marked with a bronze memorial. *State Street.*

The grave of Milton Bradley, a printer who created what was to become the largest game manufacturing company in the world, is located here in the city where he came up with the idea of his first product in 1860: The Checkered Game of Life. A big hit, it was followed by Yahtzee, Candy Land, and other games. The Milton Bradley Company was sold to Hasbro in 1984. *Springfield Cemetery.*

Sterling

The largest exhibition of rare farm animals in North America, Davis Farmland has Highland cattle, St. Croix sheep with hair instead of wool, sheep with six horns, long-haired donkeys, 2,000-pound cattle, and other livestock, some among the last of their kind. *Route 62; daily 9:30 to 4:30 Memorial Day through Labor Day, then Thursday through Sunday 9:30 to 4:30 until October 31; 978-422-6666.*

Mary, on whom "Mary Had a Little Lamb" purportedly was modeled, was Mary Elizabeth Sawyer, and the little lamb was a newborn on her father's farm that was rejected by its mother. Mary nursed it to health, and it became her constant companion, following her to school one day in 1816. Although she claimed she made it up, Sarah Josepha Hale, who wrote the famous nursery rhyme in 1830, had come to Sterling and likely heard about the incident or read a poem about it written by one of Mary's classmates, John Roulstone. Either way, the town has staked its claim. A bronze statue of the lamb stands on the town common on Main Street, and there are plaques marking the sites of the farm and the schoolhouse, which was moved in 1926 by Henry Ford to the Wayside Inn in Sudbury. The house where Mary lived is owned by her descendants. *Redstone Hill at Rugg Road.*

Stockbridge

The house where Herman Melville wrote his classic, *Moby Dick*, is nowhere near the ocean. Yet Melville said he felt as if his room was a ship's cabin, "when I wake up and hear the wind shrieking, I almost fancy there is too much sail on the house, and I had better go on the roof and rig in the chimney." The view of Mount Greylock from the window of his study is said to have been the inspiration for the white whale. Today the study, and the rest of the house where Melville lived from 1850 to 1863, is preserved; he called it Arrowhead after the Indian arrowheads he found in the field. There is a harpoon in the corner, presumably for extra motiva-

89

Unknown New England

tion, and his spectacles and writing pens are on his desk as if he just left the room where he wrote not only *Moby Dick*, but also *The Confidence Man* and other books, and the short story "I and My Chimney," the words of which his brother later had inscribed on the Arrowhead chimney that served as its central character. *780 Holmes Road; daily 9:30 to 5 Memorial Day through October 31; 413-443-1449.*

The Titanic Museum

She was the grandest ship afloat and carried the cream of British and American society. So it seems incongruous to come across the mortal leavings of the *RMS Titanic* on the main street of a small town in New England.

Yet it is here that the international Titanic Historical Society has gathered more than 2,100 items linked to the impossible disaster, most contributed by its survivors: Mrs. John Jacob Astor's life vest, a scrap of carpet saved as a memento by a steward, a deck chair found adrift by fishermen, a breakfast menu they discovered in the pocket of a corpse; all are on exhibit, along with photographs and even letters mailed from the ship before it sailed to its doom and sank on April 15, 1912.

"It is as firm as a rock," reads one note sent ashore by a passenger when the *Titanic* stopped in Queenstown. After a near-collision in Southampton Harbor, she wrote, "I was beginning to regret being upon her, but she seems alright now."

More than 1,600 people died in, and 705 survived the sinking of the supposedly invulnerable ocean liner, whose waterproof compartments were ripped open by an iceberg. The collection was acquired from the survivors and their families. One, Selena Rogers Cook, contributed everything she took with her when she was lowered to a lifeboat from the listing ship: handkerchiefs, the comb worn in her hair that night, even the cork from the champagne she used to celebrate her rescue.

A waterstained third-class breakfast menu for April 12 survives; it was found in the pockets of a passenger whose body was discovered south of Newfoundland.

Also in the collection is a diagram drawn for investigators by the lookout, Frederick Fleet, showing the position of the deadly iceberg. Fleet, who warned the bridge, escaped. But he committed suicide, impoverished, in 1965.

The museum has postcards sent by passengers from Queenstown and Le Havre. "This is our house for the present," chirped one in a note to friends before the giant liner put to sea. She and a son survived; her husband was lost.

There is a rare piece of wood from one of the *Titanic*'s lifeboats, all of which were hidden by the White Star Line to avoid reminding travelers of the disaster. There's even a fragment of a stateroom carpet dining steward Frederick Dent Ray took home as a memento just before the ship departed. Used as stuffing in a music stool for 50 years, it was rediscovered and displayed. (Mindful that he might be called upon to serve at breakfast, Ray took only his razor from the sinking ship. Today, it also gleams from a display case.)

Two yellowing telegrams sent more than 80 years ago still cause shudders. The first, from the *Amerika* at 11:20 p.m., warns of icebergs; it was one of six such danger signals the *Titanic* would receive as she raced toward the fateful collision.

"Safe," assures the second, wired by a crewmen to his wife the next day.

The Titanic Historical Society museum is in the rear of Henry's Jewelry Store at 208 Main Street in Springfield's Indian Orchard section. It is open Monday through Friday 10 to 4, Saturday 11 to 2 in July and August, then Monday through Friday 10 to 4, Saturday 10 to 3. Call 413-543-4770.

The summer estate and studio of Daniel Chester French, who sculpted the Minuteman statue in Concord and the likeness of Abraham Lincoln in the Lincoln Memorial, Chesterwood houses 500 pieces of sculpture, casts, molds, and studies,

Unkown Central and Western Massachusetts

in one of the largest collections devoted to a single American sculptor. French spent summers here to work surrounded by the quiet of the gardens he laid out himself, where there now are summer exhibitions of contemporary sculpture. *4 Williamsville Road; daily 10 to 5 May 1 through October 31; 413-298-3579.*

Designed in 1885 by the architect Stanford White, Naumkeag was the summer home of diplomat Joseph Choate, who collected enough fine furniture, ceramics and art on his travels around the United States, Europe and the Far East to fill all 26 rooms. The house, which has stone towers embedded with broken glass, is surrounded by terraced gardens and 40 acres of woods, meadows and pastures. *Prospect Hill; daily 10 to 5 Memorial Day through Columbus Day; 413-298-3239.*

Summer home of a wealthy New York family, Merwin House has a collection of jewelry made from human hair—often of dead relatives or friends—braided and transformed into designs that look as if they were made of fine wire. *14 Main Street; Saturday and Sunday 11 to 4 June 1 through October 15; 413-298-4703.*

Sturbridge

A collection of Russian religious icons, some more than 200 years old and brought to America by Assumptionist priests, is in St. Anne's Shrine. Among them: a relic of St. Anne given by St. Anne de Beaupre in Quebec. *16 Church Street; Monday through Friday 10 to 4, Saturday and Sunday 10 to 6; 508-347-7338.*

Sunderland

Hundreds of Atlantic salmon bred in captivity to bolster the population can be seen at the Cronin National Salmon Station, part of an ongoing effort to restore Atlantic salmon to the Connecticut River. Some of the salmon that swim upriver in the spring are held here, where their eggs are fertilized and their offspring released. *East Plumtree Road; Monday through Friday 8:30 to 4; 413-548-9010.*

The button ball tree in the center of town is the largest sycamore east of the Mississippi River. *Main Street.*

Sutton

Formed by the sudden release of water from a melting glacier near the end of the last ice age 14,000 years ago, Purgatory Chasm is a quarter-mile cleft between vertical granite walls 70 feet high. *Purgatory Road; 508-234-3733.*

Townsend

Drawn by the pine woods and remote lakes, Finnish immigrants settled here, building steam bathhouses along Vinton Pond where they could sit in 220-degree heat before taking a brisk dip in the water. The Finnish bathhouses remain, working testaments to the town's largest ethnic community. *Sauna Row Road.*

Tyringham

The studio of the sculptor of the Minuteman statue on Lexington green is an extraordinary work of art itself: a huge gingerbread-style house that belies the temperamental nature of its designer and owner, Sir Henry Hudson Kitson. The house, which Kitson christened Santarella, took three years to finish, with an 80-ton roof made to simulate thatching that required concrete footings and heavy chestnut beams to hold it up. It is surrounded by grottos and gardens. *75 Main Road; daily 10 to 5 Memorial Day through October 31; 413-243-3260.*

Uxbridge

A reconstructed section of the canal that was once the primary means of moving goods between Providence and Worcester has been restored, along with its adjoining tow path. The Blackstone Canal, built in 1828, had 18 locks to move canal boats around the dams that powered factories along the Blackstone River; the

Unknown New England

river drops 450 feet between its source in Worcester and its mouth in Narragansett Bay, farther than any other river in America except the Niagara. There is a visitor center in an historic barn. *287 Oak Street; daily 10 to 5; 508-278-7604.*

Webster

The original Indian name of Lake Webster is the longest name in U.S. geography and the fifth-longest word in the world. It's actually called Lake Chargoggagoggmanchauggagoggchaubnunagungamaug. *Memorial Beach Drive.*

Westborough

The birthplace of Eli Whitney, inventor of the cotton gin, is marked with a plaque embedded in a stone. Whitney's machine could separate the fiber of short-staple cotton from the seed, fueling the cotton industry—and, with it, southern slavery. *36 Eli Whitney Street.*

Williamstown

The Chapin Library at Williams College is the only place outside the National Archives that has original copies of the Declaration of Independence, Articles of Confederation, Constitution and Bill of Rights. Its Declaration of Independence was printed the night of July 4, 1776, and its Constitution still has the notes in the margin of George Mason of Virginia—including his objections. Mason voted against ratification. George Washington's copy of the Federalist Papers also is on display. *Stetson Hall, Main Street; Monday through Friday 10 to noon and 1 to 5; 413-597-2462.*

Among the 11,000 objects in its permanent collection, the Williams College Museum of Art boasts works by John Singleton Copley, Winslow Homer, Georgia O'Keeffe, Edward Hopper, Andy Warhol, Picasso, and Marc Chagall. *Lawrence Hall, Main Street; Tuesday through Saturday 10 to 5, Sunday 1 to 5; 413-597-2429.*

Robert Sterling Clark, heir to the Singer sewing machine fortune, lived in Paris from 1911 until 1921, and began an art collection there that later would form the basis for the Sterling and Francine Clark Art Institute, a hidden jewel of a museum with 32 Renoirs, and works by John Singer Sargent, Winslow Homer, Edgar Degas, and others. It also has the painting *Virgin and Child Enthroned,* one of only three works in North America by Piero Della Francesca. *225 South Street; daily 10 to 5 July and August, then Tuesday through Sunday 10 to 5; 413-458-2303.*

Winchendon

Once a toy-making center, Winchendon commemorated its sesquicentennial in 1914 with a 12-foot hobby horse, which took five months and 3,200 feet of two-inch pine to make. *Route 202 at Route 12.*

Worcester

Worcester's extraordinary but little-known contributions to American technology and culture are represented in the Worcester Historical Museum. The museum has the earliest known typewriter, made in 1847 by Charles Thurber, who called it Thurber's Patent Printer; only two were built, and the other is in the Smithsonian Institution. There are also some of the original copies of the famous smiley face, one of the most popular icons of the 1960s and 1970s, developed in Worcester by commercial artist Harvey Ball. Also on display: a high-pressure suit made for pilots by Worcester's David Clark Company, a one-time corset plant that became the manufacturer of the first anti-gravity flight suits and the space suit used on the first U.S. space walk and in the Gemini and Apollo programs and the space shuttle. Nearby is a full-sized model of a landing strut from the space shuttle built by the Wyman-Gordon Company of neighboring North Grafton. The museum has some of the first monkey wrenches, produced in Worcester by brothers Lucius and Aury

Unkown Central and Western Massachusetts

Coes, the inventors of the monkey wrench; and some of the first barbed wire, also invented here. Worcester was a center of the valentine industry in the United States after a woman named Esther Howland got an English valentine in 1847 and began to make her own and sell them through her father's stationery store. That gave way to the New England Valentine company, which became the largest greeting card company in the world until a war-time paper shortage forced it to shut down in 1942. The museum has an extensive collection of the first valentine cards. *30 Elm Street; Tuesday through Saturday 10 to 4, Sunday 1 to 4; 508-753-8278.*

The golf course where the Ryder Cup began, the Worcester Country Club hosted the inaugural United States-versus-Britain match in 1927. The Americans won. The event is named for Samuel Ryder, a self-made Englishman and golf fanatic who put up the money toward the solid gold trophy and paid for the British team's passage. *2 Rice Street.*

Isaiah Thomas's pen was as mighty as the swords raised in anger at British rule over the American colonies. Thomas published a newspaper in Boston called *The Massachusetts Spy* that exposed the misdeeds of the British and led as much as anything to the American Revolution. His print shop, now the Union Oyster House, would become known as the Sedition Foundry, and he was forced to smuggle his printing press to Worcester when hostilities began. The printing press that helped foment the American Revolution is in the American Antiquarian Society, the nation's first antiquarian society, which Thomas founded and which still occupies its original 1812 building. The society has the largest collection of printed U.S. history materials through 1877. *185 Salisbury Street; Monday, Tuesday, Thursday, and Friday 9 to 5, Wednesday 10 to 8; 508-755-5221.*

The only museum devoted to indoor plumbing, the American Sanitary Plumbing Museum has antique toilets, a 19th-century wooden two-seat outhouse, sitz baths, even antique toilet paper. It also has plumbing tools, a 1920s version of a dishwasher, a prison toilet, and a piece of the wooden underground water main that carried water from Jamaica Pond to central Boston in the 17th century. The gift shop sells such books as *Flushed with Pride: The Story of Thomas Crapper*. *39 Piedmont Street; Tuesday and Thursday 10 to 2 September through June; 508-754-9453.*

Unknown Connecticut

It's no wonder some of Connecticut's best attractions aren't known: They're underground (or underwater). There's a state prison that was built in the tunnels of an abandoned copper mine, for instance, the first submarine ever used in warfare, and the world's first nuclear sub. This nautical and military history also means that you can see America's biggest and grandest tall ship here. There's a tavern with a Revolutionary War British cannonball still lodged in the wall, a makeshift prison where the unsung Hessian allies of the British were held, and museums of military vehicles, aircraft, the fife and drum, the Purple Heart, and evidence that was used in the Nuremberg trials of Nazi war criminals after World War II.

Which is not to say there haven't been plenty of peacetime contributions. Here you'll find the nation's first Impressionist art colony, the largest collection of British art outside Great Britain, America's first law school, the birthplace of the American Episcopal Church, the real Pepperidge Farm, the site of the first transatlantic shortwave radio broadcast, Marie Antoinette's harpsichord, and a castle with a re-creation of Sherlock Holmes's fictional sitting room at 221-B Baker Street. There are museums devoted to the American barbershop, the insurance industry, and nuts; and the world's largest collection of mounted dinosaurs.

An extraordinary variety of famous people came from, or lived in, this state, and many of their homes are now museums, among them P.T. Barnum, Mark Twain, Harriet Beecher Stowe, the man who discovered Antarctica, Whistler's mother, an African prince who worked his way out of slavery, an opera star who got her start in Vaudeville, and America's most infamous traitor, Benedict Arnold.

Ansonia

The birthplace of George Washington's aide-de-camp and America's first ambassador, General David Humphreys, is equally interesting for the often overlooked monument nearby to a little-known Episcopal priest. Immediately after the Revolutionary War, Humphreys was sent to negotiate commercial treaties in Europe, and in 1791 was named U.S. minister to Portugal. It was during the war that the Reverend Richard Mansfield, a loyalist whose church stood across the street, was caught sending a letter to the enemy naming local agitators. Patriot militiamen came to arrest him in the middle of his sermon, which he abruptly interrupted, fleeing in mid-sentence. Later allowed to return, Mansfield ultimately served 72 years, making him the longest-serving pastor of a Christian congregation in the Western Hemisphere. A monument stands on the site of his pulpit; the church itself has been moved and now is next door to the General David Humphreys House. Also inside: part of the uniform worn by *USS Constitution* Captain Isaac Hull, hero

Unkown Connecticut

of the War of 1812 victory over the *HMS Guerriere*, who was also born in what is now Ansonia. *37 Elm Street; Monday through Friday 1 to 4; 203-735-1908.*

Bloomfield

A 1930 Farmall steel-wheeled tractor that ran on kerosene is among the items on display in the Farm Implement Museum. There also is an odd corn-sheller that dates to 1862, and a home-made cotton gin. *156 Wintonbury Avenue; Tuesday through Sunday 9 to 5 April 1 through October 31; 860-242-1130.*

Bridgeport

Phineas Taylor Barnum was among the greatest entrepreneurs in U.S. history, earning a fortune feeding Americans' insatiable appetite for the odd and exotic. The legacy of P.T. Barnum, creator of the "Greatest Show on Earth," is the subject of the Barnum Museum here, near where he was born. In 1870, when he was 60, Barnum founded P. T. Barnum's Grand Traveling Menagerie, Caravan and Circus. What is less known is that he became mayor of Bridgeport in 1875 and served in the Connecticut General Assembly. The museum has Pa-Ib, a 2,500-year-old Egyptian mummy; a two-headed calf; the suit worn by General Tom Thumb when he was presented to Queen Victoria; and a "Fiji mermaid," created by sewing the head of a monkey onto the body of a fish and portrayed by Barnum as a half-man, half-fish from the South Seas. Barnum's grave, with its suitably huge tombstone, is in Mountain Grove Cemetery at 2675 North Avenue. *820 Main Street; Tuesday through Saturday 10 to 4:30, Sunday noon to 4:30; 203-331-1104.*

Bristol

The first museum in America devoted entirely to clocks and watches, the American Clock and Watch Museum celebrates the once-dominant local industry. The 1,700 clocks and 1,600 watches on display include clocks made by Bristol's famous E. Ingraham & Company to commemorate the Spanish-American War, with a likeness of Admiral George Dewey and a motif of the battleship *Maine*; and a tower clock made for a church steeple by E.B. Dennison, whose other work includes the famous mechanism at Parliament House in London that rings Big Ben. *100 Maple Street; daily 10 to 5 April 1 through November 30; 860-583-6070.*

The New England Carousel Museum boasts one of the world's largest collections of carousel art, most of it hand-carved by master craftsmen. Many of the pieces here are under restoration in workshops open to the public. *95 Riverside Avenue; Monday through Saturday 10 to 5, Sunday noon to 5 April 1 through November 30, then Thursday through Saturday 10 to 5, Sunday noon to 5; 860-585-5411.*

Canterbury

Southern states were not alone in passing early laws preventing blacks from being educated. When Prudence Crandall opened the first academy to for black women in New England in 1833, the Connecticut General Assembly immediately passed a law specifically designed to stop her. Crandall defied the law and prevailed in court, but townspeople set fire to the school, forcing it to close. Charred floorboards remain in the building, now the Prudence Crandall Museum, which tells the story of blacks in pre-Civil War Connecticut and includes a sampler made by Crandall and a letter she received from Mark Twain. Guilt-ridden descendants of the mob that rioted against the school successfully petitioned the state to provide a $400 annual pension for Crandall in 1886. *Route 14 at Route 169; Wednesday through Sunday 10 to 4:30 February 1 through mid-December; 860-546-9916.*

One of the world's largest collections of antique trucks, the "Haul of Fame" has more than 60 vehicles, including a 1917 Mack truck with solid rubber tires and carbide-flame headlights that had to be individually lighted with a match. There also is

Unknown New England

a 1939 Mack truck that hauled cannons for defense along the East Coast during World War II. *Route 14A; Tuesday 8:30 to noon and 1 to 3:30; 860-546-6733.*

Cheshire

An unparalleled museum of comic strip, cartoon, western, TV and advertising memorabilia, the Barker Character, Comic and Cartoon Museum displays 50,000 items from the private collection of a commercial animation art studio owner, beginning with the first American comic hero, Richard Felton Outcault's "Yellow Kid," which appeared in 1896 in New York's *Sunday World*. The museum has "Amos 'n Andy" dolls, a rare Toonerville Trolley, Beetles bobbin'-head dolls, a room-full of PEZ dispensers, and display cases literally crammed with merchandise relating to mythic American heroes from the Lone Ranger to Superman. Each has a price tag, not because they're for sale—they're not—but to show the extraordinary value of these collectibles. *Route 10; Tuesday through Saturday 11 to 5; 203-699-3822.*

In 1822, Connecticut towns chipped in to pay for a canal from New Haven to Northampton, Massachusetts. Called the Farmington Canal, the artificial water route took 13 years to build, with lock basins constructed meticulously of brick. The *Amistad* slaves were taken on this canal in 1839 on their way to be tried for seizing the ship that brought them as hostages from Africa. Left untouched for a century, the last surviving portion of the central Connecticut canal is now the Lock 12 Historical Park, with a functioning wooden lock door and a restored lock-keeper's house that hearken back to the days when artificial inland waterways were the major means of transportation. *Route 10; daily dawn to dusk; 203-272-2743.*

Cornwall

Dudleytown is Connecticut's own ghost town, settled in 1738 atop Coltsfoot Mountain but abruptly abandoned after a series of murders, suicides, illnesses, and other catastrophes. With its homes now fallen into ruins and its streets no more than narrow trails choked with vines, Dudleytown is in the Dark Entry Forest Wildlife Preserve, a popular spot with birdwatchers—and ghost hunters. A television crew investigating the legends reported seeing a shadow rising from a cellar hole, and suffered inexplicable equipment problems that forced the project to be canceled. Others have told of strange animals in the woods. *Dark Entry Road.*

Coventry

Nathan Hale was a schoolteacher when the urge for adventure drew him to become a spy near the outset of the Revolutionary War. Caught by the British, he was hanged the next day, September 22, 1776, purportedly proclaiming: "I only regret that I have but one life to lose for my country." (The line was not original; it was paraphrased from Joseph Addison's *Cato*, a popular play at the time.) Hale was 21. Nathan Hale's Bible, his silver shoe buckles, and his deer-hide covered trunk, left behind before he set out on his spy mission, are in the Nathan Hale Homestead, his family's house. Although Hale never lived in the house, pieces of his birthplace were incorporated in the construction, including his only known likeness, scratched from life on the back of a door. *2299 South Street; Wednesday through Sunday 1 to 4 mid-May through mid-October 15; 860-742-6917.*

The dolls and toys that fill the Special Joys Museum are displayed not on shelves, but in tiny vignettes with doll-sized accessories and furniture—a hat shop, for example, a grocery store, and a kitchen. There are other unusual touches, including a wax doll from 1860—and a photo of it being held by the child who owned it then. *Route 41; Thursday through Sunday 11 to 4:30; 860-742-6359.*

Danbury

Vehicles used by many of the combatants during World War II—including a German staff car that was operated in North Africa—are in the Military Museum of

Unkown Connecticut

Southern New England, the nation's largest private museum collection of heavy fighting vehicles and artillery pieces. The museum has more firepower than some small nations. Highlights include a 1917 Renault tank, a Sheridan tank, the only known operational M-18 tank destroyer, and one of only six prototypes of a NATO main battle tank, the MBT70, which was never produced. *125 Park Avenue; Tuesday through Saturday 10 to 5, Sunday noon to 5; 203-790-9277.*

Charles Edward Ives was an insurance broker who also composed music so outstanding that his *Symphony No. 3* won the Pulitzer Prize—40 years after it was written. That's because much of what he wrote would not be heard until Ives retired from music and business in 1930. His works, including the *Concord Sonata*, came to be championed by such conductors as Leonard Bernstein, and Ives now is considered the most significant American composer of the late 19th and early 20th centuries. The house where Pulitzer Prize-winning composer Charles Ives was born is preserved as a museum. *5 Mountainville Avenue; by appointment; 203-743-5200.*

Once known as the hat capital of the world, Danbury produced six million hats a year at its peak at the beginning of the 20th century when the hat business began to fall off—thanks mainly to the invention of the automobile. Artifacts of the hat industry are preserved in the Dodd Hat Shop, a museum run by the local historical society, which has hat-making tools including smoothing instruments called tollikers and runner-down sticks, which attached the crown to the brim. *43 Main Street; Wednesday through Sunday 1 to 5 April 1 through December 31; 203-743-5200.*

East Granby

When the nation's first chartered copper mine gave out in 1773, the state came up with a novel use for the site: a prison built in the abandoned tunnels of the underground mine. Among others, British loyalists were held here during the Revolutionary War, though many escaped. New-Gate Prison closed in 1827, but the guard house remains, along with the ruins of the workshops, hospital, kitchen, and chapel. Two of the cells are visible to guests, who can descend into the tunnels down a stairway that replaced the original rickety ladders. *Newgate Road; Wednesday through Sunday 10 to 4:30 mid-May through October 31; 860-566-3005.*

East Haddam

In the cemetery at First Church is the grave of an African prince who worked his way out of slavery. Broteer, renamed Venture Smith, was the son of a prince of the Dukandarra tribe in Guinea; he was captured and enslaved at six in 1734. Known for his great size—he weighed more than 300 pounds—he caused so much anxiety among his owners that he was able to buy his freedom at the age of 31 for 71 pounds, two shillings. He eventually also liberated his two sons, his daughter Hanna, his pregnant wife, and their unborn child. Smith died in 1805. *Route 151.*

The Goodspeed Opera House, the oldest opera house in America that still stages original musical theater, has also served as a meat market and a riverboat passenger station since its opening in 1877; the tall wooden Victorian building looks a lot like an old passenger steamboat itself. But its principal contribution was to premier such original musicals as *Man of La Mancha* and *Shenandoah*. Tours include the green room with its 1850 wooden bellows organ and a chaperone, or "mother-in-law," chair, with three seats—one for the mother of the woman being courted. *Route 82; tours Saturday 11 to 1:30 and Monday 11 to 3 mid-June through Columbus Day; 860-876-8664.*

Unknown New England

East Haven
The Shore Line Trolley Museum has about 100 classic trolleys, most built between 1878 and 1962, including the world's oldest rapid transit car and the first electric freight locomotive. Many still run, and guests can take a ride on a three-mile loop. There's also a rare parlor car, snow plows, horse-drawn trolleys, and antique buses. *17 River Street; Sunday 10 to 5 in April, Saturday and Sunday 10 to 5 in May, daily 10 to 5 Memorial Day through Labor Day, Saturday and Sunday 10 to 5 through October 31, Sunday 10 to 5 in November; 203-467-6927.*

Enfield
Sergeant Elijah Churchill of Enfield volunteered to lead raids that captured two British-controlled forts during the Revolutionary War, both against great odds. To reward Churchill's heroism, George Washington created the Badge of Military Merit, the precursor of the military decoration called the Purple Heart. The National Purple Heart Museum displays service memorabilia—and a replica of Churchill's Badge of Military Merit. *1296 Enfield Street; Monday through Friday 9 to 3; 860-745-2321.*

Essex
Incredibly, the world's first submarine used as an offensive weapon in warfare dates to September 7, 1776. That was the day the *American Turtle* attacked the 64-gun British flagship, *HMS Eagle*, as she lay at anchor in New York Harbor. The *Turtle* was an afterthought; its designer, David Bushnell of Saybrook, Connecticut, had first come up with the idea of attaching a mine to the hull of an enemy ship. The problem of getting it there without detection required the invention of the one-man midget submarine that also was the world's first screw-propeller-driven vessel. The operation itself turned out to be an anticlimax. Manned by Sergeant Ezra Lee, who cranked the propeller by hand, the *Turtle* carried the mine to the ship, but it quickly drifted away and exploded harmlessly. A full-scale model of the first sub used in combat is at the Connecticut River Museum, housed in an 1878 steam-boat warehouse, which also has ship models and other artifacts from the steam-boat era. *67 Main Street; Tuesday through Sunday 10 to 5; 860-767-8269.*

Fairfield
So good was the bread baked by Margaret Rudkin for her children, she started selling it at the local grocery store in 1937. As the business grew, Rudkin named it for the farm where she lived—which, in turn, was named for the majestic sour-gum, or "pepperidge" tree that shaded the front yard. The real Pepperidge Farm remains, just as it appears on the packages of the baked goods sold by the company Rudkin founded. Much of the land has been sold off and is a gated subdivision, but the vine-covered stone farmhouse survives, along with the old tree and about 25 acres of the farm, now privately owned. The grocery store where Rudkin sold her loaves is Mercurio's, on the Post Road. *Sturges Highway at Ridge Common.*

When the Connecticut Audubon Birdcraft Museum was founded as the nation's first privately owned songbird sanctuary, Fairfield was a rural town. Now the sanctuary is a sweet-sounding urban oasis. The museum is unique for its Frederick T. Bedford Collection of African Animals, game trophies taken in 1937 on the East African plains, including antelope, lions and a cheetah. There are also mounted birds, including the extinct passenger pigeon and heath hen. *314 Unquowa Road; Tuesday through Friday 10 to 5, Saturday and Sunday noon to 4; 203-259-0416.*

Farmington
Designed in part by Theodate Pope, one of the first licensed female architects in the United States, as a retirement home for her iron-mogul father, the 29-room, columnaded Hill-Stead Mansion remains just as the Pope family left it—complete

Unkown Connecticut

with one of America's finest collections of French Impressionist masterpieces by the likes of Monet, Manet, and Degas. The garden was designed by landscape architect Beatrix Farrand. *35 Mountain Road; Tuesday through Sunday 10 to 5 Memorial Day through Columbus Day, then Tuesday through Sunday 11 to 4; 860-677-4787.*

Greenwich

On the night of December 11, 1921, FM radio inventor Edwin Armstrong and five other men accomplished a first-of-its-kind feat here that has largely been forgotten: they transmitted the first transatlantic shortwave radio broadcast, in Morse code, from Greenwich to Ardrossan, Scotland. The message? "Hearty congratulations." The experiment gave rise to the amateur, or "ham" radio, move-ment. It also made possible the pre-satellite broadcasting of news between the United States and Europe. A stone marks the site from which the broadcast was sent. *Clapboard Ridge Road at North Street.*

It's the hillside setting of the Bush-Holley House, with its colorful flowers and vine-colored grape arbor, that helped make this the first Impressionist art colony in the United States; today the house displays the art work that resulted, by such American Impressionists as Childe Hassam, John Twachtman, and Walter Allen Fitch. The house itself became an inn in 1882, where many of the artists stayed, and in 1891 Twachtman established a summer art school in the adjoining barn. There are also artifacts here relating to Greenwich history, including lottery tickets sold in 1776 to raise money for the Revolutionary War. *39 Strickland Road; Tuesday through Sunday noon to 4 March 1 through December 31, then Saturday 11 to 4, Sunday 1 to 4; 203-869-6899.*

Groton

On June 14, 1952, the keel of the sixth ship of the United States Navy to bear the name *Nautilus* was laid by President Harry Truman at the Electric Boat shipyard here. Six years later, the *Nautilus* accomplished the first crossing of the North Pole by ship, a feat made possible by the use of nuclear power to propel its engines. The world's first nuclear-powered submarine, the *Nautilus* now rests at anchor at the Submarine Force Museum, the only submarine museum operated by the U.S. Navy. The entire 319-foot sub, decommissioned in 1980, is open to the public, right down to the original torpedoes and the pin-ups over the sailors' berths. The museum also has four midget submarines used to attack ships at anchor by the Italians, Japanese and Germans during World War II; a model of the fictional *Nautilus* from Jules Verne's *20,000 Leagues Under the Sea*; and a full-sized replica of the command and attack centers of a World War II-era American sub. *Crystal Lake Road; Wednesday through Monday 9 to 5, Tuesday 1 to 5 May 15 through October 31, then Wednesday through Monday 9 to 4; 860-694-3174.*

A little-known massacre of 88 Americans by a superior force of British troops under hero-turned-traitor Benedict Arnold, is commemorated by a 135-foot monument here. Arnold ordered his soldiers to storm Fort Griswold on Groton Heights on September 6, 1781; when American commander Colonel William Ledyard presented his sword in surrender, he was stabbed in the back with it. The British then killed or wounded nearly all the men in town, piling the wounded into a cart and rolling it into a tree. One of the American heroes: Jordan Freeman, Ledyard's black servant, who tried to hold off the British with a whaling lance. *Monument Street at Park Avenue.*

Guildford

Eli Whitney may be best-known for inventing the cotton gin, but he was equally important for perfecting the potential of the interchangeable part in manufacturing. In 1797, Whitney proposed making rifles for the government, speeding

Unknown New England

their assembly to a pace of 10,000 rifles within 28 months. By comparison, the three existing federal armories had managed to turn out barely 1,000 in the previous three years. Though it actually took him nearly 10 years to provide the guns, Whitney proved the value of his manufacturing ideas. <u>A contract musket made with interchangeable parts by cotton gin inventor Eli Whitney</u> is in the Henry Whitfield State Historical Museum, which occupies the oldest building in Connecticut and <u>the oldest stone house in New England</u>, built in 1639. The museum also has a 1582 German-made Wheelock musket like those carried by early settlers, and a Brown Bess musket from the Revolutionary War. *248 Old Whitfield Street; Wednesday through Sunday 10 to 4:30 February 1 through mid-December; 203-453-2457.*

Hadlyme

Gillette Castle, a medieval-looking structure 200 feet above the Connecticut River, took 22 stonemasons five years to build and cost $1 million, an enormous sum at the time it was completed in 1919. Gillette had earned his fame and fortune portraying Sir Arthur Conan Doyle's famous Sherlock Holmes character on the stage, and was as recognizable in his time as Basil Rathbone would become during the age of film. His fantasy castle looks like a movie set, with walls of granite, oak beams, grand staircases, and balconies. But perhaps the most interesting feature is <u>a re-creation of Sherlock Holmes's fictional sitting room at 221-B Baker Street</u>, just as Doyle described it. Gillette died at 84 in 1937, his only companions six servants and 17 cats. *67 River Road; daily 10 to 5 Memorial Day through Columbus Day, then Saturday and Sunday 10 to 4 through Christmas; 860-526-2336.*

Haddam

The "poor man's salmon," shad swim upstream to spawn, just like their better-known fellow species, and have been a mainstay of this area since native Americans planted poles in the river and strung nets across to catch them; to this day, the town seal still has a shad in the middle of it. Now <u>the Museum of Shad</u> recounts this history, with nets, rods, reels, boning knives, and shad darts—cylindrical hooks that are used to snag the fish as they make their way upriver. You can find the museum, in a former barbershop, by looking for the 20-foot shad boat outside, given by the fisherman who built it. It's open during shad season. *212 Saybrook Road; Sunday 10 to 4 mid-April through June 30; 860-267-0388.*

Hamden

<u>The site of Eli Whitney's firearms factory, where he pioneered the use of interchangeable parts</u>, is now a museum devoted to the prolific inventor. It was here that Whitney proved the value of mass production. *915 Whitney Avenue; Wednesday through Friday noon to 5, Saturday 10 to 3, Sunday noon to 5; 203-777-1833.*

Hartford

When agents of James II tried to seize Connecticut's royal charter in 1687, stripping the colony of some of its rights, the document was spirited away and hidden in an oak tree. The "charter oak" became a Connecticut landmark, and when it was toppled during an 1857 storm, its acorns, leaves, and lumber were gathered as keepsakes. <u>Pieces of the original charter oak</u> made into picture frames, miniature furniture, and the handle of a Colt revolving pistol, are in the Museum of Connecticut History. Housed in the State Library and Supreme Court Building, the museum also has the royal charter itself; the state's original copy of the U.S. Declaration of Independence, Constitution and Articles of Confederation; and diaries and other mementos preserved by Connecticut soldiers from the infamous Andersonville Prison in the Civil War. It also boasts <u>the Colt's Patent Firearms Manufacturing Company Factory Collection</u> of early prototypes made by Colonel Samuel Colt, the inventor of the revolver, and the original "Rampant Colt" statue that once

Unkown Connecticut

adorned the Colt factory in Hartford. *231 Capitol Avenue; Monday through Friday 9 to 4, Saturday 9 to 3; 860-757-6533.*

The linen waistcoat worn by Colonel William Ledyard when he was killed with his own sword after surrendering Fort Griswold in Groton to the British, is among the items on display in the museum of the Connecticut Historical Society. The sword holes are still evident. The museum also has a redcoat worn by a lieutenant in the British Army, a scarlet cloak worn by 22-year-old Deborah Champion when she smuggled secret documents from New London to George Washington in Boston, and the largest collection of 18th- and 19th-century New England inn, hotel and tavern signs. *1 Elizabeth Street; Tuesday through Sunday noon to 5; 860-236-5621.*

The Old State House is the site where General George Washington first met with the French armies under Rochambeau to propose the Yorktown strategy that ended the Revolutionary War; the building itself is notable as the first public commission of architect Charles Bulfinch, who would later design the U.S. Capitol; an original Gilbert Stuart portrait of Washington hangs on the yellow-painted walls.

The Museum of American Political Life

Political dirty tricks date back a lot earlier in American history than Richard Nixon. As early as 1840, Whig presidential candidate William Henry Harrison and his supporters portrayed incumbent Martin Van Buren as a champagne-drinking aristocrat living in luxury while the nation suffered a depression. Harrison, who was depicted as a man of the people born poor in a log cabin—though he was actually a Virginia blueblood raised in a palatial James River plantation—won the election.

The story is recounted in the Museum of American Political Life at the University of Hartford, an unusual—and virtually unknown—collection of political memorabilia and history dating back to President George Washington. The 60,000 campaign artifacts begin with buttons from Washington's jacket, which he gave away as souvenirs. There are nylon stockings with the motto "I Like Ike," a JFK lapel pin in the shape of a PT boat, a Jimmy Carter wind-up peanut doll, even a political button from around 1920, after women got the vote, depicting a man in an apron. "I want to vote," it says, "but my wife won't let me."

The collection is arranged around a life-sized torchlight parade, the political mainstay of the 19th century, when festive marches followed campaign "stump" speeches. In this parade, a crowd of followers listen to a candidate who bears a striking resemblance to the populist William Jennings Bryan—which leads to another little-known American political tale.

Bryan was the model for, of all things, the cowardly lion in the *Wizard of Oz*, a hidden message to which author L. Frank Baum eventually confessed. Baum marched in one of those parades for Bryan in the campaign for president against William McKinley in 1896. The allegorical interpretation: Dorothy, an average American, looks for the Emerald City—Washington, D.C. On the way, she loses her magical shoes, which in the book are silver to represent the system of currency based on silver, and follows the yellow brick road: the gold standard. The scarecrow is an American farmer, the tin man an eastern industrial worker, and the cowardly lion Bryan (a gentle prod, since Baum thought his candidate lacked courage). In the end, populism is defeated, and Dorothy returns to Kansas.

It goes to show: In literature as in politics, things aren't always what they seem.

The Museum of American Political Life is in the Henry Jack Gray Center at the University of Hartford, 200 Bloomfield Avenue, Hartford; open Tuesday through Friday 11 to 4. Call 860-768-4090.

Unknown New England

Just as interesting is Joseph Steward's Hartford Museum, a display of curiosities originally exhibited in the 18th century and painstakingly reassembled here, including <u>a stuffed two-headed calf, a two-headed pig, and a Bengal tiger</u>. *800 Main Street; Monday through Friday 10 to 4, Saturday 10 to 3; 860-522-6766.*

Hartford dentist Horace Wells discovered the use of nitrous oxide, or "laughing gas" as a medical anesthetic in 1844, but he was derided as a fraud after a botched demonstration. Wells moved to New York, where he became addicted to sniffing chloroform, and was jailed after throwing acid at passersby during an apparent drug-induced delirium. He committed suicide by anesthetizing himself, cutting open his leg, and bleeding to death. <u>The story of the hapless discoverer of anesthetic</u> is told in the Menczer Museum of Medicine and Dentistry, run jointly by the Connecticut medical and dental societies, which has Wells's diary—mostly listing debts he believed he was owed. There also is a re-creation of a 1920s dentist office accurate right down to the spit bowls; an amputation kit used during the Revolutionary War, which consists primarily of a saw and a knife big enough to cut a roast; instruments from around 1800 used for cataract surgery, which was conducted without anesthesia at the time; and an extraordinary set of glass eyeballs peering out of a velveteen case, some made to appear so natural they're bloodshot. *230 Scarborough Street; Monday through Friday 10 to 4:30; 860-236-5613.*

Mark Twain loved to complain about the house he built in Hartford, where he lived from 1874 until 1891, and where he wrote *Tom Sawyer*, *Huckleberry Finn*, and *The Prince and the Pauper*. "I have been bullyragged all day by the builder, by his foreman, by the architect, by the tapestry devil who is to upholster the furniture, by the idiot who is putting down the carpets, by the scoundrel who is setting up the billiard-table—and he has left the balls in New York," Twain wrote. <u>Mark Twain's billiard table</u> remains in the eight-gabled, Gothic Revival-style house, which is open to the public; he claimed "the game of billiards has destroyed my naturally sweet disposition." Also here is <u>Twain's bed, where he wrote his autobiography, and where he died in 1910</u>. Twain bought the bed in Venice, and it has a headboard so ornate he said he slept with his head at the footboard so he could see what he had paid for. There are also cherubs on each of the four posts, which Twain's three daughters liked to remove, bathe and take for carriage rides around Hartford like dolls. *351 Farmington Avenue; Monday and Wednesday through Saturday 9:30 to 5, Sunday noon to 4 January through April and November, then Monday through Saturday 9:30 to 4, Sunday noon to 4; 860-247-0998.*

Twain's neighbor, Harriet Beecher Stowe, is remembered for writing *Uncle Tom's Cabin*, but Stowe was also a painter, gardener, and feminist, all of which is evident in the home where she lived until her death in 1896. In addition to her desk and writing tables, the Stowe House is filled with her oil paintings; she designed the gardens personally. *77 Forest Street; Monday through Saturday 9:30 to 4:30, Sunday noon to 4:30 Memorial Day through Columbus Day, then Tuesday through Saturday 9:30 to 4:30, Sunday noon to 4:30; 860-522-9258.*

Although America's first fire insurance company was set up by Benjamin Franklin in Philadelphia in 1752 to respond to fires at the homes of policyholders, Hartford would become <u>the birthplace of the modern American insurance company</u> with the opening of The Hartford in 1810. It remains the capital of the insurance industry. The Hartford also began by specializing in fire insurance, and an exhibit in its headquarters includes an unparalleled collection of fire apparatus, including a New York-style pumper with goose-neck snorkel from about 1855, leather fire buckets, and fire trumpets used to give instructions before the days of two-way radios. There is also <u>Abraham Lincoln's fire insurance policy</u>, and the policy issued

Unkown Connecticut

to Robert E. Lee. *690 Asylum Avenue; Monday through Friday 8 to 4; 860-547-5000.*

The Wadsworth Atheneum includes one of the oldest art museums in the United States, and it is far from undiscovered. Inside, however, is a less-known collection of works by black artists, and <u>artifacts related to the takeover of the slave ship *Amistad*</u> by its African hostages in 1839—including shackles, leg irons, and advertising art with stereotypical images of blacks. The African-American collection includes works by black artists including Robert Scott Duncanson, Charles Ethan Porter, Henry Ossawa Tanner, and Allan Rohan Crite. *600 Main Street; Tuesday through Sunday 11 to 5, Saturday and Sunday 10 to 5; 860-278-2670.*

Freedom of religion hasn't always been a sacred tenet of American society. After coming to Connecticut to escape religious persecution, Congregationalists set up their own virtual theocracy. The state constitution prevented Catholics, Jews and Methodists from worshiping in public until a group of Jews appealed to the General Assembly in 1843. Lawmakers agreed to make an exception allowing for one synagogue to be built. <u>Connecticut's first synagogue</u>, which opened in 1876 in its symbolic location beside the site of the famous Charter Oak, has been restored to its original appearance; now the Charter Oak Cultural Center, it is used for meetings and performances. (Original religious artifacts moved with the congregation to a new home at 701 Farmington Avenue, where there is also a small museum.) The synagogue also had the state's first Jewish cemetery. Buried there, among others, is Gerson Fox, owner of G. Fox, once the largest department store in New England. *21 Charter Oak Avenue; Monday through Friday noon to 5; 860-249-1207.*

The huge Victorian monuments of Cedar Hill Cemetery include <u>the graves of J.P. Morgan, firearms inventor Samuel Colt, poet Wallace Stevens, and Thomas Gallaudet</u>, founder of the school for the deaf named for him. *453 Fairfield Avenue.*

<u>The nation's oldest municipal rose garden</u>, the Elizabeth Park Rose Garden was given to the city in 1894 by industrialist Charles Pond in honor of his wife. The 102-acre garden was designed by Frederick Law Olmsted's landscape design firm in Boston, and boasts 800 varieties of roses. *Prospect and Asylum Avenues; daily, dawn to dusk, greenhouses Monday through Friday 8 to 3; 860-242-0017.*

With its 48 hand-carved antique horses and two chariots, the Bushnell Carousel is <u>one of only three operating carousels in the world made by the master craftsmen Solomon Stein and Simon Goldstein</u>. Russian immigrants, Stein and Goldstein became famous for the wild-eyed steeds they carved. They made only 17 carousels in their careers; the Bushnell was built in 1914. *Bushnell Park; Tuesday through Sunday 11 to 5 May 1 through Columbus Day; 860-585-5411.*

Up to 100 tons of trash a day from 55 towns comes to the Connecticut Resources Recovery Authority to be recycled, and you can watch from a glassed-in visitor center also known as <u>the Temple of Trash</u>, which has exhibits about recycling and garbage. *211 Murphy Road; Wednesday through Friday noon to 4 September through June, then Tuesday through Friday 10 to 4; 860-247-4280.*

Ivorytown

<u>The only museum in the world devoted to the fife and drum</u>, the Museum of Fife and Drum has a drum played at the Battle of Bunker Hill and another on the battlefield at Gettysburg, along with music, uniforms, swords, medals, and other artifacts. Patriotic fife-and-drum music plays in the background. *63 North Main Street; Saturday and Sunday 1 to 5 June 30 through Labor Day; 860-767-2237.*

Unknown New England

Kent

Book illustrator and author Eric Sloane not only collected early American hand tools; he arranged them into designs for display. The Sloane-Stanley Museum, in a former barn, has tools including pitchforks, axes, scythes, sawhorses, hay rakes, and even an unusual dog-powered butter churn. Many were made by the Stanley Tool Company, which is based in New Britain, and all were organized by Sloane, a reproduction of whose studio is also on display. *Route 7; Wednesday through Sunday 10 to 4 mid-May through October 31; 860-927-3849.*

The Connecticut Antique Machinery Association Museum exhibits steam and gas tractors and a working narrow-gauge railroad. *Route 7; Wednesday through Sunday 10 to 4 May 1 through Columbus Day; 860-927-0050.*

Lebanon

When self-taught physician Dr. William Beaumont treated Alexis St. Martin, a young French Canadian fur trapper who had been shot in the stomach during a fight, he discovered something extraordinary: the digestive process could be observed through the wound. Beaumont used the opportunity to study St. Martin's stomach for 11 years, revolutionizing knowledge of the human digestive system. The home of the father of the physiology of digestion, the Dr. William Beaumont Birthplace exhibits Beaumont's wooden travel trunk, medical instruments of the era, and a re-created doctor's examination room of the early 19th century. *169 West Town Street; Saturday 1 to 4 mid-May through mid-October; 860-642-7247.*

Lebanon was an unsung center of the American Revolution, thanks to its place as home of the only colonial governor who supported the War for Independence, Jonathan Trumbull. Trumbull didn't just lend moral support; the set up a storefront war office that scrounged supplies for the troops, organizing cattle drives to provision the hungry men at Valley Forge. Governor Trumbull's war office now is in a museum, the Jonathan Trumbull Jr. Trumbull House, set up just as it looked then, complete with the governor's chair. Virtually every influential figure of the era came through the doors here, including George Washington, Benjamin Franklin, Thomas Jefferson, and the Marquis de Lafayette. Trumbull's son, John, became one of the nation's best-known artists and painter of the famous work depicting the signing of the Declaration of Independence, now in the Yale University Art Gallery. *West Town Street; house Tuesday through Saturday 1 to 5 May 15 through Columbus Day, war office Saturday and Sunday 1 to 5 May through October; 860-642-7558.*

Litchfield

America's first law school, the Tapping Reeve House and Law School began in 1773 when Tapping Reeve took on a single student: his brother-in-law, Aaron Burr. Before that time, lawyers learned their trade by apprenticing with practicing attorneys. But as Reeve enrolled more students and developed lectures using British law books, his school attracted students from all 13 states. By the time it closed in 1833, when conventional universities got into the business, it had turned out two vice presidents, 130 congressmen, three Supreme Court justices, six Cabinet members and 14 governors. The museum has Reeve's podium, the original classroom, the students' bound leather notebooks and diaries, and a recounting of the hardships people faced to travel here for study over the nascent transportation system. *82 South Street; Tuesday through Saturday 11 to 5, Sunday 1 to 5 mid-April through November 30; 860-567-4501.*

Madison

Although the Confederacy had seized the ironclad ship *Merrimack* near the outset of the Civil War, Union Army officials were skeptical about building addi-

Unkown Connecticut

tional ironclads of their own. It was Cornelius Scranton Bushnell who personally persuaded President Abraham Lincoln to build the *USS Monitor*, and then only after agreeing to raise the $275,000 construction price himself and complete the project within 100 days. It took 110. The *Monitor* was launched on January 30, 1862, and fought the *Merrimack*, renamed *Virginia*, in one of the most famous naval vessels in history one month later off Hampton Roads, Virginia. A model of the *Monitor*, which later sank in a storm, is in the house where Bushnell was born, the Allis-Bushnell House, now a museum. Also on display here: the telegram Lincoln sent him after the battle at Hampton Roads, jokingly ordering nine more *Monitors* to be delivered the next day. Bushnell went on to become president of the Union Pacific Railroad. *853 Boston Post Road; Wednesday, Friday and Saturday 1 to 4 May 31 through Srpteember 30; 203-245-4567.*

Manchester

Nineteenth-century fire departments often had two sets of apparatus: one to fight fires, and one to enter in parades, often at torchlight, a popular form of entertainment at the time. The latter included ornate hand-painted hose reels with etched glass lanterns. Not one, but two "parade hose reel" fire wagons are in the Connecticut Fire Museum. There are 17 vehicles in this 1901 firehouse, including a 20-foot 1861 hand-pumper that took 40 men to operate, and a 1921 Ahrens-Fox fire engine. There is also fire alarm equipment, leather hoses, and old wooden water mains. *230 Pine Street; Friday and Saturday 10 to 5, Sunday noon to 5 mid-April through mid-November; 860-649-9436.*

Mashantucket

Built with profits from the tribe's casino and resort at Foxwoods, the Mashantucket Pequot Museum includes a life-sized replica of a 16th-century Pequot village in the last days before white settlement, along with artifacts including cooking utensils, blankets, toys, and other items unearthed from a nearby 9,000-year-old hunting camp and Pequot fort. *110 Pequot Trail; daily 9 to 5; 800-411-9671.*

Meriden

The only museum devoted to the American barber shop, the National Shaving and Barbershop Museum has 5,000 pieces of barber shop memorabilia, including razors, chairs, shoeshine stands, barber shop advertising, and—of course—barber poles. *39 West Main Street; Friday through Sunday 10 to 3; 203-639-9778.*

It was an odd beginning for an opera star: Born in Meriden, Rosa Ponselle started her career in vaudeville, where her voice caught the attention of Enrico Caruso when she played the Palace in New York. She debuted in opera at the Met as nothing less than Caruso's leading lady in Verdi's *La Forze del Destino* in 1918, and was an overnight sensation. The Rosa Ponselle Museum commemorates the woman whose voice was considered one of the most beautiful ever recorded, with the grand piano from her music room, a chandelier, and some of her gowns. *39 West Main Street; daily 10 to 4; 203-639-9778.*

Middletown

Brigadier General Joseph K.F. Mansfield began his Civil War career by overseeing the defense of Washington in 1861, and ended it in 1862 at Antietam, where he became one of only 18 Union generals killed or mortally wounded in battle—in his case, shot through the lung by an enemy rifleman concealed in a thicket. "I shall not live," he said as he was carried away. "Oh! My poor family!" Mansfield's house here is a museum of Civil War uniforms, photographs, and weapons, including the general's sword. *151 Main Street; Sunday 2 to 4, Monday 1 to 4; 860-346-0746.*

Unknown New England

Montville

The legacy of the Mohegans, the tribe whose story was the subject of James Fenimore Cooper's *The Last of the Mohicans* is chronicled in the Tantaquidgeon Indian Museum. The Mohegans split off from the Pequot in 1638 under a chief named Uncas. Notwithstanding the title Cooper gave his 1826 book, there still are surviving Mohegans, and they operate this museum about the tribe's culture and history. *Route 32; by appointment; 860-848-9145.*

New Britain

Begun in 1903 as an art and reading room for new immigrants, the New Britain Museum of American Art is the oldest museum in the world devoted solely to American art. Among the artists represented are Mary Cassatt, John Singer Sargent, Georgia O'Keeffe, Andrew Wyeth, and Thomas Hart Benton, whose mural series "The Arts of Life in America" is a highlight. *56 Lexington Street; Tuesday through Friday noon to 5, Saturday 10 to 5, Sunday noon to 5; 860-229-0257.*

New Haven

Yale's Peabody Museum has the largest collection of mounted dinosaurs in the world, including a 67-foot brontosaurus, its backdrop the Pulitzer Prize-winning mural "The Age of Reptiles," probably the best-known painting of dinosaurs ever made. Most of these bones and fossils were collected in the 1870s by Othniel Charles Marsh, nephew of financier George Peabody, who led four expeditions of Yale students into the still-wild American West in search of fossils. There are also collections of minerals, including the first recorded meteorite in America, which fell on Weston, Connecticut, in 1807. *170 Whitney Avenue; Monday through Saturday 10 to 5, Sunday noon to 5; 203-432-5050.*

A piece of the fabric skin of the *Spirit of St. Louis* autographed by Charles A. Lindbergh is one of the artifacts in the principal depository of Lindbergh's papers, the Sterling Memorial Library at Yale. The collection also includes the tie Lindbergh wore on his transatlantic flight, his personal diaries and logbooks. The materials are displayed periodically, generally around Lindbergh-related anniversaries, in the Memorabilia Room. During other times, the room contains artifacts relating to the history of Yale. *130 Wall Street; Monday through Friday 9 to 5; 203-432-1744.*

The Beinecke Rare Book and Manuscript Library at Yale University has one of the world's last surviving Gutenberg Bibles, the first Western book printed from movable type. The Bible, which dates from 1455 and is one of 21 known in existence, is on display on one of the library's two floors of exhibit space, along with a folio edition of John James Audubon's *Birds of America*, and two Louis XVI children's armchairs upholstered with petit point worked by Alice B. Toklas over designs by Pablo Picasso. *121 Wall Street; Monday through Friday 8:30 to 5, Saturday 10 to 5 (closed Saturday when the university is not in session); 203-432-2977.*

Marie Antoinette's harpsichord is among the extraordinary musical instruments in the Yale Collection of Musical Instruments, which also includes a drum from the American Revolution, and violins by Stradivari and Stainer. *15 Hillhouse Avenue; Tuesday through Thursday 1 to 4; 203-432-0822.*

The Yale Center for British Art houses the largest collection of British art outside Great Britain, with paintings by Hogarth, Gainsborough, Reynolds, Stubbs, Constable, and Turner. *1080 Chapel Street; Tuesday through Saturday 10 to 5, Sunday noon to 5; 203-432-2800.*

Unkown Connecticut

Founded in 1881 by a local priest as a fraternal order of Roman Catholic men, the Knights of Columbus has become the largest organization in the Catholic church, and is still based in Hartford. Its 23-story headquarters has a museum with an original cross from the statue of Christ the Redeemer atop St. Peter's Basilica, presented as a gift by Pope John Paul II. Also in the large collection: the chalice of James A. Healy, the first black bishop in America, who was bishop of Portland, Maine, beginning in 1875. *1 Columbus Plaza; Monday through Friday 8 to 4:30; 203-772-2130.*

President George W. Bush was born on July 6, 1946, in Grace-New Haven Community Hospital (now Yale-New Haven Hospital) at Cedar and York Streets.

New London

America's biggest and grandest tall ship, *Eagle* was originally commissioned in Hamburg in 1936 as *Horst Wessel*, which trained German navy cadets before World War II. Seized by the United States, it now serves as the training ship at the U.S. Coast Guard Academy here, which also has a museum of the history of the Coast Guard and its predecessors—the Life Saving Service, the Steamboat Inspection Service, the Lighthouse Establishment, and the Revenue Cutter Service—including the original figurehead from the *Eagle*, models of Coast Guard icebreakers, one of the only first-order Fresnel lighthouse lenses on display in the United States, World War II propaganda posters and movie posters from unlikely Hollywood adventure films about the Coast Guard. Among them: *Don Winslow of the Coast Guard* and *Sea Spoilers* with John Wayne. The *Eagle* is open for tours when it's in port, generally from late summer through early spring. *15 Mohegan Avenue; Monday through Friday 9 to 4:30, Saturday 10 to 5, Sunday noon to 5; 860-444-8511.*

For most people, the famous story of the rebellion by Africans being taken into slavery on the schooner *Amistad* in 1839 ends with the U.S. Supreme Court decision that granted them their freedom. Here's what happened to the actual ship: Charged $1.50 per day in dockage by the city fathers for its berth behind the New London Custom House, it was finally sold at auction in 1841 for $450. That's part of the history of what is now the nation's oldest operating custom house, today the New London Maritime Museum, which includes the original king's grant to New London, the flags flown by America's Cup winners *Magic* (1870) and *Columbia* (1871), a model of the *Amistad*, and a bust of Cinque, the slave rebellion's leader. The grand Greek Revival-style custom house was designed by Robert Mills, architect of the Washington Monument and the U.S. Treasury, and has doors made of planks from the *USS Constitution*. *150 Bank Street; Monday, Wednesday through Friday 1 to 5, Saturday 10 to 5, Sunday 1 to 5; 860-447-2501.*

America's "navy" during the Revolutionary War consisted in great part of privateers commissioned to harass British ships. The headquarters for this effort in Connecticut was the Shaw Perkins Mansion; built in 1756, it is one of only a handful of 18th-century stone houses remaining in the state, and its construction helped it survive the burning of the city by British troops under Benedict Arnold in 1781. Inside, among other things, is a silver setting looted from a British ship by an American privateer. The silver was the property of Virginia's Loyalist colonial governor, Lord Dunmore, who was trying to send it home to England for safekeeping. *11 Blinman Street; Wednesday through Friday 1 to 4, Saturday 10 to 4; 860-443-1209.*

The boyhood home of playwright Eugene O'Neill, Monte Cristo Cottage was named for his actor father's best-known stage role. It was far from a happy house; the dysfunctional Tyrone family of his *Long Day's Journey Into Night* is based on O'Neill's years here with his alcohol- and drug-addicted parents and brother. There

Unknown New England

also is a statue of O'Neill at age 7. *325 Pequot Avenue; Tuesday through Saturday 10 to 5, Sunday 1 to 5 June 15 through September 1, then Tuesday through Friday 10 to 5, Saturday and Sunday 1 to 5 through mid-October; 860-443-0051.*

Norwich

Convinced his military genius was unappreciated by his fellow Americans, Benedict Arnold offered his services to the British during the Revolutionary War. Torn about its role as birthplace of the nation's most famous traitor, Norwich has grudgingly erected a marker on the site of the house where Arnold lived from the time he was born in 1741 until he was 21. Because federal law prohibited the name Benedict Arnold from being chiseled into stone or metal, authorities removed the tombstones from the grave of his father, also named Benedict Arnold; his mother's gravestone remains. The hero-turned-traitor himself was buried in England, where he fled. The house was torn down in 1854. *Washington Street at Arnold Place.*

It seemed like a good idea at the time: Textile heir William Slater hired an expert in antiquities from Boston's Museum of Fine Arts in 1888 to assemble plaster duplicates of the finest Greek, Roman, and Renaissance sculpture in Europe, including Michelangelo's Pieta and the Venus De Milo, each cast from the original. Once the classic statues were complete, they were arranged in Slater's new museum on the grounds of Norwich Free Academy and the proud directors took a tour—only to realize that many of the figures were nude! Horrified, they added plaster fig leaves to the offending statues. The fig leaves remain, symbols of Victorian prudishness. The Slater Memorial Museum has expanded to include guns, scrimshaw, and original fine art, including one of the best collections from the Hudson River School. *108 Crescent Street; Tuesday through Sunday 1 to 4 July and August, then Tuesday through Friday 9 to 4, Saturday and Sunday 1 to 4; 860-887-2506.*

Old Lyme

When business went bad for Florence Griswold's sea-captain father, she turned their 1817 Georgian-style mansion into a boarding house, gradually becoming known among artists attracted to the colorful landscape. Childe Hassam, Willard Metcalf, and William Chadwick came to visit. So did President Woodrow Wilson, whose wife was a painter. When "Miss Florence" died in 1937, the appreciative artists turned the mansion into the Florence Griswold Museum, which has more than 900 paintings, drawings, watercolors and prints by them and other artists. The works not only hang on the wall; they include the walls themselves, painted in whimsical scenes over the years by the artists who lived here. The extraordinary private Impressionist art and furniture collection of the Hartford Steam Boiler Inspection and Insurance Company has also now been moved to this museum from Hartford. *96 Lyme Street; Tuesday through Saturday 10 to 5, Sunday 1 to 5 April through December, then Wednesday through Sunday 1 to 5; 860-434-5542.*

Orange

Invented in Vienna and named for an abbreviation of the German word for peppermint—pfefferminz—PEZ candy was designed as a mint for smokers, and in 1948 it began to be distributed in dispensers that looked like cigarette lighters. Once little flip-top heads were added, PEZ became an American legend (and valuable collectible)—and still is, to the tune of three billion pieces sold per year. The hometown of PEZ is Orange, where the candy is produced and put into dispensers, though the interior of the factory is off limits to the public. *35 Prindle Hill Road.*

Ridgefield

British troops intent on destroying supplies stored in Danbury for the Continental Army on April 27, 1777, found their route blocked here by a delaying action,

Unkown Connecticut

which they easily crushed; 18 of the American victims of the battle were buried together in a mass grave, now commemorated with a marker near Gilbert Street at Route 116. Before they left town, the British turned their cannon on the Keeler Tavern, whose owner, Timothy Keeler, was suspected of making musket balls in the basement. The tavern, now a museum, still bears a distinctive memento of that day: <u>a British cannonball lodged in the wall</u>. *132 Main Street; Wednesday, Saturday and Sunday 1 to 4 February 1 through December 31; 203-438-5485.*

Rocky Hill

Workmen digging at the site of a new state office building in 1966 made an incredible discovery here: <u>2,000 dinosaur tracks estimated to be 200 million years old</u>. Construction was stopped, and the site became Dinosaur State Park, <u>one of the largest dinosaur track sites in North America</u>, with a geodesic dome over about 500 of the tracks—some of them three-toed and as much as 16 inches long—a full-sized reconstruction of a meat-eating dilosophaurus, and life-sized triassic- and jurassic-era dioramas. There also is <u>an arboretum with more than 250 species of living plants that were around at the time of the dinosaurs</u>. *400 West Street; Tuesday through Sunday 9 to 4:30; 860-529-8423.*

Salisbury

Before he went on to Vermont and fame as leader of the Green Mountain Boys, Ethan Allen took a one-third interest in a blast furnace here that drew on the rich local iron ore deposits to <u>become the single most important supplier of cannon to the Continental Army during the Revolutionary War</u>. The Salisbury Cannon Museum recounts the history of the furnace that supplied more than 800 cannon during the war, arming both land and sea forces. The site of the blast furnace itself is marked, along with the barracks where 40 guards were stationed to protect the operation, and the hill where the cannon were tested. After the war, the furnace was used to make household goods, most notably pocket knives. The museum, in the original 1768 iron master's house, boasts a seven-hole outhouse and the pocket knife manufacturing company's exhibit from the 1876 Centennial Exhibition. *Route 44; Saturday and Sunday noon to 5 mid-June through Columbus Day; 860-535-0566.*

Stafford Springs

<u>One of the last remaining Depression-era Civilian Conservation Corps camps in Connecticut</u>, the New England Civilian Conservation Corps Museum at Camp Connor now is a museum of the program that put unemployed men to work—in this case, helping develop the Shenipsit State Forest. The museum is in the large original building used by the forestry staff and Army personnel who supervised the work, and has surprises including a uniform from the baseball league that was organized to keep the workers occupied in their free time at this remote camp. There is a mess hall table, bunk, personal scrapbooks and, outside, a 1930s Cletrac bulldozer and road grader that were used to build the trail system in the state park. *Route 190; daily noon to 4 Memorial Day through Labor Day; 860-684-3430.*

Stonington

Quick: Who discovered Antarctica? Every other explorer who stumbled across a new continent is a household name, but Nathaniel Palmer, a sealing captain who is given credit for discovering Antarctica on November 17, 1820, is virtually unknown; briefly known as Palmer Land, even the Antarctic Peninsula was renamed in 1964 by international agreement. <u>The home of the man who discovered Antarctica</u>, at least, is now a museum in his honor, with several pieces of his original furniture, including his square grand piano. There also remains an Antarctic island called Stonington. *40 Palmer Street; Tuesday through Saturday 10 to 4 May 1 through October 31; 860-535-8445.*

Unknown New England

In the darkest days of the War of 1812, five British warships fresh from the burning of Washington lined up off the coast at Stonington on August 9, 1814, and attacked the town. The three-day bombardment is commemorated in the Old Lighthouse Museum, housed in the first government-operated lighthouse in Connecticut, built in 1823. Among other things, it has a rare Congreave rocket, a bottle rocket-type incendiary device used by the British with the wooden launching stick still attached; and whaling gear, including harpoons and whale oil. From the octagonal tower of the distinctive granite lighthouse, which is no longer used, are views of three states: New York, Rhode Island, and Connecticut. *7 Water Street; daily 10 to 5 July and August, then Tuesday through Sunday 10 to 5; 860-535-1440.*

Anna Mathilda McNeill Whistler lived here from 1832 to 1837 with her husband, an engineer who worked on the Providence-to-Stonington railroad. Later, in Massachusetts, she would give birth to a son, James Abbott McNeill Whistler. The home of Whistler's mother is identified with a marker. A later owner of the house was Stephen Vincent Benet, poet, novelist and short-story writer best known for his "John Brown's Body," about the Civil War. *Wall and Main streets.*

Storrs

An archive of materials used in the Nuremberg trials of Nazi war criminals after World War II, the Thomas J. Dodd Research Center at the University of Connecticut is named for one of the American prosecutors. It has chilling photographs of evidence against the Nazis, including soap made from corpses, poison gas used in extermination camps, and steel clubs manufactured by Krupp for concentration camp guards. The photographs and other items are on periodic display, alternating with artifacts from other of the university's collections. *405 Babbidge Road; Monday 10 to 7, Tuesday through Friday 10 to 4, Saturday noon to 4; 860-486-2524.*

Stratford

Invented by Russian immigrant Igor Sikorsky, the first practical helicopter flew here on September 14, 1939, marking the start of Stratford's key role in the helicopter industry; Sikorsky Aircraft and Avco, which made helicopter engines, both were based here. Now the town is home to the National Helicopter Museum, the only museum devoted exclusively to helicopters. Housed in a 19th-century train station, the museum follows the development of the helicopter from Leonardo da Vinci to the present day, and includes the cabin of a Sikorsky S-76 helicopter, turbine engines made by Avco, rotor blades, and models—though not that first Sikorsky, which is in the Henry Ford Museum in Michigan. *2480 Main Street; Wednesday through Saturday 10 to 4 Memorial Day through mid-October; 203-375-5766.*

A 10 foot-by-16 foot Confederate flag is part of the eclectic collection of the Catherine B. Mitchell Museum; it was captured by Stratford native Captain William Barrymore, who commanded the *Julia* in the 1862 blockade of Charleston. There is also a 17-star flag from the War of 1812, an 1815 regimental standard and paper lanterns inscribed "Union Forever." *967 Academy Hill; Wednesday, Saturday and Sunday May 1 through October 31; 203-378-0630.*

The 12-foot "Trashosaurus," made from garbage, is the centerpiece of the Children's Garbage Museum, where kids can crawl through garbage in transparent tunnels running through a huge replica of a compost pile. The museum also has an enclosed glass walkway overlooking the busy neighboring recycling plant. *1410 Honeyspot Road Extension; Wednesday through Friday noon to 4; 203-381-9571.*

Terryville

Lock-making was once Connecticut's biggest industry; Terryville alone had 40 lock makers, including Eagle Lock. Today it is home to the Lock Museum of Amer-

Unkown Connecticut

ica, which has 22,000 locks, keys, door knobs, safes, and handcuffs. Among them: the original patent model of the cylinder pin tumbler lock designed by Linus Yale Jr., in 1865—considered the greatest invention in the history of lock-making. On the other hand, the museum also has a 4,000-year-old Egyptian-made wooden pin tumbler lock, which uses similar technology. It is the nation's largest collection of locks and keys. *230 Main Street; Tuesday through Sunday 1:30 to 4:30 May 1 through October 31; 860-589-6359.*

Tolland

With its own forces overextended, the British government hired soldiers from the German state of Hesse-Kassel to help it fight the American Revolution; Hessian officials agreed to the arrangement because it allowed them to maintain huge armies while the British paid them for it. About 20,000 Hessians fought in the Revolution. Thousands were taken prisoner, principally at the Battle of Saratoga in 1777. The Benton Homestead, now a museum, served as a makeshift prison for 22 Hessians and two officers taken in the Battle of Saratoga. For 18 months, the captives lived a relatively comfortable existence in the large cellar, working on local farms to pay their keep. They are believed to have built the fieldstone floor and left a faint charcoal message, still undeciphered, on the parlor floor joists. *Metcalf Road; Sunday 1 to 4 mid-May through mid-October; 860-870-9599.*

Artifacts from Tolland's industrial past, including belts used to drive machinery in water-powered mills, are on display in the Old Tolland Jail, built in 1856 and used until 1968. The 32 cells remain, along with the cushy Victorian-style warden's home. *Tolland Green; Sunday 1 to 4 mid-May through mid-October; 860-875-3544.*

Torrington

The ruins of the birthplace of John Brown, the abolitionist hanged for leading a slave rebellion at Harper's Ferry, Virginia, in 1859, remain and are marked by a stone with an inscription. Brown lived in the house until he was 5. It burned down in 1918, but the outline of the foundation remains. *John Brown Road.*

Washington

The Gunn Memorial Library and Museum is a treasure trove of relics including a chair made of Texas steer horns owned by P.T. Barnum, epaulets worn by the Marquis de Lafayette, a walking stick cut from a willow tree planted by George Washington, and a piece of Henry David Thoreau's doorsill from his cabin at Walden Pond. *5 Wykeham Road; Thursday through Sunday noon to 4; 860-868-7756.*

A re-creation of a 17th-century Algonquian village, complete with longhouse, is the centerpiece of the Institute for American Indian Studies. There are also artifacts dating back 10,000 years, and a replica of an archeological dig. *38 Curtis Road; Monday through Saurday 10 to 5, Sunday noon to 5; 860-868-0518.*

Waterbury

After Charles Goodyear discovered the process for vulcanizing rubber in 1839, he spent the rest of his life trying to promote his invention. A rubber desk made by Goodyear for display at the Crystal Palace in London in 1851 was one such attention-getting stunt—and it is one of the exhibits in the Mattatuck Museum, which also has a prized art collection and materials related to the area's industrial legacy. By 1880, three-quarters of all products made from brass or copper in the United States came from Waterbury, and the museum has household items and furnishings made here, including early cameras, clocks and tableware. The art collection boasts works by John Trumbull, John Twachtman, Yves Tanguy, and Alexander Calder. *144 West Main Street; Tuesday through Saturday 10 to 5 July and August, then Tuesday through Saturday 10 to 5, Sunday noon to 5; 203-753-0381.*

Unknown New England

West Hartford
The birthplace of dictionary pioneer Noah Webster is furnished just as it was when he was born there on October 16, 1758; he would remain until 1774, and went on to write America's first dictionary. *227 South Main Street; Monday through Sunday 1 to 4 September through June, then Monday, Thursday, and Friday 11 to 4, Saturday and Sunday 1 to 4; 860-521-5362.*

Westbrook
The largest international organization of military historians, the Company of Military Historians has a museum in its headquarters here with the world's largest collection of U.S. military uniforms and insignia, along with military vehicles from Jeeps to tanks. *North Main Street; Monday through Friday 9 to 5; 860-399-9460.*

Wethersfield
Determined to strike a final blow against the British in the colonies' quest for independence, George Washington met here with his French ally, the Comte de Rochambeau, May 19, 1781, in the home of merchant Joseph Webb; together they planned the strategy that would defeat the British at Yorktown. The site of the Yorktown Conference that led to the end of the Revolutionary War remains, complete with the table on which the plans were laid in the parlor—now known as the Council Room—and the chairs where Washington and Rochambeau sat. Five months later, on October 19, 1781, the general and the count accepted the final formal surrender of the British troops. The houses on either side of the Webb's have also been restored and are open during the same hours, collectively called the Webb Deane Stevens Museum. *211 Main Street; Wednesday through Monday 10 to 4 May 1 through October 31, then Saturday and Sunday 10 to 4; 860-529-0612.*

Winchester
A private collection begun in 1949 and now open to the public, the Kerosene Lamp Museum in a former general store and post office has 500 lamps from as early as 1852, when kerosene was patented and began to replace whale oil for lighting; there's also a whale oil lamp from 1834. *Route 263; daily 9:30 to 4; 860-379-2612.*

Windsor
Tobacco isn't only grown down south; it's a major industry in north central Connecticut and central Massachusetts, as the Luddy/Taylor Connecticut Valley Tobacco Museum bears witness. When farmers first imported a leaf from Sumatra to use as a cigar wrapper—the most important part, since it carries most of the flavor—they found it burned in the hot summer sun unless grown under cloth tents for shade. Once the growers figured that out, the so-called Connecticut shade leaf became the premium wrapper tobacco of choice. The man who sold the tents, John E. Luddy, left the trust fund that pays for the museum. The museum, in two restored and one replica tobacco shed, includes live tobacco plants, grown from seeds so small they have to be mixed with clay even to be seen. *Northwest Park; Tuesday through Thursday and Saturday noon to 4 March 1 through mid-June and September 1 through mid-December, Monday, Friday, Saturday noon to 4, Tuesday, Wednesday, Thursday 10 to 4 mid-June through August 31; 860-285-1888.*

Windsor Locks
The New England Air Museum isn't just an assemblage of puny single-engine planes. In addition to a B-29 Superfortress and a Sikorsky "Sky Crane" helicopter, it has the only remaining American-built commercial trans-ocean four-engine flying boat, the Sikorsky VS-44A *Excambian*, a mammoth but elegant classic 80 feet long and 16 feet wide that took 80 volunteers 10 years to restore. The era of the flying

Unkown Connecticut

boat was the most glamorous in aviation; while slow, these huge craft offered spacious accommodations modeled after the interiors of ocean liners. The museum's two massive buildings hold 75 aircraft in all. Among them: a Sikorsky S-16 biplane built in 1915 in pre-revolutionary Russia and last flown in 1924 for the Bolsheviks during the Russian civil war. It was the first Russian fighter actually built in Russia. There is also a wood-and-canvas Bleriot XI monoplane from 1909, and a replica of the three-winged Fokker DR-1. *Route 75; daily 10 to 5; 860-623-3305.*

Woodbury

The birthplace of the American Episcopal Church was the "glebe," or farmhouse, where the Reverend John Marshall was elected the first American bishop of the church in 1783. Today, the Glebe House is furnished as it was when Marshall lived there with his wife and nine children. In 1926, a celebrated garden was added, designed by famed English horticulturist and writer Gertrude Jekyll. It is the only garden in the United States designed by Jekyll, widely considered the greatest gardener of the 20th century. *Hollow Road; Wednesday through Sunday 1 to 4 April through November; 203-263-2855.*

Woodstock

Dry goods merchant Henry Bowen's Gothic Revival-style summer "cottage," built here in 1846, was not meant to be subtle. To start with, it had medieval-seeming arched doors, lawn tennis courts, and polo fields. The house itself, along with most of the furniture, was painted pink. And Bowen threw the biggest Fourth of July celebrations in the country, with two fireworks displays over two days (though no alcohol, since Bowen was a teetotaler). Four presidents slept here at one time or another, drawn to the Independence Day galas: Benjamin Harrison, Ulysses S. Grant, Rutherford B. Hayes and William McKinley. Today the Roseland Cottage is open to the public. It also has the oldest indoor bowling alley in a private residence in America; President Grant bowled a strike here on July 4, 1870. *Route 169: Wednesday through Sunday 11 to 4 June 1 through mid-October; 860-928-4074.*

The Photomobile Model Museum is filled with working models of solar electric cars, boats, planes, trains and magnetic-levitation, or mag-lev, super high-speed trains. *1728 Route 198; Saturday 10 to 5, Sunday noon to 5; 860-974-3910.*

Unknown Maine

Mainers seldom boast, so it's no wonder many of their historic contributions have been overlooked. It was in Maine, for instance—not Plymouth, Massachusetts—that the English planted their first colony in America. The first naval battle in American history was off the coast of Maine five days before the Battle of Bunker Hill, and the nation's first amphibious assault took place along the Kennebec River, led by Benedict Arnold, who was a hero long before he was a traitor. The oldest surviving Catholic church in New England is not in Boston, but in Maine.

It's a region of extremes—the world's highest tides, the easternmost point in America, the highest waterfall in New England—and its rocky shores and northern forests have attracted artists such as Winslow Homer, whose studio has been preserved. Writers also have found inspiration here, from William Dean Howells to E.B. White, Rachel Carson, and even Clarence Mulford, creator of the cowboy hero Hopalong Cassidy. (Although he had no link to Maine, one Maine museum has a blue marlin caught by Ernest Hemingway while he was writing *The Old Man and the Sea.*)

Maine may have been the farthest from the fighting, but it had a surprisingly large role in the Civil War, beginning with the writing here by Harriet Beecher Stowe of the influential *Uncle Tom's Cabin* and ending with General Robert E. Lee's surrender to Maine's greatest hero, Joshua Chamberlain at Appomattox Courthouse. Abraham Lincoln's first-term vice president was Maine's Hannibal Hamlin. A tiny Maine museum even has a plaster cast of Lincoln's face and right hand made the month he won the Republican presidential nomination.

There are countless other landmarks in Maine of little-known American history, among them the almost comical Aroostook War, a border conflict that could have led to greater fighting but in the end claimed only two casualties: a cow shot by mistake, and a soldier who died of pneumonia. Maine museums have so many pieces of the battleship *Maine,* whose sinking sparked the Spanish-American War, it seems the whole ship could be reassembled from them.

Maine's communities of French Acadians are cousins of the Louisiana Cajuns, its Swedish immigrants introduced alpine skiing to the United States, and its black citizens built one of the nation's first black churches.

This state's many hidden jewels attest to these unsung events, and to such hardy industries as lumbering, lobstering and shipbuilding. Its nooks and crannies also hide the legacy of ingenuity that helped to conquer this hostile landscape, with inventions ranging from the earmuff to the tracked-wheel log hauler—devised to haul heavy logs through roadless woods—which was the direct precursor to the military tank. It was this kind of resourcefulness that built an iron foundry in the

Unkown Maine

isolated north woods and an entire railroad to carry lumber in a wilderness so remote it's still known only by its map coordinates and can be reached only by canoe. This inventiveness also has made Maine the nation's largest *maker* of canoes, the toothpick capital of the United States and the birthplace of the frozen French fry.

Of course, while Maine might embrace the new, it's also slow to abandon the old. It has the oldest continually operated shoe store, the world's last community of Shakers, and the nation's last hand-cranked telephone switchboard. There are collections of classic cars, trolleys, antique snowmobiles and vintage planes, representing the region's major role in the history of aviation. Several of the many historic transatlantic flights that left from launching sites in Maine are commemorated here, as is the first transatlantic balloon crossing. Goggles worn by Wiley Post, the first man to fly around the world, are in one small Maine town, and the crate used to ship Lindbergh's *Spirit of St. Louis* home from Paris in another; copies of the Maine-made boots he wore on his historic trip are in a third. Other museums commemorate the Maine man who was the navigator on the first flight to cross the Pacific, and Maine's own Admiral Robert E. Peary, the first man to reach the North Pole.

Allagash

Only one luckless man from this tiny, isolated town was killed in World War I or II: Milford Pelletier, who died in 1944 while serving on the aicraft carrier *USS Wasp*. Pelletier's letters and paraphernalia are in the <u>Allagash Historical Museum</u>, a log house similar to those built by the earliest settlers here in rugged northern Maine. There are also artifacts relating to the lumbermen drawn here by the thick forests, and the rivermen who guided the logs downriver to mills downstate, including heavy poles used to dislodge them when they jammed up in the big rapids on the St. John River. (If the poles didn't work, the logs were moved with dynamite.) The old propeller over the door is all that's left of a rickety pontoon plane that flew lumbermen and sportfishermen to the isolated Chamberlain Lakes in the 1930s and 1940s. *Route 161 near the St. John River bridge; Saturday noon to 4 and Sunday 12:30 to 4:30 May through September; 207-398-3335.*

Alna

The engine house and station of the old <u>Wiscasset, Waterville & Farmington Railway</u> have been restored by rail buffs into a museum about the narrow-gauge line that ran from Wiscasset to Albion and Winslow beginning in the late 1890s. Inside is an engine built for this line in the early 1900s, and a huge Vulcan Iron locomotive that originally hauled freight around the Charlestown Navy Yard in Massachusetts. The museum also has the flat car used to tear up these very rails when the line was closed in 1934. *Route 218; Saturday and Sunday 9 to 5 May through Columbus Day, then Saturday 9 to 5; 207-882-6897.*

Andover

The <u>first satellite television transmission in history</u> was beamed to Pleumeur-Bodou, France, from the Andover Telstar Tracking Station on July 10, 1962, via Telstar I, the world's first communications satellite. The site was chosen because it allowed the satellite to be tracked for the maximum distance in its south-to-north orbit above the East Coast. Tracking Telstar required a 38-ton antenna in a giant dome that was the largest air-inflated structure in the world, 161 feet high. Although the dome is gone, the station is still operated, today by WorldCom. The local high school is called Telstar High School. *Route 120 on the road to Roxbury Pond.*

Ashland

The hardest part of harvesting trees for lumber in New England's northern woods was moving them to downstate mills, a problem that was ultimately solved

Unknown New England

by the invention that would serve as the precursor to the bulldozer and the military tank. It was the Lombard log-hauler, a steam-driven crawler-type tracked-wheel tractor patented in 1901 by Mainer A.O. Lombard, which could travel over snow and through thick forests with no hint of roads. Eighty-three Lombard log haulers were made, three for export to Russia; only three remain in the world, and one is here at the Ashland Logging Museum. The museum also has an intact logging camp; the bough mattresses in the bunkroom make it evident that lumbermen did not crave comfort, but the cookroom, original from the ovens to the muffin tins, shows how much they liked to eat. *Garfield Road; Wednesday through Friday 1 to 4 Memorial Day through Labor Day, then Friday 1 to 4; 207-435-6039.*

Auburn

Throwbacks to a bygone age of transatlantic propeller flight, two elegant four-engine Lockheed Constellation Super Starliners are parked like giant twin mirages in the last place you'd expect to find them: the Auburn-Lewiston Municipal Airport. With their spindly legs, triple tail and trademark undulating fuselages—designed and developed by Howard Hughes—these huge aircraft were among the most beautiful ever built, so distinctive they look as if they might momentarily disgorge Marilyn Monroe into a crowd of waiting press photographers. Even though the roomy planes could carry up to 99 passengers, some on fold-down beds in first class, their usefulness was cut short by the advent of the transatlantic jet. Only 44 of the propeller-driven Model 1649A Constellations like those parked here were manufactured, and only four serviceable 1649As are left in the world. Of the two in Auburn, one was was flown by Lufthansa until 1966, later serving as the private plane of the chancellor of then-West Germany. The other was delivered to TWA in 1957. They were brought here by a collector. *East Hardscrabble Road.*

Augusta

Before he was a traitor, Benedict Arnold was a hero, thanks mainly to the 1775 Revolutionary War expedition he commanded to take control of Quebec from the British. The invasion was a failure, but Arnold managed to prevent the British from pursuing him into New England. The expedition's staging point on the Kennebec River is now the site of an all-but unknown 1920s memorial to Benedict Arnold; no one is really sure who put it there. *Kennebec River, behind 6 Williams Street.*

Remember the *Maine*? The captain's silver setting from the USS *Maine,* the battleship whose unexplained sinking in Havana Harbor on February 15, 1898, began the Spanish-American War, was salvaged from the bottom and can be seen in Blaine House, the Maine governor's mansion, which is open to the public. The stately white wooden house, built in 1833, also played a large part in the beginnings of the Republican Party. Its one-time owner, newspaper editor James G. Blaine, was co-founder of the GOP in 1856, served as speaker of the House, U.S. senator and secretary of state, and came just short of the White House, running unsuccessfully against Grover Cleveland in 1884. The desk he used as a senator is on display, and on it a card dated April 7, 1865, allowing "the bearer, Mr. Blaine, to pass from City Point to Richmond and return." It is signed by Abraham Lincoln. The grounds of the house were designed by Frederick Law Olmsted. *192 State Street; Tuesday through Thursday 2 to 4; 207-287-2301.*

It's hard to miss the Vietnam-era UH-1 "Huey" helicopter and the post-World War II M-48 tank at the gate at Camp Keyes, but many people overlook the Maine Military Historical Society Museum behind them. Arranged chronologically beginning with a 1763 flintlock used in the French and Indian War, the museum's most prized possession beside the helicopter and the tank is a .32-caliber revolver that belonged to Joshua Chamberlain. Maine's greatest hero, Chamberlain led the fa-

Unkown Maine

mous 20th Maine Regiment that, after running out of ammunition, beat back repeated Confederate assaults on Little Round Top with bayonets to help reverse the tide of battle at Gettysburg and later accepted General Robert E. Lee's sword of surrender at Appomattox Courthouse that ended the Civil War. The unexpectedly large museum also has an exhibit relating to the first-of-its kind detachment Chamberlain established to collect, identify and bury the dead; this after Mainers who fought in the Second Battle of Bull Run were horrified to discover unburied corpses of their comrades killed in the First Battle of Bull Run. There are also artifacts relating to the unsung Maine Coast Artillery, a volunteer unit that manned fortifications along the jagged shoreline until well after aircraft made such static defenses obsolete in the 1940s. Some of the men were so bored they volunteered to fight abroad. *Camp Keyes, Upper Winthrop Street; by appointment; 207-626-4338.*

It was while defending Little Round Top on July 2, 1863, that Chamberlain, armed only with a saber, was confronted by Lieutenant Robert Wicker of the 15th Alabama Regiment, who fired his .36-caliber revolver. But Wicker missed and, as Chamberlain recounted, "seeing the quick saber-point at his throat, reverses arms, gives sword and pistol into my hands, and yields himself prisoner." The battle continued to rage, however, so Chamberlain held on to the pistol, which, he later said, "I thought might come in handy." Today the ordinary-looking gun with the extraordinary history has found its way to the Maine State Museum, which covers 390 million years of northern New England history beginning with *pertifica quadrifaria*, the state fossil and one of the oldest known ferns, discovered in north central Maine. The museum also has a 40-foot section of the square-rigged cargo ship *St. Mary*, and the Maine Lion, one of the oldest surviving steam locomotives. *State House Complex; Monday through Friday 9 to 5, Saturday 10 to 4, Sunday 1 to 5; 207-287-2301.*

The last of the original fortifications built during the French and Indian War, in this case to protect the Kennebec River, Old Fort Western includes what are believed to be the nation's oldest surviving wooden military buildings. It is certainly New England's oldest wooden fort, dating to 1754. The fort's original purpose was to induce white settlers to the hostile woods and harsh climate of inland Maine, which had trouble attracting virtually anyone—even with the offer of 250 acres apiece of free land—until after the fall of Quebec in 1769. Soldiers in period costume re-enact drills on Saturdays. *16 Cony Street; daily 1 to 4, Memorial Day through July 3, Monday through Friday 10 to 4, Saturday and Sunday 1 to 4, July 4 through Labor Day, Saturday and Sunday 1 to 4, Labor Day through Columbus Day; 207-626-2385.*

When a 10-year-old schoolgirl from Manchester, Maine wrote a letter to then-Soviet President Yuri Andropov in 1983 appealing for peace, it propelled her into the middle of the Cold War. A statue of Samantha Smith releasing a dove memorializes that girl, who was invited by Andropov to visit the Soviet Union and denounced by some in the United States as an unwitting pawn in a propaganda game. Smith died in a plane crash when she was 13. *State House Complex.*

Bailey Island

The 1928 Cobwork Bridge linking Bailey and Orrs Islands is the only bridge of its kind in the world, built of granite blocks in a honeycomb pattern that allows the tides through without carrying away the road. *Route 24.*

Bangor

One of the great 19th-century "palace hotels," the Bangor House was one of the nation's most flagrant speakeasies during Prohibition, when it continued openly

Unknown New England

selling alcohol in exchange for a twice-a-year court fine. Widely emulated by other restaurants and hotels in Maine, this came to be known as "the Bangor Plan." No less a critic than the hatchet-wielding prohibitionist Carrie Nation griped that the then-manager of the Bangor House was the country's most notorious peddler of the demon rum. President Ulysses S. Grant stayed here when he came to open the European-North American Railroad. So, later, did Theodore Roosevelt, Oscar Wilde, and world heavyweight champion John L. Sullivan. *Main and Union streets.*

Nineteenth- and early 20th-century small towns that didn't have room for their own jails used a portable contraption invented by Mainer Sanford Baker called a tramp chair: a steel chair with straps used to hold unfortunate miscreants for short periods. Convicts dubbed it the "terror of the tramps." Two are known to survive, one in the Smithsonian and the other in the Bangor Police Museum. *Bangor Police Headquarters, 35 Court Street; Monday through Friday 9 to 5; 207-234-2394.*

Once the lumbering capital of the world, Bangor chose to commemorate its 125th anniversary in 1959 by commissioning a 31-foot, two-and-a-half-ton statue of the legendary lumberman Paul Bunyan. The kitschy monument, by J. Norman Martin, is made of fiberglass wrapped around a metal frame. *Lower Main Street.*

Appropriate to the climate, the largest collection of antique snowplows and snowplowing equipment in America is on display at the little-known Cole Land Transportation Museum, which also has one of only two surviving Stanley Steamer delivery vans (the other is in Belgium) and the nation's most complete collection of early freight vehicles, from horse-drawn wagons to 18-wheelers. There's a 1943 tractor truck that carried hundreds of thousands of tons of military supplies to airfields in Bangor, Houlton and Presque Isle, specially fitted with two-speed rear axles to surmount the Maine hills. In all, the museum has more than 200 vehicles. Maine's only World War II veterans' monument is outside, a statue depicting a local man named Charlie Flanagan driving a Jeep. Flanagan was killed in action in Germany. *405 Perry Road; daily 9 to 5 May 1 through Columbus Day; 207-990-3600.*

It's a long way from Bangor to Hollywood, never mind deep space, but the world's only full-sized replica of the bridge of the *USS Enterprise* from the original *Star Trek* television series is stored in a nondescript building at Bangor International Airport. Built by vocational school students as a project, the realistic bridge is displayed most years at the Bangor State Fair, with costumed *Star Trek* fans as "crew members." *County fairgrounds, first week in August.*

Neither history, nor Abraham Lincoln, were kind to Hannibal Hamlin. Hamlin served as vice president during Lincoln's first term beginning in 1861, only to be dumped in favor of Andrew Johnson in his second; it would be Johnson who succeeded Lincoln, while Hamlin returned to Bangor. Hamlin's home at 15 Fifth Street remained in his family until 1933, when it was given by his son to the Bangor Theological Seminary to be used as the residence of the seminary's president. There is also a statue of Hamlin by sculptor Charles Tefft on Bangor's Kunduskeag Mall.

Kindly Bangor residents contributed $100,000 for relief after the Great Chicago Fire of October 1871. But then-Mayor Samuel Dale is suspected of having used some of the money instead to decorate his house for a party before the visit that fall of President Ulysses S. Grant. (He inadvertently neglected to invite Grant who, when summoned at the last minute from the Bangor House, cantankerously came to Dale's party through the front door, and left immediately through the back). Soon after suspicions of embezzlement were raised, Mayor Dale was discovered dead in the upstairs bathtub, apparently having poisoned himself. Called the Thomas A. Hill House for another of its owners, the home is now the museum of the

Unkown Maine

Bangor Historical Society, filled with memorabilia including petticoat mirrors, angled so women could see if their slip was hanging out of their hoop skirts. *156 Union Street; Tuesday through Saturday 10 to 4 April through October, Tuesday through Friday noon to 4 November and December; 207-942-5766.*

If you look hard enough at the spooky Italianite villa on West Broadway, bats and spiders begin to appear. It isn't your imagination; they're part of the design of the wrought-iron fence around the home of horror writer Stephen King, a mansion originally built in 1857. While there is no "pet sematary," the Mount Hope Cemetery by the Penobscot River at the city's edge was used in the movie of that story.

A Lockheed P2V-3 patrol aircraft once based at the Brunswick Naval Air Station, and a Stinson 10A flown by the Civil Air Patrol off the coast of Maine, are part of the collection of the Maine Aviation Historical Society, which preserves airplanes and artifacts from Maine's aviation history. There is also a full-sized mock-up of an aircraft cockpit and exhibits relating to Maine "bush pilots" and pioneering transatlantic flights from Old Orchard Beach. *Maine Avenue, Bangor International Airport; Saturday and Sunday 8 to 2 Memorial Day through Columbus Day; 207-941-6757.*

A monument with the bronze shield from the bow of the *Maine* memorializes the battleship. *Davenport Park.*

Bar Harbor

The only museum devoted exclusively to Maine's Native American history and culture, the Abbe Museum is also one of the best small museums of anthropology in New England, one of the oldest in Maine, and one of only two private museums in national parks; the other is the Borax Museum in Death Valley, California. The Abbe has largest collection of Maine Native American basketry, woven from such materials as sweetgrass and birch bark, and Indian costumes adorned with beads made from shell, clay, bone, stone and copper. There is a 3,000-year-old flute made from a bone of a swan, and an 18th-century powderhorn believed to have been owned by Chief Orono of the Penobscot Tribe. *Sieur de Monts Spring, Acadia National Park; daily 9 to 5 July and August, then daily 10 to 4; 207-288-3519.*

They may look like mice, but the transgenic rodents on display at Jackson Laboratory have human DNA. They're bred here and used in genetic research by scientists around the world for research into cancer, heart disease, diabetes, reproductive disorders, anemia, and AIDS-related immune defects. Founded in 1929, this independent, non-profit institution operates the world's largest frozen mouse embryo repository, and houses one of the world's first transgenic mouse facilities, where human genes can be inserted into embryos of mice. Live transgenic mice are in a labeled glass display case in the lobby, which is open to the public. *600 Main Street; summer visitor program Wednesday at 3 July and August; 207-288-3371.*

In whale evolution, the missing link was *ambulocetus*, a whale that could walk on land, believed to have lived some 49 million years ago in what are now the Mediterranean Sea and Indian Ocean. An intermediate step between land and marine mammal, *ambulocetus* had hooves, ear flaps, webbed feet, and fur. It has been resurrected in a full-scale model at the George B. Dorr Museum of Natural History at the College of the Atlantic, which also has the only existing mounted skeleton of a True's beaked whale, so named because it has a snout like a dolphin's. *105 Eden Street; Monday through Saturday 10 to 5 mid-June through Labor Day, then Thursday through Saturday 10 to 4, Sunday 1 to 4; 207-288-5395.*

The Beatrix Farrand Garden at the College of the Atlantic was created by Farrand, one of America's pre-eminent landscape designers, in 1929. With more than 50 varieties of roses, it was the prototype for Farrand's famous rose garden at

119

Unknown New England

<u>Dumbarton Oaks</u> in Washington, D.C. A friend of Henry James and a niece of Edith Wharton, Farrand created gardens for the Rockefellers, Morgans, McCormicks and other Social Register types. *Route 3; 207-288-5015.*

How do lobsters reproduce? Very publicly, at the Oceanarium Lobster Hatchery. The oceanarium hatches lobsters and returns them to the ocean. Lobsters as young as two weeks old are on display, however, with shells so transparent you can see their beating hearts. The facility includes <u>the Maine Lobster Museum</u>, with variously colored, odd-shelled living lobsters from all over the world. *Route 3; Monday through Saturday 9 to 5 June through October; 207-288-5005.*

New York Governor and U.S. <u>Vice President Nelson Rockefeller's birthplace</u> was the estate known as the Briars, which his parents rented because their pediatrician was vacationing near here the summer Nelson was born in 1908. It was later the home of Evelyn Walsh McLean, then-owner of the Hope Diamond. *Wayman Lane.*

The Mount Desert Island Biological Library, on land donated by John D. Rockefeller, is <u>one of the world's oldest and foremost marine biological research institutes</u>. Founded in 1898 as a summer school for college biology students, the lab is now known worldwide for its work in such areas as electrolyte physiology. It has a research aquarium of live dogfish, skate and other marine mammals. *Old Bar Harbor Road; tours Wednesdays 1:30 July and August; 207-288-3605.*

Belfast

The Scotch-Irish who settled in this town brought old divisions with them; half wanted to call it Belfast, half Londonderry. The issue was decided on a coin toss. Today the Belfast Historical Society and Museum boasts an eclectic collection that includes a case full of Maine make-do household items built from scratch by cash-poor locals—among them, <u>a clothesline made of human hair</u>—and the prescription counter from Poor's Drug Store, founded in 1814 and the oldest operating drug store in the United States when it shut down in 1979. (Belfast also has <u>the nation's oldest operating shoe store</u>, Colburn's, founded in 1832.) There are oils and waterscapes by seascape and landscape artist Percy Sanborn, who lived here, including his painting of the *Ivanhoe*, a ship built in Belfast. The bell and quarterdeck plate from the missile frigate *USS William Beazie Pratt* commemorates the Belfast native and Navy admiral who served as secretary of defense between World War I and II; Pratt's house, with the rose garden he began, is on Primrose Hill. *10 Market Street; Saturday and Sunday 1 to 4 Memorial Day through mid-October; 207-338-2078.*

Bethel

So giddy was physician Moses Mason at having been elected to Congress in 1833, he brought his autograph book and collected the signatures of virtually everyone he met in Washington—including every fellow congressman at the time. The resulting collection, with the <u>autographs of John C. Calhoun, Daniel Webster, Andrew Jackson, James Madison and Martin Van Buren</u>, and is on display at the Dr. Moses Mason House. The 1813 Federal-style house also has Mason's moose antler chair, and some of the only surviving folk murals by Rufus Porter, an itinerant artist most of whose work elsewhere has been painted or papered over. *14 Broad Street; Tuesday to Friday 1 to 4; 207-824-2908.*

Boothbay

Maine's inland towns were too heavily wooded and sparsely populated to allow or justify standard-gauge rail connections, so cheaper narrow-gauge lines were built between the 1870s and 1930s on tracks just two feet apart (compared to the traditional four feet, eight and a half inches) to the Rangeley Lakes, the northern forests, slate mines and granite quarries. The Boothbay Railway Village commemo-

Unkown Maine

rates these railroads, operating <u>a narrow-gauge steam train in a living historic train set</u>: a re-created turn-of-the-century Maine town that includes the original 1870 Thorndike and 1911 Freeport railroad stations, a bank, hotel, barbershop, and large collection of antique cars and other vehicles—among them, a 1929 Packard Custom Eight limousine with the distinctive "goddess of speed" radiator ornament. *Route 27; daily 9:30 to 5 Memorial Day through Columbus Day; 207-633-4727.*

You can <u>pet a live shark</u> at the Marine Resources Aquarium. Sharks, skates and other sea life fill seven "touch tanks" at the facility, operated by the Maine Department of Natural Resources and overlooking picture-postcard Boothbay Harbor. There are tours of the marine research labs on weekdays, and the aquarium loans out rods, reels, tackle boxes and maps to local fishing spots. *McKown Point Road; daily 10 to 5 Memorial Day through September 30; 207-633-9542.*

First produced for the opening of the famous Poland Spring Hotel in 1876, glass bottles in the shape of the biblical figure Moses have become collectors' items, and <u>the world's largest collection of Moses bottles</u> is at the Poland Spring Museum. Produced until 1972, Moses bottles were used at various times for Poland Spring Water, gin and whiskey, in a variety of shapes, sizes and colors. *53 Commercial Street; daily 9 to 6 spring and fall and 9 to 9 summer; 207-633-4225.*

A shell museum in coastal Maine should be filled with shells from the New England coast, right? Not if it's the Kenneth E. Stoddard Shell Museum. Stoddard was a Navy Seabee who traveled the Pacific during World War II and collected thousands of shells, including <u>one of only three known perfect specimens of the "glory of the sea</u>," a cone-shaped snail shell. The collection is displayed in a 56-foot reproduction of a covered bridge built with wooden pegs instead of nails. *Hardwick Road and Route 27; daily 10 to 10 May 1 through October 15; 207-633-4828.*

Bradley

When nine pulp, paper and timberland companies jointly established an experimental forest in the 1940s to study lumber management techniques, they set aside 265 acres for the <u>Maine Forest and Logging Museum</u>. Reconstructed on the site of an 18th-century water-powered sawmill, the museum has a blacksmith shop, trapper's line camp, and reconstructed log cabin. The remains of the original settlement, on Blackman Stream off the Penobscot River, also can be seen, and there are hiking trails into the experimental forest, now owned by the University of Maine and co-managed by the U.S. Forest Service and the logging industry, where there are hardwoods, pine trees, hemlocks, fir, spruce, maples, birches, and spring wildflowers. Woodsmen's teams from area universities still hold periodic chopping competitions and, in the winter, vintage sleighs take visitors on snow rides through the woods. *Route 178; daily dawn to dusk, sleigh rides Sundays 10 to 3 on the first and third Sunday of the month December through March; 207-581-2871.*

Brewer

The <u>forerunners of the Boy Scouts</u> were the Brewer Congregational Scouts, organized on October 25, 1909 by a British-born immigrant minister who copied the Boy Scout model from his home country five months before the incorporation of the Boy Scouts of America; to this day, Brewer boasts Boy Scouts of America Troop 1, whose legacy has been memorialized in photographs in the Clewley Museum, an eclectic collection that includes an antique hearse, and memorabilia relating to Joshua Chamberlain, who was born at 350 North Main Street and raised at 80 Chamberlain Street—including Chamberlain's shoulder boards and his original Civil War battlefield promotion to general, handed to him on the spot when he was wounded at Petersburg and not expected to survive. *199 Wilson Street; Tuesday and Thursday noon to 3 July and August, then Tuesday noon to 2; 207-989-7468.*

Unknown New England

Brewer's hometown hero, Joshua Chamberlain, is memorialized in a bigger-than-life statue a few blocks from the house where he grew up on a knoll designed to look like the battlefield at Little Round Top. *Freedom Park.*

Bridgewater
The second-story outhouse in the old town hall, built in 1894, is the highest in the county, and is listed on the National Register of Historic Places. (It also remained the only bathroom in the building until 1998.) *Main Street.*

Bristol
The largest and strongest fort in America when it was built in 1692 at the mouth of the Pemaquid River, Fort William Henry is a wide stone tower 28 feet high; the replica that stands today was built in 1908 and is the centerpiece of the Colonial Pemaquid State Historic Site, which displays some of the 75,000 artifacts found by archeologists relating to a succession of early white settlements on this, the northeastern edge of British colonial control. John's Island, just offshore, was named for the Pilgrim John Smith, and was the home in the 1930s of heavyweight boxing champion Gene Tunney. *Route 130; daily 9 to 5 Memorial Day through Labor Day; 207-677-2423.*

The tidal salt pond and forest where influential marine biologist and author Rachel Carson conducted the research for her 1955 book *The Edge of the Sea* is now known as the Rachel Carson Salt Pond Preserve, a conservation area owned by The Nature Conservancy and dedicated to Carson. *Route 32; 207-729-5181.*

Brooklin
E.B. White, author of the children's classics *Charlotte's Web* and *The Trumpet of the Swan,* lived on a farm on Route 175 from 1939 until his death in 1985. He and his wife, also a writer, are commemorated in the E.B. and Katherine White Garden at the Friend Memorial Library, which has two original framed Garth Williams illustrations from White's 1945 book *Stuart Little* and signed first editions of all of White's works which, until recently, still circulated in the tiny community. *Route 175; Tuesday, Friday and Saturday 10 to 4, Wednesday 10 to 9, Thursday 10 to 6 July 4 through Labor Day, then Tuesday, Friday and Saturday 10 to 4, Thursday 10 to 6; 207-359-2276.*

Brooksville
South Brooksville today looks much the way it did when author Robert McCloskey used it as the setting for the classic children's book *One Morning in Maine*, right down to Condon's Garage, now run by the son of the story's kindly Mr. Condon. The little girl of the book was McClosky's daughter, Sally.

Brownville
The Katahdin Iron Works near isolated Silver Lake laid bare entire forests by smelting iron in a blast furnace that consumed 10,000 cords of wood per year. The trees have grown back and the stone blast furnace has been restored along with one of the 14 beehive-shaped kilns that burned the lumber into charcoal. At its 19th-century peak, the facility produced 20 tons of raw iron daily and was surrounded by a village of 200 people, and a railhead. The village, too, was made of wood, and has completely disappeared. Just beyond the site, which is managed by the Maine Bureau of Parks and Lands, is the entrance to remote Gulf Hagas, known as Maine's Grand Canyon, and Screw Auger Falls. *Route 11; 207-941-4014.*

Brunswick
Few towns in America played as great a role as Brunswick in the Civil War; it was here that Harriet Beecher Stowe wrote her powerful *Uncle Tom's Cabin*, which helped incite the war, and where Joshua Chamberlain, who accepted Robert E.

Unkown Maine

Lee's sword of surrender at Appomattox Courthouse, lived for much of his adult life. The Federal-style <u>Harriet Beecher Stowe House</u>, originally built in 1807 for the pastor of the Baptist church, was the author's home while her husband taught religion at Bowdoin College. Henry Wadsworth Longfellow also lived there when he was a student at the school. The house is now owned by the college. *63 Federal Street.*

The Joshua Chamberlain House, rescued from demolition in 1982, has been transformed into a museum devoted to the one-time Bowdoin College <u>rhetoric professor-turned-Civil War hero and governor of Maine</u>, who bought the home in 1859 before marching off as a volunteer officer in the 20th Maine Regiment to fight at Antietem, Shepherdstorn Ford, Fredericksburg, Chancellorsville, Gettysburg, Mannassas Gap, and Petersburg and accepting the surrender of the Confederate infantry at Appomattox Courthouse on April 9, 1865—surprising everyone by ordering his troops to salute the defeated southern forces. Chamberlain fought in 24 major battles, was wounded six times and had six horses shot out from under him. He was elected governor in 1867 and became president of Bowdoin in 1871. The eight-room museum includes displays relating to Chamberlain's long and varied career, including original Civil War uniforms. The chimney is decorated with a Maltese cross, Chamberlain's wartime Fifth Corps insignia. *226 Maine Street; Tuesday through Saturday 10 to 4 June through September; 207-729-6606.*

The estate of a Victorian-era sea captain has been so perfectly preserved in the Skolfield-Whitter House, it looks as if the occupants might return at any moment and resume their daily lives. That's because the entire 17-room house was abruptly shut down in 1925 by the grieving widow of its final owner and left <u>sealed until it was reopened as a museum</u> in 1982. Intact down to the spices still in the kitchen spice rack, this time capsule of a home has its original furnishings and fixtures, and even the receipts for materials used in its construction by Captain Alfred Skolfield, a wealthy descendant of one of the area's earliest settlers. The house was inherited by Skolfield's eldest daughter, Eugenie, and her husband, Dr. Frank Whittier, <u>one of the founders of forensic medicine</u>, credited with the discovery that every bullet has a different signature. Their daughter, Dr. Alice Whittier, was <u>Maine's first woman pediatrician</u>. It was Eugenie Whittier who, on her husband's death, could no longer bear to stay in the home, and had it sealed shut. *161 Park Row. Tuesday through Saturday 10 to 3 Memorial Day through Labor Day; 207-729-6606.*

The <u>drum that urged the 20th Maine Regiment into battle</u> on Little Round Top at Gettysburg is part of the collection of the Pejepscot Museum, a collection of 50,000 local historical artifacts. The museum is in a house built in 1862 for Samuel Skolfield, brother of sea captain Alfred Skolfield, who lived next door. *159 Park Row; Tuesday through Friday 9 to 5, Thursday 9 to 8, Saturday 9 to 4; 207-729-6606.*

For decades, skeptics disputed whether Admiral Robert E. Peary really was <u>the first man to reach the North Pole</u>. There was little doubt about it at his alma mater, Bowdoin College, home of the Peary-MacMillan Arctic Museum, <u>the only museum in the nation devoted exclusively to the Arctic</u> and polar regions. The Navigation Foundation eventually put the controversy to rest by upholding Peary's claim that, in 1909, he had reached the pole. The museum is also named for Peary's protégé and fellow Bowdoin graduate Donald B. MacMillan, who accompanied Peary on his 1909 trek. The displays include one of the five sleds Peary had with him when he reached the pole, along with both adventurers' photographs, personal journals, instruments, and artifacts collected by them and later expeditions. *Hubbard Hall, Bowdoin College. Tuesday through Saturday 10-5, Sunday 2-5; 207-725-3416.*

Unknown New England

The polar bear became the Bowdoin College mascot in the 1920s, inspired by a gift from Arctic explorer Donald B. MacMillan, Class of 1898: a full-grown stuffed polar bear he brought back from a 1914-1917 expedition to the Arctic. MacMillan killed the bear in 1915 while in North Greenland. *Morell Gymnasium.*

One of the earliest museums in the United States, the Bowdoin College Museum of Art has one of the oldest and richest collections of art at an American college—begun in 1811—with 14,000 objects, including American colonial portraits by John Singleton Copley and Gilbert Stuart, Winslow Homer woodblock prints, works by Rockwell Kent, and Renaissance paintings; a 19th-century Bowdoin grad working in what is now Iraq contributed Assyrian reliefs from the Palace of Ashurnasirpal. Thanks to Brunswick's antislavery tradition, the museum has one of the earliest collections of African-American art. The museum is housed in an 1894 building designed by McKim, Meade and White that is itself an architectural landmark. *Walker Art Building; Tuesday through Saturday 10 to 5, Sunday 2 to 5; 207-725-3275.*

Bryant Pond

The little panel bristling with wires and switches in the Bryant Pond Telephone Museum has a lot of history behind it: When it was disconnected on October 11, 1983, it was the last hand-cranked telephone switchboard in North America. The operators, who worked out of the Bryant Pond Telephone Company owner's living room, had to turn a crank to make the line ring. *Rumford Avenue; Tuesday through Friday 1 to 4 July through September; 207-667-9491.*

Bucksport

The largest collection of home movies in North America is held by Northeast Historic Film in the restored 1916 Alamo Theatre. The nonprofit archive gathers and preserves film and videotape particularly relating to northern New England, including television broadcasts beginning in the 1950s; it has film and videotape not available anywhere else, from a turn-of-the-century home movie production of *Snow White and the Seven Dwarfs* to footage of small-town parades, and a Maine-made 1909 motion picture by silent film director Lawrence Trimble about a dog who saves his owner by digging for clams. Most of the collection is available for viewing, along with post cards of New England theaters, antique movie posters and other memorabilia. *379 Main Street; Monday through Friday 9 to 4; 207-469-0924.*

Calais

Not one country, but two—the United States and Canada—can trace their origins to the all-but-forgotten 1604 settlement established on the St. Croix River estuary by the French explorers Pierre Dugua Sieur de Mons and Samuel Champlain. The French dubbed the territory l'Acadie, or Acadia, the name it still bears, and it was one of the first European settlements on the Atlantic coast of North America. From here, Champlain explored and mapped the Bay of Fundy and the coast as far south as Cape Cod, well before the British came ashore at Jamestown or Plymouth. The settlement was abandoned in 1605, though the expedition ultimately led to the founding of Quebec. The St. Croix Island International Historic Site was made a U.S. national monument in 1949. *Route 1; daily dawn to dusk; 207-288-3338.*

Canaan

Charles A. Lindbergh's famous 1927 nonstop transatlantic flight was strictly one-way; he returned home with his plane by ship. The crate that carried home the *Spirit of St. Louis* has been converted into a hidden-away museum that is a shrine for aviation buffs. The cottage-sized pine box was used to ship the fuselage of Lucky Lindy's plane home to the United States from Paris. Painstakingly restored, it now houses a small Lindbergh collection, including a framed front page of the European edition of the May 22, 1927, *New York Herald Tribune*, which reported the historic landing; and charts and maps of Lindbergh's exploits. Canaan holds a "Crate Day" every June. *Easy Street; by appointment; 207-474-9841.*

Caribou

Appointed American consul to Tunisia in 1797, William Eaton took it on himself to recruit an army of eight U.S. marines and 400 mercenaries after Barbary pirates enslaved 300 American seamen who were shipwrecked in 1805. Eaton's motley force became the first U.S. military unit to raise the American flag on foreign soil, rescuing the sailors and capturing Dernah, also known as Tripoli; the battle is memorialized in the U.S. Marine Corps anthem ("From the halls of Montezuma to the shores of Tripoli ... "), and Eaton was given 10,000 acres in what is now called Caribou in reward. His portrait hangs in the Caribou Historical Center, a log cabin similar to the one built by Eaton. The eclectic collection also includes a wreath of human hair and other artifacts that reflect this remote community's potato farming and logging history, among them a horse-drawn, one-row potato digger and a high-wheeled bicycle used around 1885 to carry the mail. *1033 Presque Isle Road; Tuesday through Saturday 9 to 5 in June, July, and August; 207-498-3095.*

One of the finest fossil collections in the United States is housed in the Nylander Museum, named for Swedish immigrant and naturalist Olof O. Nylander, who collected most of it. Nylander worked for the U.S. Geological Survey and found fossils of starfish in Aroostook County that previously were not thought to exist in North America. The fossil also was named after him. The museum has shells from around the world; stuffed animals, birds and prehistoric marine life; and specimens of starfish, sea urchins and land snails from five continents. *657 Main Street; Tuesday through Sunday 12:30 to 4:30 Memorial Day through Labor Day; 207-493-4209.*

Casco Bay

Josephine Peary, the wife of Admiral Robert E. Peary, spent the summer in their home on Eagle Island while her husband was making his way to the North Pole, and it was here that newspapermen arrived to tell her he had reached his goal. "What do you have to say now, Mrs. Peary?" they asked. "I say, 'Come on boys, let's have a drink!'" she reportedly replied. Though he bought it in 1877 after graduating from Bowdoin, this 17-acre island became Admiral Peary's summer home in 1904, and it was here that he planned his expedition to the pole. Designed with porthole windows, the home is meant to resemble the prow of a great ship. It also has a stone turret that served as a library, where Peary wrote about his expeditions. The island can be reached by private boat, or by ferries that leave from Bailey Island, Freeport, Harpswell, and Portland. *Daily 9 to sunset June 15 through Labor Day; nesting grounds for eider ducks, the island's hiking trails remain closed to visitors through mid-July to protect the ducklings; 207-624-6075.*

Castine

Fort George, an earthworks built in 1779 to protect British interests in Maine and Canada during the Revolutionary War, would witness the worst naval defeat in U.S. history when 42 American vessels trying to dislodge the tiny bastion found themselves bottled up and destroyed in the Penobscot River by a superior British fleet on August 14, 1779. *Battle Avenue and Wadsworth Cove Road.*

The most advanced training ship in the nation, the 500-foot, $110 million *State of Maine* was built as an oceanographic research vessel for the U.S. Navy and now is operated by the students of the Maine Maritime Academy. The academy also has the 88-foot schooner *Bowdoin*, originally built for Arctic explorer Donald Mac-

Unknown New England

Millan in 1921, which sailed to the Arctic 26 times. The *Bowdoin* is built almost entirely of oak covered by two-inch sheathing to protect the hull from ice. There is a display of Arctic-era *Bowdoin* memorabilia in the lobby of the academy's Leavitt Hall, and the ship itself is usually in the harbor; the *State of Maine* is open for tours on weekends except during its annual training cruise from late April to late August.

Opened in 1833, the Castine post office is the oldest U.S. post office in continuous use. The building itself dates to 1814, when it was a custom house. The original postal window is in the lobby. *Main Street.*

The Wilson Museum, a restored home, is indicative of the beautiful Georgian and Federal-style buildings in Castine, with a small but eclectic collection of historical objects including antique hearses and ship models. The museum also maintains the 1665 John Perkins House next door, the oldest existing home in town, which has a silver platter given to the then-owner by the occupying 29th British Regiment, which was quartered there during the War of 1812. *Perkins Street; Tuesday through Sunday 2 to 5 Memorial Day through September 30; 207-326-8545.*

Cushing

One of the most familiar icons in American art, the Olson House was the backdrop for the Andrew Wyeth masterpiece *Christina's World*, which he painted in 1948. The home of Wyeth's friends Christina Olson and her brother, Alvaro, the weathered farmhouse dates from the late 1700s; Wyeth used an upstairs room as a studio and pictured the house in several other works. "I'd always seem to gravitate back to the house," he once said. "It was Maine." The painting itself is in the Museum of Modern Art; the house is owned by the Farnsworth Homestead and Museum. *Hathorn Point Road; daily 11 to 4 Memorial Day through Columbus Day; 207-596-6457.*

Eastport

At 29 feet, Eastport boasts the highest tides in the world, so huge there was a local industry in scuttling obsolete ships at high tide, then scavenging them on the beach; the *USS Constitution* was headed for just such a fate when it was saved by preservationists. These vast fluctuations have created the largest tidal whirlpool in the Western Hemisphere, the Old Sow, which comes alive beginning two hours before each high tide—and a 1930s scheme to harness for electric power the 70 billion cubic feet of seawater that enters Passamaquoddy Bay with every incoming tide. Engineer Dexter Cooper, who honeymooned near Eastport, managed to enlist the federal government in his idea of damming Passamaquoddy and Cobscook bays and generating electricity by releasing the tide through turbines on Moose Island. Several dikes were actually built before the Quoddy Tidal Power Project was abandoned. The tiny Quoddy Maritime Museum has a rock-and-cement working model of the dam, and a desk from the battleship *Wabash*, one of the many vessels scuttled here. *Water Street; daily 10 to 4 Memorial Day through Labor Day; 207-853-0911.*

An American officer recounted having his tea on the porch of the barracks at Fort Sullivan one day during the War of 1812 when he saw the British fleet approaching. He also wrote that the garrison of 60 soldiers never fired a shot, and the British occupied the town for the next four years. The officer's diary is in the Barracks Museum of the Border Historical Society along with a model of the 1809 fort, from which only the foundation of the powderhouse remains. *Washington Street; daily 1 to 4 June though August; 207-853-2328.*

Edgecomb

Built in 1808 to protect Wiscasset, one of the most important shipping centers north of Boston, Fort Edgecomb was never attacked. And it's a good thing; the

Unkown Maine

eight-sided blockhouse-style fort was often manned by drunks off the streets and convicts sprung from prison whenever British ships threatened during the War of 1812. A third of these men deserted. British prisoners also were held here, though many of them escaped. An original musket from the fort is at Colonial Pemaquid. *Route 1; daily 9 to 5 Memorial Day through Labor Day; 207-882-7777.*

Ellsworth

Enthusaists including a former curator of Boston's Museum of Science have assembled a collection of pre-digital electro-mechanical telephone switching systems probably unique in the world at the New England Museum of Telephony, housed in the old central office of the Island Telephone Company, which served this area. Telephone communication changed little since it was invented in 1876 by Alexander Graham Bell until the time it was replaced by digital technology in 1983, and the museum has examples of the manual and eletromechanical switches, analog long-distance transmission systems, and vacuum tube repeaters used during most of that time, including old-fashioned central switchboards. *166 Winkumpaugh Road; Thursday through Sunday 1 to 4 July through September; 207-667-9491.*

General David Cobb, an aide-de-camp to General George Washington during the Revolutionary War, was by all accounts a generous man, among the evidence for which is "Woodlawn," also called the Colonel Black Mansion, which he gave as a gift to his son-in-law, Colonel John Black. The 1827 brick Georgian and its 300-acre estate are extremely well-preserved; even the linens are original. No expense was spared; wealthy in his own right thanks to his large timber forest holdings, Black furnished the home with Hepplewhite, Queen Anne, and Chippendale furniture. Also on display: a miniature of Washington presented to Cobb after the Revolution. *Route 172; Monday through Saturday 10-5 June through October; 207-667-8671.*

The Hancock County Jail looks like the most comfortable ever built, until you realize you've entered through the Victorian-era quarters of the sheriff and his family, who shared the building with the inmates. The brick-and-granite jail, built in 1886, was operated until the late 1970s; it's now the museum of the Ellsworth Historical Society. Among the artifacts in the collection are medals awarded by the French government to Frank Whitmore, a local man who died fighting with the French Foreign Legion during World War II before the United States entered the conflict; and a chair from the American Hotel, which was torn down in 1918 and the lumber sent to Europe for the war effort. *State Street; Tuesday and Thursday 10 to 3 July and August; 207-667-4468.*

After a brief career as an educator—and a nervous breakdown—Cordelia J. Stanwood returned to her childhood home and began a second profession as a self-taught ornithologist and wildlife photographer, using her own back yard as her laboratory. Now the property serves as a sanctuary for sick, injured and orphaned birds: the Stanwood Homestead Museum and Wildlife Sanctuary, a 165-acre haven for blind ducks, lame owls, one-winged doves and other enfeebled fowl. Also here are more than 900 of Stanwood's original photographic plates. *Outer High Street; daily 10 to 4 Memorial Day through Columbus Day; 207-667-8460.*

Eustis

The communities of Dead River and Flagstaff are Maine's own ghost towns, wiped out by the construction of the Dead River hydroelectric dam in 1950. A memorial room with records and documents from the towns makes up part of the Dead River Historical Museum in a former church built in 1878. There also are mementos of J.P. Morgan's vacation home in Flagstaff; and a Caribou jacket given by eskimos to Sam White, a Eustis native who was one of the first bush pilots in Alaska. Eustis had another celebrity native: an abandoned fawn rescued by the son

Unknown New England

of the local game warden, which was used as the model for Bambi in the Disney animated film of that name. The fawn's real name was Joe Pete. *Main Street; Saturday and Sunday 11 to 3 Memorial Day through Labor Day; 207-246-2271.*

Exeter

Only 98 Lincoln Zephyr V-12 limousines were ever made; one is part of the extensive collection of the Memory Lane Museum of Antique Cars. Bought new by a society matron in Boston, the 1940 Zephyr is one of more than 100 cars, from Studebakers to DeSotos, in the museum's three buildings. There's a 1938 Chrysler Royal sedan, a hand-cranked 1931 Ford Model A coupe with a rumble seat, a 1941 silver Packard, a 1957 Chevrolet Bel Air and a 1964 Mercury Comet convertible. *Stetson Road; Wednesday through Sunday 10 to 5 Memorial Day through Labor Day, then Friday through Sunday 10 to 5 until Columbus Day; 207-379-4600.*

Fairfield

A blue marlin caught by Ernest Hemingway while he was writing *The Old Man and the Sea* is among the many jewels of the hidden L.C. Bates Museum of natural history and culture on the isolated campus of a school for disadvantaged children. Really a museum of a museum, this extraordinary collection was sealed off in 1950 for financial reasons and reopened decades later exactly as it had been left, with antique cabinets of glass and golden oak and stuffed Maine wildlife displayed in habitats with perfectly preserved backdrops painted by the American Impressionist artist Charles Hubbard. One of the most unusual items: a 19-foot lacquer screen made in 1691 to mark the retirement of a wealthy Chinese government official. There are also hunting implements of prehistoric people, plus colorful minerals, butterflies, bugs and fossils including mammoth and mastodon teeth. Among the stuffed birds in the collection are the extinct passenger pigeon and Carolina parakeet. The top floor is a gallery focusing on Maine art; the bottom, a sampling of antique horse-drawn vehicles, among them a shay used in Boston's Scollay Square around 1785. *Good Will-Hinckley School, Route 201; Wednesday through Saturday 10 to 4:30, Sunday 1 to 4:30 April 1 through November 30; 207-453-4894.*

Farmington

The first, and still one of the most glamorous, opera divas in America had her origins in the humble farmhouse overlooking the Sandy River that is now the Nordica Homestead Museum. Lillian Nordica, whose real name was Lilly Norton, was born in this house in 1857 and would go on to sing in Boston, New York, Paris, St. Petersburg, and London, before she died after a shipwreck in the South Pacific in 1914. The home was bought by fans in 1927, and has been slowly and painstakingly restored and filled with costumes, props, playbills, and the many tributes Nordica received from fans including millionaires and emperors: a lacquered teakwood table that was a gift from the empress of China, for example, a tiara from the queen of England, and a giant jewel-encrusted throne from an admiring Diamond Jim Brady. Nordica—the stage name, which means "Lily of the North," was given to her by her Italian voice coach —made her debut in *La Traviata* at Brescia, Italy, in 1879. Critics marveled at the range and power of her voice. She was the first American woman asked to perform at the Bayreuth Festival, and sang as La Gioconda in the opening of the Boston Opera House; the gown she wore that night is on display. So are her costumes from *Isolde* and *Aida*, the chain of armor and trick sword she carried as Brunhilde, ostrich-feather fans, and costume jewelry that spills from credenza-sized jewelry boxes. Shipwrecked near Java, Nordica was rescued but did not recover, and was buried in London; a single pressed lotus flower from her bier was returned to her home. The auditorium at the nearby campus of the University of Maine, and the troop ship *SS Lillian Nordica*, were named for her. Built in Portland in 1944, the ship has since been decommissioned, but its nameplate hangs in the museum. *Holley Road; Tuesday through Saturday 10 to noon and 1 to 5, Sunday 1 to 5 Memorial Day through Labor Day; 207-778-2042.*

Farmington native Chester Greenwood was the archetype of Yankee ingenuity. He held the patents on the whistling tea kettle, for example, and the shock absorber. But Greenwood is best known locally as the inventor of the earmuff. Ice skating one bitterly cold Maine winter's day in 1873, Greenwood came up with the idea of Greenwood's Champion Ear Protectors, as he came to call them; he was only 15 at the time. One of Greenwood's original earmuffs can be seen in Titcomb House, the historical society museum, on Academy and High streets; some of the elderly volunteers will recount how their mothers sewed earmuffs out of beaver fur and black velvet for house money. Greenwood's mansion, now privately owned, is on a bluff above the Sandy River on Farmington Hills Road just east of Intervale. Farmington holds a Chester Greenwood Day the first Saturday of December. Local livestock parade down Main Street wearing earmuffs, and anyone whose ears are bare is fined; the proceeds go to a food bank. *4 Academy Street; Wednesday and Saturday 11 to 2 mid-June through mid-September; 207-778-2835.*

The equally prolific Leonard Atwood was the inventor of the variable-tension fishing reel, flexible hose and improvements to the mechanical hoist elevator. Local legend has it that Atwood also was a bigamist, with a wife in Massachusetts and another in the white colonial where he lived in Famington Falls. *Croswell Road.*

Farmington also produced John Stevens, chief engineer of the Panama Canal; a seven-ton stone serves as a memorial to Stevens on the Farmington campus of the University of Maine, his alma mater. *Abbott Park.*

Fort Fairfield

It may be stretching things to call the 1839 border conflict between the United States and Canada a war, since it was undeclared and bloodless. The only casualties were a soldier who died of pneumonia, and a cow shot by mistake. But in northern Maine, it's still recalled as the Aroostook War, declared over a boundary dispute between Maine and New Brunswick. A deal brokered by General Winfield Scott averted a wider war with Britain, and the dispute was sent to a boundary commission, where it was settled three years later. The compromise added 7,000 square miles to the United States. Fort Fairfield Blockhouse was built during the conflict to prevent the Canadians from moving lumber on the Aroostook, which was blocked with a boom. This fort is a replica; the original was torn down for its timber. *Main Street; by appointment; 207-472-3802.*

Fort Kent

French Acadians living in the British colonies were deported in 1755 because of the imminence of war with France; some went to Louisiana, where their descendants are more widely known as Cajuns, but many others fled north up the St. John River into the rich timberlands of northern Maine. When the 1839 Aroostook War began, the Acadians built the Fort Kent Blockhouse at the fork of the Fish and St. John rivers. The fort has since been restored. Still loyal to its Acadian heritage, Fort Kent holds a Mardis Gras festival each February. *Block House Street; 207-941-4014.*

The old Bangor and Aroostook Railroad Depot has been converted into the Fort Kent Historical Society Center, where exhibits are housed in the original two waiting rooms—one for men and one for women. In the station agent's office in the middle are the original railroad lanterns, signals, ticket stamps, telegraph, uniforms and timetables dating from around the time the building opened in 1902. Also on display: Fort Kent's original hand-cranked telephone switchboard, which was used until the early 1960s. *Market Street; daily noon to 4 in July; 207-834-5258.*

Unknown New England

The less-famous but equally kitschy cousin of the West's Route 66, U.S. Route 1 begins here on its 2,209-mile journey to Key West, Florida. Long ago bypassed by the impersonal interstates, Route 1 passes an unbroken rhythm of diners, hotels and souvenir shops, most now fading reminders of its heady origins back in 1922.

Freeport

A baseball, photographs and personal checks signed by Babe Ruth are on display in a quiet corner of the L.L. Bean store, missed by most customers. An avid hunter, Ruth was a friend of L.L., who held onto the autographed checks instead of cashing them. *Main Street, Discovery Pond Entrance; always open.*

Fryeburg

Fryeburg is the unlikely hometown of Clarence Mulford, creator of Hopalong Cassidy, the cowboy hero of 28 western novels and almost as many films; with his quick-draw shooting, he was considered "the epitome of gallantry and fair play." Mulford himself moved west for a while, but didn't like it, and returned home. He lived directly across the street from the public library, which has a room full of Mulford memorabilia including his rifles, models he made of a covered wagon and a steamboat, and color plates from the illustrations in magazines and books where the Hopalong Cassidy stories were published. (Mulford also is buried in Fryeburg. His grave is in Pine Grove Cemetery.) *98 Main Street; Monday 5 to 8, Tuesday and Thursday 9 to 5, Wednesday 9 to 8, Saturday 9 to 2 July 4 through Labor Day; Monday hours change to 4 to 7 Labor Day through July 4; 207-935-2731.*

Named for French and Indian War hero Joseph Frye, Fryeburg has a museum with a pitcher Frye's wife brought with her when they settled here. It also boasts a "life mask" of Abraham Lincoln: a plaster cast taken in April, 1860, in Chicago. Only two were made; the other is in the Smithsonian. The Fryeburg museum also has the chair in which Old Abe sat while the mask was being made, and a cast of his right hand made by Volk in May, 1860, the month Lincoln won the Republican presidential nomination. *96 Main Street; Wednesday 9 to noon, Thursday 1 to 4; 207-935-4192.*

After graduating from Bowdoin College in 1877, future polar explorer Robert Peary lived for two years in what is now known as the Admiral Peary House. Inside is a seven-foot statue of the admiral carved, oddly enough, with a chainsaw; and a replica of his ship, the *Roosevelt*, detailed down to the dogsleds on the deck. The rambling Victorian is today a bed-and-breakfast inn. *9 Elm Street; 207-935-3365.*

Locals say the glacial outcropping called Jockey Cap is the world's largest boulder. Whether that's true or not, there once was a tow rope to take skiers to the top in winter months, and a viewfinder at the summit, erected in memory of one-time resident Admiral Robert Peary. The visor that gave the rock its name has fallen off, but it's still possible to find a series of caves along an ancient Indian trail.

Gorham

The hand-cranked Edison gramophone with the speaker trumpet in the parlor really works, and there's a piece of hardtack from the Spanish-American War upstairs in the Baxter House, a museum left by one-time Portland mayor and philanthropist James Phinney Baxter for generations of his Gorham neighbors to bring their treasures. Baxter made his fortune by introducing hermetically sealed cans to America just before the Civil War, just when the Army needed food that would keep. *67 South Street; Tuesday and Thursday 10 to 2 July and August; 207-839-5031.*

Unkown Maine

Gray

Opened in 1931 to raise pheasants for Maine hunters, the Maine Department of Inland Fisheries and Wildlife Game Farm began to take in <u>injured, orphaned and confiscated wildlife</u> in the 1940s. Now called the Maine Wildlife Park, it has about 60 rescued animals including mountain lions, bobcats, black bears, coyotes, lynxes, moose, wild turkeys, bald eagles, and owls. One of the moose was found on a roadside after its mother was frightened away by traffic; one of the eagles impaled itself on a broken branch, and another was found with an infection from a gunshot wound. *Route 26; daily 9:30 to 4 April 15 through Veteran's Day; 207-657-4977.*

Greenville

The cookbooks in the kitchen of the Eveleth-Crafts-Sheridan Historical House begin with the instructions for butchering the main course. They're part of the eclectic collection of the Moosehead Historical Society, located in this restored late-19th-century mansion. In the carriage house is a batteaux, or riverboat, used on log drives down the Kennebec River and on Moosehead Lake. Lumbermen would ride the boat, which resembles a sea dory with a pointed bow and stern, pulling wayward timber from the banks. *Pritham Avenue; Wednesday through Friday 1 to 4 mid-June through September 30; 207-695-2909.*

Early 20th-century industrial barons and their families once spent summers at the grand hotels and fishing camps of Moosehead Lake, including the 425-room Mount Kineo Hotel, which had a golf course and a yacht club. They got there on <u>the steamboat *S/S Katahdin,*</u> which carried saws and horses for the area's lumbermen on one deck and, on another, elegant millionaires in a wood-paneled salon appointed in green velvet and black leather. The hotel, whose guests included Theodore Roosevelt, went bust with the Depression, and the *Kate*, as the familiar steamship came to be called, was used to haul timber on the lake until environmental laws put an end to the log drives in 1975. Since restored, the *Kate* takes visitors on lake cruises; the nearby Moosehead Marine Museum exhibits paraphernalia including flatware and furniture from the Mount Kineo, and 19th- and early 20th-century paintings of the area by landscape artist Seth Steward. *North Main Street; daily 10 to 2 July 1 through Columbus Day; 207-695-2716.*

Hampden

Maine owes its very statehood, in part, to Missouri; under the Missouri Compromise of 1820, both were admitted to Union to maintain the delicate balance between free and slave states. <u>One of the parties to the Missouri Compromise</u> was Martin Kinsley, a congressman from Maine who helped negotiate the deal and whose 1794 home is preserved by the Hampden Historical Society. On the grounds of the house is <u>the original law office used from 1831 to 1860 by Hannibal Hamlin,</u> vice president during the first term of Abraham Lincoln. *83 Main Road South; Tuesday 10 to 4 April 1 through October 31; 207-862-2027.*

Disturbed by the confinement of mentally ill like criminals in jails, <u>social reformer and humanitarian Dorothea Dix</u> is credited with forcing the United States and other countries to open special hospitals for mental patients. There is a park in her memory in Hampden, where she was born on April 4, 1802. *Main Road South.*

Hancock

Pierre Monteux, French-born <u>conductor of the Paris, San Francisco and London symphony orchestras</u> retired to Hancock, where he founded the Pierre Monteux School for Advanced Conductors and Orchestra Players in 1943; his batons, including one in sterling silver given him by the London Symphony, are on display there, along with a memorial consisting only of a hand holding a baton. Monteux is buried in Hancock Cemetery. *Route 1; June, July, and August; 207-422-3931.*

Unknown New England

Houlton
A deck vent from the *USS Maine*, which blew up and sank in Havana Harbor in 1898, is among the artifacts in the Aroostook County Historical and Art Museum. There are also pictures and exhibits relating to the local military airport, where planes would be flown and then towed by land across the border into Canada to maintain American neutrality before the United States entered World War II, and the prisoner of war camp that housed about 3,500 Germans and Italians on the same site later in the war. You can also get directions here to the lonely grave of Private Hiram Smith, the only human casualty of the Aroostook War, who died of pneumonia in Houlton while helping build a road. *109 Main Street; Monday through Friday noon to 3, Memorial Day through Labor Day; 207-532-2519.*

Island Falls
One of the largest collections of its kind in the United States, the John E. and Walter D. Webb Museum of Vintage Fashion exhibits 19th- and 20th-century men's and women's clothing and accessories including wedding gowns, Prince Albert coats, early Boy Scout uniforms, Edwardian and Victorian dresses, and an especially elegant 1924 elaborate silk gown of sunburst pearls. There are also eyeglasses, shoes, spats, and ladies' "unmentionables," and a disconcerting display of hats above a line of disembodied heads on room-length shelves. *Sherman Street; Monday through Thursday 10 to 4 June 1 through October 10; 207-862-3797.*

Isleboro
The Grindle Point Lighthouse is a Pacific-style lighthouse built on the Atlantic as a prototype; unlike other eastern lights, it's square, not round. It's also the home of the Sailors Memorial Museum, which exhibits some of the original sperm oil lamps. *Gilkey Harbor; Tuesday through Sunday 9 to 4:30 July 1 through Labor Day; 207-734-2253.*

Kennebunk
Two sections of the first transatlantic telegraph cable are part of the collection of the Brick Store Museum, which fills three adjoining 19th-century mercantile buildings and an 1803 sea captain's home. The cable was laid in 1858, but lasted only three weeks; the first successful permanent cable was not installed until 1866. The museum has 40,000 other equally eclectic items, including a lock of statesman Henry Clay's hair, cut upon his death. There are also maritime paintings, portraits, and a "friendship quilt" with inscriptions of advice from residents of Kennebunk to a local man who went west for the gold rush in the 1850s. *117 Main Street; Tuesday through Saturday 10 to 4:30 June through December; 207-985-4802.*

Tiny Hatch Cemetery, an historic graveyard alongside the Maine Turnpike, has survived wildfires in the 1940s, the construction of the turnpike itself in the 1950s, and a tanker truck explosion just yards away in the early 1980s. At least 18 people are buried there, the earliest Jerusha Hatch, who died in 1814 at the age of 74, and the most recent Catherine Mitchell, who died in 1890 at the age of 63. *Mile 21.*

Kennebunkport
The rambling wood-shingled mansion with the high flagpole on Ocean Avenue was the Summer White House from 1989 to 1993, when its owner, George H.W. Bush, served as president. The Walker's Point compound and its 11-acre seaside estate, named for Bush's grandfather, was a family retreat beginning in 1902. Bush's mother, the former Dorothy Walker, married his father, Connecticut Senator Prescott Bush, in the local church.

Begun on a lark in 1939 by a handful of enthusiasts, the Seashore Trolley Museum today boasts the world's largest collection of trolley cars. The original idea was simply to save Old Car No. 31, an open trolley headed for the scrap heap at the end of trolley service between Old Orchard Beach and Biddeford; so poor were the buyers, they agreed to mow the trolley company president's lawn as payment. It would be the start of a collection that today numbers 250 vehicles, including city and suburban streetcars, rapid transit cars, electric trolley buses, motor buses, and even snow removal cars. *Log Cabin Road; daily 10 to 5 May 31 through Columbus Day, then Saturday and Sunday 10 to 5 through October 31 and in May; 207-967-2712.*

Kingsfield

The spectacular mountains ringing Kingsfield were an inspiration to the identical twin inventors of the Stanley Steamer, Freelan Oscar and Francis Edgar Stanley, and their life is recounted in the Stanley Museum, housed in the Stanley School, the creaky old converted Georgian-Style school they designed and built for their home town in 1903. The brothers' first steam car was manufactured in 1897, and nearly 11,000 of them had been sold by 1924, when they were discontinued. The museum owns Stanley Steamers made in 1905, 1910 and 1916, and even an 1895 Roper steam bicycle. Lifelong overachievers, the Stanleys also perfected the dry plate photographic process and the air brush, and built violins, and their sister, Chansonetta Stanley Emmons, was an accomplished photographer of rural life in Maine, and these achievements also are reflected. *School Street; Tuesday through Sunday 1 to 4, except in April and November; 207-265-2729.*

Kittery

In what remains perhaps the greatest underwater rescue in history, a diving bell was used successfully for the first time to rescue the men of the submarine *USS Squalus* when the *Squalus* went down off the New England coast on May 23, 1939, barely two months after it was launched from the Portsmouth Naval Shipyard. The entire nation waited anxiously to hear the fate of the officers and crew trapped 240 feet below the surface; though 26 were killed when the sub originally sank, all 33 survivors were saved, and the *Squalus* itself was refloated and returned to the Kittery shipyard, where it was refitted and renamed the *USS Sailfish*. The story had another twist: The *USS Sculpin,* which had found the sunken *Squalus* on the sea floor, was later sunk by the Japanese and her survivors sent as prisoners of war to Japan aboard an escort carrier that was sunk en route—by the *Sailfish*. A model of the *Squalus,* along with submarine clocks and other instruments, is on display in the Portsmouth Naval Shipyard Museum, a jewel of a museum in a former enlisted men's barracks that's not only hidden; it's off-limits, except one day a month. The conning tower from the *Sailfish* stands in the center of the shipyard. Also in the exhibit are naval artifacts and scale models that show the evolution of the submarine. More than 100 submarines were built here, including the *L-8*, commissioned in 1917, the first sub built in a public shipyard. The Treaty of Portsmouth was signed in the navy yard's administration building to end the Russo-Japanese War in 1905. *Gate 2, Route 103; last Saturday of each month 10 to 3 (Thursday 10 to 3 for active-duty and retired military personnel); 207-438-2320.*

The *USS Ranger*, commanded by John Paul Jones—father of the American Navy—was built for him near Badger's Island; the John Paul Jones Memorial overlooks the site of the original drydock. Legend has it that the flag aboard the ship was sewn by the women of Portsmouth who, lacking fabric, sacrificed their petticoats. *John Paul Jones Park, Route 1; 207-384-5160.*

A 13-foot model of the *Ranger* is a centerpiece of the Kittery Historical and Naval Museum, which has exhibits about local maritime history, nameplates from submarines made at the Portsmouth Naval Shipyard, and artifacts from Kittery, established in 1623 and the oldest incorporated town in Maine. *Route 1 at Rogers*

Unknown New England

Road; Tuesday through Saturday 10 to 4 June 1 through Columbus Day; 207-489-3080.

Fort McClary has guarded the approaches to the Piscataqua River since 1715, but it is perhaps most conspicuous as <u>the place where a former vice president of the United States served as a private</u>. Abraham Lincoln's first-term vice president, Hannibal Hamlin, joined up after Lincoln dumped him from the ticket for his second term. The ex-vice president served for three months at Fort McClary, working as a cook's assistant in the enlisted men's mess. Named for Major Andrew McClary, the highest-ranking American killed in the Battle of Bunker Hill, the fort was again used as an observation post during World War I and World War II. The granite walls, powder magazines and blockhouse remain. *Route 103; daily 9 to 8 Memorial Day through Labor Day, 9 to 6 Labor Day through September 30; 207-384-5160.*

<u>One of the largest and most unique collections of model trains anywhere</u>, the Railway City USA Model Railroad Museum has 5,500 square feet of working displays around a 10-by-20-foot HO gauge layout with a Boston & Maine engine, working lights, 125 buildings, and 250 human figures. Artifacts include a ticket from the last passenger train from Portsmouth to Boston and a 1934 conductor's uniform from the Boston & Maine. *Route 236; Saturday 10 to 4; 207-439-1204.*

Henry James and Mark Twain were among the literary visitors to <u>the summer home of William Dean Howells</u>, author of *The Rise of Silas Lapham* and other classics. From his library, he wrote, Howells could "see two lighthouses, one on each side of a foamy reef; three sails are sliding across the smooth waters within the reef, and far beyond it lie the Isles of Shoals in full sight. Could you ask more?" The house is now a Harvard University faculty retreat. *Route 103.*

Lewiston

Specializing in works on paper, the Bates College Museum of Art boasts <u>the largest collection of drawings by Lewiston native Marsden Hartley</u> and has prints by Impressionists and post-Impressionists including Cezanne, Gauguin and Matisse. *75 Russell Street; Monday through Saturday 10 to 5, Sunday 1 to 5; 207-786-6158.*

Like most politicians, Democrat Edmund Muskie collected rooms-full of ephemera when he was governor, senator, U.S. secretary of state and candidate for president. A sample is on display at the Muskie Archives at Bates, his alma mater, including campaign buttons, keys to various cities, donkey figurines and <u>a gold-plated hot dog</u> he was given to commemorate National Hot Dog Month. *70 Campus Avenue; Monday through Friday 9 to 4; 207-786-6354.*

Lille

Roman on the inside and Baroque on the outside, the 1909 former Catholic church now called the Musee et Centre Culturel du Mont-Carmel is <u>the only church of its kind in the world</u>. Relinquished by the parish after a membership decline, the building with this singularly distinctive architecture is now used for community events and also has a collection of Acadian furniture and artifacts. *Route 1; noon to 4 daily except Saturday Memorial Day through mid-September; 207-895-3339.*

Lincolnville

Established by the wealthy founder of the internetworking company 3Com and his wife, Kelmscott Farm conserves <u>rare and endangered breeds of livestock</u> with more than 250 animals and 20 threatened species, including Nigerian dwarf goats and nearly extinct Gloustershire Old Spots pigs. The farm is named for the summer home of William Morris, a 19th-century English social reformer who lauded old-

Unkown Maine

fashioned craftsmanship. *Van Cycle Road; Tuesday through Sunday 10 to 5 May 1 through September 30, then Tuesday through Sunday 10 to 3; 207-763-4088.*

Lisbon Falls

Even though the soft drink was invented 40 miles away in Union, the undisputed shrine to Moxie is the Kennebec Fruit Store, whose owner so loves the slightly bitter carbonated beverage he's filled every space with bottles, memorabilia—even political signs ("Vote for Jim Tierney," one says: "He's Got Moxie!")—and makes Moxie-flavored ice cream. Developed in 1876 as a nerve tonic, Moxie was one of the most popular drinks in its 1920s heyday. Sales plummeted when the formula was changed in response to competition from Coca Cola, though Moxie remains in fashion in northern New England. Lisbon hosts an annual Moxie Days celebration the second weekend in July. *Main Street; daily 9 to 5; 207-353-8173.*

Livermore Falls

The Washburn-Norlands Living History Center is a preserved Victorian-era village with a mansion, schoolhouse, library, church and working farm. The family that left it behind is an extraordinary rags-to-riches story in itself. Of the 10 Washburn children born here in poverty, one became a Civil War general, one commanded an early ironclad ship, several went to Congress, and one served as governor. *Norlands Road; daily 10 to 4 June 30 through Labor Day; 207-897-4366.*

Lubec

When you look to sea from here, the entire country is behind you; West Quoddy Head, a tiny spit of land jutting into the Atlantic, is the easternmost point in the mainland United States.

Machias

Machias was the site of the first naval battle of the American Revolution, five days before the Battle of Bunker Hill, when Colonel Benjamin Foster dared a ragged group of Patriots to follow him across a small stream and attack the British man-o-war *Margaretta*. To their surprise, they captured the ship. A marker on Route 92 records the site where Foster made his challenge. The injured were taken to Burnham Tavern, now a museum, which has a tea set from the captain's cabin on *Margaretta* and the sea chest on which a British officer lay mortally wounded. *Main Street; Monday through Friday 9 to 5 mid-June through Labor Day; 207-255-4432.*

Realizing that the British would return to avenge the *Margaretta*, the people of Machias built Fort Machias, later renamed Fort O'Brien. They were right. When the Redcoats did come back, they overran the fort, which was destroyed again during a British naval offensive in 1814. *Route 92; daily dawn to dusk; 207-941-4014.*

Madawaska

After being exiled by the British in "Le Grand de Rangement," or the great expulsion, of 1775, French Acadians settled in what is now northern Maine, placing a rough cross on the first spot they set foot in the valley after canoeing up the St. John River. A 14-foot marble cross, the Acadian Cross Historic Shrine, now marks the site where the Acadians landed. The climate was hard, and many would have starved if not for Tante Blanche, a pioneer woman who saved the struggling colony by gathering food to share. The Tante Blanche Acadian Museum, a replica of an original log cabin, includes artifacts from that time, including spinning wheels and cast-iron stoves. *Route 1, Monday through Friday 10:30 to 12:30 and 1:30 to 3:30 and Sunday 1:30 to 3:30 June, July and August; 207-728-4518.*

Unknown New England

Millinocket
So closely associated were they with the gigantic paper mills built in the late 1890s and early 1900s, communities in north central Maine still call themselves "paper towns." The biggest, Millinocket, has <u>a collection relating to the wood and paper mills</u>, including a lumberman's bearskin coat. *Municipal Building, Maine Street; Wednesday 9 to 11 and 1 to 3 May 1 through September 30; 207-723-5766.*

The astonishing sight of two giant steam locomotives in the middle of the northern Maine wilderness is testament to <u>one of the most remarkable engineering feats in New England history</u>, when a railroad 18 miles long was built through the back country to carry lumber from Eagle and Umbazooksus lakes to the Penobscot River. The engines of the so-called Pulpwood Express were taken to the site over ice during the winter of 1926, when the tracks were laid; they were abandoned seven years later. Volunteers are working to restore the trains, which still can be reached only by canoe through the Allagash Waterway, about 55 miles north of Millinocket. *Township 8, Range 13; registration required; 207-941-4014.*

The Northern Timber Cruisers Snowmobile Museum boasts <u>a collection of rare antique snowmobiles</u>, including prototypes of the first recreational models ever developed, many of which were tested in this rugged region. The museum has 32 snowmobiles made between 1951 to 1968, among them the prototypes of the 1961 Polaris Ranger and the first two snowmobiles to climb Mount Washington. It was started by the son of the state's first Polaris dealer. *Route 157; 7 to 5 Saturday and Sunday December1 through March 31; 207-723-9261.*

Monhegan
<u>Possibly the only museum that not only exhibits works of art, but was inspired by one</u>, the Monhegan Museum took its vision from a 1916 Edward Hopper painting of the island's lighthouse with its since-demolished assistant keeper's cottage. That led to the idea of reconstructing the cottage just as Hopper painted it to house the collection, which commemorates the island's famous art colony with sketches by such former residents as George Bellows and Rockwell Kent. The museum also has local historical mementos, including the American flag that covered the coffin of the lighthousekeeper's son, who died in the Civil War. *Lighthouse Hill; daily 11:30 to 3 July 1 through August 31, then 12:30 to 2:30 through September 30; 207-596-7003.*

Naples
A seven-foot <u>Oriental temple guard stolen during the 1900 Boxer Rebellion</u> by a seafaring local is in the Naples Historical Society Museum, along with a stuffed loon and mementos from the area's many children's summer camps. *Village Green; Thursday and Friday 10 to 2 July 1 through Labor Day; 207-693-4297.*

New Gloucester
Sabbathday Lake, <u>the world's last active community of Shakers</u> continues to make furniture and other products and commemorates the sect's history in America in a museum that includes Shaker variations of such inventions as the washing machine. Established in 1794, Sabbathday Lake is the last of 18 Shaker communities founded by a group of English separatists who came to America to escape religious persecution. *707 Shaker Road; Monday through Saturday 10 to 4:30 Memorial Day through Columbus Day; 207-926-4597.*

New Harbor
Best known for greeting the Pilgrims at Plymouth, <u>Samoset actually lived here</u> on Round Pond Harbor, where there is a small memorial to him. It was here, on

Unkown Maine

July 24, 1626, that Samoset executed the first property deed in New England, handing over much of the Pemaquid Peninsula to a man named John Brown. *Route 32.*

New Sweden

Northern Maine was big and very, very empty in the 19th century, when its tiny population was depleted even further by the lure of riches in the West. W.W. Thomas Jr., Maine's commissioner of immigration and a former ambassador to Stockholm, reasoned that Swedes were accustomed to the climate, so he hand-picked 51 of them to start an experimental colony called New Sweden. Those unusual beginnings are commemorated in the New Sweden Historical Museum, which has artifacts and Swedish-language family bibles brought to Maine by the original settlers. They also brought an important sport from home: skiing. The mountains nearby are the place where alpine skiing was introduced to America. The museum is at the exact spot where the arriving Swedes stopped on July 23, 1870, to give thanks for their successful voyage. Maypoles erected every June for the town's Midsommar Festival remain in place through Labor Day. *Capitol Hill Road; Wednesday through Sunday noon to 4 Memorial Day through September 30; 207-896-3018.*

Newburgh

Jabez Knowlton was a carefree traveling salesman until he met the daughter of the local tavernkeeper in 1839, married, settled down, and opened a general store. Since restored to its 1921 appearance by Knowlton's great-great nephew, the Old Country Store Museum is stocked with products that were actually sold there, or kept on inventory by the frugal Yankee proprietor who didn't like to throw anything away. There are coffee beans, cigars, kerosene lamps, ladies' hoops and bustles, gentlemen's cardboard shirt fronts, spittoons, extracts of sassafras, Colburn's Hasty Tapioca, elderberry wine, and Kickapoo Cough Syrup—19 percent alcohol. *Route 9; by appointment; 207-234-2381.*

Newcastle

The oldest surviving Catholic Church in New England is not in Boston, but here, where St. Patrick Roman Catholic Church was built in 1808 by the many Irish Catholic families that came to work in the area's shipbuilding business. The bell, cast by Paul Revere, still rings. *Academy Hill Road; daily dawn to dusk; 207-563-3240.*

Newfield

One of the most intact carousels in the nation, the 1894 Armitage-Herschell carousel still has its original 24 jumpers, four chariots and a deKliest-Limonaire organ. The carousel is the centerpiece of the Willowbrook Museum, a treasury of 19th-century rural life, with two houses, a general store, shops, and an ice cream parlor. *Elm Street; daily 10 to 5 May 15 through September 30; 207-793-2784.*

North Berwick

Begun in 1835 as a manufacturer of horse-drawn plows, the Hussey Company adapted to changing markets, going into fire escapes, then stadium seats, and today is Maine's oldest business. Its museum exhibits these products and others, including old diving boards. *Dyer Street; by appointment; 207-676-2271.*

Oakfield

A three-wheeled manually propelled pedal train car is among the items in the Oakfield Railroad Museum in the wood-frame one-time station of the Bangor & Aroostook Railroad. The car was used to patrol and inspect the tracks. The mu-

Unknown New England

seum also has the motorized car that took the place of the pedal version. *Station Street; Saturday and Sunday 1 to 4 Memorial Day through Labor Day; 207-757-8575.*

Ogunquit

A former director of New York's Metropolitan Museum of Art once called the Ogunquit Museum of American Art "the most beautiful small museum in the world." The museum is on a ledge overlooking Narrow Cove, the kind of setting that has attracted artists including Edward Hopper and Walt Kuhn to Ogunquit; it exhibits Kuhn, Thomas Hart Benton, and other 20th-century American artists. *183 Shore Road; Monday through Saturday 10:30 to 5, Sunday 2 to 5 July 1 through September 30; 207-646-4909.*

Old Orchard Beach

Old Orchard is 122 miles closer to Europe than Roosevelt Field, where Charles A. Lindbergh began his famous flight to Paris, and its hard-packed beach served as a runway for eight subsequent attempts to cross the ocean, of which four were successful. One, by a French crew, carried a stowaway, 17-year-old Arthur Schriebner of Portland, who jumped aboard unnoticed. This little-remembered history is recounted in the Harmon Memorial Museum, which also has a pair of goggles worn by Wiley Post, the first man to fly alone around the world, and who was killed in a crash along with humorist Will Rogers. There are also materials relating to Old Orchard's pier, which at 1,823 feet was the longest in the world when it opened on July 4, 1898. After a nor'easter five months later, it became the shortest. *4 Portland Avenue; Tuesday through Saturday 1 to 4 Memorial Day through Labor Day.*

Old Town

Begun in the back of a hardware store in 1898, the Old Town Canoe Company is now the world's largest canoe manufacturer. Some of its very first wood-and-canvas boats, and a birch bark canoe of unknown age and origin, are on display in its visitor center, along with an exhibit about canoe-making. *130 Middle Street; Monday through Saturday 9 to 6, Sunday 10 to 3 March through September, then Monday through Saturday 10 to 5; 207-827-1530.*

Oquossoc

Built in 1916 by fishermen and loggers, the Union Log Church is made entirely of spruce logs. The antique organ still works. *Route 16 at the Rangeley River; nondenominational services Sundays at 9 in July and August.*

Orono

Given by a wealthy alumnus, the Hudson Museum of Anthropology at the University of Maine has the largest institutional collection of western Mexican tomb figures in the United States. The large ceramic figures were buried with the dead between 300 BC and 200 AD. The museum also has one of the finest collections of prehispanic Mexican and Central American artifacts in the United States, including the only known carved precolombian emerald, made between 900 and 600 BC, and Mayan ceramic vases with painted scenes of the cosmos and the underworld. *Maine Center for the Arts; Tuesday through Friday 9 to 4, Saturday 11 to 4; 207-581-1901.*

The University of Maine Museum of Art features works by Winslow Homer, Francisco Goya, Pablo Picasso, David Hockney, and Roy Lichtenstein. *Carnegie Hall; Monday through Saturday 9 to 4:30; 207-581-3255.*

Unkown Maine

Owls Head
Some of the world's rarest aircraft, automobiles, motorcycles, bicycles and engines are on display at the Owls Head Transportation Museum, including the last surviving Fokker C.IV, one of the only five remaining Curtiss Jennies, the 1963 prototype of the Ford Mustang, and early Harley Davidson motorcycles. There are also replicas of the Clark biwing ornithopter, designed to fly by flapping its tapered wing like a bird's, and of a World War I Fokker tri-plane. The museum has one of just five remaining 1935 Stout Scarabs; only six of the automobiles, crafted by the designer of the Ford Tri-motor Tin Goose airplane, were ever built, with a streamlined airflow body and the engine in the rear. *Knox County Airport, Route 73; daily 10 to 5 April through October, 10 to 4 November through March; 207-594-4418.*

Paris
The birthplace of Abraham Lincoln's first vice president, Hannibal Hamlin, overlooks the White Mountains from Paris Hill. Just next door is the Hamlin Memorial Library and Museum—named not for Hannibal, but for Augustus Hamlin, his nephew and a local doctor. Augustus Hamlin's father, Elijah, discovered a lode of tourmaline in nearby Mount Micah; examples of the local gemstones in their rough form are in the museum, which once served as the jail. The Hamlins weren't the only famous family from Paris; so was Henry Lyon, the navigator on the first flight to cross the Pacific from California to Australia in 1928, and the museum has the trophy he got for completing the flight. *16 Hannibal Hamlin Drive; Tuesday through Friday noon to 5, Saturday 10 to 2 March through December; 207-743-2980.*

Passamaquoddy Reservation
Passamaquoddy Indians have lived in what is now Maine for thousands of years, hunting and fishing along this coast; the name means "people who fish for pollock." Passamaquoddy warriors fought alongside the colonists against the British during the American Revolution; one is said to have shot the captain of the British ship *Margaretta* off Machias during the first naval battle in American history. A monument at Pleasant Point commemorates the Passamaquoddys' contribution to the Revolution. The Wapohnaki Museum on the Passamaquoddy Reservation exhibits life-sized depictions of key people in the tribe, including a storyteller, hunters, and fishermen, and has a display about ongoing work to save the Passamaquoddy language by creating a dictionary. *Route 190; by appointment; 207-853-4001.*

Patten
The Lumbermen's Museum in Patten, once a major center of the industry, is a full-sized replica of an 1820 Maine logging camp. There's a working sawmill, a huge collection of lumbering tools, and heavy equipment including horse-drawn sleds, batteaux, and a rare Lombard steam log hauler with caterpillar treads that served as the basis for the military tank and bulldozer. The museum also has an equally rare gasoline-powered Lombard. *Shin Pond Road; Tuesday through Sunday 10 to 4 July and August, Friday through Sunday 10 to 4 September 1 through Columbus Day and Memorial Day through June 30; 207-528-2650.*

Pemaquid
A 28-pound lobster caught in a fishing net is one of the more unusual items in the Fishermen's Museum, located in the Pemaquid Point Lighthouse. The lighthouse, built in 1827, also has a Fresnel lens, charts, nets, and buoys. *Route 13; Monday through Saturday 10 to 5, Sunday 11 to 5 May through October; 207-677-2494.*

Perry
Named for U.S. Navy Commodore Oliver Perry, this town is equally famous for being the exact midpoint between the equator and the North Pole; the precise spot

Unknown New England

is marked by a red granite monument on Route 1. It was Perry who, after defeating an entire British squadron during the War of 1812, wrote: "We have met the enemy and he is ours."

Phippsburg

This, not Plymouth, is the site of the first English settlement in the Northeast and, along with Jamestown, the first in North America; both Jamestown and the Popham Colony, under the command of George Popham, were established in 1607, a full 13 years before the famous Pilgrims came ashore. This was also the place where American shipbuilding began with the construction of the first ocean-going vessel ever built in North America, the 60-foot *Virginia*, in which many of the Popham colonists hurriedly sailed home to England after experiencing their first harsh Maine winter. (A model of the *Virginia* is in the Maine Maritime Museum in Bath.) Popham didn't expect to be forgotten; on his deathbed, he is reputed to have said: "I die content. My name will always be associated with the first planting of the English race in the New World." In fact, so overlooked was he by history that a parking lot was built above the spot where Popham is believed to have been be buried. The semicircular Fort Popham was built in 1861 to protect the Bath shipyards and Augusta during the Civil War, but it was never finished, making it possible to see the workmanship and architectural features that went into the thick walls and circular staircases. Hidden on a nearby hill is an added bonus: Fort Baldwin, a coastal battery with reinforced bunkers, gun emplacements and a five-story observation tower to watch for the periscopes of enemy submarines during World War II. About 50 paces up Sabino Hill, beyond the parking lot, is the granite block intended to be the keystone at Fort Popham. Now it's the solitary memorial to the Popham Colony. *Route 209; daily 9 to dusk Memorial Day through September 30; 207-389-1335.*

Pittston

The first amphibious military assault in American history was launched in nothing more substantial than a fleet of 200 flat-bottomed river boats and birch-bark canoes beginning from an inconspicuous embankment on the Kennebec River: Colonel Benedict Arnold's expedition to take Quebec from the control of the British in 1775. The idea was that, with the British dislodged, thousands of Canadians would join the rebellion. Arnold led 1,000 soldiers up the Kennebec and Dead rivers into Canada. Facing starvation, half his army would desert, however, and the French Canadians turned out to be unenthusiastic about the rebellion. The ill-fated expedition is commemorated at the Major Reuben Colburn House, the museum of the Arnold Expedition Historical Society. Colburn was the boatbuilder who supplied 200 batteaux for Arnold's campaign, but he used green pine and oak and too few nails and many of the boats fell apart. The joke was on him, though; his bill went largely unpaid. The 1765 house displays the expedition doctor's medicine spoon and the remains of a 1760 batteaux and a birch bark canoe similar to what Arnold used. *Arnold Road; Saturday and Sunday 10 to 5 July and August; 207-582-7080.*

Poland

The Maine State Building, which represented the state of Maine at the 1893 Chicago Expedition, has been reassembled on the grounds of the former Poland Spring Resort, where it now serves as a museum. It tells the history of the famous 350-room hotel, which burned down on July 4, 1975, and Poland Spring Water, once bottled exclusively as a therapeutic tonic for guests and served to them by a tuxedo-clad waiter straight from the spring. *Preservation Way; daily 9 to 1 July and August, then Saturday and Sunday 9 to 1 through Columbus Day; 207-998-4142.*

Port Clyde

It was at the Marshall Point Lighthouse that the actor Tom Hanks ended his fictional cross-country run in the movie *Forrest Gump*; a photograph of Hanks filming

Unkown Maine

the scene now hangs in the Marshall Point Lighthouse Museum, a collection of local artifacts relating to the granite-quarrying and fishing industries, including early lobster traps made out of tree boughs. The coastal town has long attracted writers and artists including N.C. Wyeth and Sara Orne Jewett, who wrote her book *The Country of the Pointed Firs* there; the museum has Jewett's autograph. *Port Clyde; daily 1 to 5 and Saturday 10 to 5 June 1 through September 30, Saturday and Sunday 1 to 5 May and October; 207-372-6450.*

Porter

The Parsonfield-Porter Historical Society, in a house built in 1875, has the piano, a bookcase and some furniture from the home in Portland where Henry Wadsworth Longfellow lived after graduating from Bowdoin College. The items were rescued when the house was demolished. *Main Street; by appointment; 207-625-4667.*

Portland

Among the most overlooked monuments to black history in America, the Abyssinian Meetinghouse was one of the nation's first black churches, a station on the underground railroad, and a platform for famous abolitionists. Built in 1826 by black seamen in the merchant and coastal ferry fleet, it started to decline after the wreck of the steamship *Portland* in a gale in 1898 killed all 192 passengers and crew, including 30 members of the congregation. *Newbury Street.*

The author of Maine's first-in-the-nation prohibition law, Neal Dow is considered the father of Prohibition and his 1829 mansion is kept as a museum by the Women's Christian Temperance Union. A founder of the Prohibition Party, Dow also was a fervent abolitionist who served as a general in the Civil War and became the only high-ranking Union officer captured by the Confederacy, whereupon he antagonized both his captors and his fellow prisoners by endlessly preaching temperance (and purportedly hoarding blankets) until he was exchanged for General Robert E. Lee's nephew. The Neal Dow House displays his prison-issue shirt and Confederate swords he collected. *714 Congress Street; Monday through Friday 11 to 4; 207-773-7773.*

Benedict Arnold's journal from his luckless expedition to Quebec in 1775 is preserved in the Maine Historical Gallery of the Maine Historical Society, third-oldest historical society in the country. The journal was contributed by Aaron Burr, later vice president of the United States and the man who killed Alexander Hamilton in a duel; Burr was one of the volunteers in Arnold's Quebec campaign. The society also has an original copy of the Declaration of Independence, and a lock of George Washington's hair. It maintains the boyhood home of Henry Wadsworth Longfellow next door. *489 Congress Street; gallery Monday through Saturday 10 to 5, Sunday noon to 5 June through October, then Monday through Saturday 10 to 5, house Monday through Saturday 10 to 4 Sunday noon to 4 May 1 through October 31, Saturday 10:30 to 2:30 in November, daily noon to 4 in December; 207-774-1822.*

Before the telegraph was invented, port cities erected observation towers to watch for incoming ships; Portland Observatory is one of the finest, and the nation's last remaining ship-to-shore watchtower, built in 1807 on Portland's highest hill. Anchored in rock, the seven-story tower had a 30-mile view out to sea from the glass cupola at its top. It was the idea of retired naval Captain Lemuel Moody, who is buried at the foot of the hill. Operated until the end of World War II, and occasionally used later by police on stakeouts, it is now being restored. *Munjoy Hill.*

Narrow-gauge trains once used to haul lumber through the north Maine woods now run through Portland on 3,000 feet of track laid between the Maine Narrow

Unknown New England

Gauge Museum depot and Fort Allen Park, with views of Portland Harbor and Casco Bay. The three working steam locomotives, caboose, and coaches originally operated between 1880 and 1943. *58 Fore Street; daily 10 to 3; 207-828-0814.*

Born Sean Aloysius O'Feeney, motion picture director John Ford lived as a boy in Portland's Irish district. Ford won back-to-back Academy Awards for *The Grapes of Wrath* in 1940, and *How Green Was My Valley* in 1941. He also made *The Searchers*. A statue of Ford in a director's chair commemorates his birth here. *Fore Street.*

Housed in an old holding cell, the Portland Police Museum features a wall of confiscated weapons including a 1930s-era Thompson submachine gun and displays about notorious local crimes and criminals like the terrorists who stored an arsenal of weapons and explosives on Munjoy Hill in the 1970s. *109 Middle Street; Monday through Friday 8 to 3; 207-874-8300.*

George Tate worked for a contractor that provided masts for the Royal Navy in the 1750s, and he fancied himself a representative of the crown, so he incorporated fake architectural features into his house to reflect his self-importance, including an indented gambrel roof to give the illusion that there was a third floor; it's actually the attic. Tate's house, overlooking the mast yard, also has more expensive windows in the front, where they would be seen, than in the back. *1270 Westbrook Street; Tuesday through Saturday 10 to 4, Sunday 1 to 4 June 15 through September 30; Friday and Saturday 10 to 4, Sunday 1 to 4 in October; 207-774-6177.*

An unexpected collection of African tribal art fills the two-room Museum of African Tribal Art, including ceremonial masks and shrines, as well as contemporary African art in revolving exhibitions. *122 Spring Street; Tuesday through Saturday 10:30 to 5; 207-871-7188.*

Portland's Morse-Libby House is one of the finest surviving examples of a Victorian-era house and furnishings in the United States, built as a summer home just before the Civil War by New Orleans hotelier Ruggles Morse. It's also known as the Victoria Mansion. *109 Danforth Street; Tuesday through Saturday 10 to 4, Sunday 1 to 5 May through October; 207-772-4841.*

Before recordings, municipal organs served as substitutes for symphony orchestras, and were outfitted with the sounds of instruments from snare drums to xylophones, all played from a keyboard. Portland's restored 1912 Kotzschmar Memorial Organ was the second-largest organ in the world when it was installed in Portland City Hall Auditorium in 1912, and is one of only three surviving municipal organs in the United States; the others are in San Diego and Cleveland. The 50-ton instrument, with 6,612 pipes as tall as 32 feet, can be made to sound like a bass drum, Turkish cymbal, marimba, and glockenspiel. It was given to the city by Portland native Cyrus Curtis, publisher of *Ladies Home Journal* and *The Saturday Evening Post*. *Merrill Auditorium, Congress Street; demonstrations some Thursdays at noon and weekly concerts Tuesdays at 7:30 mid-June through August 31; 207-883-9525.*

Like other tourists, veterans of the Civil War-era Fifth Maine Regiment spent their vacations on Peaks Island, once known as the Coney Island of Maine, with roller coasters, boardwalks, hotels and summer theaters. In 1888 the Fifth built a Queen Anne-style house on the island, now part of Portland; today it serves as a museum of the regiment's history. The museum has not only bullets, but entire trees with bulletholes in them from the Battle of Gettysburg. Nearby are the massive fortifications of Battery Steele, an abandoned World War II artillery emplace-

Unkown Maine

ment that protected Casco Bay with two 16-inch battleship guns that could fire a 2,000-pound shell 26 miles. *45 Seashore Avenue; daily 11 to 4 June through Labor Day, then Saturday and Sunday 11 to 4 through Columbus Day; 207-766-3330.*

A 6-inch gun from the battleship *Maine* is in Fort Allen Park. A porthole, telegraph, window frame and the key to the ammunition locker of the famous ship is on display in the Cumberland Club on High Street.

Presque Isle

Maxie Anderson Memorial Park marks the launch site of the first successful transatlantic balloon flight, the trip of the *Double Eagle II*, which lifted off from here on August 11, 1978, and landed 60 miles north of Paris six days later. Anderson was one of the three-man crew of the 112-foot-high helium-filled balloon. A statue of the ballon is the park's centerpiece. *Spragueville Road.*

Prospect

The largely intact 1844 Fort Knox, named for first U.S. secretary of war Major General Henry Knox, who came from Thomaston, was one of the strongest and most powerful ever constructed, built of granite from nearby Mount Waldo. Among its unique features are two of the only five granite spiral staircases in the country. It is also the only Maine fort with its original cannon emplaced, including two 15-inch Rodmans that needed seven people to load and fire their 315-pound shells. *Route 174; daily dawn to dusk, May 1 through November 1; 207-459-7719.*

Prospect Harbor

When Maine's famous Perry's Nut House closed its doors, ephemera fans feared that the world's biggest nut collection would be split up. But the unrivaled assemblage of every known nut on earth is back on display in an old general store, thanks to a local businessman. *DiMarco Realty building, Main Street; 207-963-5540.*

Prouts Neck

The studio of Winslow Homer still has the sign the curmudgeonly artist kept on the door warning of snakes and mice to discourage curious admirers from interrupting him. A former stable, the studio also served as Homer's home from 1883 until 1910. He lived there almost like a hermit while painting his oils and watercolors of Maine seascapes. There are two watercolors by his mother, but no originall works by Homer. However, his brush and paints are displayed in the studio, which is open to the public. *5 Winslow Homer Road; daily 10 to 5 May through October.*

Rangeley

Antique chain saws dating back to the 1940s and paintings of the Maine woods have been assembled in the Rangeley Region Logging Museum. *Route 16, Saturday and Sunday 11 to 2 July 1 through Labor Day; 207-864-5595.*

The Rangeley Lakes Region Historical Society has artifacts and records relating to the era of big hotels and sporting camps, fishing, hunting, logging and railroads and the famous woman fly-tier Carrie Stevens. Housed in a 1905 classical revival-style building, it also has outboard motors dating from the 1930s and a collection of bird's eggs representing every northeastern bird, including carrier pigeons, which the Smithsonian Institution once tried to wrest away. *Main Street; Monday through Saturday 10 to noon mid-June through Labor Day; 207-864-5647.*

Unknown New England

Raymond
Now a community function hall, <u>Nathaniel Hawthorne's boyhood home</u>, was later used as a church and a stagecoach stop. Hawthorne lived here from the time the house was built in 1812 until 1823. *Hawthorne Road.*

The Wilhelm Reich Museum
One of the greatest scientific controversies in American history was rooted in the unlikely setting of the Rangeley Lakes, and the home and laboratory of the colorful protagonist remains to prove it. He was Wilhelm Reich, an Austrian-born protégé of Sigmund Freud whose lifelong study of the sexual orgasm led in the 1940s to a theory of cosmic energy he said could be harnessed to improve health, extend life and even run space ships. Understandably controversial, his work landed him in a federal prison, where he died.

Before he did, however, he built Orgonon, a magnificent estate in Rangeley at whose apex stands his Frank Lloyd Wright-style home and laboratory, designed for him in 1948 and left exactly as it was when he was taken away for the last time in the 1950s. His Philco radio, his record collection and even the local telephone directory for 1954 sit in his office as if awaiting his return. But when he did come back to Orgonon, it was to be buried in a huge stone tomb above which rises his bronze likeness glaring out at a spectacular view of the unspoiled lakes and mountains.

In the inconspicuous but impeccably preserved jewel of a museum, visitors can decide for themselves whether Reich was one of the greatest scientific minds in history, or if he was a fraud who stole from poor and desperate patients—and whose erratic behavior proved that he was insane.

Attracted to Freud's concept of psychic energy, or libido, Reich studied the minute electrical charge on the surface of the human body before, during and after the orgasm, which he concluded was a necessary means of releasing energy that would otherwise build up and create a psychological imbalance.

Reich arrived in the United States at the outset of World War II and extended his work to propose that the electricity released by living organisms was everywhere in the atmosphere. He called it "orgone energy" and built six-sided orgone energy "accumulators" to collect and concentrate it. People who sat inside these cubes, he said, could increase their resistance to illness and extend their lives, in somewhat the same way cancer patients benefit from radiation.

The government brought suit, however, alleging there was no such thing as orgone energy, and that Reich was a fraud. Refusing to defend himself, he was eventually sentenced to federal prison, where he died in 1957.

Reich's house is built from huge stones taken from the foundation of a barn that was once on the property. It holds a collection of instruments, inventions, papers and equipment he used in his experiments—including an orgone meter, which supposedly measured the energy field. An enclosed roof deck, where he had planned a telescope observatory, has unimpeded vistas of the lakes.

The volunteers, and the narrated slide-show introduction, brook no disbelief about Reich and his work, but articles and court documents related to the controversies are displayed discreetly in a quiet space beneath the stairs.

The Wilhelm Reich Museum, Dodge Pond Road, Rangeley; Wednesday through Sunday 1 to 5 July and August, Sunday 1 to 5 in September; 207-864-3443.

Rockland
Endowed by the heirs to a limestone and shipping fortune, the Farnsworth Museum has <u>one of the largest collections of art by the three generations of the Wyeth family</u>—N.C., Andrew, and Jamie Wyeth—with more than 4,000 works by Andrew Wyeth alone. The collection also includes some of the great names in 18th-

Unkown Maine

and 19th-century art, including Gilbert Stuart, Fitz Hugh Lane and Winslow Homer, American Impressionists and contemporary artists including Rockland native Louise Nevelson. *352 Main Street; art galleries daily 9 to 5 Memorial Day through Columbus Day, then Tuesday through Saturday 10 to 5, Sunday 1 to 5; homestead daily 10 to 5 Memorial Day through Columbus Day; 207-596-6457.*

The Shore Village Museum boasts <u>the largest collection of lighthouse artifacts in the United States</u>, including foghorns, rescue gear, and lighthouse lenses dating back to 1790. Housed in a former Coast Guard barracks, it also features Coast Guard artifacts and the bell from <u>the original Nantucket lightship, sunk in 1934 in a collision with the *Titanic*'s sister ship, *Olympic*</u>. *104 Limerock Street; daily 10 to 4 June 1 through mid-October; 207-594-0311.*

Rockport

The 1978 granite statue of Andre memorializes the famous harbor seal that was adopted by a family in Maine in 1961 as a pup and, until his death in 1986, swam 230 miles "home" to Rockport every April. *Rockport Harbor.*

A restored 1770 farmhouse, the Conway Homestead was the home of William Conway, <u>a Union officer who refused to lower the American flag at Pensacola Navy Yard</u> when commanded to do so by Confederate troops during the Civil War. The neighboring museum has an extraordinary four-foot ship model that took one man 20 years to build, with hand-carved figures, carpeting in the deckhouse, and a table set for dinner in the captain's cabin; called the *Minnie Gurney,* it is based on no known actual ship but apparently was named for the builder's sweetheart. *Route 1; Tuesday through Friday 10 to 4 July and August; 207-236-2257.*

Rumford

The first Democratic U.S. Senator elected in Maine history and a 1972 candidate for his party's presidential nomination, <u>Edmund Muskie</u> was born in Rumford on March 28, 1914. Muskie also served as governor. Despite this record, he elicits mixed reactions in his home town, which depended on transporting logs down rivers—a practice he helped end to stop pollution. *8 Hemingway Avenue.*

Saco

The Factory Island Fishway, built so that a hydroelectric dam wouldn't block migrating herring, shad and salmon in the Saco River, is <u>an elevator for fish</u>. The water-filled contraption lifts the fish over the dam to spawn. *Main Street.*

The <u>oldest incorporated city in English-speaking North America</u>, Saco received its royal charter in 1642 under the name Georgiana. Its history is documented at the York Institute Museum, which has <u>the largest collection of portraits by deaf artist John Brewster Jr.</u> *371 Main Street; Tuesday, Wednesday, Friday and Sunday noon to 4, Thursday noon to 8; 207-283-0684.*

Searsport

Focusing on the evolution of sailing vessels from the 17th century to the present, the Penobscot Marine Museum, housed in 13 historic buildings, has <u>one of the finest collections of marine paintings, photographs and artifacts in the country</u>, including 60 fully rigged models of ships built in the Penobscot Bay yards. *Church Street; Monday through Saturday 10 to 5, Sunday noon to 5 Memorial Day through Columbus Day; 207-548-0334.*

Skowhegan

The Margaret Chase Smith Library has a collection of artifacts relating to the career of <u>the first woman elected to both houses of Congress</u>—including Margaret Chase Smith herself; Smith's ashes are among the artifacts on display, which in-

Unknown New England

clude a pin she was given with the symbol of the Apollo program taken into space. The library was built next door to the home where Smith lived. *56 Norridgewock Avenue; Monday through Friday 10 to 4; 207-474-7133.*

South Berwick

The author Sarah Orne Jewett knew firsthand about the 19th-century Maine farmers and townspeople that populated her books, including *The Country of the Pointed Firs*; she spent most of her life in the 1774 Georgian mansion that now is the Sarah Orne Jewett House museum, traveling with her country-doctor father to inland farms and coastal towns. Here Jewett's grandfather, Captain Theodore Jewett, entertained her with tales of running away to sea as a young boy, and his trips to Europe and the Orient. The psychedelic wallpaper looks as if its from the 1960s; it actually was hung here in the 19th century. *5 Portland Street; Wednesday through Sunday 11 to 4 June 1 through mid-October; 207-384-2454.*

Seal Cove

In automaking, the period before chrome was made available for trim is called the brass era (nickel was also often used), and one of the foremost collection of brass-era antique cars is in the Seal Cove Auto Museum, the private collection of Paine Furniture Company founder Richard C. Paine Jr. Most of the 98 automobiles, two trucks and 35 motorcycles here were built before 1915; they include the world's only surviving 1914 Findlay Robertson Porter touring car and the only two remaining Chadwicks in existence, and a 1910 runabout—the first supercharged car, which could travel an unheard-of 115 miles per hour. *Pretty Marsh Road; daily 10 to 5 June 1 through mid-September 15; 207-244-9242.*

South Berwick

South Berwick was home to America's first water-powered sawmill, built in 1634, and many of the items on exhibit in the Counting House Museum relate to this and the area's subsequent industrial activity. The museum itself is in an old textile mill counting house, or office. Also in the collection is a gundalow, a shallow-draft flat-bottom boat used in the area for more than 200 years; gundalows had sails, but generally relied on the tides to take them up and down the river. *Route 4; Saturday and Sunday 1 to 4 July 1 through September 30; 207-384-0000.*

South Bristol

Rebuilt from the 1826 original, the Thompson Ice House commemorates the family-run company that harvested ice from an artificial pond for sale to lobstermen, fishermen and hotels for nearly 160 years before shutting down in 1984, long after the invention of refrigeration. Volunteers still harvest the ice each February, and store it in the building until July, when they use it for an old-fashioned ice cream social. The ice house displays harvesting tools and an antique icebox. *Route 129; Wednesday, Friday and Saturday 1 to 4 July and August; 207-644-8551.*

South Portland

Because it was the major deep-water port closest to Europe that didn't freeze in the winter, Portland Harbor was one of the biggest producer of Liberty ships during World War II; unsung South Portland yards alone built 336 Liberty ships, or 10 percent of the total. Workers' uniforms, badges, tools and plans from this era are in the Portland Harbor Museum, which also has portions of the *Snow Squall*, an America-built clipper ship found in the Falkland Islands long after it was thought that no clippers remained in existence. Portions of the bow of the ship, which was built in Portland in 1852 for the California gold and China trades, are on exhibit. Housed in the cannon repair shop of 19th-century Fort Preble, which stood on this

Unkown Maine

site, the museum is near the only caisson-style lighthouse in America accessible by foot; the rest are offshore, but the Spring Point Ledge Lighthouse can be reached across a breakwater. *Fort Road; daily 10 to 4:30 June through September, Friday through Sunday 10 to 4:30 October, November, April, and May; 207-799-6337.*

Southport

Collected in Indonesia, India, and other exotic places, the 19th-century butterfly collection in the Southport Memorial Library includes at least 100 tropical butterflies that are labeled and catalogued, and hundreds more laid out in a pattern behind glass—a Victorian-era pastime. *1032 Hendrick's Hill Road; Tuesday and Thursday 9 to 11, 1 to 4, and 7 to 9, Saturday 1 to 4; 207-633-2741.*

So realistic are the wooden carvings at the Wendell Gilley Museum of Bird-carving, they look like real birds that have been stuffed and mounted. The museum has more than 200 works by the world-renowned birdcarver, and active carving shops. *4 Herrick Road. Tuesday through Sunday 10 to 4 June 1 through October 31, Friday through Sunday 10 to 4 May, November and December; 207-244-7555.*

Standish

Frances Marrett moved back to her family manse after teaching at the Perkins School for the blind, and the Frances Marrett House is filled with letters and mementos from Helen Keller, her most famous student. There is also a child's rocking horse upholstered in real pony skin. *Route 25; Saturday and Sunday 11 to 4 June 1 through mid-October; 207-642-3032.*

Strong

When Charles Forster traveled to Brazil in the 1860s, he was impressed by the hand-whittled wooden toothpicks used there. So he returned to Maine, invented a way to produce toothpicks mechanically, and opened the factory that has made this the toothpick capital of the world. To introduce the toothpick to America, Forster paid some Harvard students to dine at Boston's Union Oyster House, after which they loudly demanded toothpicks until the management agreed to buy some. Forster Incorporated remains America's largest maker of toothpicks by far, turning out close to 30 million per day—virtually every toothpick made in America. *30 Norton Hill Road.*

Thomaston

Once called "the most beautiful house in Maine; perhaps the most beautiful house in all of New England," the 22-room estate called Montpelier was built in 1793 by General Henry Knox, Revolutionary War artillery commander and first U.S. secretary of war. Knox was the hero who dragged 59 cannon nearly 300 miles from Fort Ticonderoga to New York to break the British siege of Boston in 1775. He later founded the military academy that would become West Point, and even served as acting president of the United States for a few days during a yellow fever epidemic in the capital. His home, now the General Henry Knox Museum, featured such luxuries as whale oil chandeliers and a double flying staircase under a skylight. It is filled with original furnishings and Revolutionary War mementos; Gilbert Stuart's portrait of Knox hangs above one of the circular marble fireplaces. *Route 1; Tuesday through Saturday 10 to 4, Memorial Day through September 30; 207-354-8062.*

The vintage mahogany Chris Craft wooden boat that delivered the mail in the film *On Golden Pond* is in the Maine Watercraft Museum, which exhibits 130 classic, rare, and one-of-a-kind Maine guide boats, rowboats, birch bark and canvas canoes, dories, duck boats—even antique outboard motors. Many can be borrowed and rowed or paddled along the St. John River. *4 Knox Street Landing; Wednesday through Sunday 10 to 5 Memorial Day through Columbus Day; 207-354-0444.*

Unknown New England

Thorndike
An odd stew of <u>stoves, musical instruments and antique cars</u> is the subject of the Bryant Stove and Music Museum, which has stoves dating from the 18th century, nickelodeons, a calliope and, in a Quonset hut, a 1916 Reo, Model T Ford and two Model As. *Rich Road; Monday through Saturday 8 to 4:30; 207-568-3665.*

Van Buren
The Maine Acadians, <u>the northern cousins of the Louisiana Cajuns</u>, celebrate their culture at the Acadian Village, which consists of 16 reconstructed and relocated buildings including a church made out of logs—with an interior as fine as a cathedral's. *Route 1; daily noon to 5 mid-June through mid-September; 207-868-5042.*

Vinalhaven
The mysterious pre-Indian Red Paint people, who are believed to have reddened their faces with iron ore, were the first visitors to Vinalhaven Island as many as 5,000 years ago; like the modern-day residents, they fished and dug for clams. Later settlers branched out into quarrying and other industries, one of the most lucrative the production of twine nets with tassels worn by horses to keep flies away. The Vinalhaven Historical Society and Museum has horse nets and other artifacts from the extraordinarily productive history of the island, named for the attorney, John Vinal, who represented residents in their 1785 attempt to secede from Massachusetts. <u>Vinalhaven quarries produced the granite for such landmarks as the Washington Monument</u>, the base of the Brooklyn Bridge, the Chicago Board of Trade, and the Cathedral of St. John the Divine in New York. *High Street; Tuesday through Saturday 11 to 3 mid-June through Labor Day; 207-863-4410.*

Washburn
When a Pennsylvania food processing company set up its factory here near the potato fields in the late 1940s, it would forever distinguish Washburn as <u>the birthplace of the frozen French fry</u>. That history and more is recounted in the Benjamin C. Wilder Farmstead Museum, a farmhouse that was one of the first homes built when the town was just the Salmon Brook Settlement. *Main Street; Wednesday 8 to 11, Sunday 11 to 4 mid-June through Labor Day; 207-455-4339.*

Waterville
<u>A major collection of American art</u>, the Colby College Museum of Art displays works by Mary Cassatt, John Singleton Copley, Winslow Homer, Gilbert Stuart, and Andrew Wyeth. European paintings and Impressionist art by Courbet, Gauguin, Monet, Picasso and Renoir is shown every two years for one semester. *Colby College; Monday through Saturday 10 to 4:30, Sunday 2 to 4:30; 207-872-3228.*

After his son was killed in an airplane crash in 1960, scientist and businessman Roger Babson gave 500 shares of the American Agricultural Chemical Company to Colby and several other colleges to pay for anti-gravity research. The condition was that the school erect <u>a monument to anti-gravity study</u>, which Colby did. The shares were worth $2.7 million by 1995, when they were cashed in to pay for science equipment and facilities. As for the anti-gravity stone, it was repeatedly, and ironically, tipped over by generations of wise-cracking students until it was finally cemented to a granite base tucked away beside the campus tennis courts.

<u>A complete 19th-century apothecary</u> with a soda fountain and cases made of mahogany and brass and stocked with patent medicines, oils, herbs and extracts has been faithfully reassembled inside the Redington Museum and Apothecary, a home built in 1814 that also exhibits a rare Willard clock. *62 Silver Street; Tuesday through Saturday 10 to 2 Memorial Day through Labor Day; 207-872-9439.*

Unkown Maine

Wells
Named for the marine biologist and author of *Silent Spring* and *The Sea Around Us*, the Rachel Carson National Wildlife Refuge has 1,600 acres of marshland with more than 250 species of birds, including Canada Geese, green-winged teal, and a variety of songbirds. *Route 9; daily dawn to dusk; 207-646-9226.*

Started as a hobby, the collection of antique automobiles at the Wells Auto Museum speedily became New England's largest display of brass-era classic cars, including Stanley Steamers, Rolls Royces, Baker Electrics, Gearless Metzes, Packards and Pierce Arrows—45 makes in all, the oldest dated 1900 and the newest 1963. Less well-known is the museum's extensive display of operating nickelodeons, antique coin games, picture machines, Orchestrions and other arcade items. *1181 Post Road; daily 10 to 5 mid-June through mid-September; 207-646-9064.*

West Forks
Near the place where two rivers meet to form the Kennebec is Moxie Falls, at 90 feet the highest waterfall in New England. An easy foot trail leads to a wooden platform overlooking the dramatic rushing falls. *Route 201.*

Westbrook
Actor and bandleader Rudy Vallee's grave is in the family plot in St. Hyacinth Cemetery. *Stroudwater Street.*

Wilton
Used from 1911 until 1937 as a boarding house for employees of the G.H. Bass Shoe Company, the Wilton Farm and Home Museum has a diverse collection relating to some of the area's most interesting people and things, including giantess Sylvia Hardy, who grew to a height of 7-foot-10 and traveled with what was then known as the Barnum Circus for 15 years, and copies of the Wilton-made Bass boots Charles A. Lindbergh wore on his historic flight to Paris. *Canal Street; Saturday and Sunday 1 to 4 July and August; 207-645-2091.*

Winslow
The oldest wooden blockhouse in the United States until it was swept away by a flood in 1987, Fort Halifax was built to guard the Kennebec River and was a waystation for Benedict Arnold's luckless expedition to Quebec in 1755. An overhanging second story let soldiers fire down at any attackers. A replica now stands on the site. *Bay Street; daily 9 to dusk, Memorial Day through Labor Day; 207-585-2261.*

Wiscasset
Housed in a wedding cake-like 1852 Victorian sea captain's home, the Musical Wonder House Museum boasts one of the world's largest collections of mechanical musical instruments: a cacophony of music boxes, player pianos, reed organs, Victrolas and birds that "sing" when tiny leather bellows pump air through brass slide whistles. *18 High Street; daily 10 to 5 mid-May through Labor Day, then 11 to 3 through October 31; 207-882-7163.*

Yarmouth
More than 41 feet in diameter "Eartha" is the world's largest globe. Made by the DeLorme mapmaking company, the globe is housed in a three-story glass atrium at the company's headquarters and turns at exactly the same speed as the Earth. At the one-one-millionth scale, an inch works out to about 16 miles, making California three and a half feet tall. *Route 1; daily 9:30 to 6; 800-642-0970.*

Unknown New Hampshire

"Live Free or Die" is this state's motto, and so great their sense of independence that its residents can't even agree on that. A little piece of New Hampshire actually broke off to form an autonomous republic in the 19th century, running its own affairs unfettered until an ill-advised invasion of Canada brought an end to the experiment. Today this legacy translates into a preoccupation with politics, and visitors can find little-known collections relating to New Hampshire's first-in-the-nation presidential primary and first-in-the-nation Election Day vote-casting. The birthplace and grave of President Franklin Pierce are here, and the pen with which he signed the Kansas-Nebraska Act in 1854.

New Hampshire's natural beauty and rural culture have inspired authors from Robert Frost to Willa Cather, and literature ranging from *Our Town* to *Peyton Place* to the American edition of "Little Red Riding Hood" and "Mary Had a Little Lamb," by a native writer who also successfully agitated for the holiday of Thanksgiving.

There are museums of snowmobiles, camping, country medicine, scouting, antique radios, cuff-links, trucks, the home front during World War II, and the only Frank Lloyd Wright House in New England open to the public.

Allenstown

Brook State Park was built by the Depression-era Civilian Conservation Corps, and still includes the camp where the workers lived, <u>one of the most complete surviving CCC camps from the 1930s</u>. Opened in October 1935 as part of President Franklin Roosevelt's plan to give public works jobs to the unemployed, the camp was occupied until October 30, 1942. In addition to four of the original cabins and barracks, the park has a museum with photographs and cross-cut saws, fire rakes, axes and other tools used here. *157 Deerfield Road; park daily dawn to dusk, museum daily 10 to 4 Memorial Day through Columbus Day; 603-485-9874.*

<u>The nation's only state-supported antique snowmobile museum</u>, the New Hampshire Snowmobile Museum has more than 80 classic machines, most of them so well-restored the display area looks like a vintage showroom. Among them: a 1953 Eliason Motor Toboggan, a 1961 Polaris Ranger, and the 22nd Ski-doo snowmobile ever sold, manufactured in 1960. While commercial snowmobiles began to be made only in the 1950s and early 1960s, the museum also has earlier machines designed to go in the snow, including a rare 1918 Lombard log-hauler, which was used in the winter to carry logs in Maine, and a Model T Ford converted by Virgil White of Ossipee to run on ice and snow, with skis in place of its front wheels. It was White who patented the word "snowmobile." *Brook State Park; Friday through Monday 10 to 4 Memorial Day through Columbus Day; 603-239-4768.*

Unkown New Hampshire

The <u>Museum of Family Camping</u> has such rudimentary outdoors gear as an 1895 sleeping bag, which weighs 20 times as much as a modern version; a 1930 Norwegian rucksack used by the famous 10th Mountain Division during World War II; a camp stove like one Admiral Robert E. Peary took to the North Pole; and a 1938 travel trailer. There is also a Camping Hall of Fame here, with such celebrated inductees as Theodore Roosevelt, camping equipment manufacturer Sheldon Coleman, and Wally Dyam, the inventor of the Airstream Trailer. *Brook State Park; daily 10 to 4 Memorial Day through Columbus Day; 603-239-4768.*

Amherst

The <u>birthplace of Horace Greeley,</u> editor of the *New York Tribune*, congressman, and candidate for president in 1872, is indicated by a state historic marker. He was born here in 1811. *Route 101 at Horace Greeley Road.*

Andover

A restored 1874 railroad station and general store, the Andover Historical Society has an original Western Union office and a 1914 caboose waiting at the platform. There's also a logboat built by settlers in 1750, which was found preserved at the bottom of a local pond. Behind the station is <u>the grave of Richard Potter, a nationally known black ventriloquist and magician who died in 1834</u>, for whom the neighborhood is named. The museum has copies of his playbills. *Route 4 at Route 11; Saturday 10 to 3, Sunday 1 to 3 May 30 through Columbus Day; 603-735-5694.*

Ashland

<u>A pair of children's shoes worn by Shirley Temple</u> is among the 2,000 artifacts in the Pauline E. Glidden Toy Museum, which also has mechanical tin toys, and vintage games including Uncle Wiggily and Old Maid. Next door is the restored home of Dr. George Whipple, who won the Nobel Prize for medicine in 1934. *Pleasant Street; Wednesday through Saturday 1 to 4 July and August; 603-968-7289.*

Boscawan

<u>A pioneer woman taken hostage by a band of Indians in 1697, Hannah D</u>uston is memorialized here near where she killed 10 of her captors and escaped. Six of those she killed were women and children, and she returned with their scalps to her home town of Haverhill, Massachusetts, to collect a bounty. *Route 3.*

Bretton Woods

On July 1, 1944, as the Nazi occupation of Europe started to be beaten back, the victorious allies met here secretly to work out a post-war economic system, restore the gold standard for the American dollar, and form the International Monetary Fund and World Bank. More than 700 delegates from 44 countries attended the Bretton Woods International Monetary Conference, which was held at the Mount Washington Hotel because it was remote and easily secured. <u>The room where the gold standard was set and the post-war international monetary system hammered out</u> has been preserved by the hotel, complete with the table on which the historic agreement was signed. *Route 302; always open; 603-278-1000.*

Canterbury

<u>More than 200 radios dating from the 1920s through the 1950s</u> are on display in the Antique Radio Museum, including a 1922 Radak, early battery-operated tube radios, a Pilot radio rescued from a ship torpedoed during World War II, cathedral beehive radios, and Bakelite plastic models. There are Zeniths, Majestics, Crossleys, Stromberg-Carlsons and Philcos, and a 1927 RCA, the first with superhetrodyne circuitry. Scratchy period music plays in the background. *164 Brier Bush Road; Tuesday through Saturday 10 to 5, Sunday noon to 5; 603-783-4405.*

Unknown New England

Charlestown

Once the northwesternmost English-speaking village in New England, Charlestown was known simply as No. 4, the fourth plantation authorized by colonial authorities in the area that is now New Hampshire. Settlers built a fort around their small community against Indian attack; in fact, the Fort at No. 4 was assaulted repeatedly in 1746, two years after it was built, and again in 1747 and 1749 during King George's War and other bloody colonial conflicts since largely forgotten. Thirteen of the original buildings have been reconstructed, and re-enactments are held. *Route 11; daily 10 to 4:30 mid-May through mid-October; 603-826-5700.*

Concord

The site of America's first presidential primary, this state now has a museum devoted to New Hampshire's distinction as the most political state in the country; in addition to the famous primary, New Hampshire has the nation's largest state legislature and gubernatorial elections every other year. The Library and Archive of New Hampshire's Political Tradition has primary posters, bumper stickers, and other memorabilia dating back to 1952, when the current system was devised; before then, delegates elected to the national conventions weren't necessarily committed to a particular candidate. There's a rare McGovern-Eagleton button dating from before Senator Thomas Eagleton withdrew as George McGovern's running mate in 1972 after it was revealed that he had been treated for depression; and ballot-counting instruments used to decide the closest senatorial election in history, between John Durkin and Louis Wyman of New Hampshire in 1976, which was decided by one vote. *20 Park Street; Monday through Friday 8 to 4:30; 603-271-2397.*

The pen with which President Franklin Pierce signed the Kansas-Nebraska Act in 1854 to forestall the Civil War (but possibly hastening it), is in the Museum of New Hampshire History, which also has furniture that belonged to Pierce, a New Hampshire native, including a chair he used in the White House. Another native son, Daniel Webster, who was born in Franklin and graduated from Dartmouth, is represented here by his flask, his watch, and a lock of his hair. There also is a swatch of silk given to a newborn girl at sea by a pirate. The pirate, Don Pedro, agreed to spare the lives of everyone on the ship if the girl was named Mary after his mother, and he gave her the silk to be made into her future wedding dress. It was, and the dress was also used by the daughter, granddaughter and great-granddaughter of the woman who would come to be known as "Ocean-Born Mary." *6 Eagle Square; Monday through Wednesday, Friday and Saturday 9:30 to 5, Thursday 9:30 to 8:30, Sunday noon to 5 July through mid-October, then Tuesday, Wednesday, Friday and Saturday 9:30 to 5, Thursday 9:30 to 8:30, Sunday noon to 5; 603-228-6688.*

The grave of President Franklin Pierce is in the Old North Cemetery. *North State Street at Keane Avenue.*

The grave of schoolteacher-astronaut Christa McAuliffe is in Calvary Cemetery here in her home town. McAuliffe died January 28, 1986, in the explosion of the space shuttle *Challenger*. *North State Street.*

The English boys' school influence is evident in the chapel at St. Paul's School, designed in 1888 by Henry Vaughan, architect of the National Cathedral: students and masters face each other, rather than the altar. There also is a copy of Lorenzet-ti's fresco at Assisi, and two Calders on the grounds. *Pleasant Street; 603-229-4600.*

Unkown New Hampshire

Conway
More than 65,000 cuff-links and related items are in the one-of-a-kind Cuff-Link Museum, including onyx-and-silver styled, flowers in glass, and whole alphabets of engraved initials. *71 Hobbs Street; by appointment; 603-447-8500.*

Cornish
The home of the sculptor Augustus Saint-Gaudens has been maintained as a museum to him, with copies of his most famous works from their original casts—including his 1881 statue of Civil War Admiral David Farragut, his 1897 bas-relief of the all-black 54th Massachusetts Regiment, and designs for U.S. coins. Saint-Gaudens came to Cornish in 1885, renting an old inn for the summer and eventually buying it. He designed the grounds and converted a barn into a huge studio. Saint-Gaudens died here in 1907 at the age of 59. *139 Saint Gaudens Road (Route 12A); daily 9 to 4:30 Memorial Day through October 31; 603-675-2175.*

The 450-foot bridge over the Connecticut River connecting Cornish with Windsor, Vermont, is the longest covered wooden bridge in the United States and the longest two-span covered bridge in the world. *Route 12A.*

Derry
The farm that was the setting for 43 poems by Robert Frost has been restored right down to the kerosene lamps and wood stoves like those he would have used when he lived here from 1906 until 1911. Frost farmed here while teaching at nearby Pinkerton Academy and writing the poetry for which he was to win the Pulitzer Prize four times. Excerpts from his writings mark a hiking trail. *Route 28; Saturday and Sunday 10 to 5 Memorial Day through Columbus Day; 603-432-3091.*

The Pinkerton Academy museum has photographs related to local hero Alan Shepard, Class of 1940, the first American in space; and the uniform and medals of General Mason Young, Class of 1911, who went ashore on D-Day. *5 Pinkerton Street Monday through Friday 9 to 2 Labor Day through mid-June; 603-437-5217.*

Dixville Notch
The room where the nation's first presidential votes are cast at 12:01 a.m. each Election Day is kept as a museum the rest of the time. The walls of the Ballot Room are covered with photographs of every political candidate who ever visited, most long forgotten. There's a football given by Jack Kemp, Lamar Alexander's red plaid shirt, presidential candidate trading cards, and the ballot box itself, which turns out to have been made by prison inmates. *The Balsams, Route 26; daily Memorial Day through mid-October and mid-December until March 31; 603-255-3400.*

Durham
At a time when they're tough to find even in the American West, it's downright surprising to find a herd of buffalo roaming around New England. Yet the Little Bay Buffalo Company has introduced a herd of American bison to a wildlife estate here and gives tours in covered wagons. Bison once numbered in the tens of millions, but became virtually extinct after white settlement of the West and Midwest. *50 Langley Road; daily 10 to 5 April 1 through October 31, daily 10 to dusk November 1 through March 31, observation area daily 9 to sunset; 603-868-3300.*

Exeter
An original copy of the American Constitution—one of only nine known to exist—is in the American Independence Museum, which occupies the building that served as the state treasury when Exeter was the capital of New Hampshire. Governor John Taylor Gilman lived in the house during his 14 terms as governor, ending in 1816. The complex also encompasses the Folsom Tavern, built by Colonel

Unknown New England

Samuel Folsom, where George Washington ate breakfast on November 4, 1789. Among other things, the museum has a lock of Washington's hair, and drafts of the Constitution with handwritten notes taken by New England delegates when it was being worked out by the Continental Congress. *One Governors Lane; Wednesday through Sunday 10 to 5, Sunday 11 to 5 May 1 through October 31; 603-772-2622.*

On January 5, 1776, New Hampshire's Provincial Congress adopted the first state constitution in America. There is a marker on the site of the Exeter Town House, where the document was signed. *Court and Front streets.*

Built in 1690 to protect its occupants and their nearby sawmill against the constant threat of Indian attack, the Gilman Garrison House has walls of massive logs and a pulley above the main entrance that was used to operate a reinforced door. *12 Water Street; by appointment; 603-436-3205.*

The bronze World War I memorial, "Mother Town and Soldier Son," was cast by Exeter-born sculptor Daniel Chester French, who designed the likeness of President Abraham Lincoln in the Lincoln Memorial. *Gale Park.*

Franconia

The weathered farmhouse where Robert Frost lived with his family after their return from England in 1915 now is home to a rare collection of his least-known work: Christmas card verses he wrote and printed privately for friends. Among other writings, this site was the inspiration for Frost's "Stopping by Woods on a Snowy Evening," which he wrote in the flyleaf of a book on display here, helping later to clear up some confusion about the punctuation. There are signed first editions of all his books, along with Frost's writing table, his Morris chair, and a spectacular view of the White Mountains. Frost lived here full- or part-time until 1938. *Ridge Road; Saturday and Sunday 1 to 5 Memorial Day through June 30, Wednesday through Monday 1 to 5 July 1 through Columbus Day; 603-823-5510.*

Franklin

The birthplace of Daniel Webster was here in a two-room wood-frame house his father built beside a rocky farm before going off to fight in the Revolutionary War. Webster was born on January 18, 1782, and went on to graduate from Dartmouth College and become a noted lawyer, orator, senator and secretary of state. The house has been restored to its original appearance and location, and has displays of Webster family possessions including crockery and a cradle. *Route 127; Saturday and Sunday noon to 5 Memorial Day through Labor Day; 603-934-5057.*

Fremont

Not all northerners were enthusiastic about the Civil War. In Fremont, it sparked a riot. In fact, this town has been the site of no fewer than four historic riots. When the king ordered that the best white pine trees be reserved for Royal Navy masts in 1734, for example, the locals balked and cut them anyway for their houses and other buildings. And when David Dunbar, the surveyor general, showed up to find out what had happened to the trees, he was attacked and chased off by citizens disguised as Indians near what is today Route 107 at Route 111A. Then in 1757, an armed mob threatened to kill the search party of British soldiers that had come to imprison a deserter from the French and Indian War. On July 4, 1861, while residents were raising a Union flag on a liberty pole, a southern sympathizer shot at it, and a melee ensued at what is now the intersection of Sandown Road and Route 107. And in 1874, Irish laborers building the Worcester-to-Nashua Railroad caroused through Fremont on St. Patrick's Day, leaving people injured and houses damaged. The town's tiny historical museum chronicles these disturbances.

Unkown New Hampshire

It also has pieces of a B-52 bomber that crashed in the town on August 10, 1959, with no loss of life. *225 South Road; by appointment; 603-895-4032.*

The New England Ski Museum

It's hard to believe that anybody bothered to ski for recreation in the first half of this century, at least judging by the vintage skiwear and equipment on display at the New England Ski Museum. Early skiers had to walk uphill on heavy wooden boards with primitive metal bear-trap bindings, the women dressed in heavy woolen shirts and the men in shirts and ties. Then they picked their way down logging roads or along remote crude trails they had cleared themselves. So many skiers broke their bones, they gave each other medals for it.

All of this—100 years of skis, clothes, boots, bindings, broken-bone pins and other skiing art and artifacts—is on exhibit now to modern skiers who complain if there's a line at the bar in the base lodge when the lifts close.

The museum, in a renovated highway garage at the foot of the nation's first and oldest aerial tramway in New Hampshire's White Mountains, traces the growth of the sport and the technology that fueled it—rope tows, for example, in the 1930s, windproof nylon in the 1940s, fiberglass in the 1950s, molded plastic in the 1960s.

Immigrants from Scandinavia brought downhill skiing to New England when they were hired by the northern logging companies and railroads. They formed ski clubs to cut trails through the woods in spring and summer and skied wearing their usual winter clothes, including moccasins and farm boots.

Students in the region's wealth of colleges took up the sport in the early 1900s, and many helped perpetuate it after graduating. But the greatest single boost came during the Depression, when the Civilian Conservation Corps carved downhill trails out of rugged wooded mountainsides.

C. Minot Dole, a Greenwich, Connecticut, insurance broker, organized the National Ski Patrol in 1938, and the museum has a display devoted to him with his uniform jacket still proudly sporting medals showing that he three times broke his bones while skiing. It was Dole who convinced the government in 1941 to form the 10th Mountain Division, a specialized ski infantry that came to be comprised of Ivy League skiers, cowboys, mule skinners, forest rangers and ski instructors. Nearly 1,000 were killed in the war, but they were credited with breaking the German front in northern Italy by making a 1,500-foot vertical night ascent up a rock face in the Apennine Mountains.

The 10th is generously represented in the ski museum, which displays a full set of the 122 pounds of equipment and supplies each ski trooper had to carry and charts their missions from the Alps to the Aleutians, where 23 died accidentally after finding that Japanese occupiers already had evacuated the Alaskan islands.

The New England Ski Museum is at the base of the Cannon Mountain tramway, Exit 2 on the Franconia Notch Parkway (Interstate 93) in Franconia. It is open daily noon to 5 Memorial Day through Columbus Day and December 1 through March 31. Call 603-823-7177.

Gilmanton

Welcome to the real *Peyton Place*, the inspiration for resident and writer Grace Metalious, whose 1956 best-seller was followed by a movie and TV series of the same name. "To a tourist," she once said, "these towns look as peaceful as a postcard. But if you go beneath the picture, it's like turning over a rock with your foot. All kinds of strange things crawl out." Metalious, who died of liver disease at 39, is buried in Smith Meeting House Cemetery.

Unknown New England

Grafton
The nation's first commercial mica mine, Ruggles Mine was discovered in 1803 by Sam Ruggles, who was so concerned that someone else would find it he snuck the mica at night to Portsmouth and had it shipped to relatives in England. Since then, beryl, amethyst, quartz, 150 other minerals have been mined here, leaving giant rooms and tunnels with shining walls. *Route 4; Saturday and Sunday 9 to 5 mid-May through mid-June, daily 9 to 5 mid-June through mid-October; 603-523-4275.*

Hampton
Unlike her counterparts in Massachusetts, the only person to be convicted of witchcraft in New Hampshire wasn't executed, though she may have wished she had been. Goodwife "Goody" Eunice Cole was 64 in 1658 when she was found guilty, lashed with a whip and thrown in jail after local children testified that they had seen her conversing with the devil, who they described as a black dwarf in a red cap. Blamed for the death of cattle, the loss of a fishing boat, and other catastrophes, she was jailed for 15 years while her husband's property was confiscated, leaving him destitute and landless at 88; she was even charged with the cost of keeping her in prison. In 1673, she was arrested again for having "familiarity with the devil," and when she died, a mob reportedly drove a stake through her heart. The town did eventually apologize—300 years later, in 1938—officially clearing Goody Cole of all charges, and burning copies of the trial documents. The ashes are kept in an urn in the Tuck Museum. The birthplace of Amos Tuck, co-founder of the Republican Party, is also here, at 89 Front Street, now a private home; the museum was a gift from his son, Edward, U.S. ambassador to France. *40 Park Avenue; Tuesday, Friday and Sunday 1 to 4 June 1 through Labor Day; 603-929-0781.*

Hanover
The cottage where Daniel Webster boarded during his senior year at Dartmouth College has the fire bucket with his initials on it he was required to keep filled with sand, and the desk, clock, cane stand and hat rack from the office he used when he was secretary of state. *32 North Main Street; Wednesday, Saturday and Sunday 2:30 to 4:30 Memorial Day through Columbus Day; 603-646-3371.*

Shakespeare folios, Robert Frost's notebooks, a first edition of John James Audubon's *Birds of America* originally owned by Daniel Webster, and more than 150 works printed before 1501 comprise some of the treasures of the Baker Memorial Library at Dartmouth College. Items from the collection are displayed on a rotating basis in the main corridor, including the anomometer reading from the world's greatest gust of wind: 231 miles per hour, recorded on Mount Washington on April 12, 1934. *East Wheelock Street; Monday through Friday 8to 4:30; 603-646-2037.*

With more than 60,000 objects, the Hood Museum of Art is one of the largest university art collections in America. It includes works by Rembrandt, Goya, Toulouse-Lautrec, Picasso, Matisse, John Singleton Copley, Gilbert Stuart, Frederic Remington, and Georgia O'Keeffe; a set of Assyrian reliefs dating to about 883 BC from the Northwest Palace of Ashurnasirpal II at Nimrud; and a collection of propaganda posters from the world wars. *Wheelock Street; Tuesday, Thursday, Friday and Saturday 10 to 5, Wednesday 10 to 9, Sunday noon to 5; 603-646-2808.*

Hillsboro
A one-of-a-kind collection of vintage trucks, many of them rusting and with flat tires, Kemp's Mack Truck Museum includes an early snowplow with a wooden blade, ancient earth-movers, an antique cement mixer named Stubby and 100 other classic American trucks. *21 River Road; daily dawn to dusk; 603-464-3386.*

Unkown New Hampshire

Built in 1804 by Benjamin Pierce, a hero in his own right as a general in the American Revolution and two-time governor of New Hampshire, the childhood home of President Franklin Pierce—his son—now is a museum of family memorabilia, including items from the White House. Franklin Pierce was born in Hillsboro on November 23, 1804, and moved here shortly afterwards. A Mexican War veteran, he would become known as "Young Hickory of the Granite Hills." The house has one of two copies by Pedro Gualdi of the surrender of the Mexican government to the American army in Mexico City, a sofa from Pierce's outer office in the White House, an 1852 campaign poster, and the corset he wore on horseback when he was riding in parades. There are also items relating to Pierce's three sons, none of whom lived to adulthood, including a collection of seashells he gave to his longest-surviving son, Benny, who died in a train accident when he was 11 while the family was traveling to Washington. Pierce's wife, as a result, wore black during his entire term. *Route 9 at Route 31; Monday through Saturday 10 to 4, Sunday 1 to 4 July and August; Saturday 10 to 4, Sunday 1 to 4 June and September; 603-478-3165.*

Jaffrey

Virginia-born and Nebraska-bred, Willa Cather is buried here near Mount Monadnock, with her companion for 38 years, Edith Lewis. Cather wrote the book *My Antonia* during the summers she spent here, and won the Pulitzer Prize in 1923 for *One of Ours*, based on the life of a Jaffrey doctor. She died on April 24, 1947. Local legend has it that Cather haunts the house that now obstructs her view of her beloved mountain. *Old Burying Ground, Jaffrey Center.*

Also buried in the Old Burying Ground is Amos Fortune, one of the first African-born freed slaves in America, who settled here and ran a successful tanning business, becoming one of the leading citizens and bequeathing money for the local church and schools. He died in 1801 at the age of 91.

The diary of Dr. Frederick Sweeney, a physician who served in World War I and who was the inspiration for Willa Cather's Pulitzer Prize-winning *One of Ours*, is in the Jaffrey Historical Society museum, along with a copy of the book inscribed by her to Sweeney. The collection also includes the papers proving Amos Fortune had been freed, and a lock of Paul Revere's hair. But perhaps the most unusual materials relate to the unsolved murder of Dr. William Dean on August 13, 1918, a crime purportedly committed by a spy who signaled German U-boats from the top of Mount Monadnock. Dean's body was found bound and dumped in a well the day after he mysteriously asked a summer resident to contact the authorities in Boston on her return there, and tell them he had information for them. The town banker, who showed up the next day with bruises on his face, was suspected by half the town; Dean's missing tenant, who had a German surname, by the other half. The ropes, shoes, and bloody blanket Dean was wearing when his body was discovered, examined fruitlessly by a grand jury, are all in the museum. *40 Main Street; Tuesday 10 to 6, Wednesday through Friday 1 to 5, Saturday 10 to 1; 603-532-6527.*

Jefferson

Gas balloons had been used in Europe for reconnaissance, but pioneer Jefferson-born aeronaut Thaddeus S.C. Lowe was the first to press them into service in America as the organizer of a little-known military balloon observation force for Union forces in the Civil War. Lowe even rigged up a telegraph line between his balloon and the ground, and pinpointed vulnerable Confederate camps during night flights. There is a marker near his birthplace here. *Route 2.*

Keene

Horatio Colony, a Harvard graduate and heir to a woolen mill fortune, spent his life traveling and writing historical novels about the West. He also had an eye for

Unknown New England

the unusual, and the collection he amassed is now in the 1806 Federal-style mansion where he lived, including <u>one of the foremost collections of antique cribbage boards</u>. *Horatio Colony House Museum, 199 Main Street; Wednesday through Saturday 11 to 4 May 1 through October 15; 603-352-0460.*

Littleton

So attached were they to the team of three matched bay Morgan horses they kept from 1889 until 1919, a childless couple named Wallace buried each of them under a human-style formal gravestone. *Mount Eustis Road.*

The Kilburn Brothers Stereoscopic View Factory was established in Littleton by a pair of siblings to escape having to go into their father's foundry business. It became one of the world's leading manufacturers of stereoscopes—photographs that appeared three-dimensional when seen through a viewer, a popular Victorian-era entertainment. <u>The largest public collection of stereoscopes in the country</u> is in the Littleton Public Library, which has about 10,000 of the antique images. *92 Main Street; Tuesday through Friday 9 to 7, Saturday 9 to 2; 603-444-5741.*

Manchester

<u>The only Frank Lloyd Wright house in New England open to the public</u>, Zimmerman House was designed for Isadore and Lucille Zimmerman in 1950 and built of brick and cypress wood; Wright also designed the landscaping, furniture, drapery, carpeting, and even the mailbox. Next door is the Currier Gallery of Art, another hidden treasure, with paintings by Picasso, Monet, Georgia O'Keeffe, Winslow Homer and Andrew Wyeth, and sculpture by Henri Matisse and Augustus Saint-Gaudens. *201 Myrtle Way; house by appointment, museum Sunday, Monday, Wednesday, Friday 11 to 5, Thursday 11 to 8, Saturday 10 to 5; 603-669-6144.*

<u>One of the largest collections of scouting memorabilia in the world</u>, the Lawrence L. Lee Scouting Museum has uniforms, patches, handbooks, and other memorabilia dating back to the beginning of the Boy Scouts in the United States in 1910. It also has <u>a flag carried to the moon by first astronaut and New Hampshire scout Alan Shepard</u>; and artifacts related to Robert Baden-Powell, British-born founder of the scouting movement and hero of the Boer War, including stamps issued at Mafeking during the year-long siege of that town in 1899. *571 Holt Avenue; daily 10 to 4 July and August, then Saturday 10 to 4; 603-669-8919.*

Built during the late 1800s, Amoskeag Dam blocked salmon from swimming upstream to spawn. A fish "ladder" of 54 graduated pools has since been built, with observation windows underwater to watch the fish run. There is also a visitor center with an aquarium. *Fletcher Street; daily 9 to 6 early May through mid-June for spawning season, then Monday through Saturday 9 to 5; 603-626-3474.*

Mason

<u>The home of Little Red Riding Hood</u>, Pickity Place was the model for Elizabeth Orton Jones, who adapted the original German folk tale into the Golden Book version in 1944. Orton's own home inspired Riding Hood's house, but Grandmother lived at Pickity Place, a 1788 farmhouse that is now a restaurant with Riding Hood memorabilia in the low-ceilinged room Jones used as the model for Grandmother's bedroom. The white ash tree in the yard will also be familiar to readers. *Notting Hill Road; lunch by reservation; 603-878-1151.*

Meredith

Created in 1934 by Annalee Thorndike, the Annalee doll line is equally popular with children and collectors, as evidenced by the Annalee Doll Museum, a recreation of Thorndike's girlhood home that looks like a gigantic dollhouse. There are more than 1,500 dolls here, so many that only about a third can be displayed at one time. They include dolls resembling celebrities. *Route 104 at Route 106; daily 9 to 5 Memorial Day through Columbus Day; 800-433-6557.*

Moltonborough

You'll likely be shocked ... *shocked* ... to find the grave of actor Claude Rains in New Hampshire. Famous for his portrayal of Captain Louis Renault in *Casablanca*, Rains died in 1967 and is buried in Red Hill Cemetery. *Bean Road.*

New Castle

When British troops set out for New Castle to protect the fort at Castle William & Mary on December 13, 1774, Paul Revere was sent north from Boston to warn the New Hampshire militiamen, 400 of whom raided the fort and stole gunpowder, cannon and all the small arms and ammunition they could carry off from the hopelessly outnumbered garrison of six defenders. Paul Revere's other ride, which led to one of the first overt acts of the American Revolution, helped supply the patriots with the supplies they'd need at the outset of the war that would begin four months later in Lexington and Concord. Later renamed Fort Constitution, the fort was decommissioned in 1961. *Main and Wentworth streets; daily 8 to 4:30; 603-436-1552.*

Newport

Best known as author of the poem "Mary Had a Little Lamb," Sarah Josepha Hale also was the mother of Thanksgiving, who used her position as editor of a woman's magazine called *Godey's Lady's Book* to promote the idea of the holiday until President Abraham Lincoln made it official in 1863. The Sarah Josepha Hale Room in the Richards Free Library has bound copies of the magazine, and first editions of Hale's books, including *Northwood*, an anti-slavery work that predated *Uncle Tom's Cabin*, and a letter from Edgar Allen Poe thanking her for publishing his work. The site of her home is on Route 103. *58 North Main Street; Monday 1 to 6, Tuesday and Thursday 10 to 8, Wednesday and Friday 10 to 6, Saturday 10 to 2; 603-863-3430.*

Named for pioneering New Hampshire archeologist Howard Sargent, the Sargent Museum of Archeology contains Sargent's lifelong collection of artifacts, including a piece of the *USS Constitution,* a nail from Paul Revere's house, a giant shark's tooth, and petrified dinosaur dung. There are also about 10,000 Indian objects, many of them from a well-preserved village dating from 1200 AD unearthed by a new highway and revealing that area Indians created strikingly beautiful pottery and lived in longhouses made of bark over frameworks of saplings. *10 Center Street; Tuesday, Thursday, Sunday 10 to 4; 603-229-4966.*

North Conway

A railroad station built in 1874 that looks as if it might have inspired Walt Disney, the North Conway Depot is the home of a commercial scenic railroad, but also has a museum in its restored waiting room, with old lanterns, timetables, uniforms, and other artifacts. Outside is the original four-stall roundhouse and turntable, where railway cars and engines are usually parked, including a Pennsylvania Limited Pullman parlor car built in 1898; and a freight house that serves as the home of the North Conway Model Railroad Club. It was also here that, on December 3, 1876, Alexander Graham Bell and his assistant, Thomas A. Watson, attempted the first long-distance telephone call, trying to hold a conversation over telegraph wires between the station's ticket office and Boston, 143 miles distant. They failed. *Route 16; station opens one hour prior to first scheduled departure and closes at 6 p.m. or immediately following departure of seasonal dinner train, Saturday and Sunday mid-April through mid-June, daily mid-June through October 31, Saturday and*

Unknown New England

Sunday November and December; freight house Tuesday and Saturday July 1 through Memorial Day; 603-356-5251.

Northfield
Exasperated by a state decision to build costly artificial wetlands in place of a small natural area that was filled in by a highway project, local residents have organized the Artificial Wildlife Preserve, doubtless the only protected area for nesting plastic pink flamingos. The town's tongue-in-cheek Artificial Wildlife Preserve Act of 1996 prohibits the removal of artificial wildlife from the preserve without written permission, and applies to "any natural person, including but not limited to employees of the New Hampshire Department of Transportation," who are said to have been unamused by the hijinks. So far, the hard work seems to be paying off; pink plastic eggs have even been found in several nests. *Exit 19 on Interstate 93.*

North Hampton
The grave of the poet Ogden Nash is in East Side Cemetery. *Woodland Road and Atlantic Avenue.*

Peterborough
The place where Thornton Wilder wrote *Our Town*, Peterborough was one of several New Hampshire communities Wilder depicted. The final scene takes place in Peterborough's Old Cemetery on Old Street Road; the milkman was based on Fletcher Dole, who delivered milk to the writer's colony where Wilder was staying.

Pittsburg
Tired of being forced to pay customs duties to both Canada and the United States because of a long-running border dispute, part of this small town broke off on July 9, 1832, into the independent Republic of Indian Stream, a self-governing country with its own constitution, assembly and 40-man militia. The little republic lasted for nearly 10 years until it ill-advisedly invaded Canada when a resident was taken forcibly across the border on a criminal warrant. The good news was that people finally began to pay attention, and the publicity hastened the settlement of the border dispute by the Webster-Ashburton Treaty on August 9, 1842, when Indian Spring officially became a part of New Hampshire once again. The short-lived Republic of Indian Spring is commemorated by an historical marker. *Route 3.*

Portsmouth
Conscious of the pivotal role played by the submarine in World War II, the Navy began to develop a nuclear propulsion system and a streamlined submarine hull even before the war was over. The result: the *USS Albacore*, the forerunner of the nuclear submarine, launched from the Portsmouth Naval Shipyard on October 12, 1955. The ship spent her career undergoing tests before being decommissioned in 1972. Today the *Albacore* sits permanently drydocked in a tiny park, and is open to the public. *600 Market Street; daily 9:30 to 5 Memorial Day through Columbus Day Day, then Thursday through Monday 9:30 to 4; 603-436-3680.*

Built in 1807 by merchant James Rundlet, the Rundlet-May House was far ahead of its time, with an indoor well and privy, a coal-fired central heating system, an elaborate ventilation system, and pioneering on-demand hot water. Restored to its earliest appearance, the house still has its original imported English wallpaper. There is also a cemetery on the property for the family pets. *364 Middle Street; Saturday and Sunday 11 to 5 July 1 through Labor Day; 603-436-3205.*

Rindge
The first monument to American women who gave their lives for their country, the Memorial Bell Tower was built in 1967 and is decorated with four bas reliefs designed by Norman Rockwell showing pioneer women, wartime working women,

Unkown New Hampshire

servicewomen, and Red Cross founder Clara Barton. The tower is at the Cathedral of the Pines, a memorial to B-17 bomber pilot Sanderson Sloane, who was shot down over Berlin in 1944. There's a stone in the altar given by every president since Harry Truman. *Route 119; daily 9 to 5 May 1 through October 31; 603-899-3300.*

The house where Franklin Pierce lived after leaving the Senate and returning to his home state to practice law in 1842, the Pierce Manse is a mid-1830s Greek Revival-style mansion. Inside is Pierce's tophat and a sofa he brought to the White House when he went back to Washington as the 14th president in 1853. *14 Penacook Street; Monday through Friday 11 to 3 June 15 through Labor Day; 603-225-2068.*

Salem

A mysterious collection of stone caverns and large, shaped standing boulders reminiscent of Stonehenge, Mystery Hill is believed to be at least 4,000 years old. Still unexplained, the strange arrangement has been attributed to everyone from native Americans to Irish monks to Vikings. Its monolithic stones align with sunrise and sunset during the midwinter solstice and fall equinox, and with true north. There are also underground chambers, including one dated to 710 AD, and a "speaking tube" that carries speech into what experts believe may have been an ancient altar. *Haverhill Road; daily 9 to 5 February 1 through mid-June and Labor Day through October 31, daily 9 to 7 mid-June through September 1, daily 9 to 4 November 1 through January 31; 603-893-8300.*

Stark

With a high fence and four guard towers added, a closed Civilian Conservation Corps camp was converted in 1944 into Camp Stark, a prisoner-of-war camp for German and Austrian soldiers captured in North Africa, who were put to work cutting trees in the surrounding forest. The ruins of the camp can still be seen. *Route 110.*

Stewartstown

This town is on the 45th parallel, placing it exactly halfway between the Equator and the North Pole. *Route 3.*

Sugar Hill

Celebrities including Bette Davis, Eleanor Roosevelt, Joan Fontaine, Mary Martin, and John D. Rockefeller once summered in the elegant hotels here; Davis married the manager of one, and bought a summer home so big she decorated the living room with an antique sleigh. Bette Davis's horse-drawn sleigh is now parked at the Sugar Hill Historical Museum, which also has flatware, silverware, menus, and other artifacts from the old hotels, and early skis and equipment from America's first ski school, opened here in 1929 by Austrian Sig Buchmayr at what is now Route 117 and Lover's Lane Road. In the early 1800s, Sugar Hill was a stop on the stagecoach route to Canada, and the museum has a re-creation of the kitchen from the Cobleigh Tavern, where passengers stayed overnight. *Route 117; Thursday, Saturday and Sunday 1 to 4 July 1 through October 31; 603-823-5336.*

Sunapee

On the shores of Lake Sunapee, the Sunapee Historical Society Museum focuses on the steamboats that once traversed this lake. Among other things, it has the pilot house of the *SS Kearsage,* built in 1897, which sank in 1935. *Sunapee Harbor; Tuesday, Thursday, Friday, Saturday and Sunday 1 to 5, Wednesday 1 to 5 and 7 to 9 July and August; 603-763-9872.*

Unknown New England

Sutton
Sutton is the birthplace of baking baron John Sargent Pillsbury, who moved to Minneapolis in 1855, founded the famous flour milling company that bears his name, and served as governor of Minnesota. *Route 114 at Meetinghouse Hill Road.*

Tamworth
A reminder of a faded age of medicine, the Remick Country Doctor Museum commemorates real-life father-and-son country doctors Edwin and Edwin Crafts Remick, who treated patients from 1894 to 1993. It has replicas of their offices and the original medical bags, instruments, and drugs they carried while making house calls—traveling 80,000 miles a year, on average, the father in carriages and sleds displayed here in a barn, and later in a Model T Ford converted by Virgil White of Ossipee to run on ice and snow, with skis in place of the front wheels. *58 Cleveland Hill Road; Monday through Saturday 10 to 4 Memorial Day through Columbus Day, then Monday through Friday 10 to 4; 800-686-6117.*

After the death of his daughter, Ruth, a distraught former President Grover Cleveland spent two quiet summers here in a house now privately owned. A memorial to him marks the entrance. *Cleveland Hill and Brown Hill roads.*

Tilton
The collection of antique trains at the former freight house here is not a museum; it's a depot for railroad enthusiasts who have restored, among others, a vintage plow car, a diesel engine from the old Concord-to-Lincoln line, old cabooses, and the ornate private car used by the president of the Vermont Central. *Route 11.*

Wakefield
Collected throughout their lifetimes by a pair of retired schoolteacher sisters, the Museum of Childhood has 3,500 dolls and toys, including puppets, sleds, trains, and stuffed animals, the oldest hand-made in 1869 from a sock filled with sawdust. *2784 Wakefield Road; Wednesday through Saturday and Monday 11 to 4, Sunday 1 to 4 Memorial Day through Labor Day; 603-522-8073.*

Walpole
The piano Louisa May Alcott described in *Little Women* is in the Old Academy Museum here, in the town where the Alcotts spent their summers. *Main Street; Wednesday and Saturday 2 to 4 mid-June through September 30; 603-756-3449.*

Warren
Convinced it would encourage local schoolchildren to study science, a military veteran arranged to put a Redstone rocket in the center of this small town. The towering rocket is the same type that put New Hampshire native Alan Shepard's *Freedom 7* into orbit in 1961, making him the first American in space. *Town Common.*

Warner
The Mount Kearsage Indian Museum in the foothills of 2,937-foot Mount Kearsage tells the story not only of the peoples native to New England, but across North America in displays meant to show life as it was for the continent's original inhabitants, from a simulated woodland to an open plain. Also on display are baskets, beadwork, fishing equipment, moosehair and porcupine quill embroidery, pottery, dugout canoes, and containers made of bark. *Kearsage Mountain Road; Monday through Saturday 10 to 5, Sunday noon to 5 May 1 through October 31, Saturday 10 to 5, Sunday noon to 5 November and December. 603-456-2600.*

Unkown New Hampshire

Washington
After meeting informally for years, a small group of residents here founded a new sect of Adventism in 1842 based on the belief that Christ's second coming was near, and setting the Sabbath on Sunday, the seventh day. The site of the first Seventh Day Adventist Church is opposite the town common. *Millen Pond Road.*

Wolfeboro
The home front during World War II is the unusual theme of the Wright Museum of American Enterprise, distinctive for the military tank "crashing" out of its façade. Among other things, the museum has 1940s ration stamps, gas pumps, cars, a soda fountain, Civil Defense uniforms, a console radio carrying the war news, and military vehicles including Jeeps, command cars, half-tracks and motorcycles. There's a tribute to Rene Gagnon, one of the Marines who raised the flag at Iwo Jima, with his uniforms, medals and other mementos; the only surviving American tank that crossed the Rhine; the map of Europe used by the Eighth Air Force in its ready room in England; and one of the largest exhibits about the role of women in World War II. *77 Center Street; Monday through Saturday 10 to 4, Sunday noon to 4 May 1 through November 1, Saturday 10 to 4 and Sunday noon to 4 November and February through April; 603-569-1212.*

A country dentist, Dr. Henry Libby had an unquenchable curiosity that by the end of his life had left him with a museum's-worth of natural history artifacts, from primate skeletons to stuffed alligators. Today they are displayed as he arranged them in the Libby Museum, which Libby built himself to hold his vast collection. Skeletons trace the evolution from ape to man, and there are even skeletons of rattlesnakes and caribou, plus stuffed moose, deer, birds, porcupines, and other animals. The view of Lake Winnipesaukee from the museum is unrivaled. *Route 109; Tuesday through Sunday 10 to 4 Memorial Day through Labor Day; 603-569-1035.*

Unknown Rhode Island

For New England's smallest state, Rhode Island has a lot of nooks and crannies crowded with surprises. The highly developed culture of the native Americans who lived here, for example, and were manufacturing items for trade up and down the East Coast thousands of years before Europeans arrived. These Indians resisted white settlement in the mostly forgotten King Philip's War, whose bloodiest battles occurred here—including the death of the Indian leader Metacom.

There is also an unexpected military tradition, which turned out such Revolutionary War leaders as General Nathanael Greene and General James Varnum, who George Washington called "the light of the camp" during the dark days at Valley Forge. Rhode Island produced Commodore Oliver Hazard Perry, who made the immortal report, "We have met the enemy, and he is ours," and Perry's brother, Matthew, who led the naval diplomatic mission opening Japan to U.S. trade. It is here, and not at Lexington and Concord, that the first violent acts of rebellion occurred against the crown, a full 11 years before that "shot heard 'round the world," and where the state renounced allegiance to King George III two months ahead of the Declaration of Independence. Massachusetts may be proud of the all-black regiment it sent to the Civil War, but Rhode Island had an all-black regiment in the *Revolutionary* War. The world's first school of naval warfare opened here, and Rhode Island also is the birthplace of the Seabees and the Quonset hut; a German submarine sunk two days before the formal end of World War II sits just offshore, and the state today is home to the world's largest collection of military art and one of the nation's largest collections of military uniforms.

Rhode Island has its quirky side, too, including a colorful history of political corruption: a little-known 19th-century rebellion that sought to form an independent government, for instance, and a local linked to New York's notorious Boss Tweed. There's a supposed vampire buried in one town, and a mansion that doubled as the home of a fictional vampire in another. You can also find the birthplace of horror writer H.P. Lovecraft—and the weird inscription on his grave.

There are other sites relating to the state's seagoing legacy, among them the boat shop that built eight consecutive winners of the America's Cup race. The original Gilbert Stuart portrait of George Washington used on the dollar bill is here, but you'll never find it unless you know where to look. So is a giant redwood tree 3,000 miles from its traditional habitat in California, a rough draft of the Emancipation Proclamation, the desk on which Julia Ward Howe wrote "The Battle Hymn of the Republic," and museums that focus on everything from comic books to cooking.

Unkown Rhode Island

Block Island

The German submarine *U-853* torpedoed a freighter off Block Island on May 6, 1945, just two days before the formal end of World War II and a day after having been ordered by the German Navy to surrender; she was quickly sunk by depth charges from the *USS Atherton*. Only one other U-boat was sunk after this date. One of the two last German submarines sunk by the Allies in World War II, the *U-853* still sits in 120 feet of water five miles off Block Island; you can tell where by looking for the diving boats that frequent the wreck site and are often visible from land.

The Manissean Indian tribe that once inhabited Block Island is completely gone, wiped out by the middle of the 19th century as a consequence of white settlement. Today, the lost culture of the Manissean is remembered principally in the archeological artifacts at the Block Island Historical Society museum. The first white settlers lived by farming and fishing, and the museum has harpoons once used to catch swordfish, and ceremonial sabers as much as three feet long carved from swordfish "swords" in the manner of whalebone scrimshaw. There is also a display devoted to another extinct feature of the island: the double-ender, a remarkably stable two-masted sailboat with two sterns, for which local boatbuilders became famous; the boats were a necessity here, since the island had no harbor until 1870 when its breakwater was built, and they could be hauled up on the beach. No original double-enders survive, but the museum has models. *Corn Neck Road and Ocean Avenue; daily 10 to 5 June 15 through Columbus Day; 401-466-2481.*

Bristol

As odd as it may be to happen across a sequoia tree 3,000 miles from California, it's certainly hard to miss the biggest giant redwood in the East on the grounds of the Blithewold Mansion overlooking Narragansett Bay. The tree stands more than 90 feet high. The original mansion was built in 1896 by coal magnate Augustus Van Wickle, but quickly seemed haunted. Van Wickle died, oddly enough, in a skeet-shooting accident, and the house itself burned down in 1906. But the fire was so slow-moving there was time to remove all the furniture, including the fireplaces and bathtubs, and the home was quickly replaced with the 45-room stone-and-stucco mansion that now stands on the site. The Baccarat crystal, fine china, hand-embroidered linens, family photographs and books are arranged as if the house is still lived in. *101 Ferry Road (Route 114); grounds daily 10 to 5, mansion Wednesday through Sunday 10 to 4 mid-April through mid-October; 401-253-2707.*

Endowed and partly collected by brewer Rudolf Haffenreffer, who made his fortune producing Narragansett Beer, the Haffenreffer Museum of Anthropology on Mount Hope has one of the nation's largest collections of African masks and statuary, along with native American artifacts including a full-length headdress of the type used by the Northern Cheyenne with bison horn and black-billed magpie and eagle feathers. On the grounds are a full-sized replica of a Plains Indian teepee and a Northeast woodland Indian wetu, a shelter made with saplings bent and covered with bark. *300 Tower Street; Tuesday through Sunday 11 to 5 June, July and August, Saturday and Sunday 11 to 5 September through May; 401-253-8388.*

Mount Hope was headquarters of Metacom, dubbed "King Philip" by the white settlers he terrorized, leader of the bloody 17th-century rebellion of native Americans. It is also the place where King Philip was finally killed on August 12, 1676. His head was taken to Plymouth, where his father, Massasoit, had welcomed the Pilgrims. The rocky ledge from which Metacom watched for enemy ships in Mount Hope Bay is called "King Philip's Chair." *Tower Road.*

Unknown New England

The boat shop that built eight consecutive America's Cup winners between 1893 and 1934 today houses the Herreshoff Museum and America's Cup Hall of Fame, a tribute to their designer, Nathaneal G. Herreshoff, and to the world's oldest competitive sports trophy, named for the yacht that won the inaugural race in 1851, the *America*. The jewel of the museum sits out front: *America 3*, winner of the 1992 race. The collection also includes the *Sprite*, the oldest yacht in America; and the engine from J.P. Morgan's 114-foot yacht. *7 Burnside Street; Monday through Friday 1 to 4, Saturday and Sunday 11 to 4 May 1-June 15 and September and October; daily 10 to 4 June 16 through August 31; 401-253-5000.*

The field desk carried by Civil War General Ambrose Burnside is in the Bristol Historical Society museum, along with Burnside's swords, field glasses, mess kit, and other personal possessions. Burnside moved to Bristol after the war, during which he served as commander of the Army of the Potomac. Although his military career was undistinguished, Burnside was forever immortalized by the word "sideburns," named for his bushy facial hair. He later became governor of Rhode Island, and then the state's U.S. senator. The museum, a former county jail built out of stones that had been used as ballast by Bristol sailing ships, also has ribbons, medals and badges celebrating Bristol's distinction as home of the nation's oldest Fourth of July parade, a tradition first organized by local veterans on Independence Day in 1785. *48 Court Street; Wednesday and Friday 1 to 5; 401-253-7223.*

Charlestown

One of the largest and strongest of the New England Indian tribes, the Narragansett occupied most of the land around Narragansett Bay, and claimed dominion over smaller tribes as far away as what is now Long Island, New York. With one of the most highly developed cultures of native Americans, the Narragansett traded with tribes from Florida to Nova Scotia, growing tobacco for smoking and making textiles and rope from hemp. The ancient burial ground of the sachems of the Narragansett tribe is here beside a quiet pond on a hill overlooking the ocean. The Royal Indian Burial Ground was robbed in May of 1859 by a party of nine men looking for relics said to have been buried with the chiefs; the grave robbers were considered undesirables who lived in Rhode Island's southern swamps, where the derisive term "swamp Yankee" had its origins. Criminal charges were brought, and the nine men were arraigned in Ward Hall, now the Ocean House Marina on Town Dock Road. They were acquitted. The traditional burial site, discernible by its row of raised mounds, has reverted to the Narragansett tribe. *Narrow Lane.*

Coventry

Spell Hall was the home of General Nathanael Greene, quartermaster general of the Continental Army during the American Revolution. Greene designed and built the house in 1770 and operated a foundry next door, where he made ship anchors. The youngest brigadier general in the army and confidante of George Washington, Greene was rewarded with a plantation confiscated from a British loyalist in Georgia, where he died of sunstroke two years after the war. The home has a cannon cast at the foundry during the Revolution. *50 Taft Street; Wednesday and Saturday 10 to 5, Sunday noon to 5 March 1 through November 30; 401-821-8630.*

Cranston

The Sprague Mansion was home to two governors, both of whom would also serve as U.S. senators. But it was a murder here in 1844 that resulted in an end to capital punishment in Rhode Island. The victim was Amasa Sprague, brother of William Sprague, who built the house in 1791 and went on to become Rhode Island governor and senator. An Irish immigrant named John Gordon was convicted of the killing, and was hanged, in spite of his denials. Seven years later, Gordon's

Unkown Rhode Island

brother, Nicholas, confessed on his deathbed that he was actually the murderer, and the guilt-ridden General Assembly quickly put an end to executions. The elegantly furnished family homestead reflects the vast fortune earned by the Spragues in the cotton industry. *1351 Cranston Street; by appointment; 401-944-9226.*

East Greenwich

Under a 1724 law restricting the vote to men who owned a certain amount of property, most Rhode Island residents continued to be denied the right to cast their ballots when, in 1840, frustration over this provision finally gave way to <u>a rebellion led by Thomas Dorr, who formed an independent government that elected him as its head</u>. Dorr's supporters attempted to seize the armory in Providence, but Dorr's Rebellion was thwarted by the Independent Company of Kentish Guards, a military company loyal to the governor. Dorr was arrested and convicted of treason; property restrictions remained in effect for voting in Rhode Island until 1888; and the Kentish Guards were rewarded with a new headquarters they continue to use to this day. The building includes artifacts, uniforms, and weapons from the long history of the company, founded in 1774 by General Nathanael Greene and others. Thirty five Revolutionary War officers came from this unit, more than from any other. *1774 Armory Street; by appointment; 401-295-3183.*

Housed in the one-time armory of the Varnum Continentals, an independent military unit that split off from the Kentish Guards in 1907 in a dispute over command, the Varnum Continental Military Museum has an eclectic variety of superlative military objects ranging from <u>one of only three surviving Revolutionary War artillery helmets</u> to <u>a flag flown at the Battle of Lake Erie</u>, where Rhode Island native Commodore Oliver Hazard Perry made his immortal report: "We have met the enemy and he is ours." Among the other jewels here: a 16th-century crossbow, and 500 military posters from World War I and World War II, including some by Henry Flagg, creator of the epic "Uncle Sam Wants You." *6 Main Street; by appointment; 401-884-4110.*

George Washington said he was "the light of the camp" during the dark days at Valley Forge. Thomas Paine called him the greatest orator in the new United States. But General James Varnum died of illness at only 41 while serving as a federal judge in Marietta, Ohio. Varnum's friendship with Washington is evident in the <u>eagle escutcheons that decorate his desk, the symbol of a fraternity of Washington's top officers called the Cincinnati Society</u>. The desk is in Varnum's colonial mansion, built in 1713 and now a museum. Among the items on display there: Varnum's last letter, written to his wife from Marietta giving her advice about what to do after he was dead. The other desk in the house was specially made on an unusually large scale for John Brown, first president of the Providence Bank, who was said to be so fat he filled a carriage built for three. *57 Pierce Street; Thursday through Saturday 10 to 2 June, July and August; 401-884-1776.*

The New England Wireless and Steam Museum, a complex of buildings that includes <u>the oldest working wireless station in the world</u>, tells the story of electric communication, from telegraph to television, with early radio, telegraph and television equipment—much of it invented in New England—including a so-called <u>jigger and spark set exactly like the one used by the *Titanic* to call for help on April 15, 1912</u>. *1300 Frenchtown Road; by appointment; 401-884-0545.*

East Providence

Charles Looff was so proud of the carousel he built for an amusement park here in 1894, he painted his own likeness on it. The Crescent Park Carousel is considered <u>the finest surviving example of Looff's famous carousels</u>; even the organ is carved with moving figures. *Bullock's Point Avenue; Saturday and Sunday noon to*

Unknown New England

8 Easter to Memorial Day, Friday 3-8, Saturday and noon to 8 Memorial Day through June 30, Wednesday through Sunday noon to 8 July 1 through Labor Day, Friday 3 to 8, Saturday and Sunday noon to 8 Labor Day through Columbus Day; 401-433-2828.

Exeter

Strange enough that Mary Brown and her two young daughters died only a few years apart. After the last, Mercy Brown, was buried on January 17, 1892, her brother, Edwin, also became ill. Townspeople seeking an explanation decided that the dead Mercy Brown was feeding on her living relatives, a conclusion only reinforced when they exhumed her body, which appeared to have moved inside the coffin—and *still had blood in the veins.* So they removed her heart and burned it on a rock. The grave of reputed vampire Mercy Brown was the site of another odd occurrence in 1996, when the headstone mysteriously disappeared, then reappeared a few days later. *Chestnut Hill Baptist Cemetery.*

Indian baskets made of birch bark and decorated with porcupine needles are among the items in the Tomaquag Indian Memorial Museum, whose collection was amassed by the anthropologist Eva Butler. There are also beaded belts worn by Sioux Indians around their blankets. "Tomaquag" is Narragansett for beaver; the museum was once in Beaver Valley. *390 Summit Road; by appointment; 401-539-2786.*

Glocester

The Glocester Heritage Society, a combination museum and retail shop in the 1827 Job Armstrong Country Store, has clothing worn by Colonel Reuben Steere, a dwarf billed as the world's smallest man after the death of Tom Thumb in 1883. Steere, who was 42 inches tall, returned to his hometown of Glocester after touring with the Lilliputian Opera Company, and became, of all things, the local truant officer. *1181 Main Street; Monday through Friday noon to 4; 401-568-4077.*

Jamestown

Until the Newport Bridge opened in 1969, Jamestown was linked to the mainland by ferry boats. The Jamestown Museum focuses on the history of the island ferries, with pennants, compasses—even a working speaking tube from the *Governor Carr*, a ferry blown ashore by the Hurricane of 1938. *92 Narragansett Avenue; Tuesday through Sunday 1 to 4 mid-June through Labor Day; 401-423-0784.*

The third lighthouse built in America, Beavertail Light dates back to 1749; the original wooden tower burned down in 1856. A museum in the assistant keeper's cottage has a fourth-order Fresnel lens and a plaque from the original foundation, visible about 100 feet in front of the present tower; long buried, the foundation and the plaque were unearthed by a hurricane. There are also models of every other lighthouse in Rhode Island, and photos of the lighthousekeepers and their families. *Beavertail Point; daily noon to 3 Memorial Day through mid-June and from Labor Day to Columbus Day, daily 10 to 4 mid-June through Labor Day; 401-423-3270.*

The highly advanced culture of native Americans who once lived here is on display in the Sydney L. Wright Museum, a small collection housed in the Jamestown Philomenian Library. The artifacts, dug up by archeologists, include huge soapstone cooking bowls believed to be more than 3,400 years old. *26 North Road; Monday and Wednesday 10 to 5 and 7 to 9, Tuesday and Thursday noon to 5 and 7 to 9, Friday10 to 5 and Saturday 10 to 1 June 15 through September 15, then Monday and Wednesday 10 to 5 and 7 to 9, Tuesday and Thursday noon to 5 and 7 to 9, Friday and Saturday 10 to 5; 401-423-7280.*

Unkown Rhode Island

Kingston
Unique rocks and fossils including a flexible sandstone that bends are on display in the University of Rhode Island geology department. There are also other mineral oddities, including 300 million-year-old fossils of plants and ferns. *8 Ranger Road; Monday through Friday 8:30 to 4:30; 401-874-2265.*

A living memorial to Lorenzo Kinney Jr., known as Mr. Azalea, the Kinney Azalea Gardens boast a kaleidoscope of 800 hybrid azaleas and rhododendrons. *2391 Kingstown Road; daily dawn to dusk; 401-783-2396.*

Little Compton
Charles Edwin Wilbour was a member of New York's corrupt Tammany Hall Society under William Marcy "Boss" Tweed, which looted New York taxpayers of millions of dollars. An elaborate carriage used to travel the streets of New York by a member of the Boss Tweed gang now is in his family's home, Wilbour House, which was built in 1690 and is open to the public. Wilbour would return to Little Compton with the carriage in the summers. The home also has a wreath made out of human hair dating from the 1860s, when such things were exchanged as remembrances between friends. Attached to the barn is an artist's studio built from the curved wooden hull of the *Peggotty*, a sail ferry that connected Middletown and Little Compton. *548 West Main Road; Thursday through Sunday 1 to 5 mid-June through Labor Day, then Saturday and Sunday 1 to 5 through mid-October; 401-635-4035.*

The Rhode Island Red monument commemorates the famous breed of chicken developed here for the first time in 1854. Bred extensively by the farmers in the area, the red chicken is the Rhode Island state bird. *40 Commons Road.*

A memorial monument to Elizabeth Pabodie marks the gravesite of the first girl born to colonists in New England, the daughter of Pilgrims John and Priscilla Alden. *Commons Burial Ground; daily dawn to dusk.*

Gray's Store is the nation's oldest continually operating retail store, built in 1788. It comes complete with the original local post office, soda fountain, and other antique fixtures, and still sells penny candy. *4 Main Street; Monday through Friday 9:30 to 5:30, Saturday 9:30 to 5, Sunday noon to 4 Memorial Day through Labor Day, then Monday through Friday 9:30 to 5:30, Saturday 9:30 to 5; 401-635-4566.*

Narragansett
Created in cooperation with Boston's Museum of Science, the small but elaborate visitor center at the University of Rhode Island's Office of Marine Programs was designed by a company that makes stage sets for the Disney cruise ships. Inside: a 10-foot wave tank, a stream table that shows the eddies and swirls of ocean currents, and a machine that makes sand dunes. A highlight: a deck overlooking Narragansett Bay, with binoculars provided. *South Ferry Road; Monday through Friday 10 to 2 July and August, then Tuesday and Thursday 11 to 1; 401-874-6211.*

Newport
Benjamin Franklin was apprenticed to his older brother, James, a Boston printer, until the two had a falling out; Ben moved to Philadelphia, and James to Newport, where, as the only printer in Rhode Island, he published the laws of the colony, broadsides, pamphlets and, eventually, incendiary anti-British propaganda. Benjamin Franklin brother's printing press is in the often-overlooked Museum of Newport History. The museum also has the beacon from Lime Rock Lighthouse, whose keeper beginning in 1857 was a woman: Ida Lewis, who is credited with

Unknown New England

rescuing 17 men from Newport Harbor during her career. *82 Touro Street; Tuesday through Friday 9:30 to 4:30, Saturday 9:30 to noon; 401-846-0813.*

Not all frustration with British colonial rule was expressed in printed broadsides. Sometimes it slid into vandalism and street melees. The Wanton-Lyman-Hazard House was the site of a violent riot against the British Stamp Act in 1765, when townspeople egged on by the city's merchants attacked the author of a pamphlet criticizing opponents of the crown. The house, built in 1675 and the oldest home in Newport, still bears signs of the assault: the few remaining original windows are evidence that all the rest were broken, for example, and obvious repairs show where a closet door was broken in by looters. *17 Broadway; Thursday through Saturday 10 to 4 Memorial Day through Labor Day; 401-846-0813.*

When officers from the British schooner *St. John* tried to carry off an alleged deserter from Newport on July 9, 1764, the fed-up townspeople responded by seizing Fort George on Goat Island in Newport Harbor and turning its cannon on the British frigate *Squirrel*. Eight shots were fired in the first violent act of resistance to British rule. Five years later—and still six years before the battles at Lexington and Concord—Newporters seized the ironically named British sloop *Liberty*, seizing the ship and scuttling it off Gravelly Point at the end of what is now Long Wharf.

Small as it was, Rhode Island carried on the odd custom of maintaining five different state capitals simultaneously until 1901, when Providence was finally given the exclusive honor; until then, the seat of government moved every year from one capital to another. That's how Newport comes to be the site of the nation's fourth-oldest surviving state house, the Newport Colony House. It was here that Newporters celebrated the repeal of the Stamp Act, and where the Declaration of Independence was read for the first time in Rhode Island. The building was used as a barracks by the occupying British during the Revolutionary War, and as a hospital by America's French allies after liberation. But the greatest unexpected treasure here is the original Gilbert Stuart portrait of George Washington used on the dollar bill. *Washington Square; hours vary; 401-846-2980.*

One of only 16 remaining membership libraries, Redwood Library is the oldest lending library in the United States, founded in 1747 by local landowner Abraham Redwood. The architect was Peter Harrison, who also designed the Touro Synagogue. British soldiers who occupied Newport during the Revolutionary War purportedly used the library as a brothel. They also carried off half the original books. But there are still rare editions, including a 1488 Venetian Bible, 18th- and 19th-century portraits by the likes of Gilbert Stuart, and Rembrandt Peale's painting of George Washington. *50 Bellevue Avenue; Tuesday through Thursday 9:30 to 8, Monday, Friday, and Saturday 9:30 to 5:30, Sunday 1 to 5; 401-847-0292.*

Born in South Kingstown in 1785, Oliver Hazard Perry commanded American forces in the Battle of Lake Erie during the War of 1812, defeating the British fleet there in three hours and sending the famous report: "We have met the enemy and he is ours." Perry died unceremoniously of yellow fever in Trinidad at only 34 in 1819. Commodore Perry's grave, where he was taken and reburied in 1826, is in Common Burial Ground. Also buried here is Perry's brother, Matthew, who led the naval diplomatic mission opening Japan to U.S. trade in 1853. *Fairwell Street.*

The world's first school of naval warfare, the Naval War College was opened in 1884 in a former Newport poorhouse; it has since turned out such leaders as Admiral Chester Nimitz, Admiral Admiral William Halsey Jr., and Admiral Raymond Spruance. Today that original building is a museum of naval warfare in general, and the naval history of Narragansett Bay in particular. Rhode Island created the continent's first navy in 1676 during King Philip's War, and its first ship, the sloop

Unkown Rhode Island

Katy, was also the first vessel commanded by John Paul Jones. The museum has models of the *Katy*, later renamed the *Providence*, and a model of the *USS Cushing*, the first ocean-going steel-hulled torpedo boat, built in Bristol in 1890 by the Herreshoff yacht company. It also has the first propeller-driven torpedo made in America, built in Newport in 1871, which looks like it belongs on Captain Nemo's submarine. On the grounds are two of 12 surviving Civil War-era Dahlgren cannon, a Hotchkiss revolving cannon taken from a Spanish ship during the Spanish-American War, and a Mark XIV torpedo, the premier American torpedo of World War II. *686 Cushing Road; Monday through Friday 10 to 4, Saturday and Sunday noon to 4, June 1 through September 30, then Monday through Friday 10 to 4; 401-841-4052.*

Headquarters of the Artillery Company of Newport, chartered in 1741 by King George II, the Newport Armory now houses one of the nation's largest collections of military uniforms, including the only surviving uniform worn by the late Egyptian President Anwar Sadat and uniforms worn by Dwight D. Eisenhower, Prince Phillip, Lord Mountbatten, Field Marshal Sir Bernard Montgomery, King Hussein of Jordan, Admiral Chester Nimitz, and Generals Mark Clark, William Westmoreland, Creighton Abrams, Alexander Haig, and Colin Powell. *23 Clarke Street; Wednesday through Sunday 10 to 4, Sunday noon to 4 June through September; 401-846-8488.*

Built in 1879 as a sports pavilion by summer resident James Gordon Bennett Jr., publisher of *The New York Herald*, the Newport Casino had grass courts for the trendy new game of lawn tennis, and in 1881 was the site of the first U.S. National Lawn Tennis Championship, forerunner of the U.S. Open. Today the wooden shingle-style building designed by McKim, Mead, and White houses the International Tennis Hall of Fame, the world's largest museum devoted to the game of tennis, with historic artifacts including the original patent for the game of tennis granted by Queen Victoria in 1874. The grass courts are the oldest in the world used continuously for competition. *194 Bellevue Avenue; daily 9:30 to 5; 401-849-3990.*

Courageous, two-time winner of the America's Cup in 1974 and 1977, is the centerpiece of the Museum of Yachting. There are also restored classic wooden yachts, and a hall of fame for "single-handed sailors" who have navigated the oceans of the world alone, beginning with American Joshua Slocum, the first man to sail around the world alone; his journey, in 1898, ended at Newport. *Fort Adams State Park; daily 10 to 5 mid-May through October 31; 401-847-1018.*

The oldest Roman Catholic parish in Rhode Island, St. Mary's is the church where John F. Kennedy married Jacqueline Bouvier on September 12, 1953. *12 William Street; 401-847-0475.*

John F. Kennedy called it "the most beautiful place in the world": Hammersmith Farm, the 48-acre seaside estate where JFK and Jaqueline Bouvier celebrated their wedding with 1,200 of their closest friends. The 28-room shingle-style summer house was built in 1887 by the Auchincloss family; Hugh D. Auchincloss Jr. married Jackie's mother, Janet Lee Bouvier, in 1942. But it was best known as President Kennedy's summer White House from 1961 until 1963. The gardens were designed by Frederick Law Olmsted. The estate is now privately owned. *Ocean Drive.*

With grandstands dating to 1908, Cardine's Field is the oldest surviving ballpark in America, originally used by the railroad leagues that sponsored competitions among the New York, New Haven, and Old Colony Railroads. Touring major league and Negro League teams also later played there—among them, Boston and New York ball clubs that would travel to Newport for exhibition games on Sundays

Unknown New England

when playing baseball was not allowed in their home towns—with players including Satchell Paige and Yogi Berra. *West Marlborough Street and America's Cup Avenue.*

If Carey Mansion at Salve Regina University looks familiar, it could be because it doubled as the fictional Collinwood, home of vampire Barnabas Collins in the 1960s television series *Dark Shadows*. *100 Ochre Point Avenue.*

North Kingstown

Called the Pensacola of the North at its peak during World War II, the Quonset Naval Air Station was the second largest naval air station in the world at that time (Pensacola was the biggest), responsible for overhauling and repairing Navy aircraft. F-6 Hellcats were fitted out here for service in the Pacific, where they shot down more enemy planes than any other type of plane. The U.S. Navy Construction Battalion (or C.B.) was also formed here in 1992, and it was here that the "Seabees" invented the familiar elliptical shelter known worldwide as the Quonset hut. The historic former base now houses the Quonset Air Museum, which has an extensive collection of antique military aircraft. Among them: A Hellcat raised from the ocean floor off Martha's Vineyard 45 years after it went down there, undergoing restoration in view of visitors. Also on display: a TBM 3-E Grumman Avenger torpedo bomber, the kind former President George Bush flew during the Korean War; two Vietnam-era Bell UH-1 "Huey" helicopters; a MIG-17 once flown by the Polish Air Force; and a Soviet Antonov AN-2, the largest single-engine biplane in the world, used to carry troops during the 1950s. Outside the base chapel is the original 10-foot metal model of the Seabee mascot, a fighting bumblebee with hammers and wrenches held in some of its hands and a machine gun in another. *488 Eccleston Avenue; Friday through Sunday 10 to 3; 401-294-9540.*

Scottish immigrants in 1751 came here to establish the first snuff mill in America, making finely pulverized tobacco to be inhaled through the nose by trendy colonists. But their home is famous for another reason: It was the birthplace of Gilbert Stuart, the snuffmakers' son who became one of America's foremost portrait painters, famous for his depictions of George Washington and virtually all the other notable men and women of the era in America. Washington hated posing for him. "An apathy seemed to seize him and a vacuity spread over his countenance most appalling to paint," the artist wrote. Today, Stuart's portrait of a grumpy Washington appears on the dollar bill. Although the art works here are reproductions, the original snuff mill still operates. *815 Gilbert Stuart Road; Thursday through Monday 11 to 4, end of April through October 31; 401-294-3001.*

Built around 1750, the house at Casey Farm was the center of a plantation. Its most interesting moment came in 1777, when a party of British marines came ashore after learning that some Patriots was staying here. The house was riddled with bullets, all but one of them quickly patched: a British shot that pierced the door, which has been kept as a memento of the battle. *2325 Boston Neck Road; Tuesday, Thursday and Saturday 1 to 5 June 1 through October 15; 401-295-1030.*

The 1707 Old Narragansett Church is one of the nation's oldest Episcopal churches and has the oldest church organ in America, made in 1680. *Church Lane; Friday through Sunday 11 to 4 July and August; 401-294-4357.*

A teeming mass of 60,000 brook and rainbow trout of all sizes, raised to stock Rhode Island ponds and streams, can be visited at the Lafayette Trout Hatchery. *465 Hatchery Road; daily 8 to 3:30; 401-294-4662.*

Pawtucket

After losing its American colonies in the Revolutionary War, Britain was not about to surrender its industrial dominance, so it banned the export of machines—

Unkown Rhode Island

and skilled mechanics. Samuel Slater, a 23-year-old laborer in an English textile mill, defied the law by disguising himself as a farm worker and stealing away to Rhode Island, where he built a spinning mill to produce cotton yarn in water-powered machines, beginning the transformation of the Blackstone River Valley from a farming region into one of the nation's great industrial centers. America's first factory, the Slater Mill Historic Site now houses a museum devoted to this industrial milestone, with a water wheel that still powers lathes and drills. The original two-story mill, which was 42 feet long and just 29 feet wide, still stands at the center of a number of subsequent additions. The adjoining Wilkinson Mill, built 20 years later, shows the eventual switch from wood to stone to reduce the chance of fire. *67 Roosevelt Avenue; Tuesday through Saturday 10:30 to 3, Sunday 1 to 3 June 1 through October 31, then Saturday 10 to 5, Sunday 1 to 5; 401-725-8638.*

Begun with the handprints of the actors Dustin Hoffman, Dennis Franz, Sean Nelson, and director Michael Corrente of the 1996 film *American Buffalo*, the Hollywood Walk of Fame celebrates movies filmed in Pawtucket. It's at a three-way intersection rather hopefully renamed Times Square. *Goff, Exchange, and Broad streets.*

Portsmouth

The desk on which Julia Ward Howe wrote "The Battle Hymn of the Republic" and other of her personal items are in the Portsmouth Historical Society Museum, a former meeting house built in 1865; Howe lived a few doors down on Union Street until her death in 1910. There is also a case full of musket balls from the Battle of Rhode Island, fought here during the Revolutionary War. *870 East Main Road at Union Street; Sunday 2 to 4 Memorial Day through Columbus Day; 401-683-9178.*

Rhode Island's only major land battle of the American Revolution on August 29, 1778, was not the Patriots' proudest moment. Four thousand of their French allies sailed away to Boston in a huff just before the fighting started because of a dispute with the American commander, General John Sullivan. Another 5,000 colonial troops deserted. One bright spot was the tenacious spirit shown by a unit of freed blacks, the First Rhode Island Regiment, under Colonel Christopher Greene, who three times turned back British forces trying to flank the American line centered on Butts Hill Fort. In the end, the British won. Butts Hill Fort is still discernible off Sprague Street, and there is a memorial to the black soldiers of the Revolutionary War on the site that was the center of the battle. *Route 24 at Route 114.*

Providence

Established in 1638 by Roger Williams after he was banished from Massachusetts by the Puritans, the First Baptist Church is the oldest Baptist church in America. The current building dates to 1775, and has the requisite white steeple, columns and archways and box pews under a Waterford crystal chandelier. It was also here that the denomination split into northern and southern Baptists over the issue of slavery. *75 North Main Street; tours Monday through Friday 9:30 to 3:30 July and August, then Monday through Friday 9:30 to 3:30; 401-454-3418.*

The Old State House is where the General Assembly of the Colony of Rhode Island renounced allegiance to King George III two full months before the Declaration of Independence, passing the Rhode Island Renunciation of Allegiance on May 4, 1776, and essentially becoming the first free republic in America. The Assembly Room, where the vote was taken, is open to the public. *150 Benefit Street; Monday through Friday 8:30 to 4:30; 401-222-2678.*

The world's largest collection of military art, the Anne S. K. Brown Military Collection at Brown University includes 12,000 prints, drawings and watercolors and

Unknown New England

18,000 albums, sketchbooks, and scrapbooks by ordinary soldiers and military artists. Among them: original drawings of the D-Day flotilla converging on the beaches of Normandy, watercolors of the Battle of Iwo Jima by a Marine Corps artist, and sketches of a German prisoner-of-war camp by an American pilot shot down over Munich. The collection also includes 5,000 miniature lead soldiers from England, France and Germany in the years leading up to World War II. *20 Prospect Street; Monday through Friday 9 to 5; 401-863-2414.*

John Brown was a big guy, and in more ways than one. The first Providence merchant to become involved in the lucrative China trade, Brown became extraordinarily wealthy. He was also six feet tall and weighed well over 200 pounds—gigantic in his day. Brown's mansion is equally larger-than-life, though it gets only a tenth as many visitors as nearby museums. The house, built in 1786, has some of Brown's original furniture, and his waistcoat, which gives a good idea of his girth. The nearby Aldrich House, headquarters of the Rhode Island Historical Society, is also home to the Rhode Island Heritage Hall of Fame, which salutes such famous Rhode Islanders as *New Yorker* writer S. J. Perelman and William Blackstone, the state's first white settler, who moved to Rhode Island from Boston when other Puritans moved in and spoiled the neighborhood. *52 Power Street; Tuesday through Friday 10 to 5, Saturday and Sunday 1 to 5 March 1 through December 31, then Friday and Saturday 1 to 5, Sunday 1 to 4; 401-331-8575.*

The Culinary Archives and Museum at Johnson & Wales University

The Smithsonian of food, the Culinary Archives and Museum at Johnson & Wales University is a feast of cooking appliances, cookbooks, menus, eating utensils, and other collectible comestibles. The largest collection of culinary recipes and objects in the world, it once brought Julia Child near tears when she paused before a 1909 stove that was the same model she used when she first learned to cook.

The collection was amassed by another great chef, the late Louis Szathmary, owner of the famous Bakery restaurant in Chicago, who died in 1996. It took several trailer-trucks to carry the collection to Providence from the 31 rooms above the Bakery where Szathmary—whose motto was, "To live is to eat"—had stored it.

There are food-related items from almost every American presidency, proving that the way to a chief executive's heart apparently is through his stomach: George Washington's newspaper advertisement for a cook, a note from President Ulysses S. Grant asking his wife to send up champagne and cake for the Cabinet, President Dwight D. Eisenhower's recipe for beef stew, and one of only three surviving autographed menus from Abraham Lincoln's second inaugural dinner; Lincoln stuffed pastries in his pockets at the formal affair to take home to his son, Robert.

Letters in the collection serve as evidence of the central role of food in history: a dispatch from Napoleon, who took time out from the Egyptian campaign to demand that his bakers be paid; a note from Ernest Hemingway requesting a recipe, and one from Thomas Edison telling about his father's dietary peculiarities; dinner invitations to and from the likes of John Hancock; and a description by John Montague, the Earl of Sandwich, detailing his invention of the luncheon food that bears his name—when, during an all-night card game, he asked for a second slice of bread to accompany his cold lamb so he wouldn't get grease on his fingers.

The museum has the first electric toaster, produced in 1906; 30,000 menus from history's greatest restaurants, clubs, cruise ships and railroads; and those nostalgic stoves used everywhere from naval ships to Julia Child's girlhood kitchen. *The Culinary Archives and Museum at Johnson & Wales University is at 315 Harborside Drive, Providence; Tuesday through Saturday 10 to 4; 401-598-2805.*

Unkown Rhode Island

Not only does the Annmary Brown Memorial look like a mausoleum; its benefactors, General Rush Christopher and Annmary Brown Hawkins, are actually entombed inside. But the building also houses 526 of the earliest books ever published, beginning with the pioneer printer Gutenberg, making it one of the world's largest collections of books printed before 1500. There are also European and American paintings from the 17th through 20th centuries, including works by Van Dyck and Rubens. *21 Brown Street; Monday through Friday 1 to 5; 401-863-1518.*

Named for a Brown University alumnus who served as Abraham Lincoln's personal secretary, the John Hay Library has one of the largest collections of materials relating to Lincoln, including a rough draft of the Emancipation Proclamation, handwritten dispatches sent to generals in the field during the Civil War, a bronze casting of Lincoln's head made the week he was nominated by the Republican Party, and a death mask taken after his assassination. The library also has the papers of Providence native and fantasy writer H.P. Lovecraft, and one of the world's largest collections of comic books: 60,000 of them, donated by a software engineer and comic art enthusiast. *20 Prospect Street; Monday through Friday 9 to 5; 401-863-2146.*

Built in 1891, the Ladd Observatory at Brown University looks like something Jules Verne might have imagined: an intact 19th-century observatory where astronomers searched for evidence of life they believed existed on Mars. Still in use, the original 15-foot telescope is a twin of the one at the U.S. Naval Observatory in Washington, D.C. It is turned by a hand-cranked wheel under a dome that revolves with the use of ropes and pulleys. The observatory also helped tell time in an era when clock settings differed wildly from one city to another; before the standardization of time, it might be 6 a.m. in Washington when it was 6:22 in Providence. To solve this problem, Brown astronomers sent a message by telegraph to City Hall every day at noon to set the time. The custom continued until the 1940s. *210 Doyle Avenue; Tuesday dusk until 10; 401-863-2323.*

Ever since a man named Walter Scott began to offer food from a converted horse-drawn freight wagon in Providence in 1872, New England has been the capital of the American diner. The American Diner Museum preserves the history of roadside diners with a collection of full-sized working diners and artifacts including vintage booths, stools, and menus. Two of the diners are at the future home of the museum in the former Narragansett Electric power plant on South Street. The rest are in a Fall River, Massachusetts, warehouse, where several can be seen undergoing restoration. *110 Benevolent Street; by appointment; 401-331-8575.*

Collected principally by amateur archeologists, the artifacts in the Hudson, Fuller, St. Pierre and Chace Collections of Rhode Island Archeological Materials show, among other things, the evolution of a soapstone quarry where native Americans were manufacturing items for trade as early as 1500 BC—around the same time Moses and the Israelites left Egypt. The quarry was in the area that is now Oak Lawn Street in Cranston. Among the products made there from the dark rock: smoking pipes, bowls and kettles. *600 Mt. Pleasant Avenue; by appointment; 401-456-9694.*

The birthplace of horror writer H.P. Lovecraft is at 454 Angell Street, where he was born on August 20, 1890. He was buried in 1937 in Swan Point Cemetery under a gravestone that reads, oddly, "I AM PROVIDENCE."

At 900 times actual size, the world's largest scale model of a termite, Nibbles Woodaway, graces the roof of a pest control company off Interstate 95. The 58-foot bug had a cameo in the 1994 film *Dumb and Dumber. 161 O'Connell Street.*

Unknown New England

South Kingstown
The brightly lit and spacious cells used to hold women at the Washington County Jail seem downright pleasant compared to the dank, dark, unheated, dungeon-like men's cells in the basement. Today, the jail is a museum, complete with the original iron-barred men's cell block. The women's quarters houses artifacts telling the history of the unusual northern plantation society that existed here, where wealthy landholders held slaves and raised horses, cows and sheep. There is a painting on glass of South Kingstown native Commodore Oliver Hazard Perry, and the newspaper reporting his death in Trinidad of yellow fever; and a re-creation of the Rose Sisters Hat and Fancy Goods Shop, a local store run by women in the 19th century at a time when few women had property or businesses. *2636 Kingstown Road; Tuesday, Thursday and Saturday 1 to 4 mid-May through October 31; 401-783-1328.*

Laid out in 1929 by the same firm that was then helping to design Colonial Williamsburg, the interior of the Museum of Primitive Art and Culture resembles a southwestern Spanish mission, with exposed ceiling beams, white mock adobe walls, a red-tiled floor and decorative windows. And the collection is as abrupt and unexpected as the architecture. Among other things, there are American Indian, South Seas, African and other ancient artifacts, including <u>15,000-year-old tools from the Paleolithic-era caves of Europe; a tablet written in 4041 BC by a tax collector in cuneiform</u>, one of the earliest kinds of writing; and <u>a shield used by headhunters in the Philippines</u>. *1058 Kingstown Road; Tuesday through Thursday 11 to 3, Wednesday 11 to 2 Labor Day through Memorial Day; 401-783-5711.*

Warwick
Bad enough that the *HMS Gaspee* was sent to Rhode Island by King George III to enforce the hated Stamp Act taxing all legal transactions in the American colonies; her commander, William Dudingston, harassed and delayed even ships with all their paperwork in order. On June 9, 1772, one such vessel, the *Hannah*, led the pursuing *Gaspee* onto the shallows of what is now called Gaspee Point, where a band of Patriots burned it and took the captain and his crew prisoner. It was <u>one of the first violent acts of rebellion against the crown</u>—three full years before the battles at Lexington and Concord. A monument marks the site. *Peck Lane.*

Westerly
Built in 1867, the Flying Horse Carousel is <u>the oldest surviving carousel in the United States</u>. Each of its 20 horses is hand-carved, with manes made of real horse hair. The carousel is the only one left in the country to which the horses are attached only at the top, making them fly outward when it's spinning as riders reach for the brass ring. *Bay Street; daily 1 to 9, June 15 through Labor Day. 401-596-7761.*

Joshua Babcock went into business as a storekeeper, since his house was strategically located in the middle of the town. That's also why Benjamin Franklin, while serving as the nation's first postmaster general, gave Babcock the commission to run the local post office. It was the beginning of a long friendship between the two men, and the reason that the Babock-Smith House has <u>lightning rods furnished by Benjamin Franklin</u>. The home, built in 1734, is now a museum. *124 Granite Street; Sunday 2 to 5 May 1 through June 30 and Labor Day through October, Wednesday and Sunday 2 to 5 July 1 through Labor Day; 401-596-4424.*

Woonsocket
Drawn by work in the mills between 1840 and 1920, French Canadians came to make up about 70 percent of the population of Woonsocket. Their history here is the subject of the Museum of Work and Culture in a renovated former textile mill

Unkown Rhode Island

that carries visitors from a replica of a farmhouse in Quebec to the shop floor of a Woonsocket factory, narrated by the voices of real-life workers. The museum includes two looms and a spinning machine, the façade of the kind of triple-deckers that were home to many of the laborers, a 1920s schoolroom where students were banned from speaking French, and a re-creation of a union hall. Working conditions led to the rise of the Independent Textile Union and, ulti-mately, the Great Textile Strike of 1934, which shut down mills along the East Coast; Woonsocket saw the greatest violence, which left one worker dead and prompted textile owners to permanently close their mills. *42 South Main Street; Monday through Friday 9:30 to 4, Saturday 10 to 5, Sunday 1 to 5; 401-769-9675.*

Unknown Vermont

Sure, its quaint towns were models for Norman Rockwell, Robert Frost and Grandma Moses—all of whose work is well-represented here in out-of-the-way places—but tranquil Vermont has also produced an astonishing number of people who made history elsewhere. Two presidents were born here, Calvin Coolidge and the long-forgotten Chester Alan Arthur (though there is evidence his birthplace was across the border in Quebec, and that he therefore served illegally). So were Lincoln debater Stephen Douglas, bandleader Rudy Vallee, tractor magnate John Deere, Admiral George Dewey, the founders of *The New York Times and* the *New York Herald Tribune,* and both Joseph Smith, the founder of the Mormon Church, *and* his successor, Brigham Young. Rudyard Kipling wrote *The Jungle Books* not in India, but in a quiet Vermont town, and Justin Morgan bred his famous horses here. One Vermonter took her Yankee thrift to such lengths the *Guinness Book of World Records* named her the most miserly woman in the world.

Vermonters have hung on to more than their money. Small museums and collections around the state boast such extraordinary artifacts as Abraham Lincoln's trademark stovepipe hat, and a portrait of him made entirely of beetle and moth wings. There's Mussolini's telephone, a piece of Hitler's desk, the wheel from Dewey's flagship at the Battle of Manila Bay, Ernest Hemingway's fishing tackle, an 1851 daguerreotype of the moon, Elvis Presley's gallstones, and Ethan Allen's bar bill.

Incredibly, there was a Civil War battle here, the northernmost skirmish of the war, though it has been largely forgotten. There are relics of the 14 years Vermont was a republic independent of both the British colonial authorities and the new post-revolutionary nation. A whale was mysteriously discovered here, 150 miles from the nearest ocean, and Vermont has the largest quarry in the world, the oldest log cabin in America, and a fully furnished authentic European castle.

Equally interesting are the people laid to rest here, including a supposed vampire, an Egyptian mummy, and Baron and Maria von Trapp, whose escape from Nazi-controlled Austria inspired *The Sound of Music*. Then there is the odd memorial to Army Private William Scott. His claim to fame? Falling asleep on guard duty.

Arlington

Norman Rockwell lived in Arlington from 1939 to 1953, and used local people and buildings as the models for his distinctive work. The town that was a model for Norman Rockwell has reproductions of his locally inspired paintings on display at the Rockwell Exhibition and Gift Shop, including "Freedom of Speech," one of Rockwell's World War II "Four Freedoms" series, which features the town hall; and "Shuffleton's Barber Shop," where he set his memorable image of a boy getting his

Unkown Vermont

first haircut. Today the barber shop on Old Mill Road is a variety store; Rockwell's home at 2 River Road is a bed-and-breakfast inn. *Route 7A; daily 9 to 5 May 1 through October 31, then daily 10 to 4; 802-375-6423.*

Barre

The largest quarry in the world, the Rock of Ages Quarry has been in use since 1885; the company provided the granite for Grand Central Station, the steps of the U.S. Capitol, and other buildings. Today the largest producer of memorial stones in North America, the quarry has a visitor center and tours of its active quarry, 60 stories deep. There's a scale model of the quarry made for the 1939 New York World's Fair, the original wooden derricks and steam locomotives once used to lift the massive blocks from the depths, and geologic displays. *773 Graniteville Road; visitor center and original quarry Monday through Saturday 8:30 to 5, Sunday noon to 5 May 1 through October 31; 802-476-3119.*

Barre's skilled granite workers have decorated its Hope Cemetery with hundreds of one-of-a-kind hand-sculpted grave markers in the shape of everything from a broken heart to a couple sleeping to a favorite car. *Route 14.*

Bennington

The grave of poet Robert Frost, who died in 1963 at the age of 88, is in Old Bennington Cemetery. *Route 9.*

A farmer's wife and mother, Anna Mary Robertson Moses began a career as a folk artist when she was already in her 70s and a grandmother. The world's largest public collection of works by Grandma Moses is in the Bennington Museum, which has 38 of her rustic paintings and the tilt-top table where she painted them. The one-room schoolhouse she attended is on the grounds. The museum also has the gun that fired the first shot at the decisive Revolutionary War Battle of Bennington on August 16, 1777, as well as a drum and a pair of buckskin trousers worn by one of the Green Mountain Boys. The door of the Catamount Tavern, which was frequented by the boisterous Green Mountain Boys, is also on display, along with Ethan Allen's bar bill. Only one automobile was ever commercially manufactured in Vermont, the sleek and pricey Martin Wasp made between 1920 and 1925, and the museum has the only surviving Martin Wasp in the world. *West Main Street; daily 9 to 6 June 1 through October 31, then daily 9 to 5; 802-447-1571.*

Brandon

Best-known for his debates with Abraham Lincoln in 1858 when both were running for Senate from Illinois, statesman Stephen Douglas was actually born here on April 23, 1813. He moved to Illinois in 1820, was elected to the Senate, and authored the Kansas-Nebraska Act allowing voters in new territories to decide whether to enter the Union as free or slave states. Douglas held off Lincoln's challenge to his Senate seat, but lost the presidential election to Lincoln in 1860. His birthplace still stands. *2 Grove Street.*

On February 25, 1837, Thomas Davenport successfully used an electromagnet to turn a drill at 450 revolutions per minute. A marker stands on Route 73 at the site of his blacksmith shop, the place where the world's first electric motor was invented. Davenport is buried in Pine Hill Cemetery. *Route 7.*

Brattleboro

By 1850, the expanding American middle class was restless to make showcases of their homes. Anticipating this, plumber Jacob Estey began to build reed organs, equally prized for their snob appeal and entertainment value, which produced the same sound as pipe organs but took up less space. The instruments would be sold all over the world for a century. The Brattleboro Historical Society

Unknown New England

has <u>50 Estey organs</u>, housed in the old factory building. It also has brochures distributed by Dr. Robert Wesselhoeft, whose Brattleboro Hydropathic Establishment attracted wealthy patrons from 1846 to 1871 for dips in the town's cold natural springs and a brutal exercise regimen of dubious value to their health. *230 Main Street; Thursday 1 to 4, Saturday 9 to noon; 802-258-4957.*

Brattleboro-born Jim Fisk and a compatriot, Jay Gould, used money they embezzled from stockholders of the Erie Railroad in a ruinous 1869 attempt to corner the gold market; the scam would come to be known as the Black Friday Scandal. A charming tycoon who was partial to silk tophats, Fisk redeemed himself by organizing relief for victims of the great Chicago fire in 1871. Fatally shot the next year by a rival suitor of his mistress, he was returned to his home town to be buried. <u>The grave of robber baron Jim Fisk</u> is in Prospect Hill Cemetery. *South Main Street.*

Bridgport

Button Bay State Park takes its name from <u>naturally occurring buttons</u>: small disks of clay through which reeds grow, leaving holes. Indians and settlers sewed them to their clothes; they can still be found in shallow brooks here. *5 Button Bay State Park Road; daily dawn to dusk mid-May through Columbus Day; 802-483-2001.*

Burlington

One of the great figures of American history, Ethan Allen led a citizens' militia to take Fort Ticonderoga, the first crown property to fall to the Americans during the Revolutionary War, then lugged the cannon to Boston where it was used to break the British siege. <u>The home of the hero Ethan Allen</u> survives, a simple wooden cabin he built himself surrounded by a sheep fence. *Route 127; Monday through Saturday 10 to 5, Sunday 1 to 5 Mother's Day through Columbus Day, then Saturday and Sunday noon to 4; 802-865-4556.*

In 1849, workers building a railroad from Burlington to Rutland unearthed the bones of a gigantic animal 10 feet below the surface in a thick blue clay. Closer examination led to an even more astonishing realization: It was <u>a whale that lived in Vermont, 150 miles from the nearest ocean</u>. The discovery of the whale, christened Charlotte after the town where it was found, proved that an arm of the saltwater sea extended into the Champlain Valley following the retreat of the glaciers 12,500 years ago. <u>The bones of Charlotte the whale</u> now rest in the Perkins Geology Museum at the University of Vermont, whose elegant antique wooden display cases also hold fossils of small sea creatures found around Vermont. *Colchester Avenue; Monday through Friday 8 to 5, Saturday and Sunday 9 to 5; 802-656-8694.*

The Robert Hull Fleming Museum boasts <u>the only mummy on display in Vermont</u>, in this case of a woman who died in the 6th century BC. There are 19,000 objects here spanning the history of civilization, among them a 9th-century BC Assyrian relief from a palace in what is today Iraq, Sumerian cuneiform tablets, Chinese Tang Dynasty Tomb figures, and Japanese prints, including the complete *53 Stages of the Tokaido* by Hiroshige. *Colchester Avenue; Tuesday through Friday 9 to 4, Saturday and Sunday 1 to 5 Labor Day through April 30, then Tuesday through Friday noon to 4, Saturday and Sunday 1 to 5; 802-656-0750.*

A <u>plastic solar barn</u> houses more than 200 dairy cows, horses, sheep, goats and pigs in the experimental farm at the University of Vermont's Miller Research Center. Part of the dairy herd is also used by students in their own cooperative business. The barn is open to the public. *Spear Street; daily 8 to 5; 802-862-2151.*

Unkown Vermont

Charlotte

Six acres of wildflowers farmed for their seeds create a landscape of extraordinary colors, with hepatica, white trillium, yellow marsh marigolds, bloodroot, red poppies, daisies, wild sunflowers, daisies, black-eyed susans, goldenrod, and other varieties around meandering walking trails at the Vermont *Wildflower Farm, which produces more than nine tons of seeds annually, sold through a catalog. Route 7; daily 10 to 5 early April though late October; 802-425-3500.*

Colchester

An Iraqi anti-aircraft gun captured during the Gulf War is among the broad collection of artifacts in the little-known Vermont Veterans Militia Museum at Camp Johnson, a National Guard base. There's also an American soldier's uniform dating from the War of 1812, M-47 and M-60 tanks, and aircraft including a Vietnam-era F-4 Phantom and UH-1 "Huey" helicopter, a tank with cleats for traction in the snow used by the famous ski-borne 10th Mountain Division during World War II, and the uniform of Florence MacAllister, one of the first women to join the Marines—during World War I. *Pearl Street; 10 to 3 Monday through Wednesday; 802-654-0360.*

Craftsbury

The John Woodruff Simpson Library is itself an oddity, occupying a one-time general store with books arranged on the original grocery shelves. It also has an eclectic museum of artifacts collected mainly by its benefactor, heiress Jean Simpson, including the wedding bodice of a Revolutionary War-era woman acquainted with George Washington, a bullet from the battlefield at Waterloo, a World War I shell casing, and South American ceremonial headdresses, machetes, and necklaces made from turtle shell and crocodile teeth. *Main Street; Wednesday and Saturday 9 to noon, 2 to 5 and 7 to 9:30, Sunday 12:15 to 1:30; 802-586-9692.*

Derby

The Haskell Free Public Library and Opera House is the only structure of its kind along the entire 5,525-mile U.S.-Canadian border that is half in Canada and half in the United States. The 1904 building was a gift from a Canadian widow whose husband was American, and who didn't want to offend her friends in either country. So the front door is in Vermont, and the back door in the province of Quebec; the opera house stage is in Canada, while most of the 400 seats are in the United States; and the library lobby is American territory while the book stacks are Canadian. The border is marked by a black line across the reading room floor. The library is officially a no-man's land, so patrons need not report to Customs before or after using it. In fact, three court proceedings have been held here in which either a witness or defendant would not or could not leave or enter the United States or Canada. On-the-border construction has been banned since 1925. *Caswell Avenue; Tuesday, Wednesday, Friday and Saturday 10 to 5, Thursday 10 to 8; 802-873-3022.*

Dummerston

British author Rudyard Kipling was born in Bombay and set his adventures in far-flung foreign countries. So it may come as a surprise that Kipling wrote most of his exotic stories in the quiet confines of Vermont. The house where Rudyard Kipling wrote *Captains Courageous* and *The Jungle Books*, and other of his most famous works, is now a self-catering holiday rental with many of the original furnishings. Kipling came there after marrying Brattleboro native Carrie Balestier in 1892, but left again in 1896 because of a quarrel with his brother-in-law. He called the home Naulakha, after a palace near Lahore in India. *707 Kipling Road; 802-254-6868.*

Unknown New England

Fairfield

This was <u>the birthplace of the often-forgotten 21st president of the United States, Chester Alan Arthur</u>. Or was it? Scholars have raised the possibility that Arthur, son of a Baptist minister, was actually born in Dunham Flats, Quebec, 15 miles from the Vermont border, and served as president illegally. Vermonters delight in the controversy, and, as a memorial to Arthur, have built a re-creation of the parsonage where his family lived. What is known for sure is that Arthur came into the world October 5, 1829—he would later lie about his age, attracting more suspicion—and was living in the parsonage by 1830. He was nearly brought down over the question of his nationality when he was selected to be James Garfield's running mate, but the controversy died out because Garfield was healthy and Arthur was not considered likely to become president. But in 1881, Garfield was assassinated, and Arthur was sworn in. Arthur died two years after leaving office—but not before burning his personal papers. *Route 36; Wednesday through Sunday 11 to 5 late May through Columbus Day; 802-828-3051.*

Ferrisburgh

Owned from the 1790s until 1961 by four generations of a family of abolitionist Quakers, the Rokeby House is one of the best-documented stops along the Underground Railroad that spirited fugitive slaves to Canada before the Civil War. *Route 7; Thursday through Sunday 11 to 2 mid-May through mid-October; 802-877-3406.*

Glover

Founded in 1962 on New York City's Lower East Side, the Bread and Puppet Theater is famous for its giant puppets, some with heads as big as 18 feet from chin to forehead; it was visible in its early years in street protests against the Vietnam War. The company moved to Vermont in 1974, and its retired puppets, masks and props are on display in a converted hay barn, with performances in the summer. *Route 122; daily 10 to 5 mid-May through mid-October; 802-525-3031.*

Grand Isle

Built of hand-hewn logs in 1783 by frontier surveyor Hebediah Hyde Jr., the Hyde house is <u>the oldest log cabin in America</u>. *36 East Shore South; Thursday through Monday 10 to 4 July 4 through Labor Day; 802-828-3051.*

Groton

This small town has <u>a monument to a Civil War soldier who became famous for falling asleep on duty</u>. William Scott was saved from the firing squad by President Abraham Lincoln in what was seen at the time as a gesture of humanity and compassion, though later evidence indicates the whole incident was staged as an cautionary example to the other troops. Scott was discovered asleep on duty at 4 a.m. August 31, 1860, while helping guard a bridge over the Potomac River. Court-martialed, he was sentenced to be executed and on September 9, he was stood in front of a firing squad when the officer in charge declared: "The president of the United States has expressed a wish that, as this is the first condemnation to death in this army for this crime, mercy may be extended to the criminal." The general in charge of the Vermont brigade later wrote in a letter to a friend that there was never any intention of having Scott shot, and Lincoln was in on the ruse. Scott went back into battle and was killed in action in Virginia. *Route 302.*

Huntington

The Birds of Vermont Museum is a collection of <u>nearly 200 wood carvings depicting the state's birds in their natural habitats</u>, along with endangered and extinct species from across the continent, surrounded by a 32-acre bird sanctuary. *900 Sherman Hollow Road; daily 10 to 4 May 1 through October 31; 802-434-2167.*

Unkown Vermont

Island Pond
A nondescript house set back from the road was <u>the birthplace of actor and band leader Rudy Vallee</u>. Born Hubert Prior Vallee on July 28, 1901, Vallee appeared in 40 films beginning in 1929, but remembered his roots, returning to his home town with his band in 1932 to put on a concert. *Dale Avenue.*

Isle La Motte
The French, not the English, were the first whites in Vermont, and St. Anne's Shrine marks <u>the site where Samuel Champlain came ashore in 1609</u>. A fort built in 1666 was the southernmost outpost of the French in Canada at that time, and artifacts recovered by archeologists from the ruins are on display. The first Catholic Mass in Vermont is believed to have been held here, and the walls of the 1892 chapel are hung with crutches and other items left by people who claim to have been cured of their ailments while visiting. *West Shore Road; daily 9 to 7 mid-May through mid-October; 802-928-3362.*

Ludlow
Black River Academy, where Calvin Coolidge went to high school, is now a local history museum. Among other exhibits, it displays the school books Coolidge used. *14 High Street; noon to 4 Tuesday through Saturday; 802-228-5050.*

Lyndon
Lyndon State College was originally housed in <u>the former summer mansion of Theodore Vail, founder of AT&T</u>. Vail hatched plans here that led to the creation of the American Telephone and Telegraph Company in 1885, connecting the various Bell System lines into a national network. Guests at his home, which he called Speedwell Farms, included President William Howard Taft and banker J.P. Morgan. Although the building was dismantled in 1974, Lyndon State maintains a small museum to Vail, with bookcases and other architectural features of the house preserved, including the oversized chair Taft used. *Vail Center; 802-626-6200.*

Manchester
<u>Ernest Hemingway's fly fishing tackle</u> is one of the exhibits at the American Museum of Fly Fishing, <u>the world's largest collection of angling and angling-related objects</u>, which has more than 1,200 fishing rods, 400 reels, and thousands of flies chronicling the history of fly fishing beginning in the 16th century. In addition to Hemingway's, the museum has the <u>fly fishing tackle of famous Americans including Dwight Eisenhower, Herbert Hoover, and Samuel Morse</u>, and the work of master fly tiers. *Route 7A and Seminary Avenue; 10 to 4 weekdays; 802-362-3300.*

Successful in his own right as president of the Pullman Railroad Car Company, Robert Todd Lincoln, son of President Abraham Lincoln, built an opulent 24-room Georgian Revival-style summer home overlooking the Battenkill Valley in 1902, and named it Hildene. Though Robert Lincoln burned most of his personal papers in the fireplaces here—including those relating to his controversial decision to institutionalize his mother, Mary Todd Lincoln—he meticulously documented the construction of his home, which has been restored using the original plans. Among the contents: <u>President Lincoln's stovepipe hat</u>, one of only four known to remain in existence. *Route 7A; daily 9:30 to 4 mid-May through October 31; 802-362-1788.*

Marlboro
The Southern Vermont Natural History Museum displays the work of 19th-century taxidermist Luman Nelson, including hundreds of songbirds, waterfowl, shorebirds, eagles, a black bear, and the extinct passenger pigeon, heath hen and Eskimo curlew. There are also live hawks and owls on display. *Route 9; daily 10 to 5 Memorial Day through October 31, then Saturday and Sunday 10 to 4; 802-464-0048.*

Unknown New England

Middlebury

Henry Sheldon didn't make history. But he did collect it. An unassuming town clerk and railway agent, Sheldon singlehandedly amassed what would become the contents of the remarkable but little-known Sheldon Museum, <u>the oldest community-based museum in the United States</u>, chartered in 1882. He collected Egyptian hieroglyphics, paper currency from every nation in the world, autographs of all the American presidents and European monarchs, fragments of important buildings, a wine bottle holder used by Lafayette in 1824—even his own teeth. Many of the items still have his handwritten descriptions attached. Across the street was <u>the blacksmith shop of tractor magnate John Deere</u>, born in Rutland on February 7, 1804, who later produced the first commercially feasible, self-scouring steel plow from a broken saw blade and establishing the company in Moline, Illinois, that bears his name. The museum has some of the tools Deere used in his shop. *1 Park Street; Monday through Saturday 10 to 5; 802-388-2117.*

West Cemetery looks like any other quaint New England graveyard—until you notice the Egyptian hieroglyphics. There, between Emma Moody (died 1838) and Caroline Hawley Mead (died 1894) is Amun-Her-Khepesh-Ef, (died 1883 BC). The story of this <u>3,800-year-old Egyptian mummy buried in a Vermont cemetery</u> begins with Henry Sheldon, who bought it from traders in 1886. It became so heavily damaged that the trustees of Sheldon's museum cremated the remains and buried the ashes underneath a stone marker with a Christian cross, an Egyptian ankh and a drawing of an ibis. "Amun-Her-Khepesh-Ef," it reads. "Aged 2 years. Son of Sen Woset, third king of Egypt, and his wife, Hathor-Hotpe, 1883 BC." *Route 30.*

The Middlebury College Museum of Art has a unique collection of early experimental photography, including <u>a rare 1851 daguerreotype of the moon</u>. It also has a substantial collection of modern art by Alexander Calder, Jasper Johns, Robert Rauschenberg, Willem de Kooning, Berenice Abbott, and others. *South Main Street; Tuesda through Friday 10 to 5, Saturday and Sunday noon to 5; 802-443-5007.*

The <u>monument to anti-gravity study</u> on the Middlebury College campus was a condition of a gift from businessmen Roger Babson of 450 shares of stock to be used for anti-gravity research after Babson's son died in a plane crash in 1960. It is there, the inscription says, "to remind students of the blessings forthcoming when a semi-insulator is discovered in order to harness gravity as a free power and reduce airplane accidents." *Old Chapel Road.*

Middlesex

A 1930s Civilian Conservation Corps camp, Camp Meade now houses <u>a museum devoted to the Depression era and the American home front during World War II</u>, complete with ration books, victory bonds, a USO canteen, and the sound of big-band music. There are also working tanks and other military vehicles from World War II, the Korean War, and Vietnam, including an F-86D Saber jet, a 1942 Jeep, and a 1942 M5A1 Stuart light tank. The Camp Meade Victory Museum also has <u>the leather cover from Hitler's guest book at Berchtesgaden</u>, "liberated" by a local GI. *Route 2; daily 9 to 5 mid-May through mid-October; 802-223-5537.*

Montpelier

While the Ku Klux Klan is best known for its activities against blacks in the South, it had thousands of members in Vermont during the 1920s and early 1930s who persecuted Jews, Roman Catholics, and non-northern European immigrants. The Vermont Historical Society Museum has <u>a white hood worn by a Vermont member of the Ku Klux Klan</u> in 1925. Among the other unexpected relics here is <u>a pass signed by President Abraham Lincoln on April 13, 1865, the day before he was assassinated</u>, allowing a Vermont businessman to enter Mobile, Alabama, through

Unkown Vermont

Union lines and check on a hotel he owned there. *109 State Street; Tuesday through Friday 9 to 4:30, Saturday 9 to 4, Sunday noon to 4; 802-828-2291.*

Admiral George Dewey, who was born in Montpelier, saw to it that his home state got <u>a sunken enemy cannon dredged up after the Spanish-American Battle of Manila Bay</u> on May 1, 1898, at which Dewey commanded the victorious American fleet. The trophy sits on the lawn of the Vermont State House. *115 State Street.*

Newport
There's more than books in the Goodrich Memorial Library: There's a collection of animals and birds stuffed between 1900 and 1940, including a 10-foot alligator, preserved in glass cases. The alligator, its tag reads, was killed by a D. W. Hildreth on the Miaka River, Florida, on March 11, 1906. *202 Main Street; Monday through Wednesday and Friday 9 to 5, Thursday 9 to 8, Saturday 9:30 to 3; 802-334-7902.*

North Hero
<u>The Royal Lipizzan Stallions' summer home</u> is here on a quiet farm owned by the direct descendants of Knight Ritter von Schoevel, who was given the powerful and graceful horses by Austrian Emperor Ferdinand II to ride into battle in the early 1600s. Rescued after World War II by General George S. Patton, the few remaining Lipizzans tour in spring and fall, but in the summer can be seen on the Atkin Herrmann Farm. *Route 2; performances Thursday and Friday at 6, Saturday and Sunday at 2:30 July 4 through the third week in August; 802-372-8400.*

Norwich
The nation's oldest private military college, Norwich University has a museum with an extraordinary collection of the spoils of war, including <u>Mussolini's telephone and a piece of Hitler's desk</u>, both swiped as souvenirs at the end of World War II. The museum also displays the American flag flown during the surrender of the German Army at Innsbruck to the U.S. Second Armored Division. Also here is <u>the pennant that flew from Admiral George Dewey's flagship, the *Olympia*, during the Spanish-American War Battle of Manila Bay</u>, and the *Olympia*'s ship's wheel; Dewey, a Vermont native, attended Norwich, though he did not graduate. *White Chapel; Monday through Friday 2 to 4 when school is in session; 802-485-2082.*

Orwell
The taking of Fort Ticonderoga by Ethan Allen and his Green Mountain Boys on May 10, 1775, may have been the first major American victory of the Revolutionary War, but keeping it was another matter; the fort faced the wrong direction to protect the colonies against an expected British counter-attack from Canada. So the Americans built a second fort across Lake Champlain from Ticonderoga, the long-forgotten Mount Independence, which is today <u>one of the least-disturbed military sites from the colonial period</u>—thanks mainly to centuries of neglect. Depleted by a brutal winter, the troops at Mount Independence were forced to flee when the British assault finally came on July 5, 1777, but stopped the offensive in a bloody battle at Hubbardton and then a decisive victory at Saratoga. The British remained only briefly at Mount Independence, leaving after hearing of the defeat at Saratoga, and the site is remarkably well-preserved, with trails winding past the archeological remains of the batteries, blockhouses, hospital, barracks, and other original structures. There is also a museum. *Route 74; daily 9 to 5 Memorial Day to Columbus Day; 802-585-2821.*

Pittsford
Designed to look like a 19th-century sugar house, the New England Maple Museum begins with displays of crude wooden troughs used by Iroquois Indians hundreds of years ago to catch maple sap; the Iroquois supposedly discovered the sweetening properties of maple syrup when some sap fell into a hollowed-out rock

Unknown New England

used to collect rainwater for cooking. The display ends with an exhibit of the plastic hoses and tanks used to collect the sap today. *Route 7; daily 10 to 4 mid-March through mid-May and November 1 through December 23, daily 8:30 to 5:30 mid-May through October 31; 802-483-9414.*

Washed a mile and a half down the river by an historic flood in 1927, the Hammond Covered Bridge was simply mounted on empty oil barrels for buoyancy and towed back to its original site here on Otter Creek. *Route 7.*

Plymouth

President Calvin Coolidge's birthplace and home and the site of his swearing-in remain exactly as they look when he was born here on July 4, 1872, complete with the original village church, the general store, the dance hall that served as the 1924 summer White House, and the Coolidge family cheese factory. It was while he was vacationing here that then-Vice President Coolidge learned President Warren G. Harding had died suddenly in San Francisco; he was sworn in by his father, Colonel John Coolidge, at 2:47 a.m. August 3, 1923. Coolidge was re-elected to a second term in 1924. President Coolidge's characteristically modest grave is in the family cemetery here. "If the spirit of liberty should vanish in other parts of the union and support of our institutions should languish," he once said, "it could all be replenished from the generous store held by the people of this brave little state of Vermont." *Route 100A; daily 9:30 to 5 Memorial Day through Columbus Day; 802-672-3389.*

Poultney

Originally a blacksmith shop, the local melodeon factory was opened in 1854 to build bellows-operated organs popular with people who couldn't afford a piano; operated like a giant harmonica, the melodeon played when air was pulled in, and pushed out of, a leather bellows. The fad didn't last, and the factory shut down for good when one of the owners was caught and crushed in the water wheel that drove the machinery. But five melodeons built here are on display in the Poultney Historical Society museum; two of them still work. The museum also has trays of type used by Horace Greeley when he lived here and learned the printing trade. Greeley would go on to found the *New York Herald Tribune*, and to urge a generation to "go west, young man." When he ran for president in 1872 as a Republican, he made his first speech in front of Union Academy, one of the buildings on the historical society's property. Another highlight: the antique printing press used to print the testimonials advertising Dr. Ingham's Vegetable Extract and Nervine Pain Killer, which was made of alcohol and opium; some of the letters themselves hang alongside. *East Poultney Green; Sunday 1 to 4 June, July and August; 802-287-5268.*

Poultney wasn't only home to Horace Greeley, founder of the *New York Herald Tribune*; it was also the birthplace of George Jones, co-founder of *The New York Times*. There is a marker on Jones's family's home here. *Route 140.*

A wave of Welsh immigrants settled here in the 19th century to work in the slate industry. The Welsh Room at Green Mountain College has Welsh-language documents from this era, as well as slate jewelry boxes and other items made by quarry workers. *Griswold Library; Monday through Friday 8:30 a.m. to 10 p.m.; 802-287-8309.*

Proctor

Historically the nation's largest marble producer, Vermont seems the appropriate place for the world's largest museum of marble—Proctor even moreso, since it's named for Colonel Redfield Proctor, founder of the Vermont Marble Company, who pulled strings as a U.S. senator to make sure the U.S. Supreme Court Building,

Unkown Vermont

Jefferson Memorial and other federal monuments were made of marble his company produced. The enormous Vermont Marble Museum is fronted by a giant archway of rough marble blocks that looks like something from *The Flintstones*; inside, however, the marble is polished and includes the green Veda, Champlain and Imperial Danby types found in Vermont and other kinds of marble from around the world. A highlight is the Hall of Presidents, where every former president has been chiseled from white Vermont marble. *52 Main Street; daily 9:30 to 5:30 mid-May through October 31; 802-459-2300.*

When native Vermonter Dr. John Johnson married Sarah Robins, an English noblewoman, in 1867, the couple decided to re-create a European castle in the middle of Vermont. The result: the 32-room Flemish-style Wilson Castle, complete with turrets and parapets, and full of Oriental and European furniture including a chair once used by Pope Pius XII and the case that carried Louis XV's crown jewels. The house, which took eight years to build, has 13 fireplaces and 84 stained-glass windows. *West Proctor Road; daily 9 to 6 mid-May until October 31; 802-773-3284.*

Quechee

Quechee Gorge is called Vermont's little Grand Canyon. But part of the wonder of the 611-acre site is that it is man-made. Used as an emergency spillway for the North Hartland Flood Control Dam, the gorge can fill with as much as 10 feet of water when the floodgates are closed—and did, in 1969, when a flood carried away entire houses. Pieces of houses can still be seen in the tops of the trees here. *190 Dewey Mills Road; daily dawn to dusk mid-May through Columbus Day; 802-295-2990.*

Randolph

Two entire local businesses have been completely resurrected in the Randolph Historical Society Museum: Leonard's Drug Store and Soda Fountain, and Rye's Barber Shop. The barber shop was operated on Main Street for 54 years; the drug store by three generations of druggists from 1893 to 1958. There's even a photo of the youngest druggist getting his first haircut at the barber shop. The drug store is lined with glass display cases of drugs still in their original packaging, and boxes of remedies and toiletries, and has the ornate soda fountain with heart-shaped wire seats under a ceiling fan. A working antique wall telephone connects the barber shop with a re-created parlor, where there is a sousaphone and cornet used by E.E. Bagley, composer of *The National Emblem March*, who lived in Randolph; the 1798 slate gravestone of horse breeder Justin Morgan, which was replaced in 1952 by a granite marker; and the military-style uniform worn by Randolph native Calvin Edson, the "living skeleton," who was five-foot-three and weighed 60 pounds; Edson exhibited himself around the country in the 1830s. *Salisbury Street; first Sunday of the month 2 to 4 June 1 through Labor Day; 802-728-9308.*

Ripton

The cabin where Robert Frost spent his summers from 1939 until his death in 1963 is in the Green Mountain woods that inspired many of his poems, including "Whose Woods Are These?" The trail to the cabin—which can only be seen from the outside—is marked with excerpts of his works. *Route 125; daily dawn to dusk.*

Rockingham

Born to a wealthy whaling family in New Bedford, Massachusetts, Hetty Green was so tightfisted with her inheritance that the *Guinness Book of World Records* named her the most miserly woman in the world. Although she was worth more than $7 million by her 21st birthday in 1855, she removed the candles from her cake and returned them for a refund. In 1879, Green moved to the corner of

Unknown New England

Westminster and Church streets in Rockingham's Bellows Falls section, where she was remembered for buying broken cookies to save money, returning her berry boxes for the nickel deposit, and wearing only a single black dress over and over again. Green saved more than $100 million by the time she died in 1916, making her the world's richest woman, but her house was so ramshackle it had to be torn down. The gravesite of the Witch of Wall Street is in Immanuel Church Cemetery.

Although it's hard to believe that she left anything behind, the Rockingham Free Public Library and Museum has Hetty Green's fainting couch, her glasses, and her writing desk, where she once spent two hours hunting for a missing two-cent stamp. The museum also has a stereopticon slide collection and a tree trunk from the Gettysburg battlefield with two cannonballs lodged in it. *65 Westminster Street. Friday 2 to 4 Memorial Day through Columbus Day, and by request; 802-463-4270.*

Royalton

The birthplace of the founder of the Mormon Church, Joseph Smith, is here, where Smith was born on December 23, 1805, and lived until he was 11. Though only the foundation of his parents' modest log home remain, the church has built a visitor center with a scale model of how it would have looked when he was born, and a monument whose shaft is 38 and a half feet tall—one foot for every year of Smith's life until he was assassinated in Carthage, Illinois, apparently by opponents of polygamy. It is the largest single polished granite shaft in the world. *Dairy Hill Road; daily 9 to 7 May 1 through October 31, then daily 9 to 5; 802-763-7742.*

St. Johnsbury

Founded in 1873, the museum at the St. Johnsbury Athanaeum is the oldest art gallery in America that has never been altered; "You are about to enter the 19th century," says a sign at the entrance. Built by Vermont Governor Horace Fairbanks with the money he made as the inventor of the platform scale, the athanaeum is cluttered with landscapes in heavy gilded frames hung Victorian style, one above another, and bathed in natural light from an arched skylight above a blond wood floor. The centerpiece is the dramatic "Domes of Yosemite," a canvas 15 feet wide and 10 feet high, by Albert Bierstadt, opposite the entrance. There are 100 works in all. *Main Street; Monday and Wednesday 10 to 8, Tuesday, Thursday and Friday 10 to 5:30, Saturday 9 to 4; 802-748-8291.*

Horace Fairbanks' nephew, industrialist Franklin Fairbanks, was a lifelong amateur naturalist who collected more than 160,000 objects ranging from colorful stuffed hummingbirds from around the world to artwork made of dead insects, including a portrait of President Abraham Lincoln composed entirely of beetle and moth wings. In 1889, Fairbanks built the Fairbanks Museum and Planetarium to house his burgeoning collection. Its grand Victorian exhibit hall bulges with such things as taxidermied polar beers and a passenger pigeon, and Vermont volunteer William Scott's death warrant, signed after his court martial for falling asleep on guard duty during the Civil War, and before he was pardoned by President Lincoln. *1302 Main Street; 9 to 5 Monday through Saturday, Sunday 1 to 5; 802-748-2372.*

Shelburne

There really was a Justin Morgan, and he really had a horse. There also now is a museum devoted to horse breeder Justin Morgan and his famous Morgan Horse. Morgan moved to Randolph, Vermont, in 1788 when he couldn't explain the disappearance of receipts he was supposed to have submitted as a substitute tax collector in Massachusetts. He began a stud farming business, producing a colt named Figure that was to be the progenitor of the versatile Morgan breed, which was soon

Unkown Vermont

The St. Alban's Raid

The Civil War seemed blessedly close to its conclusion, and extremely far away, as the townspeople of St. Albans, Vermont, went about their business on the afternoon of October 19, 1864. Their complacency was natural; St. Albans was 544 miles from the bloody battlefield at Gettysburg—a vast distance in those days—and news accounts indicated with enthusiasm that the South was at long last on the brink of total and complete defeat.

At 3 p.m. that day, the impossible happened: A band of Confederate cavalrymen materialized in the middle of St. Albans, and effectively, if briefly, took the town. It was by far the northernmost military action of the Civil War, though the remarkable St. Albans Raid has been almost completely overlooked by history.

Suddenly a Confederate officer named Bennett Young was standing in the street with two Colt pistols, waving them at people on the sidewalks and exclaiming: "In the name of the Confederate States, I take possession of St. Albans." On his signal, 16 of his comrades took up their positions along Main Street.

The tiny band was there as part of a plan by the desperate Confederacy to stage a series of raids along the U.S. border with Canada in the hope that Union commanders would divert thousands of troops from the fighting to guard northern towns and cities. Young and his men had arrived disguised as Canadians on a fishing party, took rooms at a local hotel, and scouted out the town, which they had chosen because it was close to the Canadian border and had three banks.

Some St. Albans men tried to defend the town by firing from alleyways and windows. Three residents were shot, one fatally, and a raider was also injured.

The raid succeeded in one of its goals: the southerners stole $208,000 from the local banks before they mounted up and fled to Canada. Once across the border, Young and his men were arrested by Canadian officials, but ultimately freed.

The St. Albans Historical Museum has a treasure trove of artifacts from the St. Albans Raid, including photos of the raiders, panicky broadsides warning other Vermont towns of what had happened—even some of the money stolen from the banks, returned years later and now framed and on the wall. A six-foot-square diorama describes the succession of events, and the escape.

The St. Albans Historical Museum is on Church Street, St. Albans, and is open Monday through Friday 1 to 4 mid-June through mid-October. Call 802-527-7933.

in demand for its stamina, speed and beauty. The National Museum of the Morgan Horse has antique carts and plows pulled by Morgans, and a cavalry exhibit with Civil War-era Morgan saddles. There are also periodic Morgan demonstrations. *122 Bostwick Road; Monday through Friday 9 to 4, Saturday 10 to 2; 802-985-8665.*

Springfield

James Hartness, a rabid inventor of machine tools, became interested in astronomy and designed his own telescope—the Hartness Turret Equatorial Telescope—in 1908. That fact, and Vermont's almost perfect darkness and clean air, have combined to make this town a mecca for stargazers, who consider it <u>the birthplace of amateur astronomy</u>. Hartness sparked a flurry of interest in telescope making among the workers in the machine shop he owned, who built an observatory and clubhouse called Stellafane, which means "shrine to the stars." Meanwhile, Hartness built his own observatory, connected to his house by a 240-foot tunnel, and constructed underground rooms to block out any light or noise (one also doubled as a bar). While Stellafane is open only sporadically, the extraordinary warren of rooms beneath Hartness's front lawn is now the R. W. Porter Museum of Amateur Telescope Making, with Hartness's original telescope and other items on

Unknown New England

display. Porter was an early leader of the club who went on to help assemble the world's largest telescope at Palomar in California. *30 Orchard Street; by appointment; 802-885-2115.*

Stowe

The graves of Baron Georg and Maria von Trapp, whose 1938 escape from Nazi-controlled Austria into Switzerland with their 10 children inspired a Broadway musical and the 1965 film *The Sound of Music*, are buried on the grounds of the Trapp Family Lodge, which they built after settling in Stowe in 1939. *700 Trapp Hill Road.*

Vermont's ski mountains gave rise to the first ski patrol, first tow rope, and first snow-farming equipment. The Vermont Ski Museum has more than 700 artifacts commemorating this history, including 1948 U.S. Olympic ski team member Becky Fraser's ski boots and bib, and the skis Andrea Meade Lawrence wore to win two gold medals. *1 South Main Street; 10 to 6 Wednesday through Monday; 802-253-9911.*

Strafford

Justin Morrill left school at the age of 15, but would almost singlehandedly make higher education available to millions of Americans. Self-taught, Morrill became a U.S. congressman and senator, and was the author of the Land Grant College Act of 1862, establishing land-grant universities including Cornell, Rutgers, the University of Pennsylvania, the University of Wisconsin, Iowa State, and the University of Vermont. He was also instrumental in the creation of the Library of Congress and the Washington Monument. Morrill built himself a 17-room mansion here, now called the Justin Smith Morrill State Historic Site, which still is furnished with original Morrill family possessions and also has campaign banners and memorabilia relating to President Chester Alan Arthur. *Morrill Highway; Wednesday through Sunday 11 to 5 Memorial Day through Columbus Day; 802-828-3051.*

Tunbridge

This was the home town of Florence Spaulding, who bought a Model T Ford in 1914 and used it to become the first woman to drive across the country. Her home survives, though it is privately owned. *Route 110 at Monarch Hill Road.*

Underhill

The product of the sugar maple tree is a multimillion-dollar industry in Vermont, and the state runs a research center to improve sap collection and syrup quality and study tree biochemistry. The Proctor Maple Research Center offers maple sugaring demonstrations and tours. *Harvey Road; by appointment; 802-899-9926.*

Vernon

The Vermont Yankee nuclear power station offers tours of the plant to visitors over 18. There also is a visitor center at the plant gates with exhibits about nuclear energy. *Governor Hunt Road; open for groups by appointment; 802-258-5796.*

Weybridge

Nearly extinct by the late 1800s, the Morgan Horse line bred by Vermonter Justin Morgan was saved mainly through the efforts of Colonel Joseph Battell, who would donate his farm to the U.S. government in 1906. The government, in turn, transferred it to the University of Vermont, which still operates a farm that breeds Morgan horses, housed in the original picturesque Battell-era corrals and barns. *Route 23; daily 9 to 4 May 1 through October 31; 802-388-2011.*

Unkown Vermont

White River Junction

While stationed in Germany during his stint in the Army, Elvis Presley purportedly had a gallstone operation, the product of which was nabbed by a quick-thinking curiosity seeker named Wilfried Greirfinger. Today, <u>Elvis Presley's gallstones</u> are in the permanent collection of the Main Street Museum of Art, a kitschy museum that also has such things as a carcass claimed to be an aquatic monster dredged from the Connecticut River, and "modern art created by accident," including a piece of warehouse shelving with a pattern left by a leaky can of enamel ("in the style of Mark Rothko," reads the notice) and a pair of Ballantine Ale cans found behind the wall of a woolen mill ("in the style of Jasper Johns"). The museum, Vermont's strangest, moves around town, and is open by appointment. *802-295-7105.*

Whitingham

<u>The birthplace of Brigham Young</u>, second president of the Mormon Church, is marked by a monument placed by his descendants. Young was born here on June 1, 1801, and led the members of the Church of Jesus Christ of Latter-day Saints from Illinois to Utah after the death of fellow Vermonter Joseph Smith. *Town Hill Road.*

Windsor

Dedicated to the history of the interchangeable part, the American Precision Museum in the former Robbins & Lawrence Armory and Machine Shop boasts <u>the largest collection of historic machine tools in the nation</u>. Founded in 1846, the armory became famous for producing the parts needed in mass production, turning out 10,000 rifles for the Union Army during the Civil War in half the time called for in the contract. Retooled after the war, Robbins & Lawrence later made typewriters, sewing machines, and even bicycles, many of which are on display here. There are also <u>gauges and other measuring devices from Thomas Edison's laboratories</u>. *196 Main Street; daily 10 to 5 Memorial Day through October 31; 802-674-5781.*

Although it helped fight off the British, Vermont remained a sovereign nation for 14 years before it joined the Union. Elijah West's Tavern was <u>the site where delegates wrote the constitution of the independent Republic of Vermont</u> on July 8, 1777. It was the first constitution on the continent to prohibit slavery, authorize a public school system, and establish voting rights for men whether they owned property or not. The table on which the document was signed is in what is now called the Old Constitution House, and the room where it was debated looks exactly as it did that day. Vermont gave in and became the 14th state in 1791. *Route 5; Wednesday through Sunday 11 to 5 Memorial Day through Columbus Day; 802-828-3051.*

Woodstock

When a series of mysterious illnesses followed the burial of a local man named Corwin (his first name has been lost to history), townspeople started to suspect the supernatural. Their suspicions were confirmed when, in June of 1830, Corwin was dug up, and his heart was found to still have blood in it—the sure sign of a vampire. The heart was removed and burned in an iron cauldron, the ashes buried beneath the town green in a 15-foot-deep hole and covered with a 7-ton slab of granite sprinkled with the blood of a sacrificial bull. <u>The grave of the vampire of Woodstock</u> is in Cushing Cemetery. The odd occurrences in town were probably actually signs of a tuberculosis outbreak. *River Road.*

A rehabilitation center for birds, the Vermont Institute of Natural Science has about 40 birds on permanent display that are unable to be returned to the wild,

Unknown New England

including owls, falcons, hawks and eagles. *27023 Church Hill Road; daily 10 to 5 June 1 through October 31, then Monday through Saturday 10 to 4; 802-457-2779.*

About the Author

A lifelong New Englander, Jon Marcus was born in Boston, schooled in Maine, and began his professional career on Cape Cod.

The editor of *Boston* magazine, Marcus has written about travel for *Yankee* and *Conde Nast Traveler*, and for newspapers including the *Boston Globe, Chicago Tribune, Los Angeles Times, Miami Herald*, and *Washington Post*. His stories on other topics have appeared in the Melbourne, Australia, *Sunday Herald Sun, The Inde-pendent* (London), and in the magazines *New York Times Upfront* and the *American Journalism Review*. A U.S. education correspondent for *The Times of London*, he began his career as a writer at *The Cape Cod Times* and has served as a full-time Boston-based reporter for The Associated Press. He has won several journalism awards including writer of the year from the City and Regional Magazine Association.

Marcus is the author of the book *Boston: A Citylife Pictorial Guide* (Voyageur Press, 1998), which *Foreword* magazine called "packed with information" and the *Fort Lauderdale Sun-Sentinel* said "brings Boston to life through interesting, little-known details." He also wrote *Lighthouses of New England* (Voyageur Press, 2001), and *The Complete Illustrated Guidebook to Boston's Public Parks and Gardens* (Silver Lining Press, 2002).

He is a graduate of Bates College in Maine and the Graduate School of Journalism at Columbia University and attended Oxford University.

Printed in the United States
1479300002B/186